Chicago Public Library

REFERENCE

Form 178 rev. 1-94

Reading Marx Writing

Melodrama, the Market,
and the "Grundrisse"

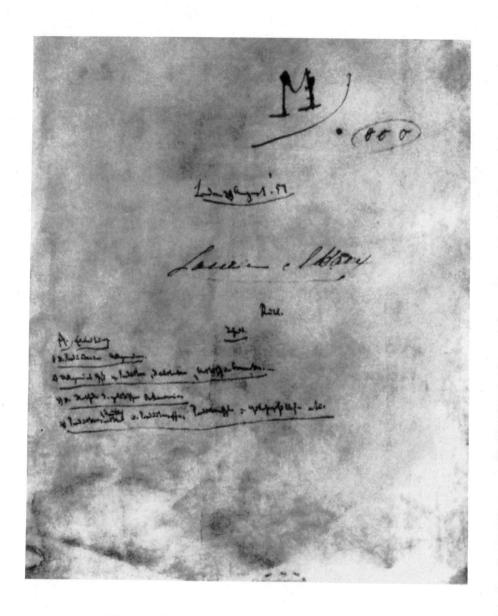

Back of the cover of Notebook M containing Marx's 1857 "Introduction."
Courtesy Progress Publishers, Moscow.

Reading Marx Writing

Melodrama, the Market, and the "Grundrisse"

Thomas M. Kemple

STANFORD UNIVERSITY PRESS
Stanford, California ... 1995

Stanford University Press, Stanford, California
© 1995 by the Board of Trustees of the Leland Stanford
Junior University
Printed in the United States of America

CIP data appear at the end of the book

Stanford University Press publications are distributed exclusively
by Stanford University Press within the United States, Canada,
Mexico, and Central America; they are distributed exclusively by
Cambridge University Press throughout the rest of the world.

For my parents

. . . .
. . . .
. . . .

Acknowledgments

On a cold December evening in 1983, John O'Neill led me into the study of his home in Toronto; I left with a copy of his book on Marx, his advice to read H. T. Wilson's work on Weber (the subject of my honors thesis), and the belief that someday I would pursue graduate studies at the Programme in Social and Political Thought at York University. Two years later, as I attended Professor O'Neill's Monday night seminars and Professor Wilson's course on critical social theory, the idea for this book was conceived. My debt to each of them is incalculable, and so their names belong at the top of this list. Many other teachers have also helped me shape my thoughts. It is a pleasure to recall the seminars I attended at Wesleyan University with Gayatri Chakravorty Spivak, James Stone, and Brian Fay, each of whom in his or her own way initially directed me on my road to Marx: the first via post-structuralist theory (she first emphasized to me the importance of Marx's *Grundrisse*), the second via social phenomenology, and the third via the philosophy of the social sciences. At York I am fortunate to have been able to attend courses given by Thomas Sekine on the Marxian dialectic of capital and H. S. Harris on Hegel's *Phenomenology*, although I cannot pretend to have fathomed everything they presented me. Kenneth Morrison drew my attention to the way "classical" social theorists like Marx have been edited and packaged for disciplinary and mass consumption, and Bryan Green's work has sharpened my sense of the methods of literary analysis and textual construction employed in sociological writing. Henry Sussman at SUNY Buffalo gave me welcome advice and needed encouragement for turning this work from a dissertation into a book, and Helen Tartar at Stanford University Press convinced me of the need for clarity and conventionality in the presentation of the visual material. Many graduate students offered challenges and new perspectives at the early stages of this project, among whom I shall name Gary Genosko, my guide and fellow traveler through the virtual worlds of French thought, and above all, Carol Moore and Geoff Miles, who have inspired some of my best insights here. Undergraduates I have taught at York University, the Oshawa campus of Trent University, and Concordia University have helped me to clarify my ideas more than I otherwise would have. My friends Cate Friesen and Cecilia Booth have opened my ears to the music beyond the meaning of words, and Julie Beebe provided many welcome distractions throughout the writing of this work. I must also thank my brothers, Jim and Marty, and my sister, Erin, for ensuring that I keep my critical reason and my common sense during my years as a graduate student. Stephen Guy-Bray's intelligence and love grace every page of this work, especially the very best ones.

T.M.K.

Contents

x   *Contents*

Tables and Figures

A Note on Abbreviations, Citations, and Translations

Citations from Marx's works are from the editions listed here, using the abbreviations and formats described. Individual works by Marx and their citation format are included in the Chronology of Marx's Works, on pp. xvi–xviii.

German Editions of Marx's Works

MEGA   1975–. *Marx-Engels Gesamtausgabe*. Berlin: Dietz Verlag. Citations give the *Abteilung* (division) in Roman numerals and the *Band* (volume) in Arabic numerals, followed by the page number: (MEGA IV/1: 350). Nearly all volumes are accompanied by a separate *Apparat* with editorial notes and sources.

MEW   1956–68. *Marx-Engels Werke*. Berlin: Dietz Verlag. Citations give volume number and page number: (MEW 36: 235).

English Editions of Marx's Works

C1   1976. *Capital*. Vol. 1, *The Critique of Political Economy*. Trans. Ben Fowkes. Introduction by Ernest Mandel. New York: Vintage Books.

C2   1981. *Capital*. Vol. 2, *The Process of Circulation of Capital*. Ed. Friedrich Engels. Trans. David Fernbach. Introduction by Ernest Mandel. New York: Vintage Books.

C3   1981. *Capital*. Vol. 3, *The Process of Capitalist Production as a Whole*. Ed. Friedrich Engels. Trans. David Fernbach. New York: Vintage Books.

CW   1975. *Karl Marx and Frederick Engels Collected Works*. New York: International Publishers.

Citations give volume number and page number: (CW 28: 549).

EW   1975. *Early Writings*. Trans. Rodney Livingstone and Gregor Benton. Introduction by Lucio Coletti. New York: Vintage Books.

FIA   1974. *The First International and After*. Ed. with Introduction by David Fernbach. New York: Penguin Books.

R48   1973. *The Revolution of 1848*. Ed. with Introduction by David Fernbach. New York: Penguin Books.

SE   1973. *Surveys from Exile*. Ed. with Introduction by David Fernbach. New York: Penguin Books.

Citations from "Grundrisse" and from Marx's Letters

Karl Marx. 1973. *Grundrisse*. Trans. Martin Nicolaus. New York: Vintage Books.

Citations give the number of Marx's original notebook in Roman numerals I through VII or M (for the first notebook, which contains Marx's 1857 "Introduction"), followed by the page number of the English translation: (VII: 704). When the German text has also been consulted, and whenever I modify Nicolaus's translation, the page number of the original notebook immediately follows the notebook number; this pagination is indicated in all standard German editions as well as in the CW translation: (VII 2: 704). Marx's own use of English words is indicated in small capitals.

——— . 1979. *The Letters of Karl Marx*. Ed. and trans. Saul K. Padover. Englewood Cliffs, N.J.: Prentice-Hall.

Letters are cited by the sender and addressee, and the day, month, and year they were written: (Marx to Engels, 15 July 1858). Here, too, Marx's own use of English words is indicated in small capitals.

Translations

As noted above, I have sometimes modified Nicolaus's translation in quoting from the *Grundrisse*. All translations from Balzac are my own. All translations of *Faust* are reprinted from Johann Wolfgang von Goethe, *Faust*, a Norton Critical Edition, trans. Walter Arndt, ed. Cyrus Hamlin, by permission of W. W. Norton & Company, Inc. Copyright © 1976 by W. W. Norton & Company, Inc.

Chronology of Marx's Works

The works below are listed in chronological order according to the date of first publication or of composition if not published in Marx's lifetime; the latter dates appear in square brackets. With the exception of the *Grundrisse* and the volumes of *Capital*, Marx's works are cited throughout the text by these dates and the abbreviations listed in the Note on Abbreviations, Citations, and Translations: (Marx [1844] *EW*: 276).

The list is interrupted twice by what I consider to be a significant turning point of particular personal, scientific, and political importance to Marx, thus dividing his lifework into three distinct phases. These events should not simply be treated as breaks in Marx's career, but rather as "biographemes" that illuminate the work in the life and the life in the work (cf. Barthes 1978 [1954], 1989).

[1840–41]	*The Difference Between the Democritean and the Epicurean Philosophies of Nature* (doctoral dissertation)
[1842]	*Excerpts on the History of Art and Religion* (Bonner Hefte)
1842	*Debates on the Law on Thefts of Wood*
1843	*On the Jewish Question*
1843–44	*A Contribution to the Critique of Hegel's Philosophy of Right: Introduction*
[1844a]	*Excerpts from James Mill's "Elements of Political Economy"*
[1844b]	*Economic and Philosophical Manuscripts of 1844*

In 1850, after emigrating to London, Marx resumes his economic studies in the British Museum. Engels moves to Manchester to manage the firm Ermen and Engels.

In 1864 Marx and Engels participate in the founding of the (First) International Working Men's Association.

Reading Marx Writing

Melodrama, the Market,
and the "Grundrisse"

....
....
....

Foreword
Ruptures-in-Reason

Ce qu'il y a de certain c'est que moi, je ne suis pas Marxiste. (What is certain is that I am not a Marxist.)

Marx to Paul Lafargue at a meeting of socialists in Paris;
in Engels to Eduard Bernstein, 2–3 November 1882

The preliminary remarks to a work, whether they be called an introduction, a preface, or a foreword, allow a reader to stand apart from what has already been completed in order to survey its overall layout, to retrace its stages of production, and to inspect its layers of composition. They provide an opportunity to savor the results of what follows or to reflect on how they might fit into some other set of themes than those already considered. And they offer a chance to get a comprehensive but brief sense of what has been the guiding thread of the work all along, either explicitly or as communicated in some other way.

Nevertheless, the reader who also happens to be the writer of these preliminary remarks has a somewhat different task from any other reader. That is, I cannot avoid trying to manage the paradox that my comments here are both a part of the work to follow (which is also a piece of my own writing) and apart from it at the same time (which is the stance I must take in trying to read it). My purpose here is primarily to encourage the reader to look forward to the text to follow, and yet I must do so in my capacity as a fellow reader who nevertheless writes about what I myself have already written. Like others before me who have tried to articulate dilemmas like these (Derrida 1981; Hegel 1977; Marx 1859), I have therefore found it necessary not only to reflect on what relationship these remarks might have to those already made in this work, but also to take up yet again the writers and texts that have been considered throughout these pages.

This book began as a study of Marx, or rather of the eight large notebooks that he filled from 1857 to 1858 and that have reached us in edited, translated, and published form under the title of *Grundrisse*, a designation Marx himself sometimes used to refer to them. But these notebooks soon became for me a kind of "pre-text" for examining the literary, political, and scientific imagination of Marx, of fiction writers he admired, and of later thinkers writing in a number of intellectual disciplines. By exploring the extent to which Marx had in mind some project or plan he did not carry through at this phase of his work, the study came to speculate on what Marx might have provided us for understanding issues he could only glimpse or not see at all: in sociology and political economy, in philosophy and literary criticism, and in critical social theory and aesthetics. Thus, the perspectives of several recent thinkers have been brought to bear on the reading of the text, just as Marx's text is brought to bear on our understanding of them. The project eventually came to explore the interpretive possibilities for approaching Marx's "Grundrisse" not as editors, translators, and other commentators have done, but to treat them as "ground plans," "outlines," and "compendia," or even as "ruptures in reason" for thinking and acting beyond Marx—each of these being a possible rendering or even mistranslation of the word *Grundrisse*, which I consider below.

The various techniques of deciphering that Marx himself developed, in contrast to those who read him, are discussed in a fairly expository way in the two chapters that make up Part II, and for this reason it might be easiest to start reading there. In the four chapters that make up Parts I and III, by contrast, a more creative attempt is made to show how the writing practices employed in Marx's plans and outlines offer new possibilities for considering specific literary works that may otherwise seem quite unrelated to his interests. In particular, Goethe's *Faust*, especially the early wine-cellar scene, and Balzac's late play *Le Faiseur* and stories from his *Comédie humaine*, particularly "Le Chef d'oeuvre inconnu" and "Melmoth réconcilié," are used to provide sounding boards for amplifying a wide range of ideas, as well as looking glasses for illuminating a number of themes, both within and outside of Marx's frame of reference. A similar use is made of a series of six more literal "illustrations" (an assortment of tables and figures) that are presented to clarify the dynamic interplay of image, music, and text in Marx's multidimensional writing. Thus, these literary works and illustrations are not just treated in a conventional way as depictions of scientific insights or even as representations of Marx's life, work, and subject of study. Above all, they are deployed as frameworks of interpretation that may be drawn from and applied to both Marx's text and the writings of others working in his wake.

If indeed a more proper introduction to this work is to be found in its middle part rather than here at its beginning, then a question might be raised about the generic status of such opening comments as these. They do, of course, serve as a preface (*Vorwort* in German) to the argument that follows in the main text, with which they share a common author. But in another sense they might also be read as a kind of foreword to a work that the writer of these lines has not written, if only because both I and my project have changed in the process of writing. Indeed, my ultimate hope is that these preliminary remarks might be considered not just as a preface to the following work or even as an introduction to those which inspired it, but also as the foreword to something some other writer unknown to me has already written or has yet to write. In presenting a book that is primarily a reading of writings by others, perhaps I should not presume upon the act of reading by which it might itself be received.

Ground Plans

To find a way into Marx's text according to the path I have marked out in this work, while also surveying it from the outside to see where it originated and where it was headed, we might take as our initial guide the first lines he wrote in these notebooks (but which were later to appear in what he came to designate as Notebook III). There is an irony here not unlike that just referred to, in that what Marx himself seems to designate as the "Avant-propos" (preface or foreword) to a work he has yet to write also appears to take the form of a foreword, or commentary on forewords, to works already written by others. Although he wrote these brief and apparently incidental remarks about two obscure political economists—Frédéric Bastiat and Henry Charles Carey—before arriving at the results he was to achieve in the *Grundrisse* and *Capital*, they seem to provide an overview of the entire edifice Marx was later to construct, to identify the particular perspective he was to take, and thus to provide the ground plan and general layout of my own work.

In 1857 Marx stepped back from his studies in political economy of the past fifteen years and tried to get a sense of the whole story, from beginning to end. He saw both its global theater and its cast of local characters, and heard a clash of petty controversies amid a distant babble of foreign tongues: "The history of modern political economy ends with Ricardo and Sismondi: antitheses, one speaking English, the other French—just as it begins at the end of the seventeenth century with Petty and Boisguillebert" (III: 884). I shall not stop here to consider the validity of this grand pronouncement or what it might have meant to Marx, who was himself not interested, in this context, in justifying it. Instead, I shall risk rewriting it according to my own interests in this work, substituting names and dates while preserving what seems to me to be the interpretive structure it suggests: The history of modern Marxist thought ends with C. Wright Mills and Henri Lefebvre—antithetical figures of whom the one speaks English and the other French—just as it began in the first half of the nineteenth century with David Ricardo and Pierre-Joseph Proudhon. Instead of trying to explain why I have chosen these particular twentieth-century sociologists at "the end," and instead of explaining why I have put these two nineteenth-century economists at "the beginning" (rather than Marx, or even Hegel, and retaining Ricardo from Marx's statement while substituting Proudhon for Boisguillebert), I shall simply state, again using Marx's own words on the same page, that the rest of the story of modern Marxist thought has been told through a "literature of epigones: reproduction, greater elaboration of form, wider appropriation of material, exaggeration, popularization, synopsis, elaboration of details; lack of decisive leaps in the phases of development, incorporation of the inventory on the one side, new growth of individual points on the other" (III: 884).

Like Marx, who goes on here to observe that "the only exceptions seem to be the writings of Carey, the Yankee, and Bastiat, the Frenchman, the latter of whom confesses that he leans on the former" (III: 883–84), so too shall I now cast in the role of the "exceptions" the writings of Fredric Jameson and Jean Baudrillard, although here I must add that it is the "Yankee" who acknowledges his debt to the Frenchman (as well as to those to whom the Frenchman also is indebted; see Jameson 1991: 399). Here, however, I shall need to offer some explanation, but again following Marx, who also elaborates on his meaning here. It may seem strange at first that an American literary critic and philosopher and a French sociologist and semiotician should initially be conceived as the exceptions, since each has been known to address themes that seem well beyond the concerns of Marx and Marxism. Where Baudrillard seems to have pursued his interests in opposition to and quite beyond anything that usually seems to be identifiably "Marxist," Jameson's career appears to focus primarily on aesthetic and literary concerns, even in his latest attempts to construct a Marxian theory of "post-modernism as the cultural-logic of late capitalism." What, then, has happened to the Marxism whose political vision has been shaped by the Soviet and Eastern European experiments with socialist economics, the creation of Chinese communes, and the fate of Third World revolutionary movements? What of the post-Leninist theories of the party and political education, of proletarian violence and revolutionary humanism? And where do these thinkers address such classical Marxist themes as class conflicts and ideological differences, the global political economy of imperialism and nationalism, and the political implications of agrarianism and accumulationism, anarchism and avant-gardism?

If nothing else, what each of these two thinkers speaks to and exemplifies in his own way is that nearly all forms of Marxism, including its weak or radical avatars in late Marxism or even post-Marxism, have themselves been packaged as intellectual commodities and integrated into established academic and political markets. This is not just another way of saying that these thinkers—along with most socialist economies of the East in the past few years, China at least since the 1970s, socialist radicals in the West since the 1960s, and many Third World countries since the Second World War—have sold Marx out and bought into the ideology of Western capitalism. It is rather a way of pointing out that Marxism can become very unshocking when it, too, is transformed into a piece of intellectual property, dissected into a million different varieties, distributed throughout the established division of academic and political labor, and traded within the existing structures of market exchange under any number of brand names. No longer do Hegelian-Marxism and Marxist-Leninism alone define the principal methods for producing Marxist science and politics, but also a consumer catalog of post-structuralist, literary, and autonomist Marxisms as well, along with an array of other "critical" approaches that may or may not come under Marxism's corporate logo.

On the one hand, Jameson has attempted to dramatize the political and theoretical issues involved here in terms of a serial characterization of postmodern cultural logics that are connected by a new global style in the media, architecture, art, and academia, and that find deepest expression in the derealization and psychic fragmentation of everyday reality. The inexorable mechanisms of this expanding process are hidden in the mediatized fictions of the market whose very unreality and unrealizability are what is really repressive about a totalizing if not totalitarian social system. Thus, in order to recover the historical roots of postmodern amnesia, Jameson envisions a critical strategy or aesthetic of cognitive mapping by means of which we may chart the pervasive spatializing and generalizing auspices of late capitalism. In this way, we might recognize and assess the gap or separation (*Trennung*) between the twin processes of global proletarianization and the globalization of markets that act together to preserve and mask, but also to intensify and subvert, the basic class structure and ideological content of capitalism.

On the other hand, Baudrillard is perhaps even more determined to dramatize the postmodern condition, but not by devising any new global framework for comprehending it as a whole. He relentlessly attacks the grand pretensions of all such totalizing theoretical models, however critical their intentions, rejecting them as ideological alibis, imaginary symptoms, and haunting after-impressions of an already dying critical culture. Against this he has invented an ingenious and eclectic array of pataphysical and fatal strategies that hold the mirror up to postmodern society and show it a sickening image of its own exterminist ethics, its savage death drives, and its forgotten symbolisms of exchange, sacrifice, and gift giving.

Like Bastiat and Carey before them, these late or post-Marxist thinkers together seem to provide us with a comprehensive picture of what Marx called those "world market disharmonies" that become fixed in economic and cultural categories as abstract relations and that have local existence on even the smallest scale (cf. III: 887). In providing us with the "ground plans" for mapping the expansive spaces of the postmodern market or for charting the fatal strategies of the "superficial abysses" of contemporary culture, these thinkers nevertheless seem haunted by the bad faith of their own unhistorical sense of the tradition of criticism to which they continue to refer but which they do not examine very closely. Like Carey with his belief in "Yankee Universality," Jameson seems able to "absorb from all directions the massive material furnished him by the old world," reading "with catalogue-like erudition" everything from Balzac to cyberpunk (a typical false distance) "not so as to recognize the inherent soul of this material, and thus to concede it the right to its peculiar life, but rather so as to work it up for his purposes, as indifferent raw material, as inanimate documentation of his theses" (III: 888). And like Bastiat with his French parochialism, Baudrillard seems to "turn away from all countries," except in cases like America, which he re-presents in terms of a science-fictional holographic simulation, that is, a "fantasy history, his abstractions sometimes in the form of supposed events, which however have never and nowhere happened, just as a theologian treats sin sometimes as the law of human existence, then at other times as the story of the fall from grace" (III: 888).

What is lost in their work is what other Marxists have been able to articulate as the cultural construct whereby, without any conspiracy, "the American Way of Life" is absorbed by the masses as the price of capitalist market freedoms while a power elite frantically escalates "the Great American Celebration" in order to enhance the cultural prestige it so desperately lacks both at home and abroad (Mills 1959, 1963: 602–3; Wilson 1977). Also stripped of its Marxian edge is a critical understanding of how the local practicalities of everyday life, such as the urban "festival" as a site for cultural revolution, provide a spectrum of ordinary and institutional responses for resisting and transforming the seductive ecstasies of postindustrial technology and media (Lefebvre 1984; O'Neill 1985). Once again using Marx's own conclusion as our model, but without further explanation (cf. III: 889), we should say that where Jameson has his antithesis in Mills, Baudrillard has his in Lefebvre, while neither seems able to recognize himself in the mirror or echo of Marx (cf. Lefebvre 1968; Mills 1962). These two "exceptions," then, not only map the political territory for us but also symptomatically dramatize certain tragic and farcical roles of its theoretical theater.

Although in Chapter 4 (and in notes 11 and 18 to Part III) I present a more detailed and sympathetic discussion of Baudrillard and Jameson, I should remark here that the former is not considered a Marxist, while the latter passionately insists that he is. Like Marx, what seems certain is that I myself am neither what the Frenchman criticizes as *marxiste* nor what the Yankee Universalist professes to be "Marxist."

Outlines

What, then, have I taken as my aim in this work, if it is neither to become a Marxist nor to confess my own Marxism? Indeed, are my efforts here to amount to anything more than a series of parallel caricatures of Marx and his contemporaries, and critics writing today? For example, when I cast Jameson in the role of Carey and Baudrillard in the role of Bastiat (or in Part II, where Robert Tucker plays "Saint Max" to Louis Althusser's "Herr Edgar"), have I simply been pretending to play Marx, imagining myself to be working in his study (as I do in Part I)? Or have I just been trying to become as much like Marx as possible, even to become more like him than he is like himself (as might be said of my role in Part III)? Perhaps my role in these prefatory comments has instead been more like Balzac's in his famous "Avant-propos" to the *Comédie humaine*, where he attempts to gaze into the deep recesses and lofty highlights of a work nearly completed while reflecting on his religious and political beliefs, sounding out what might be their ultimate meaning and future direction (Balzac 1956 [1842]).

My initial aim in this project was to return to Marx in order to recover that repressed genealogy of the "sciences of man" which brings us to the limits of human thought; this continues to be the basis of my methodology, however eclectic it has become. In the uncovering of forgotten or unconscious affiliations, not only is the haunting specter of the human sciences without "man" as their center rendered potentially thinkable, but new domains of theoretical and discursive inquiry beyond the original intentions of their founders might also be seen to open (cf. Foucault 1973, 1977 [1969, 1971]; Nietzsche 1967). Thus, I have approached Marx as a kind of logothete, a founder of a new language (cf. Barthes 1989), not simply because his polyglot articulation of the sciences and the arts literally produced as yet unheard-of ideas and entirely alien expressions that have yet to be deciphered by his anxious successors (cf. Bloom 1973). I have done so particularly because the "outlines" he left us seem to provide wide-open spaces where new reflections and resonances can find another home and a different sense. Marx's fractured but determined writing presents us with an allegory of reading that allows the works of others to be "read off" him at the same time he himself is "read off" them, thereby magnifying the common spaces between them while leaving enough room for us to make up our own Marx and leave our own marks (cf. de Man 1979). This understanding has regulated the constant flux of entering and exiting characters in my work, some of whom have speaking parts and others of whom do not, some of whom may be considered of greater or lesser stature than others, but all of whom bear some trace of Marx's radical writing. Perhaps, then, my role in bringing together such different thinkers has been captured by Goethe in his "Prologue" to *Faust*, in which Mephistopheles strikes his own bargain with the Lord in the high mountain gorges of heaven: "Say what you like, it's quite a compliment: / A swell [guy] like him so man-to-man with the Devil!" (1976: ll. 352–53; paraphrased in C1: 868).

As a way of spotlighting the open spaces in Marx's text, I have carefully sifted from it what I consider to be "foundational passages," a selection of seven sections ranging in length from about 2 to not more than 55 pages of the English translation (for an approximate total of 165 out of 800 pages; see Appendix B). These passages have not been selected simply for the way they provide a focus for discussion of Marx's key issues, nor just for the way they have been of concern to many Marxists, although this is certainly true in most cases, as I show in Chapters 1 and 6 (and in notes 2 and 12 to Part III). Most important, I have treated them as models or framing devices that are open and flexible enough to allow for the consideration of perspectives beyond or even against the grain of Marx's original intentions or the concerns with which many Marxists approach them.

To this extent, my aim here is not to be "true to Marx," nor to require of either the reader or myself a detailed familiarity with the twists and turns of his often tortured arguments or of what they have come to mean for Marxists (issues laid out in Chapters 3 and 4). Rather, my aim has been to draw out the theoretical and practical implications of these passages within and beyond Marx's overall plan, and so to suspend judgment on their political or scientific meaning just enough to sense what there is of the aesthetics and poetics of Marx's prose. Thus, I do not consider them to be the "true foundations" of Marxist science, as perhaps could be said of the passages on "method" and on "value" that are addressed in Chapters 2 and 4, respectively (M 14–20: 100–108; VII 53: 881–82). Instead, I have attempted to show how they allow us to envision the contours of a scheme or the outlines of a sketch that may be beyond Marx's own frame of reference as well as my own or any yet conceived.

This sense of the open quality of Marx's text has also determined my understanding of how such great literary figures as Goethe and Balzac are to make their grand entrances in these pages. Almost never do I assume that there must exist a direct relationship between their work and Marx's, and only as a secondary concern have I tried to trace the lines of influence or the polemical differences between them by way of a focused interpretation or a definitive exegesis. To be sure, the kind of evidence we have that Marx did in fact read the works of these writers is crucial to the use I make of them. We can be quite sure, for example, that like so many Germans of his day, both educated and uneducated, Marx would have been able to rattle off many lines, if not whole passages and scenes, from Goethe's *Faust* almost without thinking. In Part I, I have tried to show that the trace of this deeply sensed but relatively unconscious layer of his thought can be discerned in the interruption that a line from the scene in "Auerbach's Wine Cellar" makes at one point in Marx's writing. By the same token, I have found broad hermeneutic and biographical significance in a brief note that Marx wrote to Engels, a decade after completing his notebooks and just prior to publishing his great masterwork *Capital*, which makes reference to Balzac, one of Marx's favorite nineteenth-century prose writers. In it he not only characterizes his own personal situation in terms of a play by Balzac but also advises his friend to read two "little chefs d'oeuvre" by Balzac because they are "full of the most delightful ironies" (see the epigraph to Part III). In Part III, I have argued that part of the "delightful irony" here may be that these stories in an uncanny way "prefigure" what Marx was trying to express in the *Grundrisse* and could only partially achieve in *Capital*—indeed, that they provide a kind of holograph, simulation, or even substitution for what might be or would have been the work Marx wished to write throughout his career. Thus, I have used these works by Balzac and Goethe not only to set Marx's work in a new key and frame it through unfamiliar images but also to highlight the literary and fictional features that inform Marx's scientific writing.

I have therefore tried to resist whenever possible the more conventional use of literary texts as illustrations for the insights of "science," emphasizing instead the aesthetic dimensions of music, text, and image that provide structure and sense to Marx's writing and to each of the three parts of my own study (cf. Barthes 1977 [1961, 1968, 1970]). Thus, in presenting my own illustrations, as well as a setting for a song from *Faust*, I am not simply juxtaposing images with text or highlighting in a purely metaphorical way the musical dimensions of writing, as I have indicated in choosing chapter titles that may refer either to the image or song discussed in my text or to my text itself (cf. Mitchell 1986). Instead, I have tried to show how texts may literally contain images, and images, texts, in a way that problematizes the distinction of form and content (see Figure 1), how a text presented as or in terms of an image may allow us to reconfigure that text (see Table 3 and Figure 2), how an apparently "pure" image like a photograph may make sense to us only as a text or a poetic song (see Figure 3), and how a text may be pictured through a scene and interpreted as a song (in Part I). In each instance my aim has been to present in as condensed and as graphic a way as possible what other vision might be seen emerging from Marx's writing or what other sound might be heard reverberating from the voices Marx allows to bear on his thinking.

I have attempted here to recover the multiple dimensions of Marx's writing as it takes shape through imaginative figures he paints in his studio, its scientific setting or literary scene in his study room, as well as its musical overtones as an étude, even as I have also found a certain German and post-Kantian tradition of Marxian theory to be useful in developing its pedagogic aims as a *Studie*. Besides the studies of Georg Lukács and Jürgen Habermas, the lifelong work of Herbert Marcuse has done most to articulate for me the cognitive and ontological, the ethical and practical, and the aesthetic and expressive dimensions of critical thinking, acting, and speaking, the lessons from which are now somewhat abstractly presented in Table 1. However melancholic Marcuse himself became, he resisted the impulse to produce postmortem reports on the crisis of contemporary knowledge and the collapse of the modernist narratives of speculative reason and revolutionary emancipation (Marcuse 1941; cf. Lyotard 1984). Thus, he never lost sight of that tradition of Western Reason which perceives reality as an antagonistic if fragmented structure that must be "comprehended, transformed, and subverted to become that which it really is" (Marcuse 1964: 123). Rather than treat his work directly as a reading of Marx or of the other writers considered here (as I do Lukács and Habermas, for example), I have found the "Marcuse-value" of his overall project to provide me with a model for my own work—indeed, a standard that ultimately exceeds anything I have been able to achieve here.

Perhaps those writers who are the explicit focus of this work have also exceeded my abilities to make intelligent use of them insofar as I sometimes seem to forsake comprehension for interpretation and interpretation for simulation. The abstract appearance of Table 1, intended as an imaginative copy of Marx's desk and of Faust's writing table, may thus be symptomatic of my more ambitious and ultimately unsuccessful attempt to catch a glimpse of the "concrete totality" through the perspectives of writers like Goethe, Marx, and Balzac (cf. M: 101; Kosik 1976). Thus, for example, I have designed the "outlines" of my own work to reflect the pyramidal structure of Balzac's *Comédie humaine* (discussed in Chapter 4 and in note 14 to Part III), with the bottom layer consisting of moral and cultural studies (Part III), the middle one of philosophical studies (Part II), and the summit presenting the panoramic overview projected by analytical studies (Part I). Similarly, the first part of Goethe's *Faust* is the focus of my first chapter, while my remaining five chapters can be read as parallel to the five acts of the second part of *Faust,* culminating in the appearance of the Mater Gloriosa and Maria Aegyptica of the final scene in the figure of the Black Madonna (Chapter 6). Even the distribution of chapters into three main parts according to the pattern of 1, 2, and 3 has been designed to appear to correspond to the three main parts and respective divisions of Marx's 1857–58 notebooks (as presented in Table 2B).

With these—and with similar artificial devices woven into each chapter— have I done anything more than copy obsequiously the merely formal aspects of the texts I have been studying: at first taking dictation from Goethe as his confidant Johann Peter Eckermann once did (cf. Ronell 1986), later imitating Balzac's self-characterization as the secretary of modern mores (Balzac 1956 [1842]: 66), and ultimately repeating as rigid doctrines the open and flexible lessons of Marx? Might the abstract appearances of my own outlines have forced me to think and to write passively within the scenes of writing (Part I), the surfaces of writing (Part II), and the scripts of writing (Part III) that these authors have laid out for me and that I have only followed like a recipe? Perhaps these intentional though unexplored, coincidental, and apparently superficial repetitions should not disqualify me just as a Marxist but as a Goethean or a Balzacian as well.

Compendia

It is by now a commonplace for readers of Marx's writings to remark upon on their fragmentary, scattered, and condensed aspects, their overall roughness and incompleteness, and thus the difficulty of making sense of them. Perhaps the comment Marx reputedly made late in his life, that he could not assist in gathering his "complete works" because his complete works had yet to be written, could be said to apply not only to the fragmentary manuscripts he left behind and projects he left unfinished but also to those works he did see published during his lifetime, as I suggest in Appendix A. No work seems to have caused readers of Marx more difficulty than the collection of notebooks posthumously published as the *Grundrisse.* And yet the rough and unfinished quality of this text is often valued as its distinctive feature and the mark of its importance as a privileged site for reading Marx's way of managing the interplay between a radical research strategy and a will to rational presentation (Hobsbawm 1964; McLellan 1971; Negri 1984).

Like the celebrated three manuscripts he composed in Paris in 1844, these seven notebooks largely consist of long excerpts from and commentaries on works in philosophy, history, and economics. In contrast to the earlier notes, however, those of the *Grundrisse* are clearly divided into chapters (on money, capital, and value) and subsections (on production, circulation, and distribution) that serve as brief capitulations or abstract compendia anticipating the writing of his magnum opus, of which *Capital* (published a decade later) appears to have been only a part. In this mixture of chaos and order, of Marx's own writing with excerpts from others, what specifically has made this work an object of fascination both for me and for other readers of Marx?

Let us consider a reading of this text that both takes into account the difficulties readers have had in making sense of it and also defends the peculiar form in which Marx researched and wrote it. As the first translator and editor of the entire text into English, Martin Nicolaus has attempted to address the "alien character" of Marx's discourse in terms of the degree to which its revolutionary hermeneutic may be communicated both through its apparently indecipherable modes of presentation and research and through its translation into a foreign language. In the "Foreword" to his translation, Nicolaus argues that the text's "roughness of grammar," its "unfinished quality," its "rawness," its "repeated digressions . . . which chop up the continuity," its "awkward, obscure, and even altogether inaccurate formulations, endless sentences and paragraphs, irritating digressions and reiterations," and so on proclaim "on nearly every page its unripeness for print." Nevertheless, part of the reason the translation and publication of this text is such an important event in the history of Marxism is that these very features also "enhance its value as a revelation of Marx's creative mental process," and so constitute "an essential part of [the text's] significance":

Thus the *form* of the text appears as a series of obstacles only at first approach. . . . The *unity* of the structure and the method is *visible* in the *Grundrisse* on the surface; and this is its ultimately most distinguishing characteristic. . . . To grasp this unity requires reading the work as a process, a struggle with leaps and setbacks, in cognizance of origins and ends. . . . In reading the *Grundrisse*, the process and conditions of its becoming must never be forgotten, or else the perspectives it opens will once again turn into barriers. (Nicolaus 1973: 41–43)

To keep consistent with this interpretation of the significance of Marx's double strategy of research and presentation, Nicolaus's "Note on the Translation" emphasizes that nearly all of these "flaws" have been reproduced in the translation. He therefore lets Marx's sentences and paragraphs run on and break off without notice, even allowing many of the faulty calculations and mistakes in grammar to stand uncorrected. Only occasionally does he interject into Marx's rambling prose the odd explanatory footnote, and then usually just to indicate the places where Marx himself has digressed. Nicolaus's translation thus not only presents the "creative process" of Marx's reading and writing, the interruptions and resumptions that establish their rhythm, but it also tries to evoke that experience in the reading of the text by requiring the reader to take the trouble to work through Marx's impasses and elaborate the perspectives he opens.

Perhaps another mark of Nicolaus's conception of his task as a reader and translator of Marx is found in allowing the work's title, or rather, the heading given to the work by his German editors, to remain untranslated. Marx himself never really gave these notebooks a definite title, although he referred to them in his correspondence as his "Grundrisse," which Nicolaus could have translated as "rough drafts" or "outlines" (Marx to Engels, 8 December 1857; see epigraph to Part I), or as his "Heften," a word that could be translated as "notebooks" or even "installments" and that indicates the format he originally proposed for their publication (a point I return to in Chapter 3). Marx himself sometimes referred to these studies *in English* as his "principles" and his "outlines," and on the cover of the seventh notebook as "Political Economy, Critique of," options that Nicolaus also does not consider (but that the editors and translators of the *Collected Works* take as their guide, almost never calling these texts the *Grundrisse*).

Thus, Nicolaus not only uses a title that designates the roughness and incompleteness of these notebooks, but he also leaves his own translation unfinished by not translating the title (or heading) he gives them. He thereby repeats Marx's own gesture of not giving his work a title: "The lack of a title signals, at the outset, the unfinished quality of the manuscript" (Nicolaus 1973: 24), as though the translation of Marx's notebooks into English, like the notebooks themselves, should be left incomplete. In other words, not only does Nicolaus's "Fore-word" indicate that the fragmentary and condensed qualities of Marx's notebooks are an integral part of their significance, but he also allows the "word before" the English translation of this text (its "title" or "heading") to stand as a mark of the unfinished or even untranslatable dimension of Marx's work (cf. note 12 to Part III).

As a translator and reader of Marx's notebooks, Nicolaus translates them in a way that accounts for the need *not* to translate them as well, perhaps because leaving some part of them in a foreign language expresses something essential in what Marx's writing is trying to convey, or because the ideas they express are already somewhat strange. On the first page of his "Foreword," Nicolaus draws attention to the alienating effect this work might be expected to have on any readership, whether English or German, Marxist or non-Marxist. These obscure notebooks, he says, "challenge and put to the test every serious interpretation of Marx yet conceived" (1973: 7), first because they reveal Marx's intentions to present a critical compendium of political economy, and second because they seem closer to Marx's research strategies than any other work available to us.

On the last page of his "Foreword," Nicolaus calls this text "in every sense [a] *strange* product of the intellect [that] must have appeared as the reflections of some man from a distant planet" (1973: 61–62). Given their nature as a private record of Marx's reading and research "rough-drafted by [him] chiefly for purposes of self-clarification" (1973: 7), any publication, any translation, and indeed any reading of these notebooks would seem to be at cross-purposes with Marx's intentions in writing them, and thus cannot avoid stumbling upon their idiosyncratic and irreducibly alien character. Thus, as a translator who is above all a sympathetic interpreter of Marx, Nicolaus might ultimately seem to have betrayed his English readership: in his attempts to preserve what he takes to be the necessary roughness of the text in his translation of it, he may have challenged and put to the test not just every serious interpretation of Marx yet conceived, but any possible reading of Marx's text at all.

And yet Nicolaus might appear to have betrayed Marx as well by choosing to give a "smooth reading" of the text in "only one significant respect"— the very respect where his own task as an English translator is most at stake: "passages where Marx switched between German, French and English in mid-sentence are given entirely in English" (1973: 65). According to a habit that is probably nowhere more evident and difficult to treat than in these notebooks, Marx not only read several languages but frequently quoted his sources and commented on them in the language in which he read them, the dominant ones of course being German, English, and French. Thus, as a translator of Marx who also has some interpretive sense of the strange and alienating character of his writing, Nicolaus is faced with the unsolvable problem of how far to carry out his duties as translator/interpreter on behalf of a predominantly English-speaking readership. Even though he has tried to define his task as a translator to include the reproduction of the roughness and foreignness of Marx's writing, it nevertheless seems possible that in translating where Marx specifically does not, Nicolaus has tampered with an aspect of the text that gives it its "essential significance" (a worry that has often sent me back to those German editions which reproduce Marx's use of multiple foreign languages).

Nicolaus is sure to point out that Marx himself frequently translates English and French writers into his native German, sometimes even mistranslating them "in such a way as to bring out what for him were the vital points of the writer's thoughts" (1973: 66). In these instances, it appears that a certain degree of mistranslation already informs part of Marx's own interpretive evaluation of the discourses of political economy and may even allow him to open up his own perspectives. Marx's mixture of foreign languages with his own thus seems to constitute a way of writing what he reads, of reevaluating the works of others so that they can be expressed in another way, exchanged on another political and intellectual market, or characterized through another rationality than that which dominates the alien language of political economy. Producing neither a nontranslation that lacks its own voice nor an overtranslation that reduces another's words to his own unique speech (as do the Critical Critics and German ideologists discussed in Chapter 3), Marx mistranslates in a way that preserves the basic insights achieved by others while integrating them into his own theoretical discourse.

In opting both to preserve Marx's "roughness" and to translate the whole text into English (minus the "title" and a few foreign phrases), Nicolaus does seem in a certain respect to have kept consistent with Marx's own procedure in these notebooks. Perhaps this is especially true insofar as "Marx's own German version has been re-translated into English, hence the slight verbal and stylistic divergences from the original English texts" (1973: 66). That is, his decision to translate Marx's translations, rather than to reproduce original texts or even Marx's corrupted translations of them, as do other editions, is not simply a gesture on behalf of his presumably monolingual audience but also an interpretive move that reproduces Marx's own practice of subtly altering the character or style of texts written by others. As with his decision not to translate the editorial heading given to the notebooks, here too it seems that Nicolaus is concerned not just to present Marx's text as Marx himself did, but particularly to simulate or even enact it through his own translation of Marx's own representation or misrepresentation of the words and ideas put forward by other writers.

As a way of considering the ironic interpretive implications of this ambivalent fidelity and infidelity to Marx's "alien" discourse, let us look at one peculiarly revealing place in the text that draws particular attention not just to the site of Nicolaus's own practice of translation but also to our situation as readers of Marx in translation. On page 225 of the English edition, Marx describes the period preceding the development of modern capitalism as one that "opens with general greed for money on the part of individuals as well as of states." In the wake of the frantic exploration and frenzied expansion of the search for money, people do not seem aware that they have set in motion or even accelerated a process of development over which they may have little if any control: "The real development of wealth takes place as it were behind their backs, as a means of gaining possession of the representative of wealth. . . . This is why the search for and discovery of gold in new continents, countries, plays so great a role in the history of revaluation, because by its means colonization is improvised and made to flourish as if in a hothouse."

The editors of the *Collected Works* note that this passage probably refers to the discovery of rich goldfields in California in 1848 and Australia in 1851.

They also note that as early as January 1850, eighteen months after the Californian discovery, Marx and Engels were able to point to the crucial importance of these discoveries for the commercial and industrial development of Europe, as well as for stimulating the colonization of new territories in America and Asia (CW 28: 549). This interpretation is supported by the example Marx refers to in the passage I have elided, which mentions the Spanish who went directly in search of the sources of gold in the New World, not having sufficient resources of their own to trade.

Now, in all other editions of Marx's notebooks, including all of those that would have been available to Nicolaus, "the history of *revaluation*" is in fact written as "the history of *revolution*" (*der Geschichte der Revolution* in the German, at II 2). Thus, it seems that Nicolaus himself has slipped behind Marx's back and mistranslated him in an obvious (if unconscious) way. What then could be the significance, whether intentional or not, of misreading "revolution" as "revaluation," especially since these are key words in the Marxian lexicography whose meanings would by no means have been a matter of indifference to Marx?

In the same note mentioned above, the editors of the *Collected Works* also remark that the Californian and Australian discoveries spurred industrial and financial activity in the capitalist countries and so "to a certain degree contributed to the defeat of the European revolutions of 1848 and 1849" (CW 28: 549). Thus, it is as if "the history of revaluation," that is, of the expansion and intensification of the capitalist money system, was itself a factor in the "history of revolution," not just by providing an incitement to revolution (as in the wars of independence in North America) but also by bolstering the forces of counterrevolution or even by invalidating the material reasons for which a revolt might be staged in the first place (as in the European revolutions of 1848). Although Marx was certainly well aware of both these scenarios at the time he wrote this passage, his intended meaning here was clearly to make a point about the history of revolution, however much it may also have been shaped or determined, incited or blocked, by the history of revaluation, as in the search for gold in the New World and in attacks on the gold standard that may ultimately have aimed to subvert, preserve, or expand capitalism.

Insofar as we ourselves are English-speaking and specifically North American readers of Marx who approach him by way of translation, we may wish to consider whether there might be a specifically Marxian significance in Nicolaus's mistranslation that brings out what for him or for us are the "vital points" of Marx's thoughts. By going back to the "original" text (without being able to inspect Marx's manuscript, of course), I seem to have found a place where our translator himself (or perhaps some other intervening agency) has "revaluated" Marx's text, thereby submerging the history of revolution in the history of colonization and the expansion of the capitalist money system. It is as if the major political revolutions of the modern era, such as the American in 1776, the French in 1848, and the Russian in 1917, should not be considered as true revolutions in any Marxian or properly communist sense of the word, but merely as "revaluating" tactics within a larger capitalist strategy. Translating from the perspective of his own colonial American "hothouse," perhaps in some way Nicolaus hoped to introduce something new and potentially radical into Marx's discourse, to contribute to the accumulation and "revaluation" of the wealth of Marxian scholarship so that one day the "history of revaluation" might again be read in our own language as a "revolutionary story." Perhaps this is why at the end of his "Foreword," Nicolaus expresses his belief that finally, after more than a century of capitalist development and expansion, "these texts out of a London winter, long ago, are coming home" (1973: 63).

But what if this misreading were merely a mistake on our translator's part, a typographical error, or a misprint, a copy editor's oversight, a secretary's sleight of hand, a machine malfunction introducing some foreign character into the printing process, or the act of some other sinister and anonymous intervention? In what way would the consequences of such unintended "interpretations" be essentially different from those of the early capitalists in Marx's passage, for whom "the real development of wealth takes place as it were behind their backs, as a means of gaining possession of the representative of wealth"? What would the unplanned character and unexpected outcome of such accidents have to do with the fact that such a "forgery," like a counterfeit dollar, might circulate in some other market of ideas and be read, rewritten, and communicated in new ways?

Although I may sometimes have achieved no more than a childish speechlessness (*infans*) or an aesthetic fashionableness, which others may reject, clarify, or express in their own way, my aim throughout these pages has been to explore these and other "improvisations" as they emerge from our encounter with the scene of Marx writing. What more can be said will be said by other writers more articulate than I, or if not in the text to follow, then in other projects of which this is a part.[1] Like Goethe's Faust (or Balzac himself), I have in a sense never left the comfortable but sometimes confining space of the "study," sometimes searching for a new covenant or pact that would disentangle the divine and diabolical forces between myself and those whom I address, and sometimes risking enough of my reason to lay down some new law or to face the final judgment. By treading in the places of those whom I am studying (*an ihre Stelle treten*), standing apart from them, or even breaking from them altogether, I have not tried to become my ideal types, either Balzacian or Goethean, Marxist or Kemplist. There is then a sense in which Marx's "Grundrisse" may not only have served me as "ground plans" for mapping our own territory, as the "outlines" of something else in our distant horizon, and as "compendia" for abbreviating the journey getting there, but also as "ruptures-in-reason" ("Grund-risse") through which the communicative dimensions of thought turn into dementia, the rapturous delight in some new sight or sound disrupts rationality, or the destruction of a beautiful time and place forever lost to us fills us with sadness.

. . . .
. . . .
. . . .

PART I

Faust's Study

And this the man that in his study sits.

Christopher Marlowe, *The Tragical History of Doctor Faustus*

I am writing like mad all night long and every night collating my economic studies so that I at least get the outlines [*die Grundrisse*] clear before the deluge.   Marx to Engels, 8 December 1857

. . . .
. . . .
. . . .

Science, Technology, and the Song of the Cellar Rat

I

No one better than Marx has understood the general outlines of the dilemma that modern technology poses to the fate of humankind. When he withdrew from the political stage into his study after the revolutions of 1848, it was not simply because he had grown cynical about the possibility or even desirability of radical social change, but because he saw the need to explore more deeply the role of the earlier and more pervasive industrial revolution in recasting the characters and direction of the modern social drama. He intensified his studies in order to analyze more thoroughly what he had come to understand as the inherently antithetical existence of industrial society: its tendency to require longer and more intense work hours for the great mass of the population while leaving more disposable and leisure time for the few, and its mania for creating a colossal accumulation of wealth and power while enforcing a system for their unequal yet legitimate distribution. Industrial society has turned its back on its premodern past and its "undeveloped" contemporaries, but it is ultimately haunted by a lingering sense of its own primitivism: "The most developed machinery thus forces the worker to work longer than the savage does, or even than he himself did with the simplest, crudest tools" (VII: 708–9).

And yet perhaps the greatest dilemma posed to us by modern technology, which Marx already seemed to glimpse in the dark clouds of a not-so-distant future, is that the splendors of our great tools of production could well turn against their makers as instruments of destruction. Not only must technological culture attempt to manage and dispose of its monstrous excesses, but we ourselves may now be able to put an end to both the industrial mode of production itself and the world it sustains. More than ever we have the power not just to develop "the material conditions to blow this foundation sky-high" (VII: 706) but also to destroy ourselves along with it, thus making thinkable as well as possible the prospect of our own annihilation. So when Marx descended into his rat-hole apartment in London, or sat at his favorite desk in the British Museum, his desperate ambition was to compose the outlines (*die Grundrisse*) of the modern dilemma before the deluge, and thereby to clear a space for thought and reflection on a more human future (Marx to Engels, 8 December 1857; see epigraph to Part I, above).

The question we are now faced with is not just whether Marx correctly and truthfully understood the most basic parameters of his own historical situation, but whether and to what extent he might have understood ours as well. For it is not true, as some social scientists would have us believe, that the sum total of Marx's legacy to us consists of having predicted a final cataclysm from which would emerge an organized system of socialized railways, government agencies, and state-owned banks (as the ten measures in the *Communist Manifesto* seem to propose). Nor was his ultimate hope for the future simply to return to a pastoral realm of freedom in which socialist man may finally be able to hunt, fish, and criticize as he pleases (as he seems to suggest in the polemical context of the *German Ideology*). Rather, his achievement consists in conceiving a framework for understanding the permanently revolutionary character of the social drama of modernity as the "externally compelling condition" of its existence and "a question of life or death," its need to fix the relations between leisure and labor for each social class and to sustain a constant flux between the processes of production and destruction (VII: 703, 706; cf. Marx and Engels 1848; Berman 1988: 87–129).

The reasonable, free, and happy man, whether Renaissance or Socialist, is no longer the measure of the universe, the standard or model by which the things of this world are set in their proper order and proportion; rather, our machinery is itself "the measuring rod" of the development of human wealth, power, and knowledge, and the growth of technology is the norm by which we assess the progress of humanity (VII: 710). Traditional and everyday social competencies have been stripped of their relevance; science has been pressed into the service of technology, production, and politics; and all social resources have been dissected into "general productive forces of the social brain" (VII: 694) and fed into a central information system independent of human (and not just class and power) interests. Our question is not simply whether Marx was right when he stood back from the turmoils of his day, fixed his gaze on the future, and began to describe what he imagined, but how he in fact arrived at this futuristic vision of our present, what its general outlines are, and in what ways might we interpret its implications.

More than a century after Marx wrote his last word, and long after the industrial deluge of the nineteenth century and the military holocausts of the twentieth, the most difficult puzzle for us to solve may ultimately be whether we may now be at all capable of understanding Marx. For there is a sense in which the challenge that faces us in the technological reconstitution of society, nature, and politics is at the same time a challenge to the simultaneously humanist and scientific vision from which Marx never relented. Thus, we must account not only for the fact that the manual work of unskilled immediate producers in the nineteenth century has been drastically reduced, reskilled, imported from abroad, or replaced by high-level scientific labor in the twentieth century, but also for the fact that even our desire or capacity to labor (*Arbeitsvermögen*) and our will to produce have increasingly become "an infinitesimal, vanishing magnitude" (VI: 693). Besides the theoretical and analytical implications that such historical developments may have in forcing Marxists to consider a nonlabor or even leisure theory of value to serve as the new foundation for a postindustrial critique of political economy (as I suggest in Chapter 5), this emerging specter also has practical and political implications that are perhaps even more pressing, and that a Marxist approach may not be equipped to address.

Our general sense of these challenges to the relevance of Marx and of Marxism may be specified in terms of Jürgen Habermas's sketch of the salient features of the emerging technological and postindustrial society through a double process of "scientization" that evolves through the shift from early to late capitalism (cf. Habermas 1989; 1971: 94–113):

I. The scientization of technology
   A. In early capitalism, productive relations are still largely rooted in traditional ethnic and gender differences, while emerging ideological conflicts are expressed explicitly in terms of contradictory class interests.
   B. In late capitalism, such conflicts are submerged into
      1. an apparently societywide consensus about the necessity of technologically steered political and economic processes, and
      2. a belief about the inevitability of developing science-based technologies and information systems oriented more to technical criteria than to human interests.
II. The scientization of politics
   A. In early capitalism, open class conflicts are largely fought over pauperization and wealth, disenfranchisement and political power.

B. In late capitalism, such conflicts are pacified and rendered latent by
1. a strategy of state intervention in the economy designed to ensure mass loyalty through a minimum of social welfare, while
also maintaining the continuity of production and consumption
by securing new outlets for investments and spending, and
2. the state redefinition of social progress as the exploitation of scientific knowledge in the production and destruction of wealth, and of
public issues as primarily matters of private or corporate concern.

It should be remembered that these processes work not only simultaneously
and complementarily, but often in contradictory and uneven ways with respect
to one another. On the one hand, the "objective" superiority of the scientific
consciousness is achieved both by rationalizing practical issues as technical
problems of efficiency and by reconceiving the functional stability or instability
of systems as a quasi-ethical imperative. Regardless of the tactic, the result
is that all explicitly class-based ideologies come to appear irrelevant while all
social knowledge, including science, becomes potential techno-logy. On the
other hand, government activity is disembedded from public discussion by
reframing public issues as private troubles or political disputes as administrative and technical problems solvable through piecemeal social engineering. In
either case, the result is both *the depoliticization of the mass of the population*
in favor of consumption and passivity and *the retreat by government from politics* in favor of economic steering measures and social management strategies.
In short, what dies in the life cycle from "immature" to "late" capitalism is not
capitalist class structures and ideological conflicts but the historical and cultural framework of class consciousness and political action through which they
could be interpreted. Thus, the "specter" (*Gespenst*) that haunts contemporary
society is not something that has flown from the dead remains of proletarian
upheavals or political chaos (cf. Marx and Engels 1848) but the frightening
projection of our own absence from the technological production of history.

The challenge to a humanist vision of the future, and not just a Marxist
analysis of the present, has been articulated by critical social theorists in terms
of whether and to what extent the emerging technocratic rationality may be
shown to have a political dimension, and whether the very form of technology-
as-knowledge may be understood to have a political content and context within
the existing social system of domination (Marcuse 1964). If so, not only may
technocratic social strata be defined as elite class fragments and thus located
in terms of their mediated and socialized relation to the means of production
and power (Mills 1956), but even the value placed on objective knowledge and
knowledgeableness in late capitalist society may be understood as a key element of capitalist ideology (Habermas 1971). Late capitalist society can then be

reconceptualized as a social economy that has generalized and submerged—but not abolished or equalized—differences in ideology and conflicts between classes so far beyond early capitalist work and labor settings that capitalism appears as a specter or myth that is nowhere because it is everywhere (Wilson 1983). A Marxist and humanist approach to these issues therefore consists of finding to what extent and through which theoretical frameworks we may be able to study and gain critical perspective on how *the politicization of science* and science-based technology progresses in the interests of either perpetuating domination or creating the conditions for human emancipation (O'Neill 1982: 158–66).

The issues sketched here appear to be not only outside of Marx's historical frame of reference but also beyond my own capacity to develop them in the empirical detail they require. Nevertheless, it is not difficult to show to what extent Marx himself understood the theoretical complications involved, and so to have at least implicitly provided us with a framework for interpreting them that is not reducible to nineteenth-century conceptions of class and ideology. Thus, our problem here may be expressed in the open question of whether and to what extent we ourselves are capable of seeing in Marx's vision the outlines of our own dilemma, of hearing through his words the music to which we ourselves must march. The challenge, then, is not just to assess Marx's ability to understand his times, but above all to glimpse our own dilemmas through the political and sociological imagination that informed his understanding of our common history:

In machinery, the appropriation [*Aneignung*] of living labor by capital achieves a direct reality in this respect as well: It is, firstly, the analysis and application of mechanical and chemical laws, arising directly out of science, which enables the machine to perform the same labor as that previously performed by the worker. However, the development of machinery along this path [*Weg*] occurs only when large industry has reached a higher stage, and all the sciences have been pressed into the service of capital; and when, secondly, the available machinery itself already provides great capabilities [*Ressourcen*]. Invention then becomes a business, and the application of science to direct production itself becomes a prospect [*Gesichtspunkt*] which determines and solicits it. But this is not the road [*Weg*] along which machinery, by and large, arose, and even less the road on which it progresses in detail. This road is, rather, the dissection [*Analyze*]—through the division of labor, which gradually transforms the workers' operations into more and more mechanical ones, so that at a certain point a mechanism can step into their places [*an ihre Stelle treten*] (Ad ECONOMY OF POWER.) Thus, the specific mode of working here appears DIRECT as becoming transferred [*übertragen*] from the worker to capital in the form of the machine, and through this transposition his own labor capacity is devalued. Hence the workers' struggle against machinery. What was the living worker's activity becomes the activity of the machine. Thus the appropriation of labor by capital confronts the worker in a coarsely sensuous form; capital absorbs labor into itself—"as though its body were by love possessed." (VII 2: 704)

Apart from our attempts to make any factual and detailed sense of what such a paragraph might have meant to Marx in writing it, or to imagine what it might mean for us today in reading it, we may at least initially try to sense in Marx's exhilarating prose an inkling of what constitutes it as a passage from his own historical situation to our own. That is, we should recognize that the developments described here could only have suggested themselves to Marx as latent historical possibilities, and yet he is able to decipher in the direction of these tendencies a pathway or road (Weg) that leads beyond the early capitalism of his day and into the late capitalism of ours (cf. note 16 to Part III).

Marx's observations on the institutionalized application of the sciences in the service of production, the transformation of scientific invention itself into a business, and the general reconstitution of all scientific knowledge into productive knowledge for monitoring results and controlling feedback, attained practical relevance and full reality only at a stage of history much later than the one in which he wrote. At the same time, he notes that these developments have not laid the main road to progress and that there is no reason why they should necessarily be expected to do so in the future. Rather, the more basic direction of scientific rationalization is toward the intensified "dissection" or "analysis" (Analyze) of labors into an almost infinite number of discrete activities, from the most mechanical and manual to the most technically skilled and refined, so that even the scientific labors of "watching and regulating" the production process (VII: 705) will come to form part of the functional hierarchy of occupations. Thus, what Marx calls here "the workers' struggle against machinery" refers not just to the most exploited and degraded laborers in the time of the Luddites or in the London factories of the mid-nineteenth century. More generally this struggle indicates the multiplication of discrete activities on behalf of or in resistance to an expanding technological and administrative system that increasingly creates what Marx calls (in English) an "economy of power" that has the ability to render humans without value and superfluous.

Even these insights do not exhaust the imaginative resources of this remarkable passage because Marx has also projected here the image of a completely automated society, indeed, a science fiction of the technological possession of the social body. Here, it is not just a question for him of observing that scientific inventions, or what is now called research and development, can be organized into an industrial business; that all intellectual and manual work can be dissected, distributed, and integrated into the social division of labor; or even that many human faculties can be transposed or transferred (übertragt) into the capacities (Ressourcen) of machinery. Rather, Marx is really speculating on the extent to which modern technology may ultimately "step into the places" of the workers (*an ihre Stelle treten*), so that "what was the living worker's activity becomes the activity of the machine [*Was Thätigkeit des leben-digen Arbeiters war, wird Thätigkeit der Maschine*]": where humans were, so shall technology become. All capacities of the human organism, all human sensibilities might gradually be transferred to increasingly autonomous mechanical processes. The motor functions of the hands and feet, the activities of the sense organs, especially the eyes, the ears, and the skin, the energy-producing organs of the body, and the controlling and regulating powers of the central nervous system, especially the human brain, can then be separated and projected onto the technical plane of machinery. As Habermas puts it, "for the first time, man can not only as *homo faber*, completely objectify himself and confront the achievements that have taken an independent life in his products, he can, in addition, as *homo fabricatus*, be integrated into his technical apparatus" (Habermas 1970: 106).

Marx describes here a process of technological appropriation (*Aneignung*) and subsumption, of absorption and incorporation on a colossal scale, to the point where the specter of the despotic domination of a *technological body* ruled by the fluxes and flows of appended desiring-machines finally becomes a real possibility (cf. Deleuze and Guattari 1977). He imagines modern machinery as a giant automaton, "a moving power that moves of itself consisting of numerous mechanical and intellectual organs" within which labor is a mere "accessory" and "conscious link" (VI: 690, 692, quoting Andrew Ure). Indeed, as a soulless mechanism that has no regard for the human relations between society and nature, or for the proportions between body and spirit (VII: 710, quoting Robert Owen), capitalist technology appears here as a personified and artificially animated dead body with monstrous powers (cf. VII: 831). Not only may machinery confront workers in some "coarsely sensuous form" that in a vulgar sense "screws them over," but it may also appear to them through a seductive spectacle that seizes upon their bodily and imaginative resources and transforms them from the possessive individuals of property to the possessed individuals of technology (cf. Kroker 1992; Macpherson 1962). Thus, even the residually anthropomorphic image of an enlightened industrialism whose aim is human emancipation, if only for the few, would here be replaced by a mech-anomorphic specter that ultimately seduces us into toying with catastrophic scenarios of our own absence (O'Neill 1985).

Neither we nor Marx seem to have access to any clearer picture of what a world without us could possibly look like, of what sensuous form it could take, or what activities it might pursue, and so the problem we confront here is not how to interpret the meaning of Marx's message but what else might be meant by such an apocalyptic projection of our future. Recalling Marx's comment to

Engels around this time, that "I am writing . . . for me, INDIVIDUALLY, TO GET RID OF THIS NIGHTMARE" (Marx to Engels, 18 December 1857), our task may also be to see if some other latent dream content might be deciphered beyond the manifest and empirical meaning of Marx's dream text. And yet many of Marx's dream interpreters have been blind to his remarkable foresight in projecting the outlines of the human prospect. They diagnose such passages as symptoms of his limited understanding of the potential in the modern sciences to resist these processes, or as his failure of nerve in not being able to locate scientific knowledge in the sphere of human interests. As Habermas sees it, for example, the restricted view from Marx's own categorical framework requires him to reduce "the self-generative activities of the human species and its process of self-reflection to the level of the merely instrumental action of labor and production." Although in his empirical analyses Marx is able to co-ordinate his studies of human history in terms of "material activity *and* the critical abolition of ideologies, instrumental action *and* revolutionary practice, labor *and* reflection at once," in his methodological self-understanding he ultimately "interprets what he does in the more restricted conception of the species self-reflection through work alone" (Habermas 1971: 42). Marx's self-misunderstanding or even self-delusion is thus produced by his inability to find a way of conceiving the objective self-formative process of the human species (*Bildungsprozess*), including human self-reflection through the sciences, in any other way than in terms of this functional and technological worldview.

However, critics of Habermas in turn have pointed out that this reading is largely based less on any better understanding of what Marx meant or detailed insight into what Marx really said than on Habermas's own categorical distinction between the discrete and separable domains of work, including strategic and instrumental action, and interaction, including symbolic processes and communicative action (see Habermas 1970: 113). Not only does Habermas himself often seem to accept the positivist identification of the instrumental-ism of the applied sciences with science generally, but he also assumes that Marx's conception of human interaction with nature (the *Stoffwechselprozess*) is based on a rather simplistic understanding of "man as a tool-making ani-mal," itself derived from "the physical constitution of this natural being and some constraints of its natural environment" (1971: 113; cf. O'Neill 1982: 23–30). Thus, he tends to view technocratic phenomena in terms of a singular systemic entity consisting of a concrete set of operations and functions, or even as a kind of specter or myth, rather than as an inherently contradictory structure, process, or movement that is culturally and historically specific, an ideology that masquerades as a natural doctrine (Wilson 1986). In spite of Marx's explicitly critical intentions, Habermas reads his passages on scientific and technological development as unreflective observations on technological rationality that show only a partial awareness of the assumptions governing its scientistic consciousness, and that are therefore lacking sufficiently critical foundations.[1]

But we must ourselves be careful here to avoid in our understanding of Habermas the same reductionism identified in his understanding of Marx. In particular, we should note those rhetorical and tentative features of his discourse by which he grounds his own conceptual and interpretive scheme on a foundation of shaky probabilities and limited speculations (cf. LaCapra 1983: 145–83). The decisive points of his argument are not always established through a series of declarative statements, but rather in the form of conditional suppositions, counterfactual speculations, and provisionally tenable assumptions that set limits to our critique of his conclusions while challenging us to formulate alternative ones. Thus, to suppose that "*if* indeed science is to retain the meaning of modern science inherently oriented to technical control . . . then there is no more 'human' substitute," is to leave open the possibility of a "new science" not oriented toward technical control (Habermas 1970: 88; my emphasis). Similarly, to speculate that "technological development lends itself to being interpreted *as though* the human species had taken the elementary components of the behavioral system of purposive-rational action . . . and projected them one after another on to the plane of technical instruments," is to leave for later consideration how technology might also develop more in proportion to human intelligence and sensibilities (1970: 86; my emphasis). And finally, to assume for the purposes of argument that "*as long as* we regard the self-constitution of the human species through labor with respect to the power over natural processes that accumulates in the process of production, it is meaningful to speak of the social system in general and . . . in the singular," is to anticipate without dismissing some other view of both the self-formation of human capacities and the social context in which such processes take place (1971: 54; my emphasis).

Regardless of the direction Habermas was later to take his work (e.g., 1984, 1987), its roots in his reading of Marx were not entirely planted on firm empirical grounds or in a series of categorical pronouncements. Rather, he searches for and opens up interpretive possibilities that others might wish to pursue, or that may already have been opened by Marx. Thus, in this encounter of the historical past with the prospects of our present through a text of Marx, we do not simply find an instance of "misreading" that could be corrected (whether we consider Marx on the history of the human species or Habermas on Marx). More important, we approach here an open door for exploring unconscious, implicit, and even potentially subversive lines of inquiry that are already indicated in what such provocative and informed interpretations have not found time to pursue.

II

Let us return to Marx's passage by proceeding not from the conclusions of Habermas's influential reading but from the grammatical structure of the premises of this reading and the interpretive framework they imply. That is, the "if," the "as though," and the "as long as" may be understood to suggest a procedure for deciphering meanings otherwise left unexplored by both Marx and critics like Habermas. Indeed, just such a rhetorical strategy is introduced by Marx at the very climax of his science fictional delirium, in the phrase "*as though* its body were by love possessed." We have seen above the significance of the act of taking possession connoted in Marx's discourse at this point, since the paragraph begins with a reference to "the appropriation of labor by capital" and ends with an image of labor being "absorbed" into the machineries of capitalism.

In similar passages of *Capital*, Marx is even more graphic in his dramatic account of the way in which the capitalist incorporates "lifeless and objectified labor" into itself like "an animated monster which begins to 'work' 'as if its body were by love possessed'" (C1: 302, Fowkes's translation). And yet in either context it is clear that not labor but the body of capital is "possessed," in its ultimate incarnation as machinery and in some crazy or demonic way. Indeed, when we give to this expression a more literal translation by rendering *als hätt'es Lieb im Leibe* to read "as if it had love in its body," and interpret it in a vulgar and "coarsely sensuous" way that seems to run counter to the expectations raised in the rest of Marx's passage, it appears that capital is on the bottom of a coupling ruled over by labor.

It is *as if*, at this most extreme moment where the organs of human labor are being absorbed or incorporated into the mechanical body of capital, a dramatic reversal is also being effected. Indeed, it is as if Marx, without really knowing it, only half-consciously, unintentionally, or perhaps even misunderstanding himself (to use Habermas's formulation), has here suggested a direction for interpretation that would be the very opposite of, or in some sense radically opposed to, the direction in which the historical road (*Weg*) has been leading up to this point.

As Martin Nicolaus notes in his English translation of the *Grundrisse*, this phrase comes from the scene in the first part of Goethe's *Faust* that is set in "Auerbach's Wine Cellar in Leipzig" (at VII: 704), a work from which Marx, like many Germans, would have been able to recall entire scenes from memory and to recite many lines by heart. If we now try to think of what could be happening here at the very climax of Marx's theoretical reflections on science and technology, it may seem as if Marx himself, like Faust in his study, has succumbed to a situation "where thoughts are absent," and so "words are brought in as a convenient replacement," as in *Capital*, where he characterizes Proudhon's work as "scientific" more in word than in conception (paraphrasing *Faust*, ll. 1995–96; C1: 161). Or like those commodity owners who are described in *Capital* as acting before thinking, living by Faust's quasi-biblical pronouncement that "in the beginning was the deed," it is as if at this moment Marx himself can no longer think at all, but only act out through his own scene of writing a scene from Goethe's *Faust* (quoting *Faust*, l. 1237; C1: 180; cf. Derrida 1978).

If any ideas at all were passing through Marx's head at this moment, they seem to have come from someone or somewhere else, perhaps from some other ghostly voice whose words Marx takes down as if under dictation (cf. Ronell 1986). Indeed, it may be that while Marx is thinking one thing, whose meaning we can gather from his own words and their context, he also wants to express something else in some other voice, perhaps to reanimate his writing so that it may be inscribed in some other writing system or discourse network (cf. Kittler 1990). Just as for Marx it may not be a question here of analyzing, describing, or representing some process taking place outside him, either actually in the present or potentially in the future, so it is not our task here to try to understand what Marx "meant," and even less to attempt to figure out what he might have said or intended to say had he known any better. Instead of trying to read the sense of this passage, we might attempt to imagine what the scene that interrupts it looks like and thus to listen to what else it might be communicating, beyond Marx's explicit intentions or even knowledge.

Let us consider for a moment Marx's own words in the passages leading up to the one on science and technology, this time treating them not as literal descriptions of capitalist development but rather as part of an interpretive allegory for taking Marx's discourse in another direction. Our aim here is thus to recast the characters of Marx's historical drama much as he himself imagines a horrifying scenario in which capital "casts the workers as merely conscious linkages" (VI: 692). Thus, we may peer into the split (*Unterscheidung*) in the form and content of the analysis here much as Marx tries to see how capital is divided "both as regards its merely physical aspect [and as] entering into its form itself" (VII: 703). And we may try to mark this moment of interruption (*Unterbrechung*) in the flow of Marx's discourse in much the same way he notes that "the continuity of the production process and the constant flow of reproduction" are also broken into fragments (VII: 703). At stake in this allegory of reading is nothing less than the communicative dimensions that are opened through the revolutionary rhetoric of Marx's science, itself informed by an antirealist perspective on the socially constructed nature of truth and by the literary resources of his procedure of inquiry. Such an approach thus requires us to elaborate the interpretive possibilities that can be glimpsed in the discursive structure of the "as if" onto which opens the poetics of Marx's scientific prose and the dramatic structure of his political discourse.

The line from *Faust* that interrupts the continuity of Marx's passage here comes not from any long, dull speech by Mephistopheles or Faust but from the refrain of a drinking song belted out by a cheering group of tavern carousers. To interpret the role this song might play in this scene and in Goethe's *Faust* as a whole, as well as in Marx's discourse on machines, we would do well to begin not with Faust and Mephistopheles (whose relationship reaches an important new phase in this scene) but with the character of Herr Brander, who leads this song. Noting that his name in German designates a fire ship, which carries combustibles or explosives among the enemy's ships to set them on fire, we might say that his incendiary presence in this scene spreads throughout the whole of Goethe's *Faust* and into Marx's notebooks, creating an explosion each writer has barely been able to detect and whose effects they can hardly control through their subsequent efforts. From the beginning of this scene, Brander has been antagonizing the patrons of Auerbach's wine cellar by clamoring for "some pig in your poke . . . a bit of nonsense . . . a dirty joke" (ll. 2077–78), only to interrupt with a string of insults the few lines that Herr Frosch is able to croak from a satirical political ditty and a maudlin love song. Bored and disgusted with the entertainment, Brander slams his fist on the table while shouting: "Confess, I know a thing or two. . . . Attend! A song in latest vein! / Chime in with vigorous refrain" (ll. 2120, 2124–25). To the delight of everyone, he then launches into his own raunchy song about a cellar rat pursued to its death by a vengeful cook. It is the refrain from this song that chimed in Marx's head as he wrote his lines on science and technology, and thus it is the dissonant tones of this chorus in both Goethe's dramatic verse and Marx's revolutionary prose that we must now attempt to discern.

In what follows, I shall try to imagine that Marx's own writing throughout these notebooks, and not just at the place where he invokes the song of the cellar rat, is being acted out in this scene from Goethe's *Faust*. As an experiment to test how far the Marxian imagination might be stretched, I shall begin by turning Marx's passage on science and technology upside down, as it were. That is, the verses of Brander's song will be put in the place of Marx's own words while various selected sentences taken from elsewhere in Marx's notebooks will be inserted where he had put the chorus of that song. In other words, where Brander will have the floor to sing the "verses" of the song of the cellar rat, Marx will mingle among the other tavern revelers to lead the "chorus." This incongruous reversal and mixture of texts from Marx and Goethe can be justified only after experiencing their rhythm and movement together, and this will require an initial attempt to forgo the impulse to "make sense" of the historical, theoretical, or even allegorical significance of these words in their new combination. That is, to imagine this scene as if Marx, too, were caught up in its celebrations, we will need to suspend our studious concentration just enough to hear the play of call and response reverberating in the song leader's breathless story, in Marx's long-winded prose, and in the gasping cries of the dying beast that both chorus and verse can be understood to be narrating:

The Song of the Cellar Rat

Brander [verse 1]

In a cellar nest there lived a rat,	Es war eine Ratt im Kellernest,
Had butter and lard to suit her,	Lebte nur von Fett und Butter,
She wore a belly bag of fat,	Hatte sich ein Ränzlein angemäst't,
A pouch like Dr. Luther.	Als wie der Doktor Luther.
The cook had poison scattered out,	Die Köchin hatt ihr Gift gestellt;
That drove her hither and about,	Da ward's so eng ihr in der Welt,

(ll. 2126–31)

Chorus

The recognition [*Erkennung*] of the products as its own, and the judgement that its separation from the conditions of its realization is improper—forcibly imposed—is an enormous [advance in] awareness [*Bewusstsein*], itself the product of the mode of production based on capital, and as much the knell to its doom as, with the slave, awareness that he *cannot be the property of another*, with his consciousness of himself as a person, the existence of slavery becomes a merely artificial, vegetative existence, and ceases to be able to prevail as the basis for production. (IV 47: 463)

Brander [verse 2]

She hurried, scurried, pawed and clawed	Sie fuhr herum, sie fuhr hinaus,
And swilled from every puddle,	Und soff aus allen Pfützen,
The house was all scratched and gnawed	Zernagt', zerkratzt' das ganze Haus,
To soothe her frantic muddle;	Wollte nichts ihr Wüten nützen;
Tried many a leap in fear and pain	Sie tät gar manchen Ängstesprung
But all she tried was tried in vain,	Bald hatte das arme Tier genung,

(ll. 2134–39)

Chorus

(and the worker's participation in the higher, even cultural satisfactions, the agitation for his own interests, newspaper subscriptions, attending lectures, educating his children, developing his taste, etc., his only share of civilization which distinguishes him from the slave, is economically only possible by widening the sphere of pleasures at times when the business is good, where saving is to a certain degree possible). (II 27: 287)

Brander [verse 3]

In fright she sought the light of day,	Sie kam vor Angst am hellen Tag,
Came running in the kitchen,	Der Küche zugelaufen,
Fell at the stove and there she lay,	Fiel an den Herd und zukt' und lag,

With piteous gasp and twitching.	Und tät erbärmlich schnaufen.
The poisoner only laughed, she knew	Da lachte die Vergifterin noch:
She'd bit off more than she could chew,	Ha! sie pfeift auf dem letzten Loch,

(ll. 2143–47)

Chorus
The great historic side of capital is to *create surplus labor,* superfluous labor from the standpoint of mere use-value, mere subsistence; and its historic destiny [*Bestimmung*] is fulfilled as soon as, on one side, there has been such a development of needs that surplus labor above and beyond necessity has itself become a general need arising out of individual needs themselves —and, on the other side, when the severe discipline of capital acting on succeeding generations [*Geschlechter*] has developed general industriousness as the general property of the new species [*Geschlecht*]—and finally, when the development of the productive powers of labor, which capital incessantly whips onward with its unlimited mania for wealth, and of the sole conditions in which this mania can be realized, have flourished to the stage where the possession and preservation of general wealth require a lesser labor time of society as a whole, and where the laboring society relates scientifically to the process of its progressive reproduction, its reproduction in a constantly greater abundance; hence where labor in which a human being does what a thing could do has ceased. (III 23: 325)

The sense that can be made of what I have called here the "Song of the Cellar Rat," this confusion of words and music, this intertwining of Goethe's verse and of Marx's prose, and this juxtaposition of song and history, will largely depend upon our willingness to enter into that other dimension which Marx's text seems to open up but which he himself does not explore. It will require our ability to take Marx's statement that "music alone awakens the sense of music" as an invitation to retune our ears to the music beyond the meaning of words, enough to enable us to listen to the strains of a new melody, or at least of a strange and uncanny disharmony (cf. Marx [1844b] *EW:* 140–41; III: 305; Barthes 1977 [1970]).

To interpret the relationship of this song's "verses" and "choruses" with respect to the scene depicted in Goethe's text, it would seem futile, at least initially, to attempt to align the roles of the cellar rat and the cook with the respective functions of labor and capital. In the first place, such an approach would already be upset by Goethe's reference to both the cook and the rat in a way that confuses the qualities they impute to one another, in that each is perceived as enemy and poisoner of the other. In the second place, as I have already remarked, the conduct of Marx's own discourse renders the relationship between capital and labor ambiguous and potentially reversible. For example, in another related passage near the very end of his notebooks, he writes that "machines can only *arise* in antithesis to living labor, as property alien to it, and as power hostile to it; i.e. that they must confront them as capital" (VII 44: 832–33). The identity of "they" and "them" in this last statement is not clear from Marx's grammar, as the editors of the *Gesamtausgabe* point out in their comment that Marx "apparently meant the workers [they = *ihnen*] although he in fact is speaking here of living labor [it = *ihr*, the feminine pronoun corresponding to labor]" (*MEGA* II/1; *Apparat*: 967). Thus, not unlike Goethe's reference to both the cook and the rat in the feminine (*sie* = she), Marx seems to refer to both labor and capital with the same plural pronoun at precisely the moment when their perception of one another (as "machines") is most at issue. The lesson we can take from this grammatical confusion is that the meaning of this song in its new setting must first be looked for less in the psychology and identity of its characters than in the structure of its plot and the thematic development of its story line.

Approaching the song now in the most general way possible, the narrative running through each of the three verses and choruses can be read in terms of its depiction of a kind of symbolic action in which a dramatic conflict is transformed into catastrophe, or in which the poetics of vying (*streben*) is turned into the drama of dying (*sterben*) (cf. Burke 1966 [1954, 1965]). In this light, the first verse introduces a life-and-death struggle in which each side initially approaches the other through a strategy of disguise and disclosure, and then through a more active tactic of resentment and revenge (a situation signaled by the mention of Luther). In the chorus, the unequal terms of this conflict are revealed in a moment of mutual recognition, although at this point neither side has any idea of either the origins or the possible outcome of their differences. In the second verse, their frantic attempts to destroy one another eventually fade into a whimper when the weaker side collapses in exhaustion from the fight, or even begins to feel its futility (depending on whether one follows the German or the English text). The chorus in its turn narrates how the panic and exhaustion spreading on the side of the weaker one may coexist with its own mood of celebration and sense of abundance (which may nevertheless be just a constrained, parenthetical moment of relief). The crescendo leading up to the third and last verse sharpens the dramatic polarity introduced at the outset as the two combatants finally confront each other in the light of day, and the gasping sigh of the loser is answered by a burst of laughter from the winner. In the final chorus, an exhilarating if exhausting summary of the previous two choruses reveals this outcome as the fulfillment of a destiny, or even as the response to a calling (*Bestimmung*), although some doubt still remains as to whether a tragedy has turned into triumph or whether the ridiculous has emerged from redemption.

At the end of the song's performance in Goethe's text, the place of the spectators to this final scene becomes a part of the narrative and is thereby itself brought into question. The fit of laughter from the tormentor that is echoed by the final sigh of the creature who "has piped on her last hole!" (*sie pfeift auf dem letzten Loch!*), is echoed by the listeners and singers of this song, if not by the readers of the scene in which it takes place. As one disgruntled protester in the wine cellar laments, we may not only delight in the triumph of the winner but also be sickened by the cruelty the loser suffers: "A worthy pastime it would seem / To prey on helpless rats with poison!" (ll. 2151–52). But as the mocking reply to this comment by another tavern reveler seems to suggest, we might also find in the grotesque and pathetic image of the loser a mirror reflection (*Ebenbild*) of our own bestial nature: "He honors in the swollen rat / His natural kin and counterpart" (ll. 2156–57). Thus, the song of the cellar rat invites its singers and listeners not only to sympathize with the fate of these fictional characters existing in some other imaginary place and time, but also to recognize in the story it tells an allegorical account of our own historic destiny. As Marx might put it, *De te fabula narratur.*[2]

To be sure, there is certainly more than merely a general and allegorical significance to this juxtaposition of Marx's prose with the situations represented in Goethe's account of the drunken revelries in Auerbach's wine cellar. Attending more closely now to the "Goethean" depiction of the situation presented here, while not ignoring some of the "Marxian" overtones in its more dissonant and contradictory aspects, we should consider what significance this scene has with respect to the famous heroes of Goethe's work, Faust and Mephistopheles. However amusing or pathetic this scene may be to read by itself, it can also be seen to occupy a pivotal place in what others have characterized as the tragedy of historical development, in terms of which Goethe attempted to dramatize the fateful pact of humanity with the diabolical powers of modern progress (Berman 1988). How can we locate this little world of the wine cellar and of Brander, along with that other little world within it conjured through the song about the cook and the rat, within the greater world depicted in the Promethean myth of the theft of fire from the gods and the building of a new and greater world, dramatized here through Faust's will to power and knowledge (Blumenberg 1985)?

At the close of the famous study scene that immediately precedes this one, Faust had just signed his name in blood on the pact offered to him by Mephistopheles, and so we had anticipated the start of a great adventure as the devil spreads his mantle and carries our hero out of the sad dungeon of his study and into his promising "new career" (*Lebenslauf*). However, when we then descend without them into Auerbach's wine cellar, and even into the hole of the pitiful cellar rat, we seem not to have moved forward in the drama but to have regressed, not to have embarked on a voyage beyond or a leap into the future but to have made a circular return to some moment in the past (cf. Bloch 1970). Indeed, the very realism of the picture this scene presents seems to date it and render it out of place, especially since the references to Luther and Leipzig are the only explicit and literal clues in the entire work that serve to fix it geographically and historically (and were deliberately added by Goethe to his early *Urfaust* fragment of 1775). What, then, is the place of this scene in *Faust*, and what does the perspective offered in Marx's invocation of it offer to our understanding of its role in Goethe's overall vision?

When we resume the story from the point just after the cellar-rat song, we find that Faust and Mephistopheles step into the scene just at the moment when the song is finished and the drinkers are exchanging insults. As in the next scene in the witch's kitchen, which seems to project aspects of the cellar-rat song onto a fantastic plane, it is significant that Mephistopheles immediately takes the commanding role and acts as guide to Faust (another change Goethe made to the *Urfaust*). Our title character tags along behind his fiendish leader as an observer, sometimes showing some interest though more often bored with the rather plebeian antics of the wine-cellar patrons. Ultimately he looks down condescendingly on these simple people while they in turn look up with a naive sense of trust to their aristocratic-looking visitors dressed in "outlandish styles" (*wunderliches Weise*) (ll. 2168–69): "They never recognize the devil's fist / Though he may have them by the collar!" (ll. 2182–83).

With Mephistopheles at the center of the picture, our own expectations are again raised that the great powers bragged about by him in the previous study scene at the signing of the pact might soon be fulfilled. And yet his cynical reference to his disguise also alerts us to the frustration of these expectations and ultimately to the dramatic function of this scene. Indeed, like the cellar-rat song with which it opens, it may be understood to conceal a kind of creaky hinge or cracked mirror that imperfectly projects the main outlines of the drama in its entirety. With the story's diabolical center echoed and reflected off the figure of the rat as its counterpart (*Ebenbild*), this scene and this song present us with a *mise en abîme*, a *Stück in Stücken*, or a play within a play (and in pieces) that may not only indicate Goethe's intentions in the drama as a whole, but also provide the scenario for a historical drama in which Marx, too, wants to act.

When Mephistopheles goes on to sing his own little song about the well-dressed flea who becomes the king's favorite, much to the annoyance of the queen and her chambermaids, who wish to squash it, we may hear not only an echo of the cellar-rat song, and of Frosch's political song, "Oh Holy Empire dear, / What holds you still together?" (ll. 2090–91), but also a muffled hint of what will be Faust's own magnificent rise to power. Indeed, nearly all of the main events of part II are prefigured here in an oblique, caricatured, and disguised way, beginning from the scenes of act I in the imperial residence, where Faust and Mephistopheles, disguised as court dandy and jester, concoct a counterfeit scheme by reproducing the emperor's signature on the new paper currency circulating throughout the realm. When Mephistopheles performs the legendary table trick in Auerbach's wine cellar, not only are his magical powers demonstrated and his historical reputation confirmed, but so, too, are the realistic and fantastic parameters of the drama as a whole. As Mephistopheles chants his nonsensical incantations while drilling holes in the drinking table, out of which gushes the wine of each person's choice, not only does he give "proof" of the validity of the pact signed a short while ago but he also enacts a symbolic metamorphosis of Faust's own study and desk, which he now regards cynically as an illusory surface of naive happiness and a deceptively innocent space of natural freedom: "Free men, you see, at play in nature's state!" (l. 2295).

As the scene ends, Mephistopheles must play his evil prank out completely: "their bestial nature will soon be splendidly revealed" (ll. 2297–98), himself acting the role of a *Brander* by turning the wine into fire and putting everyone in a frenzy. When the angry drinkers turn on him with knives raised, he immediately conjures up misty images of a beautiful vineyard: "In this green arbor what a cluster / Of swelling grapes / what size what luster!," allowing him to vanish with Faust and thus to continue with their great adventure. What is left when the hallucination clears is a group of foolish men still reaching for grapes, only to find that they are pulling on each other's noses, a slapstick scenario into which we, too, have been led by the nose: "What of those grapes, those sights that stunned us? / And they tell you, don't believe in wonders!" (ll. 2335–36). Remembering now the grandeur of Faust's earlier hallucinations in the study, in the speeches of the Earth Spirit and the vision of the sign of the Macrocosm, or looking back on this scene from the perspectives later offered by the magnificent Walpurgisnacht scenes, Faust's adventures to the mythological underworld and his marriage to Helen of Troy, and even the very last scene of Faust's ascent to heaven, we might be tempted to rephrase that tragic sentiment expressed earlier: "A worthy pastime, it would seem, / To prey on helpless men with wine!"

I am therefore suggesting here that it would be misleading to argue, as does Georg Lukács, that the comic ending of the wine-cellar scene forms an exception to the dialectic of inner contractions at work in the other scenes of the drama, all of which end tragically or at least tragicomically (Lukács 1968: 237). The "exception" this particular scene constitutes is that it really presents only the appearance of comedy, and that its truly tragic dimension consists in the fact that these men are given virtually no share in the reality of the illusions Mephistopheles conjures up purely for his own amusement, and ultimately at their expense. In his Marxian interpretation of the drama and of Goethe's intentions in writing it, Lukács notes that Goethe sought the realization of his ideals not among men of an aesthetic consciousness but among "a certain predominantly plebeian type whose conditions denied them the highest spiritual development but whose innate ability permitted their capabilities to grow in spontaneous harmony" (1968: 231). Nevertheless, the drama played out in this little world does not resonate its own independence, harmony, and autonomy within the global perspective of the epic developments of the story as a whole, as do the tragic stories of the lives of the young Gretchen and the old Philomena and Baucis, the former left for dead in a dungeon as a consequence of Faust's thoughtlessness (but later Faust's motivation for undertaking the heroic deeds of part II), and the latter thrown out of their home and then murdered (in order to make room for building Faust's glorious new empire).

In this scene, however, the "cruel rhythm of destruction which accompanies and annotates Faust's dream of the future" (1968: 216) takes on an incongruous and perhaps even more tragic rhythm of its own, insofar as it is given no meaningful place within or in terms of the larger developmental framework of the Faustian story. Indeed, even the dynamic tension between Faust and Mephistopheles that is played out in this scene and throughout the story is literally over the heads of these men, who seem to provide mere background and local color for introducing the more epic conflict between the meaning of sensuous enjoyment in the quest for power and knowledge (Faust) and the impotent pursuit of mindless pleasures (Mephistopheles). Thus, the significance of the scene in the Faustian adventure as a whole may well consist precisely in its out-of-placeness with respect to Faust's pursuit of his dream of the future, its function as the truly diabolical pit for the senseless amusement and mindless torment of "bestial natures," and ultimately its irrelevant, excessive, and parasitical relationship to the composition of the drama as a whole.

Ironically, Lukács's own brilliant elaboration of *Faust* as an "incommensurable work" finds its most profound resonance at this deepest level of the tragedy. Very different from the drinkers' naive trust in Mephistopheles and their pathetic bafflement over his tricks is the dependence of Faust on the powers of Mephistopheles to help him to realize his will to freedom and autonomy for fear of having to return to "the desperate impotence of his study" (1968: 214). The "incommensurability" of this work therefore includes the apparently objective necessity for the realization of Faust's dream through so many individual tragic scenes and characters that may appear to be irrelevant caricatures of it. These dissymmetries and disharmonies in turn are mirrored in Goethe's own dilemma of trying to coordinate "the objective demands of expression" and his own "subjectively compelling mode of expression," including his attempts to bridge the growing chasm between the intimate worlds of love and friendship and the pressing "demands of the day." More than just

Goethe's limited bourgeois horizon (as Lukács argues), this disjunction between material and style, between subject matter and forms of expression,
and between the literary integrity and public communicability of his poetic
language ultimately denies him any more than a poetic and transcendent,
conceptual and utopian, aesthetic and formal resolution to the gaping contradictions he perceives in the depths of the modern world (1968: 227).[3]

In the very last scene of *Faust* another great chorus chants its famous hymn,
the *Chorus Mysticus*, in the high mountain gorges of heaven:

All that is changeable	Alles Vergängliche
Is but refraction,	Ist nur ein Gleichnis,
The unattainable	Das Unzulängliche
Here becomes action.	Hier wird's Ereignis.

(ll. 12104–7)

The activity, result, or event (*Ereignis*) that is fulfilled at this moment is not
just some mystical union of Faust with the Mater Gloriosa, but above all the
activity of language itself, the spirit of which is set on fire by the very incommensurability of itself and reality (cf. Adorno 1991 [1959]). The enlightened
vision that informs and motivates Faust's development may indeed be read as
a kind of scholar's tragedy staged in the confinement and solitude of the study
(cf. Kittler 1990), where thoughts seek refuge in texts and where entire worlds
and "wavering apparitions" (*schwankenden Gestalten*) (l. 1) may be conjured
from words and from books, if not from songs and wine. Thus, the drama of
Faust in his study searching for words to substitute for thoughts and striving to
put actions before words, is played out again and again in the study rooms of
such writers as Lukács and Habermas, Goethe and Marx, just as it resounds in
a different and more tragic way through the raucous songs of the wine-cellar
patrons and in the sad pipings of the dying cellar rat.

After this long detour from Marx's discourse on machines into the strange
spheres of Goethe's poetry and theater, which has forced us to retune our
ears to tones resonated in other worlds, we may now return to Marx's own
"verses" and "choruses" to the song of the cellar rat as they are played through
the overall composition of his note-books. By interpreting the meaning of
Marx's interruption here as well as the musical overtones beyond its meaning, we may again consider what Marx wanted consciously to represent here
even while unintentionally staging its reversal. Going back, then, to the place
where Marx breaks his speculations on the historical development of science
and technology with the chorus of the cellar-rat song, we shall follow the direction he indicates in the remainder of his "fragment on machines" (VII:
704–12). In doing so, we must again put our familiar sense of Marx to the
test by confronting it with the strangeness of his own digressions and flights
of fancy.

Not long after his nightmare about the technological possession of bodies and minds by the monstrous powers of capital, Marx comes to dream about the birth of *a new social body*. Through the multidimensional development and multidirectional expansion of human faculties in the sciences, in the arts, and in all spheres of human endeavor, such a body creates instruments and products that are themselves "organs of the human will over nature, or of human participation in nature . . . *organs of the human brain created by the human hand*; the power of knowledge objectified" (VII: 705–6). At the height of these revolutionary raptures, when Marx evokes an image of "the development of POWER, of capabilities of production, and hence the capabilities as well as the means of consumption" (VII: 711), he is not staging a postmodern scenario of corporate domination and bloated consumerism. Nor does he wish to celebrate the industrial reproduction of human life when he articulates this new emancipation as "the production of capital fixe, this capital fixe BEING MAN HIMSELF" (VII 6: 712). Rather, he envisions the potential emergence of what he calls "a different subject" who is free to develop in mutual relationships with others "who renew themselves even as they renew the world of wealth which they create": "for when we consider bourgeois society in the long view and as a whole, then the final result of the process of social production always appears as society itself, i.e. the human being itself in all its social relations" (VII: 712). In this way Marx describes his own abstract picture of the high mountain gorges of heaven, as if no more realistic or clearer vision of the "production of man" and of the humanistic regeneration of social relations were possible.

If we understand this vision to constitute the continuation of Marx's verses of the cellar-rat song, whose sad overtones perhaps cannot be muted by its triumphant reverberations, then how is it resolved through the choral refrains I have chosen to answer them? Turning now to the celebration called for after Marx's third and final hallelujah chorus that sings the death knell of an oppressive regime "where a human being does what a thing can do" (at III 23: 325), we find Marx reaching for his daily newspaper for a song of protest, a prayer for deliverance, and a figure of freedom. In an item from *The Times* of 21 November 1857, he hears "an utterly delightful cry of outrage" on the part of a West Indian plantation owner, whose "plea for the reintroduction of Negro slavery" is responded to by the quiet appeal of men to little more than their own freedom and their own will to autonomy. The writer of the article describes how

the *Quashees* (the free NIGGERS of Jamaica) content themselves with producing only what is strictly necessary for their own consumption, and, alongside this "use value," regard loafing (INDULGENCE and IDLENESS) as the real luxury good; how they leave to the devil the sugar and capital fixe invested in the PLANTATIONS, but rather observe the planters' impending bankruptcy with an ironic grin of malicious pleasure

[*Schadenfreude*], and even exploit their acquired Christianity as an embellishment [*Schönfarberei*] for this mood of malicious glee and indolence. They have ceased to be slaves, but not in order to become wage laborers, but instead, self-sustaining peasants working for their own consumption. (III 23: 325–26)

This, we might say, is the true celebration called for in Marx's final chorus, a refrain that echoes both the malicious burst of laughter and the final pipings of the cellar rat, and so reflects an image of a new mode of human freedom and a sign of hope for the fulfillment of a historical destiny.

But can it really be a question for Marx of returning to some pristine pastoral setting in which "peasants work for their own consumption"? Does he simply want to create the conditions for loafing and laziness, and thus for substituting leisure for labor, an aesthetic of play for an ethic of work, or even the love of labor for the promises of love's body, in a world where everyone might produce "als hätten sie Liebe im Leibe" (cf. Brown 1966)? In the conclusion to his discourse on machines, Marx also writes that "Labor cannot become play as Fourier would like, although it is his great contribution to have expressed the suspension not of distribution, but of the mode of production itself, in a higher form, as the ULTIMATE OBJECT" (VII 6: 712). Marx's project for a new science and a new technology is therefore not just a utopian conceit but is particularly a conception of the time that is needed for human beings to achieve their freedom and the place required in order to exercise it: *"free time*—which is both idle time and time for higher activity . . . discipline as regards the human being in the process of becoming, . . . practice, experimental science, materially creative and objectifying science" (VII: 712), and *"really free working,* e.g., *composing,* [which] is at the same time precisely the most damned seriousness, the most intense exertion" (VI: 611; cf. note 20 to Part III).

In a series of short newspaper articles written by another freethinking Frenchman whom Marx admired, his comrade and son-in-law Paul Lafargue, we might imagine that Marx's own *Chorus Mysticus* as it was sung for him by the free Quashees of Jamaica has been dramatized, recomposed, and amplified to almost symphonic proportions (Lafargue 1970 [1883]; an earlier version dates from 1880). To the accompaniment of what he calls "a new song with a new tune," Lafargue stages a melodrama of the regime of idleness and a courtroom saga defending "the right to be lazy," demystifying the "strange delusion" among Western people that suffering rather than enjoyment is the divine lot of humankind, and protesting against the "double madness" that requires from the working masses both overproduction and abstinence (1907: 135, 48). Like the Goethean and Marxian cellar-rat song, his musical tour de force is at one and the same time a song of retribution: "harsh and prolonged revenge [*vengeance*] . . . heaped upon the moralists who have perverted nature, the bigots, the canters, the hypocrites 'and other such sects of men who disguise themselves like maskers to deceive the world' (Rabelais)" (1907: 51–52), and a song of celebration: "On the days of great popular rejoicing [*jouissance*] . . . instead of swallowing dust as on the 15th of August and the 14th of July under capitalism, the communists and collectivists will eat, drink, and dance to their hearts' content" (1907: 52–53). But it is also a solemn requiem for the death of a monstrous life of oppression and a hymn of forgiveness expressing the jubilant remembrance of what will have been the origins of our redemption:

Under the regime of idleness, to kill the time, which kills us second by second, there will be shows and theatrical performances always and always . . . [culminating in] the great play, *Theft of the Nation's Goods*:

Capitalist France, an enormous female, hairy-faced and bald-headed, fat, flabby, puffy and pale, with sunken eyes, sleepy and yawning, is stretching herself out on a velvet couch. At her feet, Industrial Capitalism, a gigantic organism of iron, with an ape-like mask, is mechanically devouring men, women and children, whose thrilling and heart-rending cries fill the air; the Bank, with a marten's muzzle, a hyena's body and harpy-hands, is nimbly flipping coins out of its pocket. Hordes of miserable, ema- ciated proletarians in rags, escorted by gendarmes with drawn sabres, pursued by furies lashing them with whips of hunger, are bringing to the feet of Capitalist France heaps of merchandise, casks of wine, sacks of gold and wheat. Langlois, his nether garment in one hand, the testament of Proudhon in the other and the book of the national budget between his teeth, is encamped at the head of the defenders of national property and is mounting guard. When the laborers, beaten with gun stocks and pricked with bayonets, have laid down their burdens, they are driven away and the door is opened to the manufacturers, merchants and bankers. They hurl themselves pell-mell upon the heap, devouring cotton goods, sacks of wheat, ingots of gold, emptying casks of wine. When they have devoured all they can, they sink down, filthy and disgusting objects in their ordure and vomitings. Then the thunder bursts forth, the earth shakes and opens, Historic Destiny arises, with her iron foot she crushes the head of the capitalists, hiccoughing, staggering, falling, unable to flee, with her broad hand she overthrows capitalist France, astounded and sweating with fear. (1907: 53, 55–56)

We must recast our idea of Marx as a political and scientific writer in order to include an understanding of him also as a composer who strives not just to listen to the harmonies and melodies of new forms of expression but also to create disharmonies and dissonances, a new tune whose "tone [or ac- cent or emphasis: *Ton*] comes to be placed not on the state of being objectified [*Vergegenständlichtsein*] but on the state of being alienated [*Entfremdetsein*], dispossessed, sold" (VII 44: 831). To refocus our eyes on his vision and re- tune our ears to his music, we may need to magnify and amplify the outlines of the melo-drama he sketched of a different mode of production, another *Produktions-weise*, and a new melody leading us forth into the next stage of human being.

PART II

Marx's Desk

I, on the other hand, considered form as the architectonics required in the formulation of a concept, and matter as the quality required of these forms. The error was that I believed the one could and should develop independently of the other and thus I did not arrive at true form but merely constructed a writing desk with drawers which I later filled with sand.

> Marx to his father, 10 November 1837, on his attempt
> to write a systematic philosophical treatise on law

As if this rupture [*Auseinanderreissen*] had not been inverted [*umgekehrt*] out of reality and compacted [*gedrungen*] into the textbooks, but rather from the textbooks into reality, and as if the task were the dialectic balancing or equalization [*Ausgleichung*] of concepts, and not the grasping or conceptualization [*Auffassung*] of real relations!

> Marx, M 6: 90, on the abstractions of the economists

Marx Reading
On the Humanist Concept of Essence

After years of scholarly reconstruction and reinterpretation, it is now possible to imagine the progress of Marx's lifework as a series of starts and stops, transitions and turning points, interruptions and movements forward, rather than simply as an unbroken march toward enlightenment. In part, this approach requires revising the conventional view of Marx's career, which divides it into an early "humanist" phase superseded by a later "scientific" phase. In part also, it entails a more careful scrutiny of old and familiar works and a consideration of previously ignored or undiscovered texts, thereby allowing us to see the overlap of regressive and progressive moves within and around the crucial moments of Marx's career. Thus, we may follow the guiding thread that binds together Marx's corpus of knowledge in terms of the emergence of an essential truth (*Entstehung und Wesen*) by which he first established and then displaced his entire theoretical framework through a process of reading alternating with intensive periods of writing.

Using this hermeneutic approach to Marx's life and work, we may identify the great high points of his career as the *Manuscripts* of 1844, the *Grundrisse* of 1857–58, and the first edition and first volume of *Capital* published in 1867 (see Appendix A). Conceiving of the "phases" of his thought as aspects, dimensions, or points of access to a single though often incoherent textual unity, we avoid the problems inherent in trying to identify the "nature of original Marxism" or "the essential Marx," or attempting to locate an "epistemological break" or an irreversible "progress." Instead, we follow an interpretive procedure closer to Marx's own, as when he "read" a complex network of social and material relations busily operating behind the deceptive glimmer of the "text" of the precious metals (I: 173–86). In short, we may understand Marx's own theory and practice of reading as introducing us into a field of inquiry that renders problematic and expands our sense of the very meaning of what it is to read.

To take a step further the analogy with Marx's reading of the precious metals as "a social system organized through money symbols," we could say that the specific models, procedures, and materials for reading that Marx took up at each phase of his career were "by no means a matter of indifference," any more than our alphabetic or money symbols are arbitrary inventions of history (I: 145). With this in mind, let us glance at the succession or accumulation of materials on the "surface" of Marx's desk as he shaped and reworked them over the three principal decades of his career. (See Table 1; the dimensions of this table, and indeed its figural significance for Marx's project as a writing desk, will be discussed in the concluding sections of this chapter and in Chapter 3.) With regard to this table, we should recall that when Marx made his resolution in the 1840s to pursue only "positive studies"—clearing his shelves of books on literature, aesthetics, theology, philosophy, ancient mythology, and languages to make more room for those on history, political economy, and law (Marx to his father, 11 November 1837)—his decision was not simply to change his major field of study or to settle into a new area of specialization; rather, his aim was to open a new interpretive framework within which to understand the connections between these disciplines. By later identifying the basic elements of his *scientific problematic* as "use value" and "labor power" (see Table 1), his aim was not simply to reduce all thinking and modes of expression to the categories of political economy, but rather to develop a procedure for making sense of a wide range of historical events and for discussing a number of themes otherwise thought to be unrelated. Above all, by choosing to focus on and expand the boundaries of a particular discipline, the emerging field of political economy, he hoped to be in a better position to explore and redirect the more general universalist and humanist aspirations he had already pursued through the other sciences and arts.

In the decade after the defeat of the revolutions of 1848, Marx's critical project turned toward reading the historical ebbs and flows of counterrevolution and economic crisis, often by way of a careful reading of others who read these same events. His concern during this period was to develop the theory and practice of reading that he had articulated during the 1840s, but now expressed as a procedure for challenging long-held assumptions about social reality and as a method for finding provisional starting and stopping points for study: "the thing moves slowly, because subjects one has made the

TABLE 1
Marx's Desk

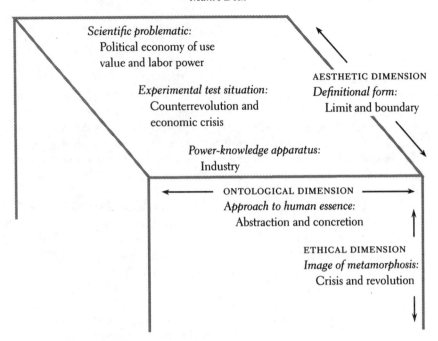

Scientific problematic:
Political economy of use
value and labor power

AESTHETIC DIMENSION
Definitional form:
Limit and boundary

Experimental test situation:
Counterrevolution and
economic crisis

Power-knowledge apparatus:
Industry

ONTOLOGICAL DIMENSION
Approach to human essence:
Abstraction and concretion

ETHICAL DIMENSION
Image of metamorphosis:
Crisis and revolution

chief aim of one's studies, at the moment one is ready for conclusions, show new aspects and solicit rethinking" (Marx to Ferdinand Lassalle, 22 February 1858). Now in exile in London, "writing like mad all night long and every night collating my economic studies so that I at least get the outlines [*die Grundrisse*] clear before the deluge" (Marx to Engels, 8 December 1857), he became almost overwhelmed by his own miserable personal situation: "I don't believe that anybody had ever written about 'money' while suffering from such a lack of money" (Marx to Engels, 21 January 1859), but comforted himself with the signs of change that he read about in the newspapers: "Though my own FINANCIAL DISTRESS may be dire indeed, never, since 1849, have I felt SO COSY as during this OUTBREAK" (Marx to Engels, 13 November 1857). The world economic crisis that hit Europe in the latter half of the 1850s was for Marx a requiem to a now dead revolution, the promise of a resurrected revolution on a larger political and economic scale, and thus an opportunity for self-evaluation and the development of a new revolutionary theory. Now putting the philosopher Hegel, the socialist followers of Proudhon, and the political economists influenced by Ricardo at the top of his reading list, Marx pursued what he called his "double labor": "(1) . . . the foundations of the economics book . . . [and] (2) THE PRESENT CRISIS," a project he undertook as much to meet his revolutionary and scientific aims as for personal reasons, "for me, INDIVIDUALLY, TO GET RID OF THIS NIGHTMARE" (Marx to Engels, 18 December 1857). Thus, within his more general problematic of reading, the period of the 1850s may be considered as that phase of Marx's work which is both mediated and disrupted by a decisive "moment of truth," that is, an *experimental test situation* whose significance for Marx was simultaneously public, intellectual, and private (see Table 1): "After all, I have the misgivings that now, having brought fifteen years of study so far, stormy movements from the outside are likely to INTERFERE. NEVER MIND. If I finish too late to find the world interested in such things, the fault is clearly my own" (Marx to Lassalle, 22 February 1858).

By the 1860s, Marx's main concern was indeed to finish this "double labor" and, more generally, to write in order to be read. His immediate aim was to communicate as well as to expand his already voluminous knowledge, by undertaking, for example, a close study of the "bluebook" reports of the factory inspectors: "I have enlarged the historical part on 'the work day,' which lay outside the original plan" (Marx to Engels, 10 February 1866). Thus he added even more subjects to his reading list: "I had to wade through the new agricultural chemistry in Germany" (Marx to Engels, 13 February 1866). At the same time he was speaking and writing for the new workers' organization: "I am in reality OVERWORKED, trying to finish my work on the one hand, and having my time extraordinarily taken up by the 'International Association' [of Working Men, formed in 1864], on the other hand" (Marx to Engels, 1 May 1865). Thus, even during this period when Marx had his hands full, his reading and writing did not follow one another in a smooth, continuous process; each new project became fraught with interruptions induced by his own poverty and poor health: "I began the copying and *styling* precisely on January 1, and the thing proceeded very smartly, as I naturally enjoyed licking the child clean after so many birth pangs. But then the carbuncles interfered" (Marx to Engels, 13 February 1866); and there also were postponements brought on by his own intellectual scruples: "I cannot bring myself to send off anything until I have the whole before me" (Marx to Engels, 1 May 1865). In this third and final phase of Marx's reading process, he reached a point where both the object and the activity of his own Promethean work schedule of academic study and political organizing eventually became subject to the same *power-knowledge apparatus of industry* (see Table 1). In other words, in his attempt to produce a representation of the structure of this apparatus (in *Capital* and other works), he could not extricate himself from his own critical and accommodative participation in the very reality he was reading and writing about. In short, as he became increasingly absorbed in his work, work came to absorb him, so that the object of his studies eventually invaded his study.[1]

I

Here we need to step back a bit from Marx's desk in order to assess what is lost in the hermeneutic appropriation of his reading practices that over the past several decades has aimed to package and circulate his lifework for a disciplinary-specific readership. An old-fashioned though still influential version of Marx's development as a reader takes as its point of departure not Marx's employment of new reading models, materials, and procedures throughout his career, but rather a kind of evolutionary life cycle from an early gestation period, where an "essential Marx" can first be identified, to an enlightened "adult" phase that is nevertheless haunted by lingering infantile "mythologies." In Robert C. Tucker's account of this development, it is as if Marx's characterization of his great book *Capital* as the "baby" he conceived from Hegel's *Phenomenology* and *Logic* should be taken literally, or rather that this work is itself the product of a childish and mythological reader who naively reads the world like a book he deludes himself into believing he is writing, producing, and changing. Thus, even in its "mature" phase, Marx's reading practice entails viewing society as an extension of his private fantasies and personal agonies, his own "inner drama" projected outward as an "image of society." In Marx's later work the social world itself appears to have a kind of "split personality," schizophrenically driven by an irrational ethic of greed in conflict with its own instincts of survival.

Being a suffering individual himself, who had projected upon the outerworld an inner drama of oppression, [Marx] saw suffering everywhere. Accordingly, relief from the suffering, liberation from bondage, was all that really mattered. What blocked the entry of man into the realm of freedom was not the continuity necessary to work for a living, but the continuing compulsion to work under the despotism of greed. (Tucker 1961: 237)

For Tucker, Marx's interpretive practice may be reduced to a *psychomythology of reading* in which what is essentially a "self-system in conflict" is "mythically" reconfigured as a "social system in conflict" (1961: 220). Marx's own "mature Marxism" thus merely retells "with added embellishments" the original dramatic story he had told in his youth "of man's self-alienation and ultimate transcendence of it in communism," although now it is expressed in terms of the social division of labor (1961: 170). This retelling is possible because Marx translated from philosophy what he was later able to read as the basic feature of modern capitalism: "Having in 1844 *translated* 'alienation' as 'division of labor,' Marx subsequently *read* the division of labor as alienation" (1961: 188; my emphasis).

Marxism here is less a political ethic than a kind of premodern moralistic "religion of revolution" that has itself issued from the modern revolution of religion, or in other words, from "man's self-realization as a godlike being or, alternately, as God" (Tucker 1961: 31). For this reason, *Capital*, a book Marx spent his entire adult life writing "under a number of different titles," may literally be understood to be the Bible of Marxism, its great Book of Revelation and Salvation (1961: 231). Tucker therefore suggests that from his own critical and enlightened vision of the myth in the man, and of the philosophical truth in the myth, Marx's interpretive strategy might be seen to consist of little more than disguising a mythological epic with a political program, and his own reading and writing merely as tactics for concealing a sacred catechism within a revolutionary ethic.

But this is the reading of Marx's own reading practices that Marx himself criticized in others as ideology. In other words, Tucker reads Marx's *Capital* as if he were Marx reading Proudhon's *Philosophy of Poverty*, a book Marx had argued is "not just a treatise on political economy, an ordinary book; it is a bible: 'Mysteries,' 'Secrets Wrestled from the Bosom of God,' 'Revelations'—it lacks nothing" (Marx [1847a] CW 6: 30). Even more to the point, the ideology Tucker imputes to Marx is not unlike that which Marx and Engels had criticized in the Young Hegelians: "The Old Hegelians had *understood* everything as soon as it was reduced or led back [*zurückgeführt*] to a Hegelian logical category. The Young Hegelians *criticized* everything by underwriting [*unterschrieben*] religious conceptions to it or by declaring that it is a theological matter" (Marx and Engels [1845–47] MEW 3: 19; CW 5: 29–30).

Specifically, then, Tucker's commentary on Marx's interpretive procedure from the 1844 *Manuscripts* to *Capital* itself appears to be modeled after Marx and Engels's critical understanding of "*Saint Max's*" (i.e., Max Stirner's) "long apologetic commentary on '*the book*' which is none other than '*the* book,' the book as such, the book pure and simple, i.e. the perfect book, the Holy Book, the book as something holy, the book as holy of holies, the book in heaven, namely, *Der Einzige und sein Eigentum* [*The Unique and Its Property*, or *The Ego and His Own*]" (Marx and Engels [1845–47] MEW 3: 102; CW 5: 117). Like Saint Max's book, which is divided into an Old Testament whose hero is "Man" and a New Testament whose hero is "the Ego, the Unique," Tucker assumes Saint Marx's great book to consist of an early philosophico-humanistic testament and a later psychomythological testament that in fact is merely the expression of Marx's own increasingly unhappy consciousness. Stripped of Marx's own critique of the philosophy of egoism and ownness in terms of the property system of ownership, or possessive individualism (cf. Macpherson

1962), Marx's "communist idea" is thus seen to be rooted in "fundamentally psychological" motivations, even for the "mature" Marx (Tucker 1961: 198).

Nevertheless, unlike Saint Max, who in the preface to his book deliberately misreads the refrain from Goethe's poetical paraphrase of Ecclesiastes in "Vanitas! Vanitatum Vanitas!"—"Ich hab' mein' Sach' auf nichts gestellt" (I have based my case on nothing)—Marx is decidedly not interested in arguing that "all is nothing to him," thereby allowing him to go on to establish a "cause" (*Sache*) based only on himself, "'on myself, on the I that is, just as much as God, the nothing of everything else, the I that is everything for me, the I that is the unique.'" Rather than delude himself into believing that "'I am nothing in the sense of void, *but* the creative nothing, the nothing from which I myself, as creator, create everything',," Marx is more concerned to produce what he calls another reading (*Lesart*) that effectively reverses the superficial meaning Stirner extracts from Goethe's poetic version of Ecclesiastes and thus exposes its essential nonsense: "I am everything in the void of nonsense, '*but*' I am the nugatory [*nichtige*] creator, the all, from which I myself, as creator, create nothing" (Marx [quotes from Stirner] in Marx and Engels [1845–47] *MEW* 3: 103; *CW* 5: 117). Stirner's book originates and terminates in a void because it pretends to create something out of nothing, that is, out of the absurd cipher he calls his "Uniqueness," his "Ego." Like Marx's Stirner, Tucker's Marx is a German ideologist, mythologically reading social alienation for his own self-alienation, the cultural education of his mind and body (*Bildung*) for the trials of his own solitary book learning. Tucker de-ciphers Marx's reading practices in order to reconstitute them as a version (*Lesart*) of or variation on the theme of *The Ego and His Own*, but without considering Marx's own reading of and response to that same theme.

It is consistent with Tucker's enlightened effort at demythologization that it eventually found its ultimate expression in the scholarly reconstitution of Marx's works into "the book," that is, the *Reader*, or more specifically, *The Marx-Engels Reader*, which was Tucker's attempt "*to place between the covers of one volume* all or nearly all of what could be considered 'the *essential* Marx and Engels'" (Tucker 1978: ix; my emphasis). The culmination of his critique of Marx would thus seem to consist of stripping Marx's own reading practices of their religious psychomythology in order to pluck out their essential core and neatly tuck away their true nature, thereby separating them from the social activities and political processes toward which they aim and through which they find their meaning. Editing and repackaging Marx's Promethean labors for a mass audience typified by "the educated person in our time, whatever his political position or social philosophy," Tucker thus capitalizes on the literary surplus value of their political irrelevance so that they may be circulated as an academic commodity on a market that is only apparently ideologically neutral.[2]

II

A more attentive and elaborate inquiry into Marx's reading practices has been undertaken by Louis Althusser. Where Tucker tries to follow the development of Marx's thought through the evolutionary framework of a mythical ego psychology, Althusser tries to purge the Marxian ego of its mythical residues in order to sift out a more properly scientific method of reading. And where Tucker argues that Marxism's religious essence is only "superficially obscured by Marx's rejection of the traditional religions" (Tucker 1961: 22), Althusser more directly challenges the "religious privileges of divine reading" in terms of a scientific critique that he argues is developed by Marx himself. In a more explicit way than Tucker, Althusser invites us to consider the relation of Marx to us who read him and of Marx to those whom he reads, through what he calls *a process of double reading*: "when we read Marx, we immediately find a *reader* who *reads* to us, and out loud" (1970: 18). His ultimate concern, then, is to show how "the Marxist theoretical concepts, in which the reality of theoretical formations in general (philosophical ideologies and science) can be considered, must be *applied to Marx himself*" (1969: 32; my emphasis). In short, he argues that we must take Marx's own procedure of reading as our guide for reading Marx himself.

Althusser insists that the essential theoretical principles of Marx's reading practice need to be rendered explicit by "an authentic reading . . . both epistemological and historical," and that this need arises because "a definition of the irreducible specificity of Marxist theory" cannot be "*read directly*" in Marx's writings" (1969: 38–39). Thus he sets out to provide just such a definition, or rather, a series of definitions, by way of a magisterial reading of Marx that places Marx's own reading principles low down in a categorical hierarchy which ultimately culminates in Althusser's own version of "Theory":

I shall call *theory* any theoretical practice of a *scientific* character. I shall call "theory" (in inverted commas) the determinate *theoretical system* of a real science (its basic concepts in their more or less contradictory unity at a given time). . . . I shall call Theory (with a capital T) the general theory, that is, the Theory of practice in general, itself elaborated on the basis of the theory of existing theoretical practices (of the sciences) which transforms into "knowledges" (scientific truths) the ideological product of existing "empirical practices" (the concrete activity of men). This theory is the materialist *dialectic* which is none other *than* dialectical materialism. (1969: 168)

Althusser says that he gets to this high plateau of Theory by a reading of Marx, who apparently did not develop his own "Dialectics" because it was "not *essential* to the development of his own theory, that is, to the fruitfulness of his own practice" (1969: 174). Since the "fruitfulness" of Althusser's own theoretical practice does seem to require such a Theory, he will cultivate what Marx left wild, thereby producing his own Fruit (Theory) from the soil of Marx's *theory* and "theory."

However, in taking Marx's own critique of theological mysticism and turning it back on what he takes to be the residues of Marx's philosophical essentialism, Althusser himself appears to be acting out the ideological role of the Critical Critic who finds in his own "abstract" experience and perception of things (i.e., Althusser's own reading of Marx) only the repetitions of an Essence, an Idea, a Concept, or a Theory of things. For Althusser, just as things are not always as they appear to be, so Theory cannot be read directly into Marx's works, and so those works must be shown or imagined to be otherwise. In other words, in order to "bear fruit," Marx's many-sided and plural "theory" or *theory* needs to be "read" through a one-dimensionalizing interpretive screen that exposes its essential meaning as Theory:

> If from real apples, pears, strawberries, and almonds I form the general idea [*Vorstellung*] "*Fruit*," if I go further and *imagine* [*einbilden*] that my abstract idea "*Fruit*," derived from real fruit, is an entity existing outside me, is indeed the *true* essence of the pear, the apple, etc., then—in the *language of speculative* philosophy—I am declaring that "*Fruit*" is the "*Substance*" of the pear, the apple, the almond etc. I am saying therefore that to be a pear is not essential to the pear, that to be an apple is not essential to the apple, that what is essential to these things is not their real existence, perceptible to the senses, but the essence that I have abstracted from them and then foisted on them, the essence of my idea—"*Fruit*." . . . Particular real fruits are not more than *semblances* [*Scheinfrüchte*] whose true essence is "*the* Substance"—"Fruit." (Marx and Engels 1845 *MEW* 2: 59; *CW* 4: 57–58)

To read *Theory* into Marx's works, in spite of or precisely because of the fact that Marx did not write *It* there, to declare *It* to be that from which Marx's own works are produced, to argue that *It* is essential to an "authentic reading" of Marx and to the specificity of Marx's "Dialectic" as its unspoken and thus inaudible presupposition, is to concoct a kind of transcendental and speculative Mystery in the very name of *Science*.

Althusser's efforts at producing a demythologized reading of Marx proceed with the aim of giving a scientific formulation to Marx's own style and principles of reading. We might ultimately characterize Althusser's critical efforts with respect to Marx much as Marx himself read the Criticisms of "one Herr Szeliga," whose own Critical Critique resulted in little more than a series of dogmatic pronouncements conjured up from a host of "Parisian mysteries": "[He] has proclaimed that 'degeneracy within civilization' [*Verwilderung innerhalb der Zivilisation*] and rightlessness in the state are 'mysteries,' i.e., he has dissolved them into the category 'mystery,' he lets mystery begin its *speculative career*. . . . Having produced the category '*Mystery*' out of the real world, he produces the real world out of this category" (Marx and Engels 1845 *MEW*

2: 59, 62; CW 4: 57, 60). Contrary to what Althusser imagines, here and in similar passages from *The Holy Family* Marx is not primarily concerned to condemn "the sin of abstraction which inverts the order of things and puts the process of the auto-genesis of the concept (the abstract) in the place of the auto-genesis of the concrete (the real)" (Althusser 1969: 187). Marx's critique here is less concerned with the difference between what is abstract (or fictional and merely theoretical) and what is concrete (and thus real and practical), than it is with the relation between differing readings of reality.

What is specifically at issue in Marx's polemic is not just a "theoretical" or "empirical" criticism of Szeliga's "Critical" reading of Eugène Sue's novel *Les Mystères de Paris*, nor is it primarily an assessment of the correctness and plausibility of Sue's melodramatic "reading" or sentimental depiction of the Paris underworld. Marx is less concerned here with whether Sue's novel portrays Parisian life in a literally "realistic" or "unrealistic" way (which is Szeliga's worry) than he is with discerning the uses of characterization and disguise in both "the contrasts of contemporary life" and the melodramatic appeal of Sue's literary craft. Marx's approach is thus in sharp contrast to Szeliga's treatment of the novel as a literal representation of Parisian life, the deceptive appearances of which are assumed to conceal an essential structure or "mystery": "Herr Szeliga does not pass from the mysteries of the criminal world to those of Aristocratic society; instead, '*Mystery*' becomes the 'invisible content' of educated society, its *real essence*. It is '*not a new twist*' of Herr Szeliga's designed to enable him to proceed to further examination; '*Mystery*' itself takes the 'new twist' in order to escape examination" (Marx and Engels 1845 CW 4: 31–32).

Rather than implicate himself in the labyrinth of this more complex hermeneutical structure of multiple readings, Althusser sets himself up to be the final arbiter between Marx and those he reads. Like Szeliga reading Eugène Sue, he thus produces his own Parisian mystery out of his reading of Marx, a Mystery he calls "Structure," and the Knowledge of the knowledge of Its truth he calls "Theory": "the truth of history cannot be read in its manifest discourse because the text of history is not a text in which a voice (the Logos) speaks, but the inaudible and illegible notation of a structure of structures" (Althusser 1970: 17). Thus he is able to argue that if Theory and Structure cannot be "read directly" into Marx, it is because they are the very presuppositions of Marx's thought that he himself was not able to see, hear, or read. Perhaps, however, like a Parisian Mystery, they were already invisible, inaudible, or unreadable to begin with.

For Althusser, Marx fits not only the loose and open definition of the reader as "one who reads" but also and more particularly its stricter and more pedantic version as a kind of lecturer, that is, "one appointed to read to others, a teacher's assistant, or one who reads lectures or expounds subjects to students" (*Webster's New Collegiate Dictionary*, 1979). Thus, when Althusser reads Marx's great book, *Capital*, he does so by way of what he calls "a truly *critical reading* . . . which applies to Marx's text precisely the principles of the Marxist philosophy, which is, however, what we are looking for in *Capital*" (1970: 74). His aim, then, is to distill "the definition of the essential principles of Marxist philosophy [and] to establish the indispensable minimum for the consistent existence of Marxist philosophy in its difference from all philosophical ideology" (1970: 33). Not unlike Tucker's strategy, Althusser's approach consists of identifying what he takes to be Marx's implicitly philosophical but residually ideological reading practices so as to reconstitute them between the covers of a great book. The *Reader* that Althusser reconstructs, however, is not a dry anthology of "readings," but rather Marx's *Capital*, a text he treats according to the pedantic definition of a "reader" as "a book of instruction and practice, especially in reading" (*Webster's New Collegiate Dictionary*, 1979). In his hands, Marx's work becomes a reading manual that Althusser, as the old soldier of Marxism who will not fade away, has somehow authorized himself to read, out loud, for our instruction.

Tucker's reading of Marx is premised on the idea that his sense of Marx's own neurotic split personality (as a reader) preserves our ability to understand the unifying "essence" of his work (as a *Reader*) through its development from youth ("original Marxism") to old age ("mature Marxism"). Althusser, on the other hand, preserves a unified sense of Marx's identity (as a reader) by splitting his work into an early phase ("ideological Marxism") and a late phase ("scientific Marxism") so as to uphold Marx's scientific authority (as it developed into a *Reader*, that is, *Capital*). For Tucker's Marx, the perceptive reading of the world seems to "break" from his representation of it as his sense of the "self-alienation of a split personality" is later conceived as "the social division of labor." By contrast, the work of Althusser's Marx seems to "break" apart from itself as he cultivates his "science" and divides it from what is merely "imaginary" and "ideological." In short, as both Marxes develop reading strategies through the course of their life-work, the one becomes a reader internally divided, and the other becomes a *Reader* split in two.[3]

III

If it is indeed true that Marx nowhere gives us a precisely formulated theory of his critical practice of reading, it is no less correct to say that reading, as with all forms of thought and action, constitutes for him part of a more positive theory and practice of perception. In his mind, we cannot just be pedantically "instructed" in reading, any more than we can simply be "taught" to think, to hear, to smell, or to feel. Although our age may one day be remembered for its insistence on the need to relearn the meaning of even "the simplest acts of existence: seeing, listening, speaking, reading" (Althusser 1971: 15–16), our senses are ultimately formed through a long history that alters their meaning and changes their ratio (Marx [1844b]). Marx insists that this process of cultural relearning should not be usurped by a professorial elite authorized to read to others; rather, he argues that it needs to incorporate the essential process by which "the educator himself must be educated," as he remarks in the third of his "Theses on Feuerbach" ([1845] EW: 422).

Thus, instead of producing yet another critical exegesis of Marx, we need first to develop a positive understanding of his concept of ideology that does not simply reduce it to the idea of an abstract and imaginary distortion behind which may be found the concrete reality. Rather, his concept calls for a critical procedure for thinking about social practices of the past, their inscription within existing relations of power, and the possibilities they contain for a more human future. For Marx it cannot be a question of finding where science "breaks" with ideology, but rather of developing a notion of ideology as the rupture between thought and action, and more specifically, the rift that occurs between theoretical concepts and the actual social relations they are intended to represent.

In Marx's view, an ideological "reading" is not one based on a misperception of reality, but rather one that presumes upon an abstracted, categorical representation of reality as the sole, authentic, and real basis of all experience and perception. An ideological reading replaces its own sense of reality with the "truth" established through preformed categories. As Dorothy Smith has shown, Marx understood the German ideologists to be operating through a set of three "tricks" that he was then able to use as both an example and *a model of misreading,* but without pretending to substitute his own scheme for measuring degrees of theoretical precision and generality (as Althusser believes; 1969: 182). This model provides us with a critical standard that is not simply a rule for deciding on the "correct" reading, but mainly a procedure for understanding even abstractly scientific and apparently neutral representations of reality as ideological practices:

Trick 1: Separate what people say they think from the actual circumstances in which it is said, from the actual conditions of their lives, and from the actual individuals who said it.
Trick 2: Having detached the ideas, arrange them to demonstrate an order among them that accounts for what is observed . . . (i.e. "making mystical connections").
Trick 3: Then change the ideas into a "person"; that is, set them up as distinct entities (for example, a value pattern, norm belief system, and so forth) to which agency (or possible causal efficacy) may be attributed. And redistribute them to "reality" by attrib-

uting them to actors who can now be treated as representing the ideas. (Smith 1990: 43–44, paraphrasing Marx and Engels [1845–47] CW 5: 62)

In this way the ideological practice of science may be conceived as a complex interpretive process of "reading the world like a text-book" and of "inscribing actualities into the discourses of the ruling relations of power." It proceeds by separating ideas from experience, abstracting them so as to introduce them into another system of interconnected ideas based in some other sphere of experience, and then "characterizing" this new abstraction as representing the real Essence or Substance, the Concept or Theory of the thing itself, the presupposition of its existence and its condition of possibility. Marx's own *problematic* thus consists less of defining the unity of and specific differences between scientific and ideological frameworks of meaning and value, theoretical formations "within which a word or concept is used and must ultimately be considered" (Althusser 1969: 253–54), than of treating both theoretical abstractions and commonsense beliefs as "problematic," that is, as "difficult to solve or decide, puzzling; not definite or settled, open to question or debate" (*Webster's New Collegiate Dictionary*, 1979). Rather than rework ideas and separate them from practices so that they might better fit into an established scientific (or ideological) system, Marx's problematic proceeds by attempting to situate human experiences and perceptions within the actual social and historical contexts from which they arise and in which they find their sense (cf. Smith 1987).

Although Marx may dispute readings proposed by others, he does not do so simply by contradicting their perception of reality or their conviction that what they perceive is real. As H. T. Wilson argues, Marx's critical and dialectical procedure begins from a principle of noncontradiction that takes our perception of reality as both given and problematic. On the basis of this principle, further theoretical elaborations may indeed be undertaken, but without the illusory assumption that a more "scientific" version of its beginnings is an a priori necessity for arriving at the "truth":

To say that the humanly perceived is real, and to make this the key element of a principle of non-contradiction as both Aristotle and Marx do, is to state that the prime root of all knowledge claims and all truth seeking lies in a given which it is literally "sense-less" to dispute. This is not to say that what we have in sense perception—observation in the common sense mode—is "truth." Political economy and the social sciences like to imply that this is a central characteristic of the people, with their "undisciplined" modes of thought and thinking, thereby lending weight to the claim that these disciplines make for a superior understanding. But all this does is to justify the heavy industry that has been built atop daily life typifications in a way which allows these disciplinary practices to hide the abject dependence of their "ideal types"—their "laws" and "hypotheses"—on these very typifications. What it really means is that this is what one proceeds from, and that it always does constitute a standard in fact. (Wilson 1991: 132)

As Marx had already argued in *The German Ideology*, the real premises from which a critical reading begins should be neither dogmatic nor arbitrary. It is not simply a question of "setting out from what men say, imagine, conceive, nor from men as narrated, thought of, imagined, conceived, in order to arrive at men in the flesh," but rather of beginning from "the language of real life" through which is expressed the consciousness of being (*das Bewusstsein*) as an already conscious being (*das bewusste Sein*). What matters is that we start out "from real corporeal [*leibhaftigen*] men, and on the basis of their real life pro-cess," from the practical and material conditions of "real individuals . . . both those which they find already existing and those produced by their activity," their actual life process, and their material and practical intercourse (*Verkehr*) (Marx and Engels [1845–47] *MEW* 3: 20, 26; *CW* 5: 31, 36).

Marx's theory of reading is thus itself grounded in a perception of history, that is, a sense of the future and a perspective on the past that are not exhausted by our analyses of them and that may in fact prove such analyses to be mistaken when confronted with our developing sense of things as they are (Merleau-Ponty 1969; O'Neill 1982: 123–50). Marx is not interested in elaborating a scientistic or pedantically bookish conception of historical events that would conceive of them independently of either the hermeneutic circle of rival inter-pretations or the utopian telos of history toward which our thoughts strive for the completion of their sense. The vocabulary of insight and revelation is only partially adequate to the complexities involved in Marx's reading practices, in-sofar as they require a reader's own inscription into a conflict of interpretations or a rivalry of readings as the irreducible context of any critical intervention.[4]

• • •

Marx's understanding of the essence in appearances as a "reading" of the human essence of appearances does not require him to adopt an essentialism that assumes a transcendental structure of Being or an immutable ontologi-cal difference. As Herbert Marcuse argues in an early essay (1968 [1936]), the Marxian concept of essence exploits the historical imbalances, or even monstrous disproportions (*ungeheueren Missverhältnis*; cf. VII 2: 705) between essence and appearance, or between actuality and possibility. The critical dif-ference between this conceptualization of the problematic of essence and all others resides first in its aspect as both an accusatory and an imperative argu-ment, that is, its rhetorical strategy to negate things as they are or have been and to demand that they be otherwise, and second in its inherently "ironic" structure, that is, in the way it contains its own negation (Marcuse 1968 [1936]: 86).

Acknowledging Marcuse's philosophical essay as our primary inspiration (along with Negri 1984: 41–58; O'Neill 1987: 72; Wilson 1991: 177–79), but taking Marx's own groundbreaking discussion of "the method of political economy" in the "Introduction" to his studies of 1857–58 as our guide, we may formulate the critical and empirical functions of the materialist conception of essence by way of the following five stages or *rules of Marxist reading*.

1. Like all human thought and action, reading begins with the perceived reality of *abstract appearances*, and thus with the concrete totality or social aggregate presupposed as their basis (M 14–15: 100–103).

2. Knowledge of abstract appearances must then be read in their connection to actual *social practices*, with even very abstract scientific categories understood to be "true in practice" within specific social contexts (M 15–16: 103–5).

3. These social practices should also be read in terms of the extent to which *real potentialities* are at work through them, since past and present social forms always already carry in them the potential (*dynamei*) of becoming other forms in the future (M 16–18: 105–6).

4. These real possibilities must then be read by locating them in the context of a social epoch understood in its *historical specificity*, that is, in terms of the particular social character that dominates all the others and determines their rank and influence (M 18–20: 106–8).

5. Ultimately, the reading process aims to comprehend such periods of history with reference to a standard of the *human essence* toward which they "unevenly" converge, as in the beautiful image of a truly human community free to develop its capacities on the basis of social conditions that it has itself created (M 21–22: 109–10).

I have expressed Marx's humanist concept of essence in terms of rules for reading not just to emphasize the hermeneutic auspices of Marx's work but also as a way of reconsidering a set of themes that recur in Marx's own reading of the history of philosophy. For him, the philosophical quest for the concrete essences behind the concealing distortions of abstract appearances must be grounded in actual social practices undertaken by specific groups of people at particular periods of history. The incongruities of essence and appearance, or actuality and potentiality, are therefore conceived through a historical relationship that can be transformed in this world by human action, and indeed as an incitement for knowledge to become a part of the practice of transformation. Tendencies conceived within a given sociohistorical formation that transcend its bad facticity in the direction of another historical structure thus provide Marx with a critical standard or model against which actual conditions may be measured. This is the case, for example, in Marx's understanding of the history of the concept of essence itself, from Aristotle's notion of *dyna-mei* as what may potentially be, to Hegel's notion of *Wesen* as "timelessly past being," recollected as the permanence and promise of what was. Marx reads their conception of a state of being in the process of becoming as an expression of the historical and utopian dimensions of human thought and action (Marcuse 1968 [1936]: 69–87).[5]

Let us briefly specify these rules through a meditation that takes as its object the scholar's own reading and writing desk, a classic example which, as already hinted in the presentation of Table 1, will prove to be "by no means a matter of indifference" (cf. O'Neill 1989b: 102; Smith 1987. 124, 133 34). That is, we shall consider the ontological dimension of the desk in terms of its nature and emergence (*Wesen und Enstehung*) as mediated through specific material and social conditions, and as an epistemological setting where a thinker works out his or her thoughts and gives them reality as language. As Marx himself once suggested to his father, a desk may be understood metaphorically to express the relationship between thought and reality precisely in the way that it provides a figure for *the content of form* (Marx to his father, 10 November 1837; see the epigraph to Part II, above). While the drawers and shelves of the desk contain printed materials and tools for thought, the desk as a whole serves a practical purpose for separating the sublime spheres of the head from the ruder domain of the feet, for creating an intermediate area between a thinker and the world, or a line of authority marking the hierarchical social relation between those on either side of it. In *Capital*, Marx invites us to consider the economist's table, first from our simplest perception of it in everyday life, and ultimately in a more complicated and even fantastic way when it is put under the optic of political economy:

It is absolutely clear that, by his activity man changes [*verändert*] the forms of the materials of nature in such a way as to make them useful to him. The form of wood, for instance, is altered if a table is made out of it. Nevertheless the table continues to be wood, an ordinary sensuous thing. But as soon as it emerges [*auftritt*] as a commodity, it changes into a thing which transcends sensuousness [*verwandelt er sich in ein sinnlich übersinnliches Ding*]. It not only stands [*steht*] with its feet in the ground, but in relation to all other commodities, it stands [*stellt*] on its head and evolves out of its wooden brain grotesque ideas, far more wonderful than if it were to begin dancing of its own free will. (MEW 23: 85; C1: 163–64)

Taking this as our example, we can follow Marx's procedure up to this point in chapter 1 of *Capital* as an application of the five reading rules from the 1857 "Introduction" as presented above. To begin with, an ordinary table or desk can be perceived according to its "abstract appearance" as a simple "thing," its sensuous "look" or its "feel," its "style," or even its "personality" as it exists within a larger social field (rule 1; cf. C_1: 125). Next, the desk can be observed to be tied to actual practices that determine its use in everyday production and consumption, as well as its value as a commodity that can be exchanged on a market (rule 2; cf. C_1: 125–28). To be sure, the desk is itself a product of human powers and faculties and was therefore at one time only potentially wood in the form of a desk, just as the latter is already potentially something else, such as a place to eat or even a piece of firewood (rule 3; cf. C_1: 128–31). This realization can be further specified in terms of the various uses of desks, the different techniques employed to construct them, or the social organization of their production and use in particular social settings and historical periods, as in the cell of a medieval monk or a lawyer's office (rule 4; cf. C_1: 131–63). Finally, we may speculate more generally on how the desk expresses material relations between persons and social relations between things, and is therefore an example of one of the multiple faces and dimensions of the entire history of humanity (rule 5; cf. C_1: 163–77). Such, for instance, might be how we think of the fictional desk on which Faust signed his fateful pact with Mephistopheles, the philosophico-historical desk on which Hegel wrote the *Phenomenology of Spirit* as Napoleon's troops entered Jena in 1807, or the *tableaux économiques* on which the political economists attempted to summarize the mediation of all life through the abstract processes of labor and trade. And such in fact may be how we understand Marx's own desk.

In his famous eleventh thesis on Feuerbach, Marx acknowledges that any "reading" of the world is inadequate without a sense of the practice of which thought forms a part, and thus without some notion of the reality toward which its own activity must aim: "Die Philosophen haben die Welt nur verschieden *interpretiert*, es kommt drauf an sie zu *verändern* [Philosophers have only *interpreted* the world in various ways, the point is to *change* it]" (Marx [1845] *EW*: 421). Marx does not wish to indicate here a division between two separate realities, as between the passivity of thought and the activity of changing the world. Rather, he attempts to negotiate the potential and actual connections between interpreting the world (*interpretieren*) and changing it or rendering it other (*ver-ändern*). The silent pause marked by the comma interrupting the eleventh thesis on Feuerbach is literally a place between "what is" and "what ought to be," or between "what is not" and "what may yet be." His sense of the relation between interpretation and change is also conveyed but less perfectly expressed in the phrase "es kommt drauf," which may designate both the idea of "coming upon" something from the past or at some time in the future, and the act of "coming at" something from here or somewhere else. Rather than insist on a "change in consciousness" or "demand to interpret the existing world in a different way, that is, to recognize it by means of a different interpretation" (Marx and Engels [1845–47] *CW* 5: 20), Marx's activist conception of knowledge aims at locating the spatial and temporal points of articulation that "unevenly" bind thought and action together: "The method of rising [*aufzusteigen*] from the abstract to the concrete is only the way in which thought appropriates [*aufzuneigen*] the concrete, reproduces it as concrete in the mind. But this is by no means the way in which the concrete itself comes into being" (M 14: 101).

In the course of the development of his work, the linking point (*Gliederung*) between his own theoretical concepts and the historical reality Marx sought to comprehend was stretched and rendered more fragile. Increasingly his task came to consist of marking dissymmetries between real social practices and the conceptualization of their development, but always through a "sense of the concrete totality" by which he might grasp their general direction and glimpse their human truth.

Reading Marx
On the Alien Character of Revolution

When we read Marx, we encounter someone who not only writes but who also reads as he writes and writes as he reads. By copying from and commenting upon what he reads as he reads, Marx *writes his reading*. His aim is to gain access to the creative, living, and innovative sources of a piece of writing by reading and rereading it, so as to break into its rationality and find a space for his own rewriting. He often copies long passages from other authors while interrupting them with his own ironic and critical remarks before elaborating his own commentary or moving on to another passage. The opening line of his celebrated 1857 "Introduction"—"The object before us, to begin with, *material production*" (M 1: 83)—not only identifies the object of his critique— what he treats as the textbook analyses of production—but also provides a sketch for his own ultimate objective, which is to show how such analyses are "produced" so that he may then be able to "produce" his own.

Reading Marx thus usually entails following Marx's own procedure of writing across the intersection of two or more different "readings." For example, he often takes as the object of his reading the commentaries of others who are also readers of texts with which he is concerned, an indirect approach he employs in considering Szeliga's reading of Sue and Stirner's reading of Goethe, as discussed in Chapter 2. In *The Holy Family* and *The German Ideology*, he is not concerned with Hegel's "original" writings per se but with those Hegelian epigones who "Critically" revise, translate, and characterize Hegel. He even implies that such commentaries often provide more insight into the mysticisms of Hegelianism than an unmediated reading of Hegel himself would yield. "The more completely Critical Criticism (the criticism of the *Literatur-Zeitung*) distorts reality into an obvious comedy through philosophy, the more instructive it is" (Marx and Engels 1845 CW 4: 7). Such rereadings aim to yield an example, a model, or even a comedy and a *melodrama of misreading* that may serve both as a place for determining differences, between an original and a copy, for example, and as a site for negotiating oppositions, between virtue and villainy, for example (cf. Bloom 1975). In this way he breaks forcefully into texts to allow his own comic irony or satirical critique to intervene and thus to expose them to a dramatic reversal and subject them to a potentially truer rewriting.

Through the process of rereading, of writing down what others have written, and of writing out the differences between his own readings and those produced by others, Marx comes to critically evaluate what he reads. This evaluative aspect of his reading and writing emerges less as a function of the codes and categories of a science or an ideology than through the act of writing itself. That is, Marx reads the texts of philosophy and political economy not as mere readerly texts for consumption and reiteration, ones he may simply choose to accept or reject according to categories he has already formed, but rather as writerly texts whose production he can creatively imagine and even transform in his own act of rewriting (cf. Barthes 1974: 4). Reading Marx thereby entails some sense of the double reading and writing process Marx himself undertakes, and thus requires an attempt to apply the principles he himself employs to our own reading of and writing about Marx (cf. Althusser 1969: 32).

If there is indeed an "epistemological break" in Marx's work, we have no access to it except through the drama of his own reading and writing process, which both breaks from the philosophical pretensions of epistemology and effects a rupture within its rationalist intentions. In Marx's reading and writing we may expect there to be at work a conflict of forces that are not simply reducible to the levels of his "text" (Althusser) or his individual "personality" (Tucker); they exist somewhere between the critical rules he sets for his own reading and his desire to write and to act, or between his will to act and the limits that determine or block action (including the action he undertakes as scholarly work). The apparent gap or "gulf" in Marx's text is the place of a real desire to bring thought and action together, and the site of a real alienation between his desk and the outside world. It is not simply the space of a "supposed twisting and inversion [*Verdrehung und Verkehrung*] . . . existing merely in the imagination," as he puts it in the "remark on alienation" from his notebooks of 1857–58 (VII 44: 831). Marx's expression of this desire and this alienation lends to his text its craziness (*Verrücktheit*) and therefore its difficulty, while enhancing its ethical dimension as well as its aesthetic dementia (cf. Table 1).

Thus, somewhere between his life and his scientific researches there is a grid of conflicting influences that cannot be resolved into the identity of a single author and a unique text operating under the same name. Rather, there is a plural Marx through which we must read a multiplicity of meanings in a scattering of marks.

I

Following Marx's procedure, our own reading of Marx might best begin not by directly interpreting his words and his works, and not by immediately reacting to the subjects he is writing about, but rather by considering his effect on other readers, Marxist and non-Marxist alike. Like Marx in his reading of the post-Hegelians, we might then find a starting point for producing an instructive reading that magnifies his sense of the "twisting and inversion" of reality as it is displayed and exaggerated through the comedy or melodrama of theory. A case in point is the irreverent and almost delirious reading of Marx that has been undertaken by Jean-François Lyotard, for whom Marx's desire, or rather, what he calls the desire named Marx, is not simply what informs the written themes that metamorphose into the political practices, ideologies, and interpretations devised by a man named Marx; rather, the desire named Marx is read by Lyotard as itself a legible text full of creative conflicts and clashing affects, a decipherable inscription that is "like a madness and like a theory." Unlike so many other readers, Lyotard does not want simply to interpret the truth of Marx or to reread and correct him, but rather to read "Marx" through the frustrations and enthusiasms of his own reading and writing, to "wonder what there is of the libido in Marx, and 'in Marx,' that means in his texts and in his interpretations, principally practices." This approach in turn affects and infects Lyotard's own wish to "succeed in disconcerting [Marx's] theoretical barrage, to fondle his beard without disrespect [*mépris*] and without devotion, without false neutrality either . . . [but] like a complex libidinal volume, to awaken his hidden desire and ours as well" (Lyotard 1974: 118; my translation).

Clearly, then, his aim is infused with not just an erotic but also a critical desire. This manifestly polemical drive also has been emphasized by Jeffrey Mehlman in his own vertiginous reading of Marx's text, less as a monument we must not deface than as a battlefield in which we must fight: "But to the extent that one has been able to work within the node or matrix of the various forces, the pursuit of the battle will take the form of a rigorous positing of the lines along which and the conditions under which the work may be *rewritten*" (Mehlman 1977: 107). The curious and conflicting mixture of political polemics and literary imagination, of philosophy and myth, and of science and religion that both Lyotard and Mehlman find in the split or rupture "in" Marx's text thus inflects their own "transformative reading" of and writing about Marx.

To use Lyotard's expression, the proper name "Marx" may be understood to function less as "the name of someone (a predicate of existence), even if that person were double," than as a kind of "tensor sign" (*signe-tenseur*) that names "both Yes and No," "both first and second," as well as "a region of the libidinal space left to the undecidability of influxes of energy, a region on fire" (1974: 72; my translation). Or, to borrow from Mehlman's terminological repertoire, "Marx" must often be read under the illicit sign of a "sinister ano-nymity" (*unheimliche Anonymität*) that the conventional laws of authority and authorship, of censorship and free speech, ultimately find intolerable (1977: 5, quoting Marx 1850 *SE*: 135). "Marx," then, is the name for a unique though unwieldy tension: a delirium that diverges into a movement of inventions, additions, and affirmations, and a designation for a consolidated act of *reason*, a movement of organization, unity, and opposition; in short, it names an act of *revolution* that is also an act of writing.

But in Marx we are not only confronted with a writer who writes himself, who reads for his own self-understanding, or who writes to relieve his desires and soothe his frustrations in page after page of tirelessly pursued analyses and digressions, proofs, and criticisms. Rather, we also encounter a thinker who struggles to communicate what he is thinking and who wants to preserve its difficulty while rendering it readable. As Robert Paul Wolff notes in his reading of the literary structure of *Capital*, Marx's project is burdened by the duty it has taken on to search for "a language whose syntactic and tropic resources are rich enough to permit him to accomplish a number of literary and theoreti-cal ends simultaneously" (Wolff 1988: 80). Thus, what Marx in fact ends up articulating is less the language of common sense or of scientific reason than an insane discourse whose irony alone can express the truth of an irrational reality.

If social reality (the political economy of capitalism) has "an irreducible element of collective communication," and if that communication itself has "something like an ironic structure" (in that it contains its own negation), then Marx must find a language that expresses both the objective, social validity of the categories operative in that reality and the inverted logic or unacknowl-edged madness (*Verrücktheit*) of those same categories. At the same time he cannot avoid expressing his own conflicting desires and hesitations in and through his attempts to address those of a potential or actual readership: "The truly crucial feature of ironic discourse that justifies the appearance/reality distinction is the asymmetrical relation between the two meanings of the utter-ance and the two audiences that receive it" (Wolff 1988: 37). Marx's text may thus be read as a communicative sign that is split by the unevenness of the desires bearing the tensor sign of its author's proper name and those desires which bear the proper name(s) of his readership. Not only does he strive to write from his own experience while also searching for self-clarification, but he also tries to articulate a language that will touch the experiences and appeal to the competencies of those who read him.

It cannot not be a question here simply of diagnosing Marx's split personality (Tucker) or of analyzing his text as if it were something that could be broken into parts that are properly scientific or improperly ideological (Althusser). Rather, we must remember that there is more than one "Marx" writing the texts we read under that singular proper name, and that those texts communicate several meanings to several readers. In taking up any particular work by Marx, then, we need to ask not just specifically to and for whom Marx writes, but also which Marx is writing. Where Lyotard will argue that Marx writes as an author with a double identity who is at the same time seduced and horrified, fascinated and indignant over the monstrosities of capital, Wolff will argue that Marx writes for a double readership: one naively bound to appearances and another more able to fathom the depths of the realities he expresses. These characterizations provide us with a clearer sense of what Stanley Edgar Hyman understood to be Marx's *melodramatic conception of scientific writing*, that is, the literary structure through which Marx imaginatively expresses his fears and desires while at the same time searching for an effective way to communicate them in the form of a scientific study and a political program:

I would suggest that we see Marx's book [*Capital*] as a melodrama called something like *The Mortgage on Labor-Power Foreclosed*. In the first act [the chapter "The Working Day"] the villain mistreats the virtuous wife and injures her poor little child; in the second act [the chapter "Machinery and Modern Industry"] the young laboring hero himself is maimed and sits paralysed in a wheelchair while the child dies; in the third act [the chapter "The General Law of Capitalist Accumulation"] they are thrown out into the snow and take refuge in a miserable hovel; in the fourth act [the chapter "So-Called Primitive Accumulation"] the discovery is made that the villain stole the mortgage originally and has no legal or moral rights over our heroes. It needs a fifth act in which the working class family is rescued and restored to its happy home, but only the proletarian revolution could produce that final curtain, and Marx could not finish *Capital* without it. (Hyman 1962: 146)

From Wolff's perspective on the hermeneutics of this melodrama, we get a picture of a readership consisting of Mr. Moneybags (and associated political economists), who would read "reason" in Marx's presentation of the rationalist logic of bourgeois political economy, and another group of readers, consisting of Mr. and Mrs. Proletariat (and associated revolutionaries and intellectuals), who would read "insanity" in those same categories. By contrast, Lyotard understands Marx himself to be playing a role in the drama, writing as both a little girl and a lawyer who are simultaneously fascinated and scandalized by the monstrous spectacle of capitalism: "Marx the little girl [*la petite Marx*], obfuscated by the perversity of the polymorphous body of capital, reclaims a great love; Karl Marx the great attorney, delegated to the accusation of the perverts and to the 'invention' of a convenient lover (the proletariat), begins to study the dossier of the accused capitalist" (Lyotard 1974: 118). Whatever specific characterizations we decide to pursue in our own reading of Marx (and to be sure, none of these readers keep consistently close to Marx's text), the general point here is that his writing stages a kind of melodramatic scenario played out not only within its own subject matter but also through its readers and writers. Whether in the same work or in different works, Marx's textual melodrama provides him with a form of self-expression and a means of self-clarification that may also have the effect of implicating us as readers in what he is writing about.[6]

II

We need now to test whether this model of reading Marx's work as a writerly text of alienation, desire, and melodramatic characterization bears any connection to Marx's own method of reading and his own style of writing. That is, we need to evaluate the extent to which Marx himself may have aimed to produce an effect of alienation (*Entfremdungseffekt*) or to cast a net of desire over his readers by "writing his reading." To do so, we must recall the effect of Marx's work on such readers as Lyotard and Mehlman, Wolff and Hyman (whose reading of Marx is explicitly determined by their own libidinal and literary, as well as scientific and political, agendas) while reevaluating the extent to which Marx's own interpretive principles may inform or redirect our interests in reading him.

Marx did not simply read "the alienation of labor" into his understanding of the "facts" of political economy, as many readers assume about his 1844 *Manuscripts*. He also conceived of the language of political economy as an alienated and alienating language, and recognized that his own humanist discourse would itself appear alien to the language of capitalist values, as he notes in his conspectus of the writings of James Mill:

The only comprehensible language we have is the language our commodities use together. . . . Our mutual alienation from the human essence is so great that the direct language of this essence seems to us to be an affront to human dignity and in contrast the alienated language of the values of things seems to be the language that justifies a self-reliant and self-conscious human dignity. (Marx [1844a] EW: 276–77)

Marx reads the texts of political economy not only as providing a theory about alienation but also as themselves an expression of alienation, as a language that seems to make sense only within a context of alienation. Against the political abstractions of the economists who read a relation between people as a relation between things, and who reduce human values to commodity values, Marx approaches the discourse of political economy critically as a *foreign language*. For Marx the critique of political economy may ultimately be possible only as a procedure of estrangement (*Entfremdung*), that is, by rendering the self-evidence, rationality, and clarity of the language of political economy unrecognizable or alien to itself.

This approach to political economy does not just have a metaphorical significance for him, by way of the analogy of human alienation (*Entfremdung*) to communication in a foreign language (*fremde Sprache*); it has literal and dramatic importance to him as well. To the peril of many of his less versatile readers, Marx was so knowledgeable about foreign languages that he often did not translate many of his sources when citing them, nor did he always write his commentaries or criticisms on them in German. As Wolff remarks in his reading of *Capital*, "At one instant [Marx] is a *polemicist*, writing to the moment. At the next, he is a *pedant*, calling down authorities in six languages from twenty countries to confirm his etymological tracings and analytical speculations" (1988: 13; my emphasis). To this we might add that at other times Marx's polyglot pedantry is woven into the very polemical fabric of his writing.

In his critique of Proudhon, for example, which Marx wrote in French, not only are specific writers associated with the field of inquiry in which they write but they are also connected by Marx to the national characteristics of the countries from which they originate, and thus to the foreign languages in which they write. He not only bestows whole bodies of knowledge with national characteristics but also assigns to individual thinkers characters who thereby play speaking parts in the staging of his own theatrical critique: "If the Englishman transforms men into hats, the German transforms hats into ideas. The Englishman is Ricardo, a rich banker and distinguished economist; the German is Hegel, an ordinary professor of philosophy at the University of Berlin" (Marx 1847a CW 6: 161). If the Frenchman in Marx's trilingual theoretical drama is indeed Proudhon, the latter in turn is merely "another Dr. Quesnay . . . , the Quesnay of the metaphysics of political economy." Thus, even though Proudhon's own "French" role is simply acted out as the imitation of a part already played by someone else, what interests Marx in Proudhon is the way the "Frenchman" has been able to take on the scientific characters of his "German" and "English" counterparts.

When constructing his system of economic contradictions, Proudhon proceeds by "talking metaphysics while talking political economy," a linguistic versatility that seems to challenge and give direction to Marx's own discourse: "Just now [Proudhon] forced us to speak English, to become pretty well English ourselves. Now the scene is changing. M. Proudhon is transporting us to our dear fatherland and is forcing us, whether we like it or not, to become German again" (1847a CW 6: 161). Besides the fact that Marx continues to write in French here, a language not that of his "dear fatherland," it is clear that he is not just concerned to identify the national characteristics of foreign ideas or the foreign character of individual thinkers. He is above all drawing attention to the being in language and the character as language of their ideas by communicating them not only in but also as a foreign language.

Although Marx is concerned here to point out the foreign character of Proudhon's poor philosophical discourse on poverty, this is not simply because he is determined to translate the Frenchman's system of thought into either his own mother tongue or his multilingual prose, thereby recasting Proudhon's work so that it can play its dramatic role in the staging of his own critical theory. On the contrary, he is highly critical of the violence done to the ideas of a thinker like Proudhon when their mode of expression is simply "translated" into more familiar characters, as he notes in *The Holy Family* at a point where he is concerned in fact to defend Proudhon against the Critical Critics:

It was not *Proudhon* himself, but "Proudhon's *point of view,*" Critical Criticism informs us, that wrote *Qu'est-ce que la propriété?* . . . As only the works of the Critical point of view possess a character of their own, the Critical characterization necessarily begins by giving a character to Proudhon's work. . . . [Herr Edgar] naturally gives it a *bad* character, for he turns it into an *object* of "Criticism." . . . Herr Edgar gives this work a character by *translating* it. . . . Proudhon's work, therefore, is subjected to a double attack by Herr Edgar—an *unspoken* one in his characterizing translation and an *outspoken* one in his Critical comments. We shall see that Herr Edgar is more devastating when he translates than when he comments. (Marx and Engels 1845 CW 4: 23–24)

Marx's attack against the Critical Critics proceeds both directly as a defense of Proudhon and indirectly through his own rival commentary that presents a mocking simulation of Herr Edgar's critique of Proudhon. Marx divides his text into "Critical translations" on the one hand, which compare the version of Proudhon's text given by the Critical Critic with Marx's own quotation in French of Proudhon, and "Critical commentaries" on the other, in which he himself provides a lengthy critical discussion of his differences with Herr Edgar. In the process, he also contrasts his own characterizations of what he calls the "Critical Proudhon" as misinterpreted by Herr Edgar with the "Real Proudhon" as cited in French by Marx. Thus, for Marx it appears that the key issue here is not simply that "translations" of Proudhon's work may in fact give it a character different from or foreign to the original, but particularly that the character of certain translations betrays their own unstated interests while revealing an instructive misunderstanding of that original. In general terms, it seems that while some ideas need to be expressed in a foreign language to preserve their uniquely "foreign" character (i.e., Marx on Proudhon), others may need to be commented upon and "characterized" without translating them in order to find dramatic expression in one's own critical discourse (i.e., Marx on Herr Edgar).

Marx not only elaborates a theory of the alien character of the discourse of political economy and the foreignness of the language of philosophy, but he also at least implicitly develops a theory of foreign languages and of their translation. His criticism of Herr Edgar and of certain other Critical Critics is not that they translate too much but that they translate too little: they characterize the thoughts of others (e.g., "Proudhon's point of view") according to their own interests without having first tried to discern the intended sense of the words through which such thoughts are expressed. The error in such an approach is that it ultimately fails to grasp the specificity of the other text's meaning, and thus lacks a sense of its own voice:

It is now clear why Critical Criticism does not give a single thought in *German*. The language of its thoughts has not yet come into being in spite of all that Herr Reichardt by his Critical handling of foreign words, Herr Faucher by his handling of English, and Herr Edgar by his handling of French, have done to prepare the *new Critical* language. (Marx and Engels 1845 CW 4: 38)

No better is a Critic such as Stirner, who "disrespects" the text's own language by translating too much, assimilating it to what he calls the divine Uniqueness or Propriety (*Eigentumlichkeit*) of his own peculiar terminological system:

A special branch of [Stirner's pseudoscience of] synonymy consists of *translation*, where a French or Latin expression is supplemented by a German one which only half-expresses it and in addition denotes something totally different; as we saw above, for example, when the word "*respektieren*" was translated "to experience reverence and fear" and so on. (Marx and Engels [1845–47] CW 5: 275)

By contrast, Marx wishes to respect the foreignness of words and meanings as they are expressed by other writers, but in a way that also allows what is distinctive about their ideas to be instructive for opening up his own critical perspective. In his struggle to make sense of the thoughts of other writers through his own system of meaning, and so to determine their place in the performance of his own discourse, Marx himself sometimes finds it necessary to characterize or even caricature them, to interpret them through his own interests, or even to mistranslate them. In such cases, the *principle of characterization* by which he tries to gather a sense of the general character of what such writers are on about must violate the *principle of nontranslation* by which he aims to understand the native sense of their ideas through their peculiar mode of expression. In short, the pedantry of nontranslation often conflicts with the polemics of characterization.

Marx himself seems to suggest that the difficulty here may reside not in what is particular about the fund of meanings and terms with which one approaches texts, but rather in the difference between thought and language itself, a difference not unlike the foreignness (*Entfremdung*) of political economy's language of facts to the humanist conception of essence. In an analogy where he compares the circulation of commodities on the market with the circulation of ideas between people, he suggests that even when words and ideas, or commodity values and money, are run through a process of "translation," the dimension of foreignness between them cannot be reduced:

(. . . Language does not transform ideas, so that the peculiarity [*Eigentumlichkeit*] of ideas is dissolved and their social character runs alongside them as a separate entity, like prices run alongside commodities. Ideas do not exist separately from language. Ideas which have first to be translated [*übersetzt*] out of their mother tongue into a foreign language in order to become exchangeable, offer a somewhat better analogy [of the relation of commodities to prices, and of money to values]; but the analogy then lies not in language, but in the foreignness [*Entfremdung*] of language.) (I 23: 162–63)

Marx is less interested here in the specific characteristics or peculiarities (*Eigentumlichkeiten*) of ideas versus language, or of values versus money, than he is in their difference, their foreignness, or their alienation (*Entfremdung*) with respect to one another. Not only does this difference form the basis for the comparison between commerce and communication (*Verkehr*) but it also allows values and meanings to be exchanged, conveyed, and rendered decipherable, whether on a market or among a group of speakers. In other words, whether the direction of "translation" is from what is "native" to what is "alien" or from one's mother tongue (*Muttersprache*) to a foreign language (*fremde Sprache*), both communication and social intercourse require one to decipher the inscription of an *alien character*.[7]

III

Here the problem of reading Marx's own style of reading, and thus of writing about what he reads, joins with the problem of the readability of Marx's writing, a problem that increasingly occupied him in his later works. How can we communicate something when we do not speak the same language or share the same thoughts? To answer that our thoughts may correspond with one another even when the languages we use are irreducibly foreign, or that communication is already part of the more general problem of the difference or foreignness of thoughts to language, only begs another question: How can we become familiar with the strangeness of Marx's writing when his intention may be to communicate the idea that meanings are often foreign to one another, or even alien to the truth?

The issues involved here are at least implicitly addressed by Marx as a methodological question concerning the manner in which his researches are to be composed and presented to the public. In the famous passage from the "Afterword" to the second edition of *Capital* (published with the new edition of 1873), he notes that there is a necessary difference between the method of research (*Forschungsweise*), by which the materials are first worked out in detail, their forms of development comprehended, and the manifold empirical connections between them tracked down, and the method of presentation (*Darstellungsweise*), by which the results of these investigations are systematically presented as an interconnected whole, as if they were "an a priori construction" (*MEW* 23: 27; *C*1: 106). This methodological distinction does not just designate two radically separate intellectual processes; rather, it marks the temporal sequence of different phases of a single interpretive procedure, as well as the simultaneous existence of distinct aspects of social reality. Indeed, the two methods betray a deeper rift already noted by Marx in his 1857 "Introduction" between how phenomena are conceptualized (presented and researched) and how they emerge socially and historically (M: 101; cf. Wilson 1991: 49).

As Lyotard puts it, in Marx's writing not only is there a "search" (*Forschung*) that is literally "set up" (*darstellt*) within and by the presentation itself; there is also a continuous process of "staging" (*Darstellung*) materials and dramatizing his relation to them within the activity of research:

Now there is in the interminable reporting of Marx's accusatory revolutionary peroration a certain power of effect: the theoretical discourse stops presenting itself according to its closure even as it *researches* this closure. What Marx perceives as defeat, suffering (and eventually sees in *ressentiment* in effect), is the mark on his work of a situation that is precisely that of capital, and which gives way as much to a strange success as to a fearful poverty: the work cannot body forth [*faire corps*] just as capital cannot. (Lyotard 1974: 125; my translation)

Marx strives to move his thoughts forward through writing while seeking out a sense of their own completion; he wants to follow through on his revolutionary aspirations while presenting his insights through the more constrained rhetoric of science. This conflict prevents him from simply describing social processes as factors to be recapitulated, enumerated, and documented as in a bureaucratic report, and forces him instead to personify them as actors taking part in a dramatic situation. But rather than represent individuals as personalities more or less responsible for the state of existing social relations (as a German Ideologist or a Critical Critic would), he deals with individuals "only as they are personifications of economic categories, the bearers [*Träger*] of particular class relations and interests," as he remarks in the "Preface" to the first edition of *Capital* (MEW 23: 16; C1: 92). In this way, he is able to recast the critique of political economy as a kind of "human comedy" where each character plays a part within the ensemble of a historical totality.

The dynamic of rehearsal and staging in Marx's work, of research and representation, includes his conflicting attempts to achieve both self-clarification and dramatic effect, and thus to maintain control over the manner in which his writings are to be read and received. As a writer, he must decide on the form his researches must take in order best to communicate his insights, and thereby to reach a sympathetic readership and an open-minded publisher. In the late 1850s, when he was putting together his still fragmentary studies in political economy, he recalled the difficulties he had in writing and trying to publish his study of Epicurus in the early 1840s, specifically in attempting to put together

the presentation of a total system out of fragments [*die Darstellung des Totalsystems aus dem Fragmenten*], a system which . . . existed only *in itself* in the writings of Epicurus but not in any known system, as is the case with Heraclitus. . . . Even among philosophers who give their work a systematic form, Spinoza for example, the real internal structure of a system is entirely different from the form in which he consciously presented it. (Marx to Lassalle, 31 May 1858)

In general terms, the "method of presentation" that gives structure to a piece of writing may itself require a different method for one's own research and writing about it. The problem for Marx is not only how the parts of his research can convey a sense of the whole of what it is about but also what kind of "part" in the whole he himself as a writer is to play in setting up the final representation.

Since research and presentation must account for the writer's as well as the reader's role in what is communicated, the "communicative dimensions" of Marx's text will take different forms of expression and have different effects depending on which work of his we are reading, insofar as we take into account Marx's own aims and target readership in writing it. For example, it has been argued that if his notebooks of 1857–58 were written for his own self-clarification and in anticipation of writing a comprehensive critique of the system of classical political economy, then the first volume of *Capital*, published a decade later, was written for the purposes of educating others, and especially for informing the political action of the proletariat, notwithstanding the uphill climb of its opening chapters. Where the former work anticipates its own completion in the writing of a book, and so bears the marks of its author's hesitations and uncertainties, the latter confidently anticipates both its own reading and the future action toward which it aims: "Whereas in the *Capital* the tone is that of an outraged Olympian, in the *Grundrisse* the bafflement shows, is worked at, and sometimes controlled by a gesture of postponement" (Spivak 1987: 55). Looked at another way, if *Capital* is motivated by Marx's wish to open the infernal gates of science to the workers, the *Grundrisse* is driven by his desire to write against the philosophers and political economists from within the cave of their own abstractions and ideologies: "It is Marx's refusal [by 1867] to continue entertaining the hope that critique might improve political economy from within that necessitated a critical theory in opposition to the traditional thinking of both the political economists and the speculative philosophers, each in their own way" (Wilson 1991: 68).

At the research stage of his studies in political economy, and specifically in the second half of the 1850s, Marx's concern with the readability of his works, and specifically their acceptance or rejection by workers, political economists, and publishers, was expressed as both a hope that his writings might one day serve the purposes of revolutionary enlightenment and a fear that in the short term they would not be well received: "In the end, and after the experience of the last ten years, the contempt of the masses, as of individuals among RATIONAL BEINGS must have grown to such an extent that '*odi profanum vulgus et arceo*' [I hate the common mob and resist it] is practically a forced wisdom of life. But all this is merely a philistine mood that will be swept away by the first stormy weather" (Marx to Lassalle, 22 February 1858, quoting Horace's *Odes*). And yet by the time he wrote the first "Preface" to *Capital* in 1867, he seemed less ambivalent in the face of the ever more remote possibility of creating a true communicative situation, or even of intervening into an existing one, now adapting a line from Dante's *Purgatorio* as his personal maxim: "*Segui il tuo corso, e lascia dir le genti*" [Go on your way, and let the people talk] (*C*1: 93). Keeping in mind the different circumstances of their composition, including Marx's intentions in writing them and the readers he wished to reach, the *Grundrisse* and *Capital* may thus be understood to mark two aspects or phases of Marx's larger critique of a system of domination in terms of its prevailing mode of repressive communication.

From the 1850s, when his economic researches were at their most intense, to the 1860s, when he also had to consider seriously their mode of presentation, Marx also seems to have shifted his thinking about the most effective publication format of his writings. The problem here involved a decision over whether it would be better to present the whole of his project through discrete pieces, thereby making allowances for the limited attention spans of his readers, or to wait and present the parts all at once and in the context of the completed whole, thereby requiring a higher level of stamina from his readers. In 1858, Marx thought it would be "most agreeable for me to publish the whole work in *Heften*" (i.e., serial issues), in the way that Friedrich Vischer published his *Aesthetics* between 1844 and 1857. Even though this would "attenuate" the subject matter and work to the "harm of the format," it would be better for "the understanding of the public," presumably since they would be able to follow Marx's own paths of discovery and moments of bafflement, if not the peculiar "Rationale" of his subject matter. Nevertheless, he also believed that "if I had the time and the means to finish the whole before giving it to the public, I would condense it greatly, since I have always liked the method of condensing" (Marx to Lassalle, 22 February 1858). With the expansion of the bookselling trade and its mass commercialization, a condensed and serial format would have seemed more likely to meet with the demands of the new reading public of the nineteenth century than would its publication in the more standard and elevated format of the economic textbook. Rather than presume upon a privileged intimacy between himself as a scholarly writer and a highly educated readership, and rather than assume the alienation of reading and writing from other social and political activities, Marx seems to have wanted at first to "capitalize" on what Charles Augustin Sainte-Beuve disparagingly called the "invasion" of *literary democracy* by an *industrial literature* geared to the anonymous masses (cf. Prendergast 1978).

In a dramatic reversal of this stance, however, and on the eve of publishing *Capital* ten years later, Marx no longer seemed able to bring himself to publish his work in serial installments, now insisting on a closer relationship between form and content, between presentation and research, although at the expense of the communicative bonds tying himself as a scientific writer to his often uneducated readers. Now comparing the serial format of publication with the "method of Grimm," whose *German Dictionary* had begun appearing in 1852 with the "A" installment, he dismissed it as "in general more suited for writings that are not dialectically constructed": "Whatever shortcomings they may have, the merit of my writings is that they are an artistic whole, and that can only be attained by my method of not having them printed until they lie before me in their *entirety*" (Marx to Engels, 1 February 1865). Rather than accommodate himself to the prejudices and short attention spans of the reading public, rather than produce a piece of economic science on the model of the *romans-feuilletons* of his day, Marx wanted to present a completed chef d'oeuvre that everyone, masses and literati alike, could admire for its aesthetic perfection, if not its scientific insights. Although Marx in fact only managed to publish a master-*piece*, that is, only the first of several planned volumes of

Capital (itself apparently part of a larger project), he continued to risk the read-ability of his intermittent writings by insisting on their presentability as a total system of thought, or even as an artistic whole. In any case, throughout these shifting reflections on the communicability of his strange and even alienating ideas, Marx's continuing desire was to present his often tortured scientific dis-course as dramatically as possible, since what was at stake in this gamble was the *revolutionary effect* of his writing on a reading public.[8]

• • •

Having taken Marx's own reading practices as our guide, and having tried to account for the intended or actual responses his writing may have on us as readers, we can now reformulate the problem of reading Marx introduced at the beginning of this chapter as a desire to decipher the alien character of revolution. It seems that Marx himself found the cryptic sign of revolution so difficult to read because it could be read only through such alienating and foreign languages as political economy and philosophy, and could be writ-ten only in terms of such peculiar polyglot discourses as he himself invented. Thus, when we read a text like Marx's *Grundrisse*, we should not simply treat it "rationally," as a work important for the edification and education of scholars or as a contribution to the science of political economy, Marxist or otherwise. We must also read it by searching for what defies or breaks with the estab-lished mode of rationality, and thus what resists clear expression and correct translation, whether inside or outside of traditional Marxist theory and poli-tics. Just as we may read Marx's magnum opus as the headwork (*Kapital*) of an Olympian mind pitted against the monstrous and intelligent mechanisms of modern capitalism, or his early studies as the work of writing hands (*Manu-scripten*) that pursue a cultural labor of self- and social transformation, so we may also read his interminable rough drafts as attempts to make revolution-ary sense from the ruptures in modern reason, and thus to find rifts in the groundwork of modern power (*Grund-risse*).

Marx's writing literally de-ciphers the fetishes of modern reason by finding a human meaning and a social substance within the abstract appearances of what passes for "rationality," rather than by decoding such appearances according to a stereotyped character that is presumed to reflect the mechanisms of knowl-edge and power (Spivak 1987: 49; C1: 167). His aim is to seek out those voids where the apparatuses of domination appear to be constructed according to a rigid rationality but may yet be quietly undone by their own "subtle viscosity" (Lyotard 1974: 126) to reveal a human trace and a radical reversal. My remarks here and in Chapter 2 on the hermeneutics of Marx's revolutionary humanism thus echo John O'Neill's reminder that "the *radical anthropomorphization* of the fundamental concepts of theology, philosophy, and political economy must stand as the central dogma of Marxist humanism." And yet for Marx the critical force of this ethic exceeds any merely utopian idealism:

This anthropomorphic dogma is more than a renaissance trope of creative hierarchy in view of what we may call its *deconstructive power*. By the latter, we refer to the analytic power of Marx's tireless critique of every binary usage which separates mankind from its humanity by compounding the separations of mind and body, male and female, owner and non-owner, individual and society. In short, every discursive production of man's self-estrangement is seized upon in Marx's emancipatory prose—in passage after passage from which any one of us can recall the exhilaration of our first vision of socialist man and of human reason cleared of thought fetishes. The "thingification" (*Verdinglichung*) of social practices and relationships to which men and women subordinate themselves is deconstructed in Marx's complete rejection of the *metaphysics of absence*. Man's absence from man is circulated throughout the commodity system and its property relations, in the state and in all the ideological discourses of philosophy, the arts, and social sciences that expand upon the absence of integral discourse for human conduct and community. (O'Neill 1987: 69)

We must read Marx not simply to the letter (as Althusser proposes but does not do, literally or even literarily) but also mindful of his silences and omissions, gaps literally written into his discourse in a way that requires its readers to amplify the human voice and magnify the vision that must come to fill them. For this reason, we often cannot avoid disrupting his own stated intentions, thereby redirecting the meanings of his words while rerouting the ways they have been received and reworked in the Marxist tradition. Even as we try to evaluate Marx's own shortcomings and omissions, we may ourselves be forced to forge our own "misreadings" of him (cf. Bloom 1975). There is a sense, then, in which remaining true to the vision and voice that sustain his writing may entail not only an understanding of Marxism beyond Marx (the traditional "revisionist" problem) but also a reading of Marx beyond Marxism, a reading that may even go against the grain of anything Marx himself was able to conceive.[9]

A certain *violence of reading* is inevitably implicated in our approach to Marx's own forceful writing and reading practices. Deciphering his cryptic script may require on our part a deliberate attempt to misread him, to mistranslate his own "sublation" (*Aufhebung*) of the meanings and intentions of the texts he reads by inducing an "upheaval" (*Auf-hebung*) in the texts by him that we ourselves are reading. And yet in doing so we are also following the sense or direction (*Sinn*) of his own writing, in the hopes not of producing "a correct reading" that reproduces his transcendent intentions, but rather of proceeding from and beyond his own principles of reading: "Every reading is an upheaval of that which is read, not in the same way, but unevenly" (Spivak 1987: 44).

When Marx considers the texts of political economy and the events of capitalist history, he "suspends" (*aufhebt*) his judgment on their ultimate value and meaning. For example, he does not project the final outcome of the process by which "capital pushes beyond national boundaries [*Schranke*] and prejudices" without also acknowledging capitalism's "permanently revolutionary" character. For the very reason that capital "carries within itself immanent limits [*Grenze*] [that] have to coincide with the nature of capital, with the essential character of its very concept," he reads in the course of capitalist development not just an inevitable cycle of intensified exploitation and expanded accumulation but also the historical potential for crises and the ethical possibility for social metamorphosis, each of which he reads as an emblem or image of revolution (IV 22: 415; see Table 1 above). At the same time, he recognizes the need for capitalism to keep enough resources in reserve to defer self-destruction and thus to ensure that its growth may resume: "These contradictions, of course, lead to explosions, crises, in which momentary suspension of all labor and annihilation of a great part of the capital violently lead it back to the point where it is enabled [to go on] fully employing its powers without committing suicide" (VII 16–17: 750). Ironically, perhaps, our model for reading Marx might be invented from the allegorical significance we can draw from passages like this one, where the limits on Marx's desire to see the object of his criticism destroyed may match those we ourselves encounter in the *crisis of meaning* that frustrates our attempts to understand him. Indeed, even the "apparent virtual repetition" in Marx's having inserted here nearly the same line again in English (as Martin Nicolaus notes in his English translation) might be read as an invitation for us to decipher the alien character of revolution in Marx's prose by returning to the sense it may make in our own language.

We only catch a glimpse of what it is to share Marx's desk, to read him reading and writing, insofar as we understand that in coming up against the limits (*Grenzen*) of existence, we must try to reconfigure them in their aesthetic dimension as boundaries (*Schranke*) whose definitional form may yet be broken, suspended, or even surpassed (see Table 1 and Part III). That is, not Marx's dense prose and impressive scholarship, or even our own theoretical imagination, but history itself may present us with the ultimate impasses we meet in trying to understand him. The "ruptures" that we may decipher in his works, the tearing of parts out of other parts (*Auseinanderreissen*), are not just symptoms of his own failure at balancing, equalizing, or compensating (*Ausgleichung*) for conceptual dissymmetries. Rather, they mark his attempts at apprehending and interpreting (*Auffassung*) actual historical relations, or social processes that have already been broken apart, inverted, and compacted into one another (*gedrungen*) on their way to becoming inscribed into texts he himself writes (cf. M 6: 90, in the epigraph to Part II above). Marx's discourse does not try to say everything, but neither does it simply reserve its ultimate meaning for pedantic statements or definitive reasons that must always be explained later. Instead, it suspends final closure enough to allow, anticipate, and even require some as yet unknown and foreign element to disrupt it, or to supplement it with a strange and revolutionary sign.

PART III

Balzac's Pact

His admiration for Balzac was so profound that he had planned to write a criticism of *La Comédie humaine* as soon as he should have finished his economic studies. Marx looked upon Balzac not merely as the historian of the social life of his time, but as a prophetic creator of character types which still existed only in embryo during the reign of Louis Philippe, and which only reached full development under Napoleon III, after Balzac's death.

Paul Lafargue, *Karl Marx: His Life and Work*

Dear Fred,

BEST THANKS FOR £20.

Letter from Kugelmann enclosed.

At this moment I can only write you these few lines as the LANDLORD'S AGENT is here and I have to act the part of Mercadet in Balzac's comedy [*Le Faiseur*] for his benefit. Apropos Balzac, I advise you to read "Le Chef d'oeuvre inconnu" and "Melmoth réconcilié." They are two little chefs d'oeuvre, full of the most delightful ironies.

Salut.

Your
K. M.

Marx to Engels, 25 February 1867

The Pyramid of Sacrifice
*Marx's Unknown Masterpiece and the
Problem of Realism*

An irony in the history of Marx's thought, and of Marxism generally, is that
what many now regard as one of Marx's most important works remained almost
completely unknown until after the Russian Revolution of 1917, considered
to be the first and most important modern revolution undertaken for explicitly
Marxist reasons. In 1923, David Ryazanov, founding director of the Marx-
Engels Institute in Moscow, announced to the Socialist Academy the discovery
of eight notebooks that Marx filled in 1857 and 1858, emphasizing the "extraordinary interest" of these notebooks for "presenting the history of Marx's
intellectual development as well as what is characteristic [*die Characteristik*]
in his work and research methods" (Ryazanov 1925: 393–94). Although Karl
Kautsky's 1902–3 edition of a version of the 1857 "Introduction" is evidence
that at least one of these notebooks had already been discovered before the
October Revolution, as a whole this apparent masterpiece hidden away in
Marx's desk drawer seems to have remained unknown to or forgotten by even
Engels, Marx's closest friend and collaborator.

Marx would have been the first to recognize the "irony of fate that the Russians, whom I have fought for 25 years, and not only in German but in French
and English, have always been my 'patrons'" (Marx to Kugelmann, 12 October 1868). That his 1857–58 notebooks were jealously guarded by the Russians
until their publication in 1939 in Moscow, that they appeared in a more accessible German-language edition only in 1953 in Berlin, and that they were
still not widely known about, read, or translated in Western capitalist countries
until the 1960s and 1970s are further ironies in the fate not only of Marx's

legacy but also of socialism and capitalism generally (see Appendix A). Like
the political revolution that drew inspiration from Marx's humanist ethic and
scientific insights, but in advance of its own economic and historical maturity,
reading Marx seems to depend upon historically ripe moments that still seem
to elude us, leaving us with the peculiar residues of an "unknown Marx."[1]

In his introduction to the first English translation of a key passage from
these notebooks, Eric Hobsbawm hints that the obstacles in reading them
are not exclusively political or intellectual but also technical, literary, and
aesthetic. Marx's "sibylline passages" are "written in a sort of private intellectual shorthand which is sometimes impenetrable, in the form of rough notes
interspersed with asides which, however clear they may have been to Marx,
are often ambiguous to us" (Hobsbawm 1964: 10). Thus, the cryptic quality
of these notebooks, complicated by Marx's hurried and messy handwriting,
would seem in part to explain why they have remained unknown or at least
largely misunderstood by readers. Indeed, as I will suggest later, it may not be
too fantastic to compare the history of Marx's unknown masterpiece, which
has only fairly recently been revealed and still remains largely misunderstood,
with the painter Frenhofer's "chef d'oeuvre inconnu" as told about in Balzac's
"conte fantastique," in that it, too, appeared to those for whom he finally unveiled it as "nothing . . . just colors confusedly amassed and contained by a
multitude of bizarre lines" (Balzac 1956 [1831]: 498). But where Frenhofer
destroyed his life's work and died in despair over not being understood, Marx
chose not to show his masterpiece to anyone, perhaps hoping that someday
some baffled but appreciative reader might recognize its significance or even
attempt to complete it.

One such reader is Martin Nicolaus, who was the first to translate the
notebooks into English in their entirety, and who has gone so far as to argue that although "Marx's script is virtually a cipher" (1973: 65), it should
still be understood as the "summit" of Marx's entire career and as the "blueprint" for the reconstruction of Marxist social science and politics: "Now that
Marx's unpolished masterwork has come to light, the construction of Marxism
as a revolutionary social science which exposes even the most industrially advanced society at its roots has finally become a practical possibility" (Nicolaus
1972: 333; my emphasis). Although "obscure and fractured," Nicolaus argues,
these notebooks present "the only truly complete work on political economy
that Marx ever wrote," in that they provide a grand sketch of his entire theory of
capitalism from its origins to its final breakdown (1972: 309). David McLellan
makes the same point in his introduction to an early selection and translation
of some of the most important passages from the notebooks: "In a sense, none
of Marx's works is complete, but the completest of them is the Grundrisse"; it
is "the central point in Marx's process of 'self-clarification,'" "the centerpiece

of his work," "the kernel of his doctrine," and is therefore "the most fundamental of all of Marx's writings" (McLellan 1971: 15, ix, 1, 2). The long and
hard climb to the heights of science to which Marx invites us in his prefaces
to *Capital* in 1867 would thus seem already to have been achieved by him in
1857 and 1858.

Ironically, although McLellan is emphatic about the centrality of this work
to an understanding of Marx's thought in particular and of Marxism in general (1971: 3), his selections from it are made up almost entirely of passages
he admits are marginal to the main economic arguments of the work. He
states that Marx's asides and digressions are ultimately of a much wider scope
than the systematic economic analyses that make up its core, and that these
"marginal" discussions indeed reveal what is most essential or central to these
more technical analyses. The notebooks then seem to be strewn with "foundational passages" that might be sifted to reveal precious conceptual stones
whose glimmer may shed light on an entire complex of characteristic traits (*die
Characteristik*) that distinguish Marx's research methods and the direction of
his overall project: "It is these digressions that give the *Grundrisse* its primary
importance and show that it is a rough draft of a far wider scope than what
was later included in *Capital*" (1971: 8). Insofar as these notebooks are "much
more than a rough draft of *Capital*," McLellan argues, "the most striking" of
these asides might be seen to be the draft plan Marx tagged onto the end of the
section from the 1857 "Introduction," "The Method of Political Economy"
(M: 108), an outline that not only presents the major divisions of Marx's critique of political economy as a whole but also is "couched in language that
might have come straight out of Hegel's *Logic*" (1971: 13). Although this outline appears in Marx's work almost as an aside or an afterthought, it seems both
to present his whole study of capitalism as a particular socioeconomic system
and to draw from or even criticize an entire universalizing system of absolute
knowledge.[2]

The trajectory of Marx's career that led up to and then surpassed what he
was able to achieve in his *Grundrisse* can be traced in more detail than is
implied in these general terms that only gloss the main phases of his lifework
(compare the "surface" of Table 1 as well). That is, we need to go beyond
the observations that these notes literally occupy a central place in the three
main stages of Marx's work, and that their cryptic and fragmented qualities
have both helped and hindered attempts to assess their broader significance.
By highlighting the salient features of the principal works that are most characteristic of each decade of Marx's career, we shall be able to test more precisely
the extent to which the notebooks are indeed "the work which more than any
other, contains a synthesis of the various strands of Marx's thought" (McLellan
1971: 15).

TABLE 2A
*The Social Phenomenology of the Class System, According to the Thematic
Organization of the* Manuscripts of 1844

FOUNDATIONS OF CAPITALIST SOCIETY		
Wages of labor	Profit of capital	Rent of land

CRITIQUE OF SOCIAL ALIENATION
Private property, division of labor, human needs, the power of money, communism, etc.

HUMANIST CONCEPT OF "ESSENCE"
Aristotelian *dynamei* and Hegelian *Wesen* as standards of human development

NOTE: Marx initially divided the pages of his manuscript into three equal columns, one for each of the three basic social classes, before addressing more general issues concerning social alienation and his own version of the humanist concept of "essence." See the presentation of this text in Marx [1844b] *MEGA* I/1.

Considering now in chronological order those works we can identify as the basic building blocks or layers of Marx's comprehensive theory of capitalism, we can begin by noting that in his *Economic and Philosophical Manuscripts of 1844,* he had initially analyzed not only how the industrial class structure was founded upon labor, land, and capital but also how these foundations were hidden under the abstract appearances of the monetary revenues corresponding to each: wages, rent, and profit (Table 2A). Going beyond the copious excerpts he took from the political economists he was studying at the time, Marx proceeded to his now famous critical discussion of the themes of social alienation before concluding with a more positive elaboration of the humanist concept of essence drawn from Aristotle and Hegel (see Part II). The result was a remarkably wide-ranging social phenomenology of the capitalist class system by which its most obvious and superficial aspects could be grounded, or phenomenologically reduced, to the concrete social totality they presuppose, as Marx clarified in his later remarks in the *Grundrisse* on "the method of political economy" (M: 100–108).

The groundwork laid in the 1840s for tracing the history of human development up to the industrial era became the starting point for the studies Marx undertook in the next decade and summarized in his *Grundrisse.* Since at this point my concern is to contrast the theoretical outlines of this work with the studies that came before and after (the details will be taken up in this chapter and in Chapter 5), it is necessary only to note how the textual organization and the theoretical scope of the materials gathered in the later manuscripts seem to follow and then surpass the earlier ones in both theme and method (Table 2B). Like their predecessors, the 1857 notebooks begin with a discussion of the monetary surfaces of capitalism ("Chapter on Money"), although here the argument proceeds not by way of a sociological and philosophical

TABLE 2B
The Morphology of Value, According to the Theoretical Scheme of the Grundrisse

III. CAPITAL		
1. *Production process* money as capital: inequality, unfreedom capital/labor relation surplus value maintained/ multiplied	2. *Circulation process* capital accumulation and reproduction (D) original accumulation (E) fixed/circulating capital (F)	3. *Capital as fructiferous* surplus value transformed into profit, interest, etc. (G)

II. MONEY	
1. Crisis and convertibility; the nature and emergence of money (C)	2. The functions of money as measure; as means or medium; as representative of value

I. VALUE
Framework of analysis:
all use values produced and realized as value

N O T E : Marx's 1857 "Introduction" to his notebooks explains the analytical priority of the concept of production with reference to other economic categories, the method of political economy, and the forces and
relations of production (M 1–22: 83–111). Elsewhere in his notes, labor in particular is elaborated as a potentially vanishing mediator in the representation and transformation of value (Spivak 1987 [1985]; Table 3). The
passages of the text marked here as C through G are identified in Appendix B and are discussed in terms of their
dramatic significance later in this chapter.

investigation of the foundations of trade and revenue, but rather as a topical commentary on the current world financial crisis, and then as a historical and theoretical analysis of the functions of money.

In the same way, the three basic elements that make up the concept of capital (which in the "Chapter on Capital" are elaborated in terms of the production, circulation, and "fructiferous" distribution of surplus value) are not developed primarily in terms of what they mean for the entrepreneurial system of industrial capital. Rather, they are presented as the highest conceptual expression of the ultimate tendencies of capitalism as a whole. Where these studies especially supersede those which came before is in the theoretical scheme Marx eventually employed to reorganize these materials in terms of the problematic of value. The incomplete and scarcely one-page section titled "Value" appended to the very end of these notebooks thus led Marx to revise his plan to reflect the formal metamorphosis of values under capitalism, according to a grammar or logic dictating that all goods be exchanged for money, and that all money be governed by the accumulation of capital. In short, while the actual contents of Marx's work of the late 1850s match almost anything sketched in the 1840s in breadth and depth, the theoretical form and orientation are both narrower and more precise.

Although the theoretical underpinnings of this value scheme served as Marx's point of departure in the following decade for the celebrated analysis

TABLE 2C
The Logic of Capital, According to the Conceptual Structure of Capital

III Doctrine of the Concept—distribution of capital
II Doctrine of Essence—production of capital
I Doctrine of Being—circulation of capital

NOTE: In actual composition, the three volumes of Marx's *Capital* deviate from the strict application of Hegel's science of logic to the doctrines of capital logic as presented here (Hegel 1969; Sekine 1984, 1986). Instead, they treat the production process after analyzing the commodity and before tracing the circulation and distribution processes of capital as a whole.

of the commodity in chapter 1 of *Capital*, in the later work he did not in the end carry through with his original plan. Rather, in *Capital* Marx attempted to synthesize both his phenomenology of class and his morphology of value into an abstract logic that would both be informed by and offer a concrete alternative to Hegel's science of logic (see Table 2C). Several generations of Marxists have commented upon this correspondence, from Engels to Lenin to Lukács, but few have studied it in detail. Nor shall I attempt to do so here, although I shall return to some of its implications in Chapter 5. Rather, my purpose is to show that what Marx himself considered to be the summit of his critique of political economy ultimately represents a further narrowing of his theoretical field, at least when considered in the larger context presupposed by his other studies, and especially when compared with his *Grundrisse*.

In the 1860s and 1870s, the point of view afforded by capital itself, rather than the broader perspectives of value and money, or of social class and the human condition, provides Marx with the conceptual focus and framework for determining the logical hierarchy of capitalist social processes. However, in spite of his tendency to formulate these processes more rigidly (here in terms of abstract doctrines on the being, essence, and concept of capital), his overriding preoccupation, evident from the actual composition of this work, is with the "production" of capital in particular and of human being in general. In short, even Marx's culminating achievement in the three volumes of *Capital* suggests his desire to build upon rather than to replace the broader foundations laid in his preceding studies.

Thus, it indeed appears that Marx's investigations of 1857–58 provide us with both an outline and a partial execution of the whole of his critical vision of the history and self-interpretation of modern society, from its beginnings to its ultimate demise. Indeed, the most comprehensive plan Marx appears to have projected seems nowhere more developed than in these notebooks, however fragmentarily. In a letter to his friend Ferdinand Lassalle as he was finishing work on his *Grundrisse*, he announced his intention to publish a threefold critique of capitalism in the form of a systematic analysis (itself in six parts, beginning with the general concept of capital and ending with a study of the world market), a critique and history of the categories of bourgeois and political economy and socialism (in the form of excerpts and commentaries), and a historical sketch of capitalist and noncapitalist ideas and social forms (Marx to Lassalle, 22 February 1858; cf. Marx 1859 CW 29: 261; Rosdolsky 1977: 10–56). From the broad sweep of its sketches, tableaux, and outlines, down to the minutest details of its polemical digressions, technical discussions, and "foundational passages," the *Grundrisse* thus seems worthy of its reputation as Marx's greatest and most comprehensive study. Or at least it appears to have provided us with a peek at what would have been his most perfect work but one that was destined to remain both an unfinished and an unknown masterpiece.[3]

I

However convincing this argument may be, we can still sense something profoundly contradictory and ironical in the idea that Marx's theoretical project is somehow contained or prefigured in the framework of his notebooks from the late 1850s. Although Marx's notes seem to have merited their estimation as a great masterwork, at the same time they are also obviously only a plan, indeed, a series of fragmented plans for a major work yet to be written. The dimensions of this project are only hinted at in various outlines, personal letters, and marginal comments that indicate he may well have been planning a work quite different from what he was eventually able or willing to produce. In other words, Marx's notebooks may indeed be "unknown" not just because so few people have read them (and even fewer have actually understood them), but also because they are at the same time merely the outlines for a work that in fact he never finished—or indeed, hardly even began.

This irony may contaminate my own attempts to depict, describe, or speculate upon in outline form what Marx's work is about, what its sources are, how he later revised it, and ultimately what it would have been about had he been able or willing to develop it further. While the discussion concerning the tables presented above is intended to sketch Marx's overall conceptual project with reference to the outlines of his major works, it also raises a number of questions regarding the relationship between the fragmentary form of Marx's text and its content, and between what it actually is and what it might have become. With this in mind, we may attempt to combine Tables 2A, 2B, and 2C in a way that reflects at a glance both the hierarchy of Marx's principal works as they progressively took on a narrower focus and the successive layering of his theory of capitalism as it developed through the three main decades of his career (Figure 1). With reference to this figure, and with one of the literal

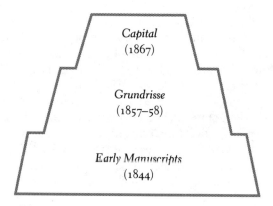

Figure 1. The pyramid of sacrifice

meanings of the German word *Grundrisse* in mind—an architectural plan or a blueprint for the construction of a building or monument—we might use this figure to consider the extent to which Marx might have provided us not just with a sketch of what he actually did make of his studies in political economy but also with what he might have constructed in some other work.

As a blueprint or architectural plan of something else, Figure 1 happens to project Marx's lifework in the form of an image, that is, a pyramid of sacrifice. Although this seems to have happened by chance, the presentation of Marx's overall theory in the shape of a pyramid may provoke some speculation about whether this figure itself might provide us with a key for making sense out of Marx's unknown masterpiece and, more speculatively, of the work he might have written. To explore this possibility, I shall cite a passing comment he made in his notes that happens to mention Egyptian pyramids. The fact that Marx himself had something to say about pyramids lends some initial support to the idea that at least a part of his overall theory may be figured through this particular image:

With kidnapping, slavery, the slave trade and forced labor, the increase of these laboring machines, machines producing surplus product, is posited directly by force; with capital it is mediated through exchange. . . . Use values grow here in the same simple relation as exchange values and for that reason this form of surplus labor appears in the slave and serf modes of production etc., where use value is the chief and predominant concern, as well as in the mode of production of capital, which is oriented directly towards exchange value, and only indirectly towards use value. This use value may be purely imaginary, as e.g. with the Egyptian pyramids, in short with the works of religious ostentation which the mass of the nation in Egypt, India etc., was forced [to undertake]; or it may be directed towards immediate utility as e.g. with the ancient Etruscans. (VII 22–23: 769)

Leaving aside for the moment the theoretical significance of these remarks at this point in Marx's argument in the *Grundrisse*, it can be asserted here that Figure 1 presents Marx's work in the form of one of its contents (a pyramid). Put another way, these comments open up for us the dimension of *the content of the form* through which we may gain access to another side of what Marx's text could potentially be about, or what we ourselves might make of it. That is, thinking about this passage through the image projected by Figure 1, the form and the content of Marx's text need not be presumed to operate separately or in some other conventional way, but may be thought about from some other perspective that allows us to imagine both how this text is constructed and how it might yet be deconstructed.

But by calling this arrangement of Marx's works "the pyramid of sacrifice," I have given to Marx's text a characterization that may also provide an approach to or emphasis on an aspect of his understanding of political economy that is different from that which dominated his own view. Looking now more closely at the contents and context of Marx's comments on pyramids, it seems that my characterization draws from themes he himself addresses, such as the problem of "imaginary use values" like the pyramids in structuring ancient economies, and, in a closely related discussion earlier on in the text, from his critique of the old idea of "work as sacrifice" as expounded by the classical political economists (VI: 610–11). Marx's observations on the Egyptian pyramids highlight their function as imaginary use values, in contrast to the more utilitarian use values of the Etruscans, while both kinds of use value are understood to organize massive armies of "laboring machines" that are sacrificed to the ruling powers of the prevailing social system.

In spite of the appearance of this passage as marginal to Marx's main concern with modern industrial capitalism, it in fact is closely tied to the broader theory he has developed concerning the symbolic use of those imaginary, non-utilitarian, and apparently arbitrary constructions that organize social relations generally. This larger framework was made evident in his opening comments in the "Chapter on Money," where he had analyzed capitalism's need for an apparently arbitrary symbol, cipher, or character that in reality could wield monumental powers for the accumulation and expansion of wealth. In both discussions his more general point is that an essential part of how a society "works" can be read in the imaginary principles and symbols through which it functions.

The figure of the pyramid of sacrifice thus draws our attention to the wider scope of Marx's more general theory of the symbolic and imaginary dimensions that give focus and form to the real organization of social life. In more familiar, Marxist terms, the figure exemplifies a basic analytical distinction that is crucial to Marx's critical theory, namely, an ideal superstructure or imaginary logic of legal, political, cultural, and religious ideas (that are themselves effective in reality and therefore not simply illusions people have about reality), and a material substructure of social and material resources organized in space and time (but that may be shaped by the prevailing illusions people have about them). By depicting the intermediary layer between the two main tiers of this social edifice, the figure of the pyramid provides both an empirical example and a theoretical symbol for Marx's topographical scheme depicting how real and ideal social forms meet at a solid, though imperfect and broken, foundation (*Grund-risse*), and perhaps also how they conceal a labyrinth of subterranean passages and hidden recesses.

In other words, notwithstanding his orthodox apologists and semiotically obsessed critics, Marx understood the capitalist economy in part as a *symbolic economy*, and conducted his own critique of political economy in part as a *theory of social symbolism*. Not only is he concerned to show how imaginary sign values and use values have an effective and real function as social symbols, but his own theory of how this happens is designed to make sense of and intervene in the laws governing those symbols. For this reason, any attempt to isolate and compare the specific organizing functions of particular imaginary use values within given historically determined social contexts (as I do in what follows) presupposes the more general problematic of the principles and laws that govern social symbolism (cf. Goux 1990; Green 1988; Simmel 1978).

In the context of Marx's critique of political economy broadly conceived, the figure of the pyramid may be creatively interpreted in general terms as an exemplary emblem for a self-sustaining socioeconomic system whose survival depended upon its organization as a culture of sacrifice and death instituted by way of socially constructed symbols. The Egyptian pyramid with which Marx was most familiar, for example, not only contained the mummified remains of the dead tyrant, his family, and his riches (often including his slaves) but also stood as a symbolic monument to the sacrifice and anonymous labor of generations of slaves—or, to use his own cynical expression, to the army of "laboring machines" whose lives were spent constructing it. As a symbol for the place of death in life, of life in death, and of a life after death, the Egyptian pyramid thus projects a succession of theoretical schemes, each embodied in stone and superimposed upon generation after generation of silent workers. It is thus not unlike the pyramid of sacrifice, its South American counterpart, which I have used to reconfigure Marx's work: "To see Cholula is to understand the relation among theory, sweat, and blood. For the pyramid was not designed for aesthetic purposes, as an exercise of *l'art pour l'art*. The meaning of the pyramid was provided by its sacrificial platform, the theory behind which was cogent and implacable: If the gods were not regularly fed with human blood, the universe would fall apart" (Berger 1974: 3). Although the site of death is a tomb within, in the one case, and a platform on top for human and animal sacrifice, on the other, in both kinds of pyramid the very form of the pyramid exerts symbolic force as a structural principle of social organization and universal order, and thereby embodies the material relations of power, knowledge, and wealth that establish a society's dominion over space and time, as well as over life and death. Thus, the pyramids provided an ideal focal point for the construction and use of massive networks of transportation, trade, and communication routes that in turn provided mechanisms of social survival and the infrastructure for social reproduction (cf. Weber 1976).

Modern capitalism, of course, has had no one monumental structure like the pyramids to serve as a symbolic focal point, a central image, and a principle of intellectual, economic, and social organization. However, Marx analyzed the symbolic functions operating in what we may understand to be its capitalist counterpart, the money symbol, in that it, too, embodies an apparently infinite range of "imaginary" functions in the survival and growth and life and death of a culture. Marx developed his theory of money not only in material terms, as a restricted economy of buying and selling, borrowing and lending, or producing and consuming, but also in view of its symbolic character as a potentially unlimited and generalizable economy of wealth, power, and knowledge. He tried to show how money is sustained as a symbolic medium necessary to the capitalist social system through the perpetuation of a class structure at the level of production (section 1 of the "Chapter on Capital"), which in turn is expanded, intensified, and even distorted at the levels of circulation and distribution (sections 2 and 3, respectively). The modern money system thus seems to project a reverse image of the ancient pyramid as a symbol of sacrifice and death in its function as a symbol for the capitalist ideology of bounty and life, but amid squalor and destruction.

Apart from whatever significance we may want to read into the fact that the image of an Egyptian pyramid is still printed on every American dollar bill, let us consider instead how Marx's metaphor of the colonial "hothouse" (*Treibhaus*) may be read as an inverted image of the pyramid symbol as it is projected onto the screen of the capitalist money system. Marx uses this figure to express the impressive development of capitalism into an apparently bountiful world market, its expansion into a global transportation system and communications network (V: 517–48), and its frantic rush to find the material resources and social symbols on which its social metabolism depends: "the search for and discovery of gold in new continents, countries, plays [a] great role in the history of revolution [or revaluation], because by its means colonization is improvised and made to flourish as if in a hothouse" (*treibhausmässig*) (II 2: 225). When considered apart from its "revaluation" through capitalist profit-making schemes, the hothouse appears simply as a structure for creating an artificial environment to allow trees and other plants to grow and bear fruit even in the most inhospitable climates and seasons. However, when viewed *sub specie capitalis*, or from the perspective of the relations of distribution of surplus value and profit, the capitalist "hothouse" may be seen to manufacture an environment for the cultivation or cultured development (*Entwicklung*) of the seeds (*Keime*) of wealth (I: 198; III: 310) into mature "plants" (or factories) that can be assured of continuously "bringing fruit" as profit, interest, and rent (VII: 745–78). Thus, at least from a capitalist point of view, there is indeed some truth in saying that money really does grow on trees.[4]

Like the ancient pyramid, this modern social factory must put masses of "laboring machines" to work, thereby perpetuating a class structure that is integral to its own "organic composition" while at the same time ensuring that the precious fruits of its harvests are not distributed to everyone in the same way, nor to all places equally. The golden apples of power, wealth, and knowledge must alternately be placed within and beyond the reach of their cultivators and caretakers, just enough to tease and tantalize them into wanting more: "A mass of parasitic bodies come to cluster around capital, and, under one or another title, they lay hands on so much of the total production so as to leave little danger that the trees will be allowed to grow [too far] over their heads" (VII 19: 757). Insofar as the economic principle of this new world order preserves the old structure of palaces next to hovels, poverty amid plenty, warfare with welfare, and a death culture within a living civilization, the capitalist "hothouse" both reverses and reinforces the image of death and sacrifice figured in the Egyptian pyramids.

Living by Adam Smith's version of Jehovah's curse on Adam, "In the sweat of thy brow shalt thou labor," the workers practice a kind of ritual of self-sacrifice: "'In his normal state of health, strength and activity, and with the common degree of skill and facility which he may possess, he must always give up the *identical portion of his tranquillity, his freedom,* and his *happiness*'" (VI: 610–11). And yet their efforts must not be wasted on "imaginary" sacrifices to the gods, as with the Egyptian kings or Etruscan priest-nobles and their pyramids (IV: 432). Rather, the fruits of their labor must be objectively realized in the market as values in the form of profit, interest, rent, and wages; that is, they must be made productive as money. Ultimately, then, not only are the products of these "laboring-machines" being cultivated for exchange on the world market, but they themselves are also being "developed" (or "underdeveloped") for universal prostitution in the global emporium (I: 163).[5]

The idea that Marx's image of capitalism's "hothouselike" expansion is an extension of the ancient figure of the pyramid of sacrifice seems to hit a stumbling block as soon as we remind ourselves of the obvious fact that the ancient civilizations which built the pyramids have long since disappeared, while industrial capitalism survives and continues to grow. Here, however, the figure of the pyramid reveals its deepest significance as a memorial to a civilization that is now dead insofar as we also recall that Marx's critical perspective on modern industrial society projects a futuristic vision of the death of capitalism. In other words, the explicit purpose of Marx's theoretical excavation of the pyramidal and apparently solid structures of modern knowledge, wealth, and power is ultimately to assist in "digging capitalism's grave," as he puts it in the *Communist Manifesto*. In the context of the nuclear age, however, we must face the possibility that the search for security and the quest for power in the global context of capitalism may entail not just cultivating the tree of life but also unthinkably catastrophic consequences that we can only glimpse in the dark afterimage of a mushroom cloud (cf. Gill and Law 1988: 360–80).

For Marx, capitalism's burial place is also an archaeological site in which the fragments of this civilization's most precious treasures, its greatest achievements in the arts, in the sciences, and in technology, are preserved from oblivion, imbued with new life, and given new uses. As the archaeologist of capitalism, Marx's first task is to detect the gaps, breaks, or rifts in the area of contact between the ruined monuments of reason and the ground on which they rest (*Grund-risse*), spaces that serve as access points to the hidden caverns and passages below the pyramid's surface where holy relics, memento mori, and precious treasures lie buried. Later, in his role as the museumologist of a dead culture, he will search through these fragments to find reasons for the decline and destruction of modern capitalism, to discern whether it was conquered or plundered, whether it died of natural causes or destroyed itself from within. In spite of the care he will have spent in excavating these relics and treasures, and in giving them a new (scientific) value and a new afterlife, Marx's archaeological labors will also have contributed to the long burial process of this dead (or dying) civilization. Thus, even looking back on it from the future, the capitalist "pyramid" will continue to function as a symbol of the relations between knowledge, wealth, and power, but now as a ruined monument that stands in memory of those whose sacrificial labors built it and of those who still work toward its excavation or destruction (cf. Lenhardt 1975; O'Neill 1976).[6]

II

At this point the perspective on capitalism as a pyramid of sacrifice might be shown to intersect with the position taken by such post-Marxist readers of Marx as Jean Baudrillard. From *The Mirror of Production* (1973) to *Symbolic*

Exchange and Death (1976), for example, Baudrillard, too, is concerned to "remember capitalism" in the future perfect tense by presenting a futuristic vision of the industrial present partly in terms of the "primitive" cultures of its noncapitalist past (and Third World "subcultures"). As a kind of postmodern primitive (Kroker 1992: 62), Baudrillard radicalizes Marx's perspective on capitalism by conducting a "spéculation à mort" into the exterminist logic of capitalism's own death culture, figured in such spectacular scenes as foreign wars, concentration camps, nuclear holocaust, urban violence, international terrorism, funeral parlors, and suicides. Ultimately, the system is haunted by the specter of its own death in primitive and barbaric scenarios of sacrificial violence, loss, and excess. This is because the distinctive characteristic of the modern age, which is only magnified in the postmodern era, is our "future anterior" view of ourselves as the subjects of future archaeology. The intensification of capitalist death culture as we reach the fin de millennium may be read as a sign that the system as we imagine it to exist is already dead, or at least creating the conditions for its own extinction.

Baudrillard's analysis begins by pointing to the break with the symbolic logic based on the exchange of use values that has been effected through the ascendancy of the economic logic of exchange value. The restrictive economic rationalities of consumption and production, he argues, contain and condemn to oblivion the primitive logics and savage scenes of symbolic exchange and destruction (*consommation*) that nevertheless continue to be presupposed, distorted, and fatally amplified: "The real rupture [within capitalism] is not between 'abstract' labor and 'concrete' labor," nor between work on behalf of the system and work for oneself, "but between symbolic exchange and work (production, economics)" (Baudrillard 1975: 42). That is, the real break effected by capitalism is between such ssocioritual exchanges as gift and sacrifice, excess and loss, contamination and taboo on the one side, and such socioeconomic processes as buying and selling, growth and recession, pollution and repression on the other. Thus, Baudrillard both accelerates and surpasses Marx's analysis in his assertion that the death of capitalism comes not only with its economic and moral bankruptcy but even more with its symbolic poverty, that is, its utter inability to find symbolic expression for the social bond without which it cannot survive.

The ongoing crisis within capitalism must be read not simply in the fall of the profit rate, in the unequal distribution of wealth, or in legitimation crises of political and moral authority, but above all in the system's failure to reproduce itself as a symbolic economy:

It is directly at the level of the production of social relations that capitalism is vulnerable and en route to perdition. Its fatal malady is not its incapacity to reproduce itself economically and politically but its incapacity to reproduce itself *symbolically*.

The symbolic social relation is the uninterrupted cycle of giving and receiving, which, in primitive exchange, includes the consumption [*consommation*] of the "surplus" and deliberate anti-production whenever accumulation (the thing not exchanged, taken and not returned, earned and not wasted, produced and not destroyed) risks breaking the reciprocity and begins to generate power. It is this symbolic relation that the political economy model (of capital), whose only process is that of the law of value, hence of appropriation and of indefinite accumulation, *can no longer produce*. It is its radical negation. What is produced is no longer symbolically exchanged and what is not symbolically exchanged (the commodity) feeds a social relation of power and exploitation. (Baudrillard 1975: 143)

As long as the ideologies that govern money exchange, stock markets, and factory production function simply as imaginary reflectors of the law of value and project only the mirror image of industrial production, then capitalism's fatal disease may be diagnosed in its inability to see its own image in those savage cultures whose symbolic laws govern the rituals of gift giving and sacrifice. Fueled by a symbolically impoverished system of uninterrupted production and reproduction, capitalist death culture thereby sustains an irrational belief in the superiority of its modernity, and a supernatural faith in its immortality.

In spite of Baudrillard's brilliant post-Marxian vision of the subversive logic of symbolic exchange deciphered from the fetish character of capitalist rationality, he nevertheless fails to see how this logic already operates within Marx's own critical theory: "If there was one thing Marx did not think about, it was discharge, waste, sacrifice, prodigality, play and symbolism. Marx thought about *production* (not a bad thing), and he thought of it in terms of value. There is no way of getting around this" (1975: 42). Thus, Baudrillard takes Marx's theory itself, and not just the capitalist ideology Marx criticized, to be a reflection of the industrial performance principle, that is, to be itself a mirror of capitalist production. He offers a restrictive, sacrificial, and even uncharitable view of Marx's economic theory by approaching it as a kind of *fetish text* that can be ceremoniously offered or "thrown up" just as Marx once claimed to have "thrown over" Ricardo's theory of profit (Marx to Engels, 14 January 1858).

Reading Marx's work only as the product of a Protestant ascetic or a Jewish iconoclast (cf. Marx 1843) and not as the imaginative work of a Catholic fetishist like himself (cf. Marx [1844b]), Baudrillard thus finds in the subtleties and niceties of Marx's analysis only a statement of the obvious, the trivial dressed up as economic science. Giving to Marx's work very little and taking from it only a frugal collection of key words, pithy phrases, and passages, his ungenerous reading makes of Marx's science a stark and almost impenetrable fortress, or even a pious and laughable religious sanctuary ignorant of its own irrelevance. Baudrillard's aim here is to reject what he takes to be the imperialist pretensions of Marx's historical materialism, which in his view is to provide a scientific key to modern social life, a Euclidean geometry of history ("Human anatomy contains a key to the anatomy of the ape"), or a two-dimensional grid for interpreting such "primitive" cultures as the Egyptian master-slave economy in terms of alienation and exploitation ("The history of all hitherto existing society is the history of class-struggles") (Baudrillard 1975: 93–95).

Insofar as Marx himself not only conceived of production in terms of value but also analyzed value explicitly in terms of its "fetish character," he did not make a fetish of production, whether industrial or ancient. When Marx held a mirror up to capitalist society, the image it reflected to him was full of "mysteriousness," "necromancy," and "absurdity." Thus, while a commodity may appear to be "an extremely obvious, trivial thing . . . its analysis brings out that it is [also] a very strange thing, abounding in metaphysical subtleties and theological niceties" (C1: 163).

If I state that coats or boots stand in a relation to linen because the latter is the universal incarnation of abstract labor, the *absurdity* [*Verrücktheit*] of the statement is self-evident. . . . The categories of bourgeois economics consist precisely of forms of this kind. They are forms of thought which are socially valid, and therefore objective for the relations of production belonging to this historically determined mode of social production, i.e. commodity production. The whole mystery of commodities, all of the magic and necromancy that surrounds the production of labor on the basis of commodity production, vanishes therefore as soon as we come to *other* forms of production. (C1: 169; emphasis added)

As Marx's comment on the absurdity of political economic categories shows, the primitive economies of fetishism, slavery, and sacrifice are not really "clarified" by the historical materialist interpretive grid of labor power and commodity value. On the contrary, his point is that the latter is exposed for its own irrationality, injustice, and even insanity (*Verrücktheit*) when viewed from the perspective of the former, that is, under the light of "other forms of production" (cf. Mitchell 1986; Wolff 1988). Marx's analysis thus presupposes a kind of historical genealogy of the emergence of "economic man" as a standing being (*Entstehung*), his subjection to the gaze of modern knowledge, and his "descent" (or "fall") and even disappearance into oblivion (cf. Foucault 1973). Just as Darwin tried to show how the anatomy of the ape can be understood as the key to human anatomy (Darwin 1871), so Marx tried to show that the master-slave relation provides a perspective from which to read the history of modern class struggles, the later stage as a more evolved and "mediated" form of the earlier one (V: 501). Indeed, from the perspective of a developed money system (which is not, of course, the only point of view Marx considers), the symbolic exchange and *consommation* of use values themselves appear as "primitive," as "abstract chaos," and even as "*madness*; madness, however, as a moment of economics and as determining the practical life of peoples" (II: 268–69).

To explore the implications of this analysis, let us imagine for a moment a very ordinary use value, such as a house. For the sake of simplicity, let us also imagine this house to be the one in which Marx himself lived and worked for so many years in London: a run-down structure made of stone, "as durable as [anything] used for machinery" (VII: 710), located in a working-class neighborhood, with a front entrance and a back door, a sparsely furnished living room, a few bedrooms, a kitchen, and a cellar (which might occasionally have been infested with rats and other vermin). Now since the living room of this house also doubled as a study (when Marx was not reading and writing in the British Museum), it served as both a place where he enjoyed and suffered family life with his devoted wife, his three adoring daughters, and his loyal maidservant, and a work site where he made his rather meager living (when he was not receiving subsidies from Engels). We should remember, however, that while he did not work simply to support himself and his family, much less his landlord and his publisher, neither did he labor simply on behalf of "the proletariat" or even "le roi de Prusse" (to use one of his favorite expressions).

However charming or horrifying this picture of Marx's domestic economy may appear by itself, what is at stake for us here is the problem of whether Marx, not just as a private family man but also as a critic of political economy, could view such things as a house, a living room, a desk, or his own writing tools only under the aspect of their utilitarian distribution and exchange as values, as Baudrillard claims (1975: 46). The question ultimately concerns whether Marx understood "the products of labor" and other use values solely within the rational scheme of their production, valorization, and consumption as useful objects and as fixed and circulating capital, or whether he may also have had a definite sense of their symbolic and even sacrificial value.[7]

In the section on "small-scale circulation" in Marx's notebooks (VI: 673–90), the family home is offered as an example of how the crude "rationality" of modern political economy can be critically exposed for its primitive mysteriousness, its idealism, and even its "fetishism":

It is not necessarily the case that *fixed capital* is capital which in all its aspects serves not for individual consumption, but only for production. A house can serve for production as well as for consumption; likewise all vehicles, a ship and a wagon, for pleasure outings as well as a means of transport; a street as a means of communication for production proper, as well as for taking walks etc. . . . The crude materialism of the economists who regard as the *natural properties* of things what are social relations among people, and qualities which things obtain because they are subsumed under these relations, is at the same time just as crude an idealism, even fetishism, since it imputes social relations to things as inherent characteristics, and thus mystifies them. (VI: 687)

When economists such as Ricardo (in the elided part of the passage above) treat the uses of things not just as they are economically and legally defined, that is, as they exist within definite social relations, but also in terms of their inherent, "natural" characteristics, they assume that the "physical properties" of even the most ordinary things are the "inherent properties" of capital's fixed or circulating components. Marx calls this the fetishistic treatment of social relations as natural phenomena, for example, when one treats a house as "fixed capital" not because it is subsumed under capitalist social relations but simply because it is thought to be more or less "durable" by nature. By contrast, Marx insists on specifying the analytical context in which a product of labor can be understood with respect to "its continued enclosure within the production process," that is, either noneconomically from the point of view of its natural or other properties, or economically from the perspective of its subsumption within the capitalist social factory (cf. Rovatti 1973).

The analytical context in which Marx "here regards capital as a process of realization and a process of production" may in fact require the consideration of such qualities as the perishability or durability of use values in the study of interest and rent: for example, when Marx's landlord keeps his property in repair or lets it go to waste, when a tenant like Marx refuses or fails to pay the rent, or when a real-estate dealer in the housing trade tries to buy or sell its property title (cf. VII: 723). But in no way are the symbolic (or even imaginary) dimensions of the concept of use value thereby foreclosed or disavowed. In the section entitled "I Value" that concludes Marx's notebooks (but that comes first in logical order), Marx argues that "although directly united in the commodity, use-value and exchange-value just as directly *split apart* [*fallen*]" (VII 63: 881; my emphasis). Although he also states in this context that the *examination* of use value may well lie "beyond political economy," this does not imply that such an investigation would necessarily lie outside the *critique* of political economy: "Above all it will and must become clear in the development of the individual sections to what extent use-value exists not only as presupposed matter, outside economics and its forms, but to what extent it enters into it" (II: 268).

Indeed, Marx himself later became increasingly interested in expanding his studies of value with respect to the place of use values not only in modern capitalist countries but also in non-European civilizations (cf. VII: 882; Marx [1879–83]). The study of use value and its communal organization, including its specifically utilitarian functions as well as its place in symbolic exchange and *consommation*, covers not just what is excluded by political economy proper but also what the presentation (*Darstellung*) of political economy ultimately presupposes, and therefore what it leaves to be elaborated in other research or in the course of its critical self-analysis. Only in this way is it possible to read how capitalism may ultimately be governed and destroyed through a crisis within its own symbolic structure and genesis.[8]

III

Marx argues that the value of a commodity "does not have its description branded on its forehead . . . [but] rather transforms every product of labor into a social hieroglyphic" (C1: 167). Baudrillard adds to this idea the injunction that we also understand that "utility (including labor's) is already a socially produced and determined hieroglyphic abstraction" and that this hieroglyph may be deciphered through the anthropology of "primitive" cultures and symbolic exchange practices. He argues that we must ultimately "break with the natural evidence of utility and . . . reconceive the social and historical genesis of use-value as Marx did with exchange value" (1975: 46). My point has been that Marx's theory of use value, as well as the use value of Marx's theory, need not be understood simply as "mirrors of production," that is, as mere reflections of the economics and economic theory of capitalist exchange value. Rather, the utilitarian and symbolic use value of Marx's theory itself may ultimately lie in our ability to "decipher" it as a kind of "hieroglyphic script" or, to draw from the discussion above, as the hieroglyphic script that covers the capitalistic "pyramid of sacrifice."

I am suggesting then that we regard Figure 1 as the architectural plan not just for Marx's theory of economics (*oikonomos*) but also for Marx's own theoretical *oikos*, his household of theory. The "use value" of this house that Marx built may ultimately allow us to read capitalism as a pyramid of sacrifice, the analysis of which implies and even requires the kind of understanding of the social and historical genesis of use value called for by Baudrillard. The utility of Marx's apparently ordinary, trivial, and simple conceptual apparatus may therefore lie in its (potential) function as a device for reading the imaginary and symbolic fetish character of capitalist values, for deciphering the cryptic hieroglyphic script that conceals even the most ordinary object and social relations. In other words, the real theoretical value of Marx's theory of value may well lie in providing us with a concept of the form of value without contents.

If so, then his initial and ultimate analytical effort consists of trying to conceive the peculiar capacity of the money symbol to reflect all social relations in the image of an alienating power and to bring all things within reach of an uncanny influence (cf. Marx [1844b]). Indeed, the unique feature of money lies in its peculiar capacity to represent *itself* as well as everything else, either through "real" and concrete materials like gold and other precious metals, or in the form of "fictitious capital" in which only the titles to properties are exchanged. Marx's Herculean task was to find a way to represent this apparent infinity in theory and to assess its sociopolitical implications in practice.

Let us try to conceive this impossible idea of a "form without content," which seems to designate the uncanny and alienating powers of money, by imagining the capital letter **A** to be superimposed upon Figure 1, thereby altering the shape of this figure to suggest something more like the Egyptian pyramids with which Marx was most familiar. To be sure, it is not just for this reason that the choice of this particular sign for the power of money is not entirely arbitrary or irrelevant to Marx's argument, since this letter **A** might also be understood to derive from the chemical symbols for gold and silver, *Aurum* (Au) and *Argentum* (Ag), or from the names for the new sources of gold and silver discovered in the early 1850s in Australia and America (I 28: 174). Marx had already made the general point assumed here in the following parenthetical remark that appears in his study of money:

(The material [such as gold] in which this symbol [for money] is expressed is by no means a matter of indifference, even though it manifests itself in many different historical forms. In the development of society, not only the symbol but likewise the material corresponding to the symbol are worked out—a material from which society later tries to disentangle itself; if a symbol is not to be arbitrary, certain conditions are demanded of the material in which it is represented. The symbols for words, for example the alphabet etc. have an analogous history.) (I: 145)

Finally, we might also note in this connection that Marx himself happened to write this capital letter **A** on the cover of the notebook from 1857 that contained his "Chapter on Money," an alternative designation to the one he eventually decided on, "Heft [Notebook] I," which together "have the character of headings or titles" (*Überschriften*), as the editors of Marx's *Gesamtausgabe* remark (MEGA II/1; *Apparat*: 781, 783 facsimile).

If we allow ourselves to judge a notebook by its cover, then this **A** might be imagined to signify Marx's theory about the signifying powers of money, the capacity of money to designate an almost unlimited number of signifieds, at least in the imagination. We might say, then, that Marx's writing attempts to superimpose this **A**—or to "overwrite" (*überschreiben*) and "underscore" its de facto superimposition—over the hieroglyphic surface of the capitalist pyramid of sacrifice. By enacting through his own writing the manner in which a text without images (the alphabetic sign of the **A**) has been inscribed over a text made up entirely of images (the script of the hieroglyph), he at the same time recounts how the history of the modern money system has been written over the stories told on the surfaces of pyramids that originate from a more ancient economic system.[9]

Insofar as Marx's own theoretical practice might be placed under the same sign as that which he is writing about, and insofar as Marx's own writing might be represented at least partly by means of what it is itself trying to represent, then we may decipher his own semiology or theory of social symbols in part through the *semiotics of his theory*. Not only does the pyramid of sacrifice then offer a potent symbol for Marx's understanding of capitalism as an economy of form without content, but also, through our representation of it in the character or cipher of an **A**, it may designate the logical and rhetorical form of Marx's critical theory itself. In short, Marx's theory of social symbolism is itself decipherable through the symbolism of his theory: this is the poetic, the prosaic, and more specifically, the literary dimension of his science.[10]

IV

If the "use value of Marx's theory" may be understood to stem from its aspect as a theoretical form without content, then this conceptual form might be considered not just in terms of its imaginary contents (as a pyramid of sacrifice) but also, through its own superficial and symbolic dimensions, as a text. This perspective leads us back to our consideration of how Marx's notebooks have been perceived by readers as a cryptic "cipher" that is difficult to understand but also may be characterized as a masterpiece in its own right. Here I shall try to show how the chaotic and seemingly indecipherable strangeness, mysteriousness, and even madness of Marx's "unknown masterpiece" participate in the thematics of the literary tradition of melodrama, as I have begun to argue in earlier chapters. Apart from the dubious shock value this switch from science to literature may have here, its aim is to show how the realism of Marx's science is achieved through many of the same critical intentions and rhetorical effects it shares with melodramatic fiction. Just as Marx's scientific and political aim was to evoke in his readers intense emotions while inspiring new insights, so too the melodramatic arts of eighteenth-century musical theater, nineteenth-century mystery stories and spy novels, and even twentieth-century horror movies, romantic serials, and courtroom dramas have tried to present as graphically as possible the most compelling social realities in the most poignant way possible (cf. Prendergast 1978).

Ironically, even the flamboyant and scandalous language of such a critic of Marx as Baudrillard seems to provide us with a point of access for reading the French accent in Marx's melodramatic literary style. Just as Baudrillard elaborates a theory of symbolic exchange as a pataphysical strategy or *science fiction* by which the system's logic may be turned against itself (1976: 12), in a similar way my characterization of Marx's text as a pyramid of sacrifice might be read as a way of staging a kind of theater of catastrophe in which scenes of death, sacrifice, and excess upset the prevailing industrial reality principle. Marx's text can thus be read as a catastrophic melodrama that not only depicts the annihilation of capitalism but also expresses his own revolutionary impatience to see this system as the victim of its own self-destruction.

Taking as our model the opening passages of a section in his notebook on the circulation process of capital, we can see that Marx's interest is not so much to analyze the buying and selling of commodities on the market as it is to show how this system carries within it explosive devices for its own ruin, and how "the realization process [*Verwircklichungsprozess*] of capital is at the same time its de-realization process [*Entwircklichungsprozess*]" (IV: 401–56; cf. Negri 1984: 85–104). The combination of Marx's imaginative revolutionary angst and his scientific rigor reveals his understanding of how the modern sense of "realism" is both defined and rendered problematic by the inherently unstable processes of the capitalist market (cf. Gill and Law 1988: 25–36). As in Marx's other foundational passages (see Appendix B), the achievement and usefulness of this excursus on crises resides less in its aspect as an account of a historical episode or a hypothetical occurrence than in its character as a sketch, a plan, or an outline of something that is anticipated but still beyond reach, as Baudrillard himself might have understood: "One takes a long time to outline the sketch of a work which, once completed, would be returned to oblivion and nothingness. But this is all wrong for the sketch already contains the whole work, and this alone is the work" (Baudrillard 1975: 165n).[11]

Provided we remember the lesson of this excursus on crises, we may read the sketches Marx made from 1857 to 1858 as a whole for the way they form a kind of tragicomic melodrama in five acts, to which I shall propose giving the title "The Curious Mystery of the Gold-Weighing Machines." In contrast to the "production" that Marx later directed for the staging of *Capital*, here our playwright seems more interested in describing the stage settings and assembling a cast than he is in actually writing scripts for the character roles of the social classes (cf. Hyman 1962: 146). As Nicolaus argues, while "*Capital* is planfully unfinished, like a mystery novel which ends before the plot unfolds . . . the *Grundrisse* contains the author's plot outline as a whole" (Nicolaus 1972: 325). Thus, Figure 1 might also be regarded as the roof or attic of a theater or playhouse for storing the texts that will serve as the script outlines, stage directions, prop orders, casting instructions, and musical scores later needed to act out a great revolutionary drama. In contrast to his desire in *Capital* to concentrate on the dramatic tensions through which the plot develops, Marx wants his "Curious Mystery of the Gold-Weighing Machines" to present a full-scale theatrical simulation of the life and death of an entire organic process (refer to Appendix B and compare Table 2B above):

Overture

Marx's melodrama opens with the sound of "world market disharmonies" accompanying a charming chorus on "the historic childhood of humanity." Parts of this piece prefigure the revolutionary crescendo that occurs later in the play (passage A at III: 886–87; passage B at M: 111).

Act I

The musical score of the overture develops here into the explosions produced from the mines that contain the glittering treasures of the fully developed capitalist economy. In the backdrop to this scene, we can make out a strange double image that combines the "economy of time" in communal association with a monstrous mechanism that "clears . . . the land of its excess mouths [and] tears the children of the earth from the breast on which they were raised" (before passage C at I: 159–73).

Act II

The rumblings from the previous act now spread far overhead in "the great thunderstorms" of modern crises, which are then tamed and disciplined to exert a "propagandistic, civilizing influence" by the exploration and development (*Entwicklung*) of the earth's resources through universal industriousness and general utility, the exploitation and domination of whole populations, and the creation of a "world market" that conquers human reality and space with time (passage D at IV: 401–15).

Act III

Here we are presented with a kind of phantasmagoric flashback to the mysterious "antediluvian conditions" leading up to the illegitimate birth scene of this "animated monster" (*beseeltes Ungeheuer*) or "forced combinatrix" of industry and objectified scientific ideas. The first "knell to its doom" is sounded when the countless workers who are forced to feed its insatiable appetite achieve an initial "advance of awareness" of their role as a mere "accessory" or "punctuation mark" for its survival. But whether it will later be destroyed by them or kill itself is here left undecided (passage E at IV: 459–71).

Act IV

The crescendo and climax of the drama are reached when the hideously distorted monster appears as " 'a vast automaton, composed of numerous *mechanical and intellectual organs* . . . subordinated to a motive force which moves itself,' " "sucking in labor as its soul, vampire-like." And yet by the end of these violent scenes we may also begin to distinguish a "picture of the coming social revolution," an image of a "different subject," the "free individual," "the human being itself in its social relations," whose life activity is not so much play as it is "discipline . . . practice . . . exercise . . . [and] composition" (passage F at VII: 690, 646, 712–14).

Act v

Finally, the spectacular "explosions, cataclysms, and crises" of the previous act culminate in "catastrophe" for the mechanical monster, the *Aufhebung*, upheaval, or "SUSPENSION" of its powers, and the "twisting and inversion" (*Verdrehung und Verkehrung*) of its final death rattle. As the smoke clears and the clouds lift, the actors in the drama, as well as the spectators and stage crew, see that they themselves have been the "animators" of this dead mechanical monster all along, and now perceive "a changed" (*veränderten*) stage of reality, a "new foundation first created by the process of history" (VII: 749–51; passage G at VII: 831–33).

Coda

By way of conclusion, we are presented with a fairly cryptic but apparently rational and commonsensical "solution" to the riddle posed by the play—"In the concept of value, its secret betrayed" (VII: 776, 881–82)—in the form of a final chorus reciting the strange allegory of the "Gold-Weighing Machines" which gives the drama its title. This last incantation seems to resonate an eerie warning (but what it means is unclear) against turning the scales of justice or upsetting the balance of truth in our desire to process all human life through a durable yet exquisitely "delicate" machine that "JUDGES FOR ITSELF" and reduces to a minimum the "PERSONAL EQUATION" (VII 64). Marx's curious melodrama thus ends not with a ringing revelation but shrouded in mysteries and riddles and "full of the most delightful ironies." [12]

The problem we now face is how to establish the relationship between the *descriptive format* of Marx's text as an incomplete and unexecuted plan, a theoretical speculation, or an empirical investigation into the history and structure of capitalism, and its *narrative structure*, through which the birth, growth, and death of capitalism are presented in a melodramatic plot that ironically depicts the triumph of moral virtue over villainy. To explore this connection, I shall need to go outside of Marx's text by treating the fiction of Honoré de Balzac, the great melodramatist of Marx's day and one of his favorite prose writers, as a kind of hermeneutic deus ex machina brought in to fix, clarify, or supplement something in Marx's text that so far has appeared to be lacking or mysterious.

Balzac's great *Comédie humaine* would indeed seem to be perfectly suited for gaining a "literary" perspective on Marx's work in that it apparently presents us with a literary analogue, holograph, or simulation of the pyramidal structure of knowledge projected by Marx's own grand theoretical scheme (cf. Wilson 1991: 76 and Figure 1 above). For example, Marx's character sketches of what he calls "the agreeable customs of life" (I: 119), in which he studies commonsense understandings of costs, prices, and wages, or where he presents his more disciplined insights into the great political and military events of the day, would seem to correspond to Balzac's elaborate "études" of contemporary manners, which he conceived as the foundation of a magnificent sociological *tableau vivant*. Similarly, Marx's more abstract philosophical and scientific reflections on commodity values and class structures seem to provide a parallel with the intermediate layer of Balzac's scheme, which is made up of fictional *études philosophiques* dealing with more refined issues which emerge from the search for truth, beauty, and goodness by way of the social media of power, knowledge, and wealth. Finally, the peak or focal point of Marx's project, which centers on the analytical constructs and conceptual logic of capitalist social processes generally, appears to be analogous to the crowning summit of Balzac's scheme, in which he planned to write a series of analytical investigations into the principles governing the social organism as a whole, including a physiology of love and marriage, an anatomy of educational bodies (*corps enseignants*), and a pathology of social life.

Like Marx's pyramid of sacrifice, Balzac's plans for the *Comédie humaine* thus appear to have been formed according to "a twofold descriptive metaphor of a picture gallery designating *Les Etudes de moeurs*, and of a monument built stone by stone, the architectural pyramid of which simulates the successive staging of the *Comédie humaine*, in its entirety. The *Etudes de moeurs* thus form its base, the *Etudes analytiques* its apex, and the *Etudes philosophiques* its median transition" (Perron and Le Huenen 1990: 216; cf. Balzac 1956 [1842]).[13]

Even the polemical intentions of Marx and Balzac motivating their presentations of modern society may be seen to reflect reverse but parallel images of one another: just as Marx's pyramid of sacrifice projects the death of capitalism by figuring the conditions of its future destruction, so Balzac's grand scheme for an "Occidental Thousand and One Nights" ultimately prefigures the decline and death of his beloved nobility, whose values were being sacrificed to the base and primitive passions gaining ascendancy among the bourgeoisie (cf. Lafargue 1890: 11; and the epigraph to Part III). Both projects thus inevitably become enmeshed in their attempts to solve *the problem of realism*, and in the difficulty of trying to represent what is in fact the case as what only appears to be such or as what may yet be otherwise. This problem forces us to consider whether the pyramidal shape of the Balzacian and Marxian human comedies may in fact only appear to reflect a realistic picture of society as it is, or as it can be projected to be through its future downfall or final demise. Indeed, such dramatic figures in Marx's work as the capitalist hothouse and gold-weighing machines clearly do not quite capture the reality of the system of industrial capitalism, any more than the virtuous and vicious caricatures that appear in Balzac's work could ever really have existed as such in nineteenth-century France. Bringing these two writers together thus seems to exacerbate and not resolve the problem of realism that defines the basic parameters of their studies. In an uncanny way their *recherche de l'absolu* through all forms of literary and scientific endeavor may only have brought them further from reality even as they approached closer to the truth.[14]

Our speculations into the broad conceptual schemes of Marx and Balzac as plausible simulations of one another magnify the problem of realism in their works by sharpening our sense of the *nonidentity* of these schemes not only with each other but also with the realities they profess to be about. Where Marx's realistic science may at first seem to present an almost exact copy of capitalist reality (an impression belied by its melodramatic rhetoric), Balzac's work reminds us of the fictionality of all forms of realism, that is, the non-identity of reality itself with our representations of and expressions for what is perceived to be real. In other words, just as earlier we speculated that Marx's theoretical scheme of contemporary capitalism may be seen to operate under the sign of the letter **A** when understood as an uncanny cipher or symbol for the imaginary and real functions of the money form, so we might now consider whether and to what extent Marx's writing may also be understood to operate under the letter **B** when understood as a sign for Balzac and as a general designation for the elaborate social fictions Marx himself employed to highlight and intensify the general problem of realism.

Here we are in the domain of Georg Lukács's influential studies in European realism, and particularly in the area of his concern to show not only how Marx's critical sense of reality may be communicated through Balzac's fictional "illustrations," but also how Balzac's critical use of realism provides an opening into the Marxist imagination. Part of his procedure involves looking for those places in Balzac's work where his failure as a writer might best be remedied or addressed through an understanding of Marx as a political thinker. He thus extends Marx's own appreciation for Balzac's "profound grasp of real conditions," as exemplified in such novels as *Les Paysans* (see C3: 138), by showing not just how "reality" is conveyed through "fiction" but also and especially how the nonidentity of the writer and what he is writing about provides a place for a specifically Marxist critique of the lost illusions or fictions that sustain modern reality: "It is precisely this discrepancy between intention and performance, between Balzac the political thinker and Balzac the author of *La Comédie humaine*, that constitutes Balzac's historical greatness" (Lukács 1950: 21; cf. Adorno 1991 [1965]: 135–36). Thus, Balzac is able to depict reality with "inexorable veracity" both in spite of and largely because of the fact his "personal opinions, hopes, and wishes" came into conflict with the demands of reality, which in turn could be shown to operate by way of certain illusions. Jameson also makes this point, although he does so while trying to argue "the sense in which Lukács is right about Balzac, but for the wrong reasons": "not Balzac's deeper sense of political and historical realities, but rather his incorrigible fantasy demands ultimately raise History itself over against him, as absent cause, as that on which desire must come to grief" (Jameson 1981: 183).[15]

Even in his early negative assessment of the *Comédie humaine* in the *Theory of the Novel* (1915), Lukács never lost sight of the profound discrepancies and nonidentities that are exemplified in Balzac's novels, including and especially the nonidentity of even realist fictions with reality itself, a contradiction he expressed as the "demonic inadequacy" or monstrous disproportion between the ideals of Balzac's fiction and the effective experience of a common basis of life. Balzac's exorbitant fantasy demands as a writer necessarily came into an inexorable conflict with the elaborate difficulties and insurmountable obstacles posed by the demands of reality itself:

For [Balzac] the subjective-psychological demonism which is characteristic of his work is an ultimate reality, the principle of all essential action which objectifies itself in heroic deeds; its inadequate relation to the outside world is intensified to the utmost, but this intensification has a purely immanent counterweight [in that] strange, boundless, immeasurable mass of interweaving destinies and lonely souls. (Lukács 1971 [1915]: 109)

Far from presenting a realistic copy or photographic image of contemporary society, Balzac's realism consists of trying to merge the elements that drive his novelistic practice with those that characterize his own social world. Thus, my case for Lukács here, that is, for a kind of "Balzacian Marxism" which acknowledges the necessity of taking literary digressions from within the main road of Marxist science (like the detour presented in these pages), is at the same time an argument for understanding the general problem of the uses of fiction in realism and of realism in fiction (cf. Jameson 1971b: 160–205).[16]

Lukács pursues the issues involved here in an important essay that asks whether even the apparently formal aspects of a piece of fiction, such as the long descriptions that dominate Balzac's work, may be crucial for conveying both its literary "realism" and its social "ideology." By way of example, he argues that Balzac allows description to predominate in his writing in a way that "provides nothing more than a base for [a] new decisive element in the composition of the novel," thereby prefiguring the main plot twists or dramatically staging beforehand the key ideological conflicts to be narrated elsewhere in the story (Lukács 1970: 118). By contrast, other novelists who are more taken by psychologistic and naturalistic forms of expression tend to employ methods of descriptive observation that only mirror the alienating still lifes of capitalist reality, hoping that such a technique will "substitute for the epic significance that has been lost": "The domination of capitalist prose over the inner poetry of life, the general debasement of all humanity—all these are objective facts of the development of capitalism. The descriptive method is the inevitable product of this development. Once established this method is taken up by leading writers dedicated in their own way, and then it in turn affects the representation of reality" (1970: 127).

Not only may the content of literary writing be ideological, but the literary forms of description and narrative may embody different ideological purposes and desires as well as different philosophies of composition. The "same" event might be presented in radically different ways, such as a horse race in novels by Tolstoy and Zola, according to whether they are narrated in the past tense from the standpoint of a participant, or described in the present tense from the perspective of a distant observer. Where a purely narrative account would aim to draw the reader into the experience of the events, emphasizing the epic significance of the minutest details in the weave of human destinies and passions, a predominantly descriptive account would portray a picturesque setting independently of its significance to the actions and lives of the characters, with details largely serving as autonomous symbols. In contrast to these literary techniques, however, the excellence of Balzac's descriptive realism consists in dispensing with the illusion of actually "being there now" or of "having been there before." Instead, he combines descriptive and narrative realism in an attempt to achieve an epic sense of the present by an ironic invocation through his writing of the simultaneity of fictional characters and historical individuals, as well as of those who read and write about them. Indeed, far from simply portraying or making present something we already know is not there, his technique of descriptive narrative or narrative description aims to exert a compelling impression on us as readers by invoking the *reality effect* of fiction itself, that is, by producing in us a sense of both the reality of and the reality in fiction (cf. Barthes 1986: 146–48).

From a Marxist or perhaps Marx's own perspective, the most interesting feature of Balzac's stories therefore may not be the attitudes toward capitalism they depict, but especially the ideological implications of their literary form, and in particular their use of description toward narrative, dramatic, and ideological ends. Even when Balzac appears to be presenting a straightforward description, his use of this apparently neutral literary form frequently has an ideological content that resonates with what he portrays elsewhere in the narrative, in a way that constitutes description as a narrative event in its own right. As Jameson argues in his analysis of a brief passage early on in *La Vieille Fille*, Balzac's deployment of the ideological codes of manners, sex, and money in the description of a house serves both to dramatize the story's main conflicts and to prefigure the sequence of events narrated later in the story. The Balzacian descriptive technique thus tries to bring into being "*a unique temporal structure*—something like *a meta-melodrama*—in which the reader's most characteristic reactions are neither hope nor fear but rather something like 'hope against hope,' a negation of some already present temporal perspective, which as soon as expectation has ratified it in its turn, will itself be the object of some new reversal 'beyond all expectations'" (Jameson 1990: 210; emphasis added).

The melodramatic effect of Balzac's writing operates not only at the level of narration and story line but also within the "partial system" of description and the multiple ideological codings that constitute it. Not only does the narrative play on the emotions and prejudices of the reader to achieve its effects, as with all melodramas, but Balzac's descriptions also literally program, frame, and set up the reader for the narrative to come by providing a formal—though no less ideological and dramatic—metacommentary on the story's central conflicts and themes. And yet, like Marx's revolutionary angst that explodes into a vision of death and destruction even as he tries to present a scientific analysis, Balzac's descriptive fanaticism also expresses a "hope against hope" that something new and unexpected might take place.

V

Let us try, then, to imagine what effect Balzac's work actually had or could have had on Marx as both a reader and a writer. Insofar as Balzac's literary scheme provides a frame for or commentary upon the general problem of realism by putting into question the very meaning and possibility of what it is to "depict" something, Marx's interest in reading Balzac's fiction need not have been limited to its uses for "illustrating" his scientific analyses and historical investigations. Thus, it cannot be simply a question here of speculating on how Balzac's fiction provided Marx with a "dramatic medium" for representing history, an "unconscious depiction" of social reality or "intertextual primal scene" of his own psychical conflicts, as Ned Lukacher has argued with respect to Marx's work of the early 1850s: "It is a question not of Marx's failure to see the post 1848 milieu for what it was, but rather of the fact that he saw most deeply into it when he 'thought' in terms of Balzac's fictional constructions. . . . History becomes accessible and assimilable to Marx not despite but *through* this memory of Balzac" (Lukacher 1986: 237). This notion of "the emergence of the 'literary' in Marx," and of Marx's "direct response to what is at once a subjective crisis and a crisis in the very notion of the historical subject" (1986: 238), seems to presume upon a fairly crude psychological portrait

that would interpret Marx's literary interest in Balzac literally as a dramatization of the relations between Marx's personal life, his social world, and his
work (cf. Seigel 1978). But this is only a part (an important part, to be sure)
of the problem that is posed to us in thinking Balzac and Marx through one
another, the other being the broader issue of the nature of their modes of
reading and research, and of writing and presentation.[17]

By the same token, the assertion of Marx's "Balzacian" or "literary unconscious" is akin to recent attempts to approach these issues from the other
direction, that is, from a perspective that tries to preserve the critical functions
of Marxism within literary analysis generally, and in particular to discern the
dimensions of a Marxist or political unconscious in Balzac's own literary creations. In Jameson's formulation of this problem, literature is portrayed as an
eloquent depiction or "textualization" of politics, with history mutely standing
by as the "absent cause" of the "Real": "History is *not* a text, not a narrative,
master or otherwise, but . . . as an absent cause it is inaccessible to us except
in textual form, and . . . our approach to it and to the real itself necessarily
passes through its prior textualization, its narrativization in the political unconscious" (Jameson 1981: 35). This manner of positing Marxist history as the
political expression for what Balzac could not articulate, or of asserting Balzacian fiction to be the literary expression for Marx's political imagination,
ultimately seems to miss the problem both Marx and Balzac are concerned
with in the practice of their respective crafts. For them, it is not a question
simply of trying to gain access to historical reality as or through texts, fictional
or factual, but particularly of discerning the fictionality of our sense of reality,
as well as the sense of reality that may be communicated through our fictions.
Rather than point from a comfortable distance to what they take to be the
inexorable force of history's rock-hard realities, they are more concerned to
develop a style and a technique, a form and a forum, for communicating an
understanding of the historical world and a picture of their place in it.[18]

In one of Marx's favorite short stories by Balzac, which the latter included
among the *études philosophiques* of his *Comédie humaine*, we seem to find an
image that not only depicts and dramatizes Marx's own reading and writing
process but also seems to configure the whole of the *Comédie humaine*. Balzac
indeed seems to have conceived the entirety of his great work less as a collage
constructed from isolated pieces than as a montage of wholes constructed from
other wholes, so that each individual story or novel would be read not only
as autonomous and complete in itself but also as projecting an image of the
whole of which it is a part (Pasco 1991). A story Marx recommended to Engels
one day in 1867 (see the epigraph to Part III), "Le Chef d'oeuvre inconnu,"
seems to go further than even this idea through its ironic commentary on an
object that might be taken to be the exemplary figure for Balzac's project as

a whole, if not of Marx's as well: the great masterpiece itself, but one that, ironically, seems to be masterly precisely because and insofar as it is a piece of something which is not, and may never be, realized. Balzac's story seems to provide us with a telling fable that relates the fates and fortunes of his own colossal work, and of Marx's as well.

As Marx's son-in-law Paul Lafargue suggests, Balzac's fantastic tale recounts the tragic fate of a painter named Frenhofer's interminable attempts to create the perfect work of art, and indeed to capture life itself through art, in a way that is reminiscent of Marx's own personal drama of trying to complete his masterwork on political economy:

One of Balzac's psychological studies, "Le chef d'oeuvre inconnu," which has been pitifully plagiarized by Zola, made a deep impression on [Marx] because it was in part a description of his own feelings. A talented painter [Frenhofer] is so tortured by the urge to reproduce exactly the picture which has formed itself in his brain that he touches and retouches his canvas incessantly, to produce at last nothing more than a shapeless mass of colors, which nevertheless to his prejudiced eye seems a perfect reproduction of reality. (Lafargue 1890: 16)

Let us consider for moment the extent to which Frenhofer's obsession with his great unfinished painting may have presented for Marx a compelling image of his own views on his unfinished and unknown masterpiece on political economy.

In 1847 Marx had mocked the "petty-bourgeois ideal of the chef d'oeuvre" as it was valued by Proudhon, who like Frenhofer, his seventeenth-century Parisian counterpart, seems able to imagine only in terms of a precapitalist, handicraft version of the masterwork: "And to realize this ideal, he can think of nothing better than to take us back to the journeyman or, at most, to the master craftsman of the Middle Ages. It is enough, he says somewhere in his book, to have created a masterpiece once in one's lifetime, to have felt oneself just once to be a man" (Marx 1847a CW 6: 190; cf. Raphael 1980). Nevertheless, some two decades later, Marx seems to have found himself in Frenhofer's dilemma, now expressing his anxious hesitation to make his works public "until I have the whole before me," or even to show them privately to Engels, his best friend. "Whatever shortcomings they may have," he writes, "the merit of my writings is that they are *an artistic whole*" (Marx to Engels, 31 July 1865; my emphasis): "Show my work! No, no! I still have to put some finishing touches to it. Yesterday toward evening, I thought that it was done. . . . This morning by daylight I realized my error" (Balzac 1956 [1831]: 486).

In Marx's own search for the absolute, which was strangely reminiscent of the quest he had earlier criticized in Democritus (Marx [1840–41]), he repeatedly deferred the completion of his magnum opus by interminably copying and styling his drafts, constantly seeking new avenues of scientific research and ways of testing his theories against the latest documents from the real world of industry and politics (see the letters to Engels from 1865–67, and Chapter 2). Like Frenhofer in his faltering ambition to capture "nature herself" through painting, Marx seemed to doubt whether a work on the incessant motions of history could ever be made adequately presentable, and may also have wondered whether his own scientific pretension to reveal the secrets of capitalist reality might itself be the ultimate obstacle: "O Nature, Nature!, who has ever followed thee in thy flight? Observe that too much knowledge, like ignorance, leads to negation. I doubt my own work!" (Balzac 1956 [1831]: 487). Similarly, Frenhofer's pathetic response to the young Nicolas Poussin's entreaties to show the work about which he has been bragging for so long indeed seems to express Marx's own reluctance to bring his great magnum opus, the first volume of *Capital*, before the critical gaze of the public: "For ten years, young man, I have been working; but what are ten little years when it's a question of fighting against nature? We know nothing of the time Sir Pygmalion used to make the only statue that walked!" (487).

Ten years separate the time when Marx first began to lay out his plans for his own great masterwork—1857—from the time he published that part of it for which he is best known but also often poorly understood—1867, the same year he happened to read these lines and recommend Balzac's story to Engels. Balzac's literary insights thus seem to have kept a decade ahead of Marx's ability to make sense of the progress of his studies. Thus, if Marx had planned to write a criticism of Balzac's work after completing his economic studies as Lafargue reports (see the epigraph to Part III), then this might have been because this best of prose writers (in Marx's view) had already provided for him the finishing touches he needed, or at least a way of seeing why there was no need for any.[19]

Like Frenhofer in his despair over being so profoundly misunderstood, Marx was devastated by the cold indifference with which the critics in 1859 received his *Critique of Political Economy*, which was written from the plans of 1857–58 (Seigel 1978: 364–65). However, in contrast to Frenhofer, Marx ultimately did not seem to believe that in revealing only a piece of his total masterwork, he would thereby spoil the integrity of his vision or forfeit the possibility that his readers might gain a sense of the "artistic whole" through one of its parts. Rather than kill himself or burn his plans and sketches, he continued to suffer and take pleasure in the exertion of his faculties through his work, pursuing his studies as both a sacrifice and a joy, and leaving the remains of his vision to the judgment of his readers and the vicissitudes of history.[20]

Whether or not Marx might have found in Balzac's story a literary image for his own personal dilemmas and scientific struggles (cf. Seigel 1978: 363–87), for us it seems that Balzac's fiction provides the most complete literary expression for Marx's own unfinished project. Beyond even this possibility, Balzac's short story may also be read as a kind of allegorical and ironical commentary on Marx's sketches for his own unknown masterpiece, in which he had hoped to produce the outlines of the beautiful picture of a "different subject," his ideal of a world without domination and exploitation (VII: 712). That is, rather than force a connection between biography, literature, and social science, we may consider whether Marx's own unknown masterpiece may be viewed not just in comparison with Balzac's story but also as the object of that story, in terms of the judgment that story seems to pass on the painter Frenhofer, his work, and his discourses on the process and products of artistic creation. Thus, the question here is how to discern what is characteristic (*die Characteristik*) about the realism in Balzac's literary fiction as well as the fiction in Marx's realistic science, and what is distinctive about the way that each employs and exemplifies a model or *apparatus of representation* (cf. Perron and Le Huenen 1990).

This perspective is anticipated in a few brief notes on Balzac's short story that are scattered among Lukács's *Studies in European Realism*. He contrasts Balzac's lively and humanist "three-dimensional, all rounded realism" with Frenhofer's ecstatic, impressionistic, and excessive "cult of the momentary mood," and compares both against the Marxist vision of "the completeness of the human personality and of the objective typicality of men and situations" (Lukács 1950: 6). Although Lukács prefers the cold light of Marx's scientific realism to the warm, mystical clouds and intense poetic colors of Balzac's emotional fictions and prejudiced ideology, he nevertheless appreciates the beauty of Balzac's own futuristic vision of man as a whole, "the partial achievement, or non-achievement of completeness in its various periods of development" as viewed through the fractured windows and the multiple perspectives of the present:

Balzac's greatness lies precisely in the fact that in spite of all his political and ideological prejudices he yet observed with incorruptible eyes all contradictions as they arose, and faithfully described them. It is true that he regarded them as destructive of "culture" and "civilization," as the prelude to the extinction of his world; but he nevertheless saw and depicted them—and in so doing achieved a depth of vision reaching far into the future. (1950: 38)

In contrast to Frenhofer's emotional, impressionistic, and "Pygmalian" realism, Balzac's literary and Marx's scientific realism achieve their depth of vision through the observation of real contradictions and with the clarity of incorruptible eyes, in spite of the best hopes or worst fears each had regarding the historical fate of this reality. Although Balzac and Marx differ in their enthusiasm or pessimism over the desirability of the possible outcomes of current conflicts, their difference lies not in precisely what they perceive, or even in how they depict what they perceive, since each "sees the same reality" with the same clarity while refusing to depict it in romantic, subjectivist-emotional terms, in short, through a "Frenhoferan" mode of representation. Although basing his assessment on almost opposite ideological reasons, Balzac would have agreed with Marx's assessment that "It is as ridiculous to yearn for a return to that original fullness as it is to believe that with this complete emptiness history has come to a standstill. The bourgeois viewpoint has never advanced beyond this antithesis between itself and this romantic viewpoint, and therefore the latter will accompany it as legitimate antithesis up to its blessed end" (I: 162). As Lukács puts it, "Le Chef d'oeuvre inconnu" thus provides "a prescient tragic-comic outline of the entire problem" of realism for the very reason that this general problem is played out in its purest and (apparently) most formal terms far from any ideological debate, and through an artistic medium that appears to be foreign to the intellectual crafts of both Marx and Balzac (1950: 6).

Let us consider now in more detail the principles of realist irony and non-identity that inform this work, in the spirit of the comment Marx made in his advice to Engels to read this story because it is itself a little chef d'oeuvre "full of the most delightful ironies" (Marx to Engels, 25 February 1867; see the epigraph to Part III). One of the story's most salient ironies resides in its curious mixture of historically real and fictional characters, scenes, and objects, which together put into question not only the reality the story represents but also its status as fiction. Balzac carefully frames his account to present a sharp contrast between actual historical persons and his own fictional personages: on the one side, Poussin and François Porbus (Frenhofer's master) were indeed real painters, while on the other, Frenhofer and Gillette (Poussin's lover), who occupy the dramatic core of the story, are fictional. So, too, is Cathérine Lescaut, the imaginary subject of Frenhofer's painting whose fictionality is further complicated by the fact that she has been conjured from Frenhofer's own imagination (and that her name recalls the fictional Manon Lescaut of Abbé Prévost). In addition, the effect of setting this fictional account involving the real Poussin in a believable but vaguely sketched period in the past—in 1612, before Poussin created the masterpieces for which he later became famous— is perhaps to confirm our sense of the actual and mythic greatness Poussin himself was later to achieve (cf. Pasco 1991: 118). This effect is only enhanced when we try to fill in the gaps of our uncertain knowledge of Poussin's personal history by speculating on whether his first brush with artistic greatness owes more to the fictional Frenhofer or to the real Porbus, both of whom may nevertheless seem equally obscure to us. By contrast, we know the supposed magnificence of Frenhofer's masterpiece only through Balzac's story about it, and indeed only insofar as we recognize the story's reality as fiction and allow its fictions to shed light on our sense of historical reality.

A further and perhaps final set of ironies lies in the extent to which Balzac's story only apparently presents itself as a dramatic narrative recounting events in the lives of its four principal characters. Just as throughout the *Comédie humaine* Balzac employs the literary technique of subordinating narrative to description, a habit that often makes reading his works exasperating if not boring, so in "Le Chef d'oeuvre inconnu" the story's simple narrative is dominated by carefully constructed descriptions and theoretical discourses, and in particular by a set of discussions concerning Frenhofer's work in progress and his ideas about art. Indeed, the story line ultimately comes to appear as only the trace or beginning of a narrative, perhaps an imaginative preface to a biography of Poussin or a philosophical speculation on a hypothetical event in art history.

Balzac limits the narrative to the telling of its most basic dramatic conflicts, which therefore lend themselves to the following brief descriptive summary presented in the form of the story's two principal parts (as Balzac indicates) and five main acts or scenes (as I suggest).

1. Having just arrived in Paris in 1612, the young, hopeful, ambitious, poor, and, at that time, unknown Poussin makes the acquaintance of the great master Porbus, but not before accidentally encountering Porbus's older master, the eccentric and mysterious Frenhofer, on the stairs outside Porbus's studio.

2. In the course of several long discussions on art that the three men subsequently engage in, Poussin's artistic potential is favorably tested in a sketch he is asked to make, and Frenhofer is eventually prodded into showing his great unknown masterpiece, *La Belle Noiseuse*, which he claims to be a perfect and more-than-lifelike portrait of Cathérine Lescaut, a woman he has conjured from his own fantasies. But he will do so only on the condition that Poussin's beautiful lover, Gillette, poses for him, believing that he must add the finishing touches to his painting only while comparing it to a real-life model of perfect womanhood.

3. Though in despair over the conflict between Poussin's ambition and his love for her, Gillette reluctantly cedes to his entreaties to pose for Frenhofer (end of the first part of the story).

4. When Gillette finally does bare body and soul to Frenhofer, he decides that his work is in fact already perfect, and so at last Poussin and Porbus are called in to view the painting. To Frenhofer's initial disbelief, followed by horror and despair, his baffled companions see "nothing" in his work except "colors, lines confusedly amassed and contained by a multitude of bizarre lines that form a mere wall of paint." And yet peeking out from the bottom of the

canvas they can also make out "the end of a naked foot" that has been perfectly depicted (*vera incessu patnit dea*).

5. The ironic denouement, which is described only after the fact and not portrayed in the narrative, occurs that same evening when Frenhofer burns his paintings and dies during the night, thereby ensuring that he and his great masterpiece will remain unknown, except as remembered by Poussin, Gillette, and Porbus, or as preserved in Balzac's story (end of the second part of the story).

In Balzac's telling of these dramatic scenes, they are not so much connected through a story line as they are conceptually organized and discursively submerged in a series of elaborate descriptions and aesthetic discussions that dominate the narrative as a whole. The descriptions of Poussin's studio early in the story, and of Frenhofer's later on, for example, as well as the long discussions on art among the three painters that are presided over by Frenhofer, present the story's main themes, which deal with such issues as the relations between art and life, ambition and imagination, love and anticipation, and thereby serve a specifically dramatic function and narrative purpose. With these passages reframing and refocusing the story's dramatic conflicts in this way, the ironic moral of Balzac's artistic fable ends up applying not just to the fate of the central character and the "masterpiece" he created, but also to Frenhofer's own creative process and the ultimately inadequate theoretical discourses by which he attempts to describe it. It is important, then, to the irony in the moral of the story that the final scene of the destruction of Frenhofer's painting and his subsequent death not be narrated either as it happens or in the past tense as an ongoing event, as are the other scenes, but only described as having already happened, after the event. In this way we are reminded that we in fact have no access to any visual image of Frenhofer's masterpiece except as he describes it to us and through the baffled exclamations of Poussin and Porbus, which in turn reach us through Balzac's creative writing.

To recall Jameson's account of Balzac's "allegorical realism," description ultimately functions as a privileged moment of authorial wish fulfillment especially when the object of the description or commentary is itself the focus for the conflicts within the narrative (cf. Jameson 1981: 155). This is the case in a particularly clear way with Frenhofer's painting, the obsessional object that forms the centerpiece of "Le Chef d'oeuvre inconnu." Around this figure an intense emotional drama is staged and elaborated not simply through the actions of characters and the development of scenes, but especially through the deployment of competing aesthetic ideologies of realism itself. Thus, the naturalism of the exact copy and the impressionism of evoking a sensation or experience are in a sense combined in the Pygmalionism of Frenhofer's attempt to substitute a representation or a model for the object from which it derives. Like scenes and dramatic conflicts in the story, these dilemmas and perspectives are conveyed less through the narrative than through Frenhofer's discourses on painting in general, and in particular on his own painting that he calls *La Belle Noiseuse*, and that I shall translate as *The Quarrelsome Beauty* as a way of designating the contested and polemical character, as well as aesthetic and seductive charms, of the story's central object.

These tensions are already intimated in Balzac's own brief description, near the beginning of the story, which depicts Frenhofer's face when Poussin first meets him on the stairs outside Porbus's studio. Here, the entire dramatic conflict, including its ironic denouement, is literally "(pre)figured" in the face with "something diabolical" about it, "withered with thoughts that hollow out mind and body equally," and illuminated with a "fantastic color" like "a painting by Rembrandt walking silently out of frame in the black atmosphere that this painter appropriated for himself" (Balzac 1956 [1831]: 476–77). Similarly, the crude contract of exchange that Frenhofer requires, that Poussin facilitates, and in which Gillette serves as token, is already dramatized by Balzac in the opening lines of the story through his description of Poussin on the threshold of Porbus's house, hesitating "with the irresolution of a lover who does not dare to present himself before his first mistress" (475). There is a sense, then, in which Balzac's story never progresses beyond the initial reluctance of this first (?) encounter, unless it does so by invoking insights, memories, and experiences in the reader that are beyond the threshold of Balzac's own intentions, plans, and wishes.

Balzac's narrative about Frenhofer's failure truly to represent reality does not just depict or narrate the cryptic and ironical structure of the *mise en abîme*, the work (the painting) within the work (the story with its descriptions and discourses), but it also literally describes and exemplifies this structure— as the scene of fiction writing within the other scenes of painting and aesthetic discourse. The story is a commentary on the fictional creations that it is about, a statement about what fiction may reveal about the nature of social relations, artistic creations, and historical facts, and therefore a metacommentary on itself as a piece of fiction as well. Its "digressions," descriptions, and commentaries on art and life ultimately seem to carry the entire dramatic burden of Balzac's short story, even while they also obliquely expound Balzac's own general theory of fiction, forming a kind of separable discursive stratum of "statements on fiction writing" that literally "explain" the text by designating it and displaying the models according to which it functions. Ultimately, then, these interventions seem to bear on the plot as much as on the text itself, creating a kind of equivalency between the story and the reality it is supposed to represent: "But one must note that this equivalency is reversible to the extent that, if the novel is given as 'real,' the 'real' in its turn is to be seen as a picture. . . . These equivalencies underscore rather than suppress the ambiguity of the novel as a representation of reality" (Van Russum-Guyon 1990: 196–97).

In "Le Chef d'oeuvre inconnu," fictional portraits—those which are Balzac's own constructions as well as the one he describes as Frenhofer's *Belle Noiseuse*—are combined with historical facts—marked by Poussin's presence in the story and by the display of Balzac's knowledge of his life—in a way that renders each reversible to the other. The "story" then turns out to be as much about Frenhofer's painting as about his discourses on how it was created (or should have been created), and as much about those discourses as about the story that would re-present them. In its attempts to expose the artificial and even ideological dimensions of a certain idea of reality and theory of fiction— here exemplified in Frenhofer's belief that he has "created" life or "captured" reality in painting—the story dramatizes the reality of its own telling within itself.

The ultimate irony of this story that so delighted Marx and prompted him to advise Engels to read it may therefore be expressed through Marx's own reference to it as a "little chef d'oeuvre," implying that the *chef d'oeuvre inconnu* of the title may ultimately refer not to Frenhofer's painting but to Balzac's story itself. And yet here, too, the irony might be understood to be reversible, so that *le chef d'oeuvre inconnu* may stand as the name for that elusive ideal of "realism" under which both Balzac and Marx labored, with *La Belle Noiseuse*, or simply **B**, as the cryptic sign of that beautiful image (*schöner Schein*) that always seemed beyond the threshold of their ability to represent it, and thus to remain virtually unknowable.[21]

• • •

Here, then, at last is the place to reveal the irony that my own designation of the *Grundrisse* as "Marx's unknown masterpiece" may be seen to stand in the same relation to Marx's text as Balzac's title does to Frenhofer's painting. My discourses on Marx's "virtual cipher," on those "sibylline passages" that have finally been unveiled to the world too late to be understood and that seem tragically fated to remain unread by most Marxists just as they lay unread by Engels, may in the end have little more effect than to enhance our vague sense of this work as a virtual masterpiece. And yet any understanding at all of what these cryptic notes are about may be possible only by way of such interpretive fictions and commentaries as those which have been spun out here, or by imagining in our own way the meaning of those designations, characterizations, descriptions, discourses, and plans they themselves ambiguously contain. Just as we may understand Frenhofer's greatness through his failure as an artist, his inability to paint what he could see in his mind's eye or describe through a theory of painting, and just as we may understand Balzac's greatness through his failure as a political thinker, his inability to reach beyond his prejudiced view of the historical progress he so deplored and yet observed with incorruptible eyes and so faithfully described, so we may now be in a position to recognize Marx's greatness through his failure as a literary writer, his inability to realize and express his inner vision of a more just and beautiful future through critical sketches in the science of political economy. Perhaps, then, we may read in Marx's decision to keep his *Grundrisse* tucked away in a desk drawer, unknown to almost everybody, in his failure to complete his great intellectual project, in his resigned decision to present only a baffling piece of his grand scheme, and even in the recent trashing of his work in political and scholarly circles—in short, in the death of Marx and the ruined monument of Marxism—not the pathetic story of Frenhofer's tragic death and the destruction of his chaotic canvas of lines and colors, but rather something like the perfect foot protruding from the lower corner of an unknown masterpiece, as if some entirely new and living being were about to emerge, the sign of a promise yet to be fulfilled.

The Ledger

Marxian Science Fiction in the Critique
of Political Economy

Marx elaborated a theory of the proletariat before he had empirically verified the real historical existence of this class, before he had read the bourgeois economists of his day, and without at the same time conceiving of a program for the exercise of this class's political power. In fact, his idea or ideal of the emancipatory mission of the proletariat never really met with his analysis of actual proletarian struggles, whether of the peasant thefts of wood in 1842 in Bavaria, the petit bourgeois revolutions of 1848 in the major cities of Europe, the legal battles over working conditions in England from the 1850s on, or the brief success of the Paris Commune in 1870–71. Marx seems instead to have emphasized the order and movement of the dialectical categories in his analysis of political economy and historical events at the expense of their socio-logical context and empirical content. He even seems to have remained under the spell of a kind of "Hegelian choreography" that led him to posit the in-creasing polarization of society into two antagonistic classes, expressed as the bourgeoisie and the proletariat in the *Communist Manifesto* (1848), and as capitalists and workers in volume 1 of *Capital* (1867), with the latter in each pair dancing the role of a successful negation (Nicolaus 1967).

The question is whether this dance is essential to Marx's theory as well as to his understanding of social reality, or whether in his better moments Marx was also able to shake its spell and go on to develop a critical theory more con-sistent with the historical facts. The usual answer given is that Marx's theory is either "dogmatic" from a scientific perspective or "immature" from an empiri-cal point of view. Either Marx only apparently solved real historical problems by straitjacketing them into a preconceived theory, and so the theory would need to be judged out of date, revised, or thrown out entirely, or else the problems with Marx's early naive idealism would need to be corrected in light of his later, more sophisticated materialism, as Nicolaus argues. Alternatively, we may understand the issues raised here to involve whether and to what extent Marx's idealism and his materialism, his scientism and his empiricism, may be purposefully and necessarily nonsynchronous with one another, and whether this nonidentity may be the mark of the theory's dependence upon a history it can never transcend entirely or know perfectly. That is, the question to ask may rather be what the implications are of a theory that puts the empirical verification of its abstractions second to a theoretical truth that anticipates (without thereby predicting) its own historical realization.

In his first and clearest articulation of the concept of the proletariat as both an empirical reality and an ethical ideal, Marx addresses some of these issues in terms of what he calls the historical and practical "anachronism" of the German status quo in spite of its "philosophical" advantage over the rest of Europe generally, and over France in particular. Simply put, what the Germans only think in advance of their own historical experience, the French already practice and experience as a part of everyday social life. In his 1843–44 "Introduction to the Critique of Hegel's *Philosophy of Right*," Marx literally introduces into Hegel's advanced philosophical abstractions an empirical and experiential notion of that-class-which-is-not-(yet-)one by way of a quite specific and concrete question: "Where is the *positive* possibility of German emancipation?"

This is our answer. In the formation of a class with radical chains, a class of civil society which is not a class of civil society, a class [*Stand*] which is the dissolution of all classes, a sphere which has a universal character because of its universal suffering and which lays claim to no *particular right* because the wrong it suffers is not a *particular wrong* but *wrong in general*; a sphere of society which can no longer lay claim to a *historical* title, but merely to a *human* one, which does not stand in one-sided opposition to the premises of the German political system, and finally a sphere which cannot emancipate itself without emancipating itself from—and thereby emancipating—all the other spheres of society, which is, in a word, the *total loss* of humanity and which can therefore redeem itself only through the *total redemption of humanity*. This dissolution of society as a particular class is the *proletariat*. (Marx 1843–44 EW: 256)

In spite of its apparent specificity, Marx's answer to his own question— "Where?"—is in fact formulated in such a way that it might seem to amount to a nonresponse: "nowhere . . . and everywhere."

This problem may only be exacerbated by his subsequent acknowledgment that "the proletariat is only beginning to appear in Germany as a result of the emergent *industrial* movement, for the proletariat is not formed by *natural* poverty but by *artificially* produced poverty" (1843–44 EW: 256). Having reached his moment of truth, he can only point vaguely (though with passionate conviction) to the place where this new historical reality may be emerging. Without actually verifying the empirical existence of the class he refers to, he can express its desires only generally—"I am nothing and I should be everything!"—and merely assert that the "dream history" of the German nation and its "actual conditions" intersect in German social reality. It appears, then, that he cannot avoid expressing the "practically real" as the creation of history, and the "empirically possible" in the form of a hypothesis or *fiction*. The question thus becomes why such abstractions from historically real tendencies, which at present are only latently possible, take on a kind of fictional character for Marx.

It is interesting to note here that even in the midst of describing real, empirical conditions, and specifically the political, economic, and social problems faced by present-day Europe (i.e., 1843–44), Marx appeals to a distinction that normally applies to what is literally fictional, that is, to literary genres. Specifically, he contrasts the "epic" features of the relation between different social strata in Germany with the "dramatic" aspects of the relations between the classes in France. On the one side, the German epic of the emerging proletariat is still informed by an old-fashioned sense of morality and honor in its display of a "modest egoism which asserts its narrowness and allows that narrowness to be used against it" (Marx 1843–44 EW: 255). This in turn seems to be the very opposite of the French dramatization of modern class struggles in which a rising new class competes with the others not simply in defense of its own needs but above all by appealing to a political ideal by which it understands itself to be the supreme "representative of social needs in general" (255). Marx's sense of the emerging class dynamics of capitalist Europe is thus more subtle and more intricate than a gloss on his "Hegelian choreography" might otherwise suggest: "Each sphere of German society must be depicted as the *partie honteuse* of that society and these petrified conditions must be made to dance by having their own tune sung to them!" (257). Our question can then be reformulated to ask what the connection may be between the literally and metaphorically fictional dimensions of Marx's theoretical abstractions, and his knowledge of empirical facts.

In 1857, when Marx was much more thoroughly immersed in his study of political economy and current events, he was still concerned to highlight what he had earlier identified as the national and literary character of abstract political and economic generalizations. At least to his mind, the narrow-minded abstractions of the German idealists now seem to have their counterpart in the French parochialism of economists like Bastiat, who in turn seem to be superseded by the Yankee universalism of economists like Carey. At the same time, Marx appears to have kept his sense of the tragicomic historical narrative or *epic drama* of social relations as expressed through these competing ideological viewpoints and pseudoscientific accounts:

All economists, when they come to discuss the prevailing relation of capital and wage-labor, of profit and wages, and when they demonstrate to the worker that he has no legitimate claim to share in the risks of gain, when they wish to pacify him generally about his subordinate role *vis-à-vis* the capitalist, lay stress on pointing out to him that, in contrast to the capitalist, he possesses a certain fixity of income more or less independent of the great ADVENTURES of capital. Just as Don Quixote consoles Sancho Panza with the thought that, although of course he takes all the beatings, he is not required to be brave. (III: 891, section "Des Salaires")

The epic dimensions of the story of modern political economy, or as Marx here expresses it, the quixotic aspect of its ideology, are thus rendered thematic in terms of a grand adventure that entails a belief in one's place in a great historical journey, along with a sense of duty to pay the price in suffering and sacrifices while sustaining a modest egoism. These aspects are dramatically characterized here as competing ideological claimants who bear specific class interests and who confront one another in an ongoing historical struggle. Where Bastiat and Carey score this musical drama to the harmony of local interests dancing to the tune of the world market, Marx composes a dissonant symphony to which wage laborers and capitalists dance out an epic-dramatic shadow play of illusions, ideologies, and fictions but where the stakes are very real.

Marx's reference to the competing perspectives of Don Quixote and Sancho Panza thus does not need to be understood as a mere literary ornamentation or illustration, but rather as an integral part of his critical apparatus for highlighting the unavoidable anachronistic and fictional aspects of what he is writing about. In his attempt to acknowledge the difference between his own conceptual abstractions and his empirical knowledge of historical reality, he implies that his own theoretical discourse has a kind of narrative structure or story line that recounts a loss of illusions or the realization of a quest. Thus, when he begins to elaborate his own countertheory of the conflict between wage labor and capital in his later works, Marx highlights not only the essential dramatic tension of this struggle but also its far-reaching epic implications, all in an effort to set his theoretical insights in the right key and his ability to communicate them to the right tune (cf. Jameson 1981: 281–99).[22]

Rather than give more examples from Marx's work, I shall summarize here what I take to be the principal starting points for assessing the outdatedness, the abstract idealism, and the fictional unreality of Marx's critique of political economy, which we must account for as we attempt to find its current relevance and empirical applicability.

1. Even when Marx gave empirical content to particular theoretical abstractions, and specified them with respect to their historical context, he developed many of the most essential aspects of his theory in advance of their historical verification or empirical falsification (for example, when he analyzed the history of the English working class as "the proletariat").

2. For this reason, then, particular formulations by Marx often appear to be abstract or even fictional with respect to the historical realities they are supposed to refer or apply to.

3. At the same time Marx often interprets historical events and communicates the meaning of social facts in terms of certain generic categories in literary fiction (for example, as tragedy or farce, epic or drama), and thus as elements in a social theater and a historical narrative.

4. Clearly, however, part of Marx's critical intent in drawing upon literary analogies is to expose the unacknowledged use of fictions in the making of science by both empiricists and idealists alike (for example, English political economists, French socialists, and German philosophers).

5. Thus, we may speculate that Marx's method consists of an empirical and scientific procedure that does not simply replace the fictions and ideologies of others with his own scientific analyses and empirical demonstrations. Rather, he tries to incorporate and surpass the limitations of many of the illusions and blind spots he criticizes, hoping thereby to project a kind of utopian vision that extends into the unknown, that is, beyond existing realities and even beyond his own sphere of knowledge.

With reference to the whole of Marx's 1857–58 notebooks, in what follows, I shall attempt to highlight the science fictional underpinnings of Marx's critique of political economy by considering his critical use of several rhetorical and literary devices that may in turn be read to form a series of ten connected "droll stories" or *contes drolatiques*. In the epilogue to this chapter, I will return to the more general problematic introduced above, but from the other side, and specifically by considering the ironic deployment of these same science fictions as they take shape in a particular literary text by Balzac. In this way I hope to show that it is not a question here of reducing science to fiction (or vice versa) but rather of understanding the extent to which both science and fiction must operate on the basis of or in terms of problematics that are specific to the other.

I

As Marx would sometimes write after a digression into matters apparently hypothetical or illustrative, "retournons maintenant à nos moutons" (let's return to our sheep, i.e., back to our subject) (e.g., VI 19: 618; VII 19: 758). Here we need to test whether Marx's "anachronistic" and "unrealistic" theory of the class structure of early capitalism may have analytical and empirical implications for our understanding late capitalism. In particular, we need to assess what relation the fictional or aesthetic dimensions of Marx's method have to his peculiar use of literary analogies and references, whether his empirical analyses are reducible to the historical context in which they were developed, and to what extent his work employs a method of approach that may extend to areas beyond his frame of reference. Our task is to explore these issues by testing the extent to which reading Marx's own rationalist constructions as *science fictions* may help us to recover their theoretical import, their critical intention, and their contemporary relevance.

I shall approach Marx's text by attending to what Jeffrey Mehlman has referred to as the "historicity of the act of reading" (Mehlman 1977: 2), and what I shall call the historico-hermeneutic structure for reading Marx beyond Marxism, capitalism, and socialism. Such a project requires inventing a way of reading the empirical realities and theoretical perspectives of our day as lying within the purview of Marx's political vision and historical circumstances, but without implying that Marx could really see into the future, and without ignoring the differences between his age and ours. This entails testing whether Marx's backward look toward the past, his theoretical regard for the present, and his utopian vision of the future together suggest a structure that could provide us with anticipatory illuminations, illustrative "indications" (*Andeutungen*), or even hypothetical "FORESHADOWINGS" of our own past, present, and future: "Just as, on the one side the pre-bourgeois phases appear as *merely historical*, i.e. suspended [*aufgehobne*] presuppositions, so do the contemporary conditions of production likewise appear as engaged in *suspending themselves* and hence in positing the *historic presuppositions* for a new state of society" (IV 46: 461). In what follows, I shall lay some stress on the "essay on precapitalist social formations" from Marx's 1857–58 notebooks (IV–V: 456–515; see Appendix B), not just because it is a crucial text for Marxian historiography (Hobsbawm 1964) but especially because it provides us with a model for approaching Marx's critique of political economy as a reading of the meaning and direction (*Sinn*) of history.

If only for the sake of clarity, though perhaps at the risk of appearing implausible right from the beginning, I shall identify the time/place parameters of this historicist reading of Marx in very specific terms: London, 1858, and New York, 1973. On the one hand, I refer to the time and place Marx stopped work on the *Grundrisse,* and on the other, I designate the time and place of its appearance in full in English (also see the discussion in the Foreword). Each date and place happens to mark a significant moment in which the crisis of capitalist power reached dramatically global proportions. For example, Marx analyzed the financial and commercial crises in Europe in the late 1850s in terms of the emerging world market and the political economy of labor power, and part of the challenge for social analysts in the early 1970s was to make sense of the global political economy of energy, both human and natural, in the wake of the crisis of American hegemony (culminating in the October war of 1973, when Arab oil interests dictated the behavior of American companies while the Israeli military agenda continued to be backed by the American government. Cf. Gill and Law 1988: 261–62). While social forecasters of the 1970s often looked back to their predecessors in the nineteenth century, including Marx, we should remember here that a third historical parameter must be dealt with insofar as Marx likewise conceived of his work in part as a reading of eighteenth-century historical events such as the French Revolution, and of political economists such as Adam Smith. Thus we have here a set of sociohistorical contexts that are also circumstances of reading and writing, each of which presupposes the one that preceded it as the condition of its possibility, as its point of departure, or as that which tends to project the outlines of an uncertain future. With these structures in place, we can begin to test whether there is anything instructive in Marx's method of reading and writing, not just for our own reading of Marx and his historical circumstances but also for what we are able to make of our own situation.

II

Marx begins his 1857–58 economic studies with a critique of the particular manner in which certain French socialists had literally "sold out" the 1848 revolution. Inspired by the establishment in 1849 of what Pierre-Joseph Proudhon called the "People's Bank," where credit would be granted to the public free of charge (*crédit gratuit,* as both Proudhon and Bastiat called it), Alfred Darimon had proposed a reform of France's financial institutions as a remedy for the economic crisis that had gripped Europe by the mid-1850s. In the opening lines of Marx's notebook, the particular object of his scorn and ridicule is Darimon's naive speculation that "The whole evil [*tout le mal*] comes from the predominance which one insists on maintaining for the precious metals in circulation and exchange" (I 1: 115; Nicolaus's translation from the French modified). Now, I shall propose not only that this speculation by Darimon from 1856 may be compared with a particular fact from 1971—President Nixon's announcement in August of that year of the end of the gold standard and the inconvertibility of the dollar—but also that the perspectives of both Darimon and Nixon may be considered within the general parameters sketched by Marx's analytical procedure. Although more than a century of historical changes and an ocean of cultural variations divide these pronouncements, the empirical differences between them should not prevent us from considering the extent to which—at least from Marx's theoretical perspective—Darimon's criticisms of the Bank of France's measures in October 1855 to "stem the progressive diminution of its reserves" may be understood finally to have been heeded by the attempts of Republican economists in August 1971 to control the rate of inflation!

We might first notice here that Marx's analysis of "THE PRESENT CRISIS" (Marx to Engels, 18 December 1857) begins with his critique of a kind of cynical and counterfeit socialism, represented in this context by Darimon and the Proudhonians, and similarly that the initial challenge to Marxists in the early 1970s was to assess their own relevance by trying to analyze an apparently cynical and counterfeit capitalism, then represented by Nixon and the Republicans. In both cases, the problem of discerning and defining the perspective of a true and authentic "socialism" seems to include the search for what is real versus what is fake, what is essential and proper, versus what is superficial and only apparent within both capitalism and socialism.

Marx's critique of Darimon consists of problematizing the latter's assumption that an absolutely fixed or controllable standard governs the relations between a historical fact, such as the particular behavior of bank officials during a crisis, and the ideological, scientific, or popular assumptions that may come to bear in "reading" them. Marx's point in his critique of Darimon is that both the policies of the Bank of France and the proposals of Darimon ultimately assume a faulty, or more precisely, a narrow and partial, understanding of the causes and effects of the current crisis. The difference between Darimon and the bank officials is that the former operates from the naive and thoroughly unfounded assumption that public need for the services of banks and other financial institutions is directly "represented" in such indicators as "the quantity of discounts extended by the bank (commercial papers, *bills of exchange* in its portfolio)" (I 1: 116). Against this, Marx points out that not only is there no necessarily "representative" relation between the interests and services of financial institutions and the public need for and use of these services, but also that in a more profound sense—and the banks themselves understand this very well—there is no necessarily "representative" relation between public need in general and the statistical self-interpretations of these institutions. Darimon, however, assumes that such indicators as the figures in a bank's portfolio or prices on the stock exchange "amount to the same thing" (*revient au même*) as the public need for financial institutions—as if these numerical indicators could be deciphered as constellations in a kind of economic astrology chart that would map public welfare and social well-being. Marx's deeper and more far-reaching angle on these assumptions already brings us close to the rationalizations that guided the political measures designed to manage the inflationary crisis of the early 1970s: in both cases, what is at least implicitly assumed is a clearly representative relation or fixed identity between "the requirements of circulation" and "public need" in particular, and between the interests of financial institutions and the interests of public welfare in general (cf. note 13 to Part III).

But as Marx points out, this is precisely what cannot be assumed: "Ce qui revient au même? Du tout" (Which amounts to the same thing? Not at all) (I 1: 116). In other words, it is not that Darimon's "statistical tableaux" comparing the bank's metal reserves with banknotes are entirely false; they are, in fact, taken from the banks' own accounts over several months (I 1–2: 116–17). Rather, they present only a part of the whole (*une partie "du tout"*), only a piece of the picture (*tableau*), and are therefore irreducibly abstract and ultimately unreal. In Marx's words, what Darimon's "statistical table" actually "amounts to," with its columns (*Rubrike*) on "metal assets versus portfolio" torn out of their necessary context, is nothing more than a "*statistical fable*" (I: 120). The moral lesson of this fable is entirely unconvincing because it does not even consider, for example, the circulation of banknotes and metal deposits, along with the disproportionate devaluations that are thereby entailed. Ultimately, these columns crumble on their own weak foundations when the ground beneath them is shaken up by certain fundamental questions (*Grundfragen*) that Darimon cannot fathom but only dumbly presuppose:

Can the existing relations of production and the relations of distribution which correspond to them be revolutionized by a change in the instrument of circulation? Can such a transformation of circulation be undertaken without touching the existing relations of production and the social relations which rest on them? . . . Various forms of money may correspond better to social production in various stages; one form may remedy evils against which another is powerless; but none of them, as long as they remain forms of money, and as long as money remains an essential relation of production, is capable of overcoming the contradictions inherent in the money relation. (I: 122–23)

Marx's questions (and his preliminary answer to them) reveal that the gold standard alone is not essential for capitalism to function, and indeed that no single particular material by its own physical properties necessarily and essentially carries either the representational functions of money or the evils of capitalism, even though some material or other must serve as a carrier (*Träger*) of capitalist relations of production.

With this larger field of inquiry opened up, we may now see the extent to which Marx has been able to displace the focus and broaden the terrain of analysis in such a way that even Nixon's announcement abolishing the gold standard in 1971, or more specifically, declaring the dollar inconvertible, may appear as the realization of a basic tendency within capitalism, one that ironically confirms the unacknowledged presuppositions of Darimon's self-styled socialist proposal of 1856. Insofar as later stages of capitalist development have demonstrated that the system may actually need to declare its standards irrelevant by rendering its own bills of exchange inconvertible (as during the late 1890s and 1929 in the United States; Gill and Law 1988: 159–90), the theoretical truth of Marx's analysis in 1856 is to this extent proved in the historical reality of 1971: in Darimon's dream of socialism without gold and Nixon's declaration of capitalism without the gold standard, the fiction of the one has become the fact of the other.

Failing a more complete analysis of his proposals, Darimon must resort to staging his own fable in the form of a "fictitious dialogue," in which the bank faces its critics, with all the *immense clameur* of a *grand débat*, but in which the bank's script is written with such false rhetorical generality (*algemeinen Phrase*) that it, too, is tacitly assumed to hold the same superstitious faith as its critic: that in "hoarding" gold it really does wield despotic control over the money markets (I: 124). In the meantime, Marx advances and expands his own analysis by displacing it beyond this particular example and beyond his dismissal of "the theoretical abstractions of the Proudhonians," "their manner of playing with the facts" (I: 119). He does so by illustrating the general problem of the convertibility of paper currency and precious metals with reference to specific historical examples, such as Scottish and English bank crises earlier in the century, and to hypothetical situations—such as socialist time chits or supposed grain crop failures (I: 127). To this we may add our own examples by citing the 1971 decision as one that simply replaced a dollar-to-gold standard (the Bretton Woods System, which Reaganomics attempted to revive) with a foreign currencies–to–dollar standard, modifying the credit and banking system but otherwise keeping the basic structures of circulation and production intact (Gill and Law 1988: 170–77). To be sure, such historical and hypothetical cases "cannot of course decide the matter, because modern credit institutions were as much an effect as a cause of the concentration of capital." Indeed, no form of money, "as long as money remains as essential relation of production, is capable of overcoming the contradictions inherent in the money relation" (I: 123).

However weak and superficial Darimon's analysis has proved to be, it has served the purpose of provoking Marx's *Grundfragen* along with a set of other considerations that have offered Marx a glimpse of the system's operation as a whole. Thus, the rest of the *Grundrisse* is structured in its entirety (fragmentarily and with numerous digressions and asides, to be sure) around a series of systematic analyses that are called for by the *Grundfragen*, from the enumeration of the functions of the capitalist money system as (1) *measure of circulation*, (2) *medium of circulation*, and (3) *material and ideal representative of wealth* (and store of value) (I–II: 187–238), to their analytical amplification in the three main sections of the "Chapter on Capital" that deal with (1) *the production process* (based on surplus versus necessary labor time, II–IV: 239–401), (2) *the circulation process* (based on industrial and commercial turnover, IV–VII: 401–743), and (3) *the distribution process* (including the accumulation, consumption, and reinvestment of wealth, VII: 745–78; see Table 2B). Although almost nowhere else in the *Grundrisse* is Marx's main concern explicitly to return to his study of the CURRENT CRISIS or to theorists writing about it, these later analyses may be read as progressive complications of Darimon's simplistic bank schemes and of the narrow assumptions that uphold their social "credibility." Through a labyrinthine series of broad historical digressions, theoretical hypotheses, and systematic arguments, Marx draws a moral lesson from Darimon's statistical fable that applies to situations well beyond those depicted in its original telling.

III

However, Marx does not in fact begin his systematic analyses until he has explored a highly speculative digression on the origins and emergence of the use of the precious metals in the circulation of money and commodities (I: 173–86). Just as Darimon has been able to make his case against the banks only by means of a statistical fable and a fictitious *grand débat*, so Marx ultimately seems to make his case against Darimon only by dropping Darimon's facts (and, for the moment, his own *Grundfragen*) in order to construct his own scientific and historical fiction of "the money-subject" (I: 167). Although Marx's digression here may appear to be little more than an impressive display of technical scholarship and intellectual thoroughness, he clearly does not believe either that he is proving anything with this investigation or that he is hypocritically making any allowances (if only for the sake of argument) to Darimon's belief that "the whole evil derives from the precious metals." Rather, I would suggest that there is an irreducible irony here in Marx's attempt to magnify the fiction of "money as (essentially) gold" and of "capitalism as an (essentially) gold-based society." Curiously, he does so not in the form of a story or narrative but by way of the sciences—through a historical, chemical, mineralogical, geological, and even etymological investigation into the origins of the use of precious metals as money. The effect of this digression is both to imply that Darimon's pseudoscientific proposals rest on little more than a crude gold fetish and to confirm the necessity of such a "superstitious belief" for the functioning of capitalism.

I am arguing that what Marx elaborates here is little more than a sophisticated version of an ancient and still popular myth presented in the guise of a scientific investigation: the story of the birth and baptism of modern society up to its emergence into a golden age (in the literal sense), its growth and confirmation through a kind of golden rule of reciprocity (money exchange), and its confession in its old age that, after all, the pursuit of money is the root of all evil, *"that accursed hunger for gold" (sacra auri fames)* (I 1: 116; I: 163, quoting Virgil). Put another way, Marx's digression on "the money-subject" as "the representing subject" (*Darstellende*) is a study of the nature and emergence (*Wesen und Entstehung*) of the precious metals or the origins of (monetary) species that proceeds in the form of *a speculative mythology of money*: What if capitalism could be understood as the sum of the physical properties and symbolic meanings of gold and silver, *aurum* (Au) and *argentum* (Ag)?

to "glitter," to "reflect all colors," and to "attract the eye"?

to resist oxidation, to be malleable, and yet difficult to melt and thus lasting?

to require "the application of so many sciences and collateral arts" to extract it from the ground, and so be rare, unique, and "far from the common herd"?

to be naturally refined, a kind of "uncombined virginal nature"? (see I: 173–86)

Are not gold and silver the "perfect" bourgeois objects and the "perfect" metaphorical expressions of bourgeois society, the exemplary symbols of its most noble or even absolute values? Are not the delicate balancing and weighing of the specific gravity (*Dichte*) of gold the perfect poetic expressions (*Dichtungen*) of the modern social bond?

Darimon's pseudoscientific view of the centrality of the financial system in modern industrial society thus overlaps with the common opinion that sees the power of money as an ostentatious display of privilege, security, and luxury, as when Baron von Rothschild puts two £100,000 banknotes in a mounted frame (I: 231), or, in the case of his fictional counterpart, when Grobseck, the rich usurer in one of Balzac's stories, turns childishly giddy at the sight of a table full of precious diamonds (C1: 735). The myth here is that the engines which drive this society are not located in the dark caves of the modern factory system, but in something more like those delicate gold-weighing machines described in Dodd's book *The Curiosities of Industry and the Applied Sciences* (London, 1854, in VII 64; see note 12 to Part III and Appendix C). With their "independent judgement" and "exquisitely sensitive balance," they provide a kind of running account or story (*Erzählung*) of the great bourgeois mythology of possessive and possessed individuals. In terms of this myth, people work hard to look like a million dollars, to be worth their weight in gold, in short, to fit perfectly into a universal order of fixed, essential types and an immobile hierarchy of possessions within which they can hardly breathe for fear of producing "minute errors": "Bourgeois morality will essentially be a weighing operation, the essences will be placed in scales of which bourgeois man will remain the motionless beam" (Barthes 1972 [1957a]: 155; cf. Kroker 1992). In the bourgeois mythology of the golden age of capitalism, which continues to provide symbolic capital to its late capitalist and postindustrial successors, "the measure of man" is cramped by a calculus of credits and debits, and crushed by its delicate machineries of sacrifices and rewards.

IV

Insofar as this digression on precious metals is essential to Marx's elaboration of economic theory as a whole, and not just to his critique of socialist economists like Darimon or his side interests in geological and economic history, it presupposes a theory of (economic) fictions that proceeds through a literal reading of economics as a kind of literary fiction. Let us digress a bit from Marx's digression in order to consider his literalization of this approach in the famous example of the "unimaginative conceits of the eighteenth-century Robinsonades," to which he refers in the opening line of his 1857 "Introduction" (M 1: 83). As he notes in a later work, even the best of the nineteenth-century political economists make use of the Robinson Crusoe story to illustrate their economic insights; Ricardo, for instance, on at least one occasion "slips into the anachronism of allowing the primitive fisherman and hunter to calculate the value of their implements in accordance with annuity tables used on the London Stock Exchange in 1817" (Marx 1859 CW 29: 300). Marx suggests that this story functions as a kind of primal myth for the political economists of the eighteenth and nineteenth centuries in much the same way that the story of Adam served as a kind of myth of origins for the Jews and Christians, or Prometheus for the ancient Greeks (I: 85). The Robinsonades project an image of the solitary Natural Individual who "produces without exchanging," consumes without the mediation of money (VII: 840), and who therefore appears to be stripped of all distinctly modern characteristics. Thus, they express the originary principle for the moral calculus that continues to animate the secular worldview of the present, much as the old Protestant ethic haunts modern society under a different guise in the new spirit of capitalism (Weber 1930: 182).[23]

As Marx shows in *Capital*, such a fiction cannot be sustained without at the same time abstracting from and reintroducing a set of extraneous and specifically modern factors that only project the present level of social development into a sentimental and naturalized version of the past:

> As political economists are fond of Robinsonades, let Robinson appear on his island. Undemanding though he is by nature, he still has needs to satisfy, and must therefore perform useful labors of various kinds: he must make tools, knock together furniture, tame llamas, fish, hunt and so on. Of his prayers and the like, we take no account here, since our friend takes pleasure in them and sees them as recreation. . . . Whether one function occupies a greater space in his activity than another depends on the magnitude of the difficulties to be overcome in attaining the useful effect aimed at. Our friend Robinson Crusoe learns this by experience, and having saved a watch, ledger [*Hauptbuch*], ink, and pen from the shipwreck, he soon begins, like a good Englishman, to keep a set of books. His stockbook [*Inventarium*] contains a catalogue of the useful objects he possesses, of the various operations necessary for their production, and finally of the labor-time that specific quantities have on average cost him. (*MEW* 23: 90–91; C1: 169–70)

Marx's notorious critique of the Robinsonades is not just another, more clever conceit designed to ridicule either Daniel Defoe (whom Marx appreciates as both a novelist and a political economist) or those scholars who may have later referred to Defoe's story in the context of their own economic discussions. Indeed, by producing his own *naturalist conceit*, his own version of the tale of the island castaway ("let Robinson appear on his island"), he is clearly concerned to elaborate on the significance of this story both for the political economists and for his own critique of them. For Marx it is less a question of finding the fiction in their theory in order to expel this fiction and establish his own science (as Althusser might have it) than it is of analyzing the function of economic fictions in the making of economic theory.

Thus, when Marx himself makes use of similar dramatic constructions, his intention is both to give an imaginative account of the connection between apparently unrelated social facts and to expose the irreducible phantasmic dimensions of all science. In *Capital*, for example, the crucial transition from the discussion of the circulation of commodities to their production is scripted as a change of scenery, and specifically as a descent from "the noisy sphere" of the market, "a very Eden of the rights of man: . . . Freedom, Equality, Property and Bentham," into "the hidden abode of production, on whose threshold there hangs the notice 'No admittance here'" (C1: 279–80). In the same passage he refers to a "certain change . . . or so it appears, in the physiognomy of our *dramatis personae*" when he shifts the spotlight from the character of the merchant to that of the entrepreneur. Insofar as the Robinsonades constitute the primal myth of political economy, these latter-day figures may be understood to be the descendants of Robinson, their primitive ancestor. Marx's task, then, would consist of producing an evolutionary account of the emergence of the species *Homo economicus* through changing stages of history and scenes of social reality, a genealogy of the descent of this species from a savage state, and its fall or even disappearance as a dying breed (cf. Foucault 1973). On a more comical note, perhaps he is telling us a tall tale of how this *"Capitales Homines"* achieved his fantastic intelligence and reached his upright posture (*Entstehung*), but at the price of having to pay a "head tax," "*'qui debent censum de capite'* . . . if one wants to descend to bad Latin" (V: 513).

Rather than dismiss the Crusoe story as a primal myth of classical political economy, Marx revives, criticizes, and then redeploys it through his own version of the labor theory of value. As he states explicitly in *Capital*, even though Robinson's labor is not itself objectified (appropriated, exchanged, etc.) as value, the case of Robinson Crusoe "contains all the determinants of value" (C1: 170). That is, the labor theory of value may be understood as a kind of socially transposed Robinsonade: just as Robinson keeps an inventory of his daily activities and possessions by making a catalog of "useful objects," "various operations" necessary for their production, and "the labor-time that specific quantities have cost on average," so must capitalist society operate on the assumption that the value of a commodity is equal to the quantity of socially necessary labor directly or indirectly spent for the production per unit of that commodity, and that the expenditure of society's productive labor will produce goods in socially necessary quantities. What else is this abstract theory, Marx seems to ask, besides the transposition of a story about the activities of a "natural" individual onto the history of capitalism?

In its most abstract and purest form, of course, the labor theory of value could really hold only in a pre- or noncapitalistic exchange economy of small producers, each of whom owns the means of production (*einfache Warenproduktion*), as Oscar Lange argued in an article titled "Marxian Economics and Modern Economic Theory" (1934–35). As a theory that posits a fixed and determined relation between labor and what is produced within specific parameters, it presupposes the same abstract conditions that led the economists to the Crusoe story, "production without exchange" (VII: 840). In this respect, Marxian economics in many ways presents an empirically more primitive, restricted, and narrow conception of capitalism, in terms of labor-capital ratios, pure competition, and natural equilibrium, than even the most simplistic classical utility theories. By the same token, the economic meaning of the labor theory of value as a theory of production *and* exchange "is nothing but a static theory of general equilibrium not essentially different from the theory of marginal utility employed by [modern] bourgeois economics in its stead" (Lange 1934–35: 194).

Indeed, as Marx interpreted it, this theory could not serve as "proof" of the exploitation of labor, or even that "labor is the source of all value" (cf. Marx 1875). This is why it might better be called the "value theory of labor," as Diane Elson argues. Although its object is indeed labor (and not prices, as so many economists after Rudolf Hilferding and Piero Sraffa have assumed), value is conceived here to be a category of both production and exchange (cf. Marx [1881a]). At the same time, this conception of value assumes "not a mechanical (articulation) or a mathematical/logical (correspondence/approximation) but a chemical and biological conception of law (crystallization, incarnation, embodiment, metabolism, metamorphosis)," the basic idea of which is "change of form" (Elson 1979: 139; see also Meikle 1985; Wilson 1991). Thus, rather than reduce social relations to natural properties, Marx deploys his own naturalist conceits as a way of imagining models and metaphors that are flexible enough to express as simply as possible the growth and metabolism of a complex social organism (cf. note 4 to Part III).

Thus, for Marx it cannot be a question here simply of reducing the complexities of industrial capitalism to the simpler elements of its precapitalist past. Rather, the peculiar nature of the abstractness and unrealism of the Marxian labor theory of value renders its empirical clarity and analytic power superior to that of modern "bourgeois economics." The explicit purpose of the theory's anachronistic abstractness is to bring the institutional preconditions of modern-day capitalism into relief, as distinct from those of simple commodity production: "It is not the specific economic concepts used by Marx, but the definite specification of the institutional framework in which the economic process goes on in capitalist society that makes it possible to establish a theory of economic evolution different from mere historical description" (Lange 1934–35: 194). Thus, the very fact that such a theoretical fiction as the labor theory of value does not strictly "apply" to the actual practice of capitalism in the way it would have in previous social formations, in Robinson's fictional case, or in an abstract theoretical system purged of empirical variables, serves as a reminder that the dysfunctions of the system are not merely historical contingencies or accidents of nature and human psychology that can be repaired. Rather, such anomalies form an inherent part of the system's institutional (dis)organization and principles of social (dis)order. Insofar as "Marx's science realized its analytic power precisely because of the *absence* of a belief in or hope for the identity between history and the appropriating capacity of the mind" (Wilson 1991: 91), we might say that the "reality effect" of Marx's theory is produced as much through its anachronisms and conceits as through its more straightforward attempts at descriptive observation, empirical documentation, or hypothetical verisimilitude.

V

As a way of elaborating upon the implications of this thesis (thus pursuing my digression from the order of presentation of Marx's argument a bit further), I present what I shall take to be Marx's more up-to-date and capitalistic version of Crusoe's "ledger" (see Table 3). I shall argue that the major difference between this ledger and its eighteenth-century precursor does not reside primarily in its relatively more modern appearance and contemporary terminology or in the obvious differences between their empirical content and their degree of complexity. Rather, their difference consists in how the later version presupposes a social relation between classes (and not just individuals) that is grounded in a specific institutional framework (and not just a natural environment). The visual format of this ledger, though somewhat obscure at first glance, is simply a balance sheet with two columns that also represent the sides of a social contract, here expressed in terms of capital and labor. Each is pitted against the other in a structural relation of credits to debits in which neither can ever win completely, although one will always win more. This is because the modern social contract, the "dead pledge of society" or capitalism's Faustian pact (*Faustpfand der Gesellschaft*) (I: 160), is signed on the text of money, through which the relative independence of each party in the bargain is ensured (and insured) along with their mutual though unequal dependence upon one other. My task here and in the remainder of this chapter will be to show how this ledger, which represents Marx's own *tableau économique* of social relations under capitalism, is the theoretical artifact at work throughout Marx's critique of political economy. It may thus be understood to provide the analytical terms, the ethical standards, and even the aesthetic model for all subsequent elaborations of Marxist political economy and cultural criticism.

We can begin our analysis of Table 3 by trying to locate what is both logically and sociologically distinctive about the structural relationship represented in the individually oriented (or Crusoean) versus the socially oriented (or capitalist) versions of the ledger. In his reconstruction of Marx's dialectic of capital, which Table 3 represents in another way, Thomas Sekine has shown, at least from a logical and purely economic perspective, how the capital/labor relation need not be represented as a political struggle between social classes in which one class has the upper hand in a situation of domination and exploitation. Rather, for precisely defined theoretical reasons, this relationship may be kept implicit as having been subsumed within in the impersonal logic of capital. The purpose of this move, he says, is "to distinguish clearly the logical constituents of capitalism from their empirical contingencies," such as the historical stages leading up to it, the political processes it presupposes and holds implicit, and, of course, the class conflicts it tries to disavow or pacify (Sekine 1984: 17).

Abstracting from Marx's already abstract scientific logic so as to construct a completely self-contained theoretical system allows us to imagine what a purely capitalist society might look like, one that is based only on commodity-economic necessities and thus freed from the direct interventions of extra-economic forces. To achieve this requires sustaining the "fiction" that several empirical variables can be assumed to work in theory although they cannot be upheld in practice (cf. Sekine 1984: 45): (1) the complete saturation of all conditions of life by commodity-economic forms, especially the capacity to labor and consume; (2) an already formed and fully developed capitalist system with no history and no local or national variations; (3) a noninterfering state that guarantees the legitimacy of the system and maintains its proper functioning without cost or force; (4) a stable, competitive market and fixed individual needs that expand uniformly with respect to one another and according to purely commodity-economic principles.

Sekine demonstrates how "the dialectic of capital" stands in for Hegel's "dialectic of the absolute" insofar as Marx's basic categories can be shown to correspond to the elementary components of Hegel's doctrines of philosophical logic (see Table 2C). However, there is this essential difference: "the concept of 'use-values' as opposed to value has a substance which is lacking in Hegel's concept of 'nothing'" (1984: 48). To this extent (and to this extent only), as a historically changeable social institution the capitalist system's "nonbeing" cannot entirely be accounted for by the consistent development of and pure application of its logic. Use values are thus not merely the ideological alibis or unavoidable by-products of capitalist production, but rather its fundamental condition of possibility: "The *true limitation* of capitalism . . . in its ideal state lies in the fact that all use-values are produced as value, i.e. produced with indifferent labor" (1984: 98–99; my emphasis). Indeed, it appears that the system works in theory because of, and not just in spite of, the fact that it cannot work in practice, and vice versa. Thus, the theoretical abstraction of the dialectic of capital shows that in spite of capitalism's dream of perpetuating itself to eternity (if only in theory), its real and fatal flaw is that it cannot avoid being haunted by the reality of its own nonbeing, and indeed, its imminent death.[24]

Taking this as our initial perspective, and turning now to the centerpiece of Table 3, we may identify what is most distinctive about Marx's theory of the labor/capital relation: *the theory of surplus value* is the theoretical abstraction or fiction that distinguishes the logical specificity of capitalism from all other

TABLE 3

The Ledger, or Marx's Economic Tableau of Capitalist Social Relations

Scheme I. *Simple Production and Realization* (algebraic equation, temporal analysis)

COLUMN A Labor	COLUMN B Capital
Presupposed components of production	
	Variable capital (v)
	Constant capital (c) (including fixed, circulating capital)
Subjective living labor	
Objectified labor (materials, tools, consumer goods, etc.)	
Logic of self-valorization	
	Profits extracted from newly created value (beyond value preserved in use of c and v)
Wages earned from necessary labor (surplus labor appropriated by capital)	
	M—money as presupposed store of value
	C—commodity exchange for c and v (labor power as capital's use value)
C—labor power as commodity (exchange value for capital)	
	...
	P—production process
	...
M—exchange with capital for wages	
	C'—new commodity = old value + surplus value
	M'—exchange for cost price + profit on market
C'—exchange for consumption goods (specific use values via market)	
	Immediate self-interest
	Large-scale circulation claim on future labor, more value
Small-scale circulation based on vital needs, expressive desires	
	Increase value of surplus labor (s): absolutely (employ more labor, prolong work) relatively (new technology, faster turnover)
Realize value of necessary labor	
Expand autonomous needs, desires	

The presupposition is the result.
The result of Scheme I is the presupposition for Scheme II.

SURPLUS VALUE
(ratio of surplus/necessary labor)

Scheme II. *Expanded/Intensified Reproduction and Realization (geometric progression, spatial analysis)*

COLUMN A Capital's falling profit rate		COLUMN B Labor's struggle over the wage
	Hypothesis	
The falling rate of profit is logically inevitable in view of capital's own methods of preservation and expansion.		The struggle over wages is ethically and rationally imperative in view of labor's own principles of preservation and expansion.
	Premises	
1. Surplus value not property of producers		1. Capitalist appropriation unjust, irrational
2. Availability of science-based technologies		2. Science-based technologies can serve needs and desires, and reduce alienating work
3. Labor power available in needed quantities and skill levels		3. Capital's limits (*Grenzen*) = labor's barriers (*Schranken*)
	Proof	
Higher profits and comparative advantage in competition are achieved by intensifying or expanding production or consumption. As a result:		Success in the collective struggle to expand needs and desires beyond production for profits and beyond the technological a priori is a real possibility, because:
1. the organic composition of capital increases (c/v)		1. the organic composition of capital must have labor as its basis
2. the rate of (relative) surplus value decreases (s/v)		2. the rate of (relative) surplus value increases with refusal of labor, nonwork
3. over time, the rate of profit inevitably falls ($s/c + v$)		3. the real interest of labor is to abolish itself as such
(Even over the vicissitudes of the business cycles of the aggregate social capital, capital's primary interest is always growth based on necessary labor.)		(These can be sung as the three verses of the cellar-rat song reproduced in Chapter 1.)

The presupposition is the result.
Repeat Scheme I at a higher level of cultural and material wealth.

social systems, and not the labor theory of value per se, which it both modifies and presupposes. Where the latter posits a relation of "necessary labor" only (a relation that may be represented by Robinson alone on his island), the former entails a structural proportion between necessary and surplus labor that must be based on a social relation. To return to the simpler terms of the naturalist conceit introduced earlier, the theory of surplus value cannot simply be illustrated by the extra work Robinson does to make life more comfortable for himself. Although the scene of Robinson alone on his island might be altered to include what Friday must do for him because Robinson requires it of him, even this situation would constitute a "relation of domination" (*Herrschaftsverhältnis*) and not of capital, and Friday might assert his will by refusing (as did the Quashees of Jamaica, III: 326; see Chapter 1). In theoretical terms, the specific substance that has "something more" than the strictly Hegelian conception of "nothing" is not simply use value in general but the use value that is labor power, the value of which is necessarily realized beyond what it is exchanged for: "Labor is not only the *use-value* which confronts capital, but, rather, it is *the use-value* of capital itself" (III: 297). On the basis of this abstract formulation the Crusoe story could be understood from the perspective of surplus value only if Robinson's control over Friday were exercised not just through the former's superior personal power and will but also in the context of the island's actual or potential use as a colonial outpost (as suggested in a recent American film adaptation, for example).

As the rest of this chapter will show with reference to Table 3, the relationship or ratio of necessary to surplus labor is grounded in both a quantitative proportion, a kind of factoring of accounts that can be measured economically and demonstrated mathematically, and a qualitative difference, that is, a power struggle for domination and control that can only be proved discursively and argued rhetorically. As a general theory positing a basic analytical distinction or difference between necessary and surplus labor, the theory of surplus value thus operates throughout all of the class relations that define the basic economic spheres: the haggling between buyers and sellers in the circulation process, the negotiations over wages and salaries between employers and employees in the production process, and the conflict of interests between lenders and borrowers in the distribution process. Indeed, it was the ultimate unworkability of the classical labor theory of value in actual capitalist practice and theory that led Marx to his great discovery of surplus value. To account for the empirical anomalies he observed in various class conflicts, he tried to test whether a structurally and logically necessary imbalance or disproportion (*Misverhältnis*) operates at the analytically distinct level of production that may be disavowed or even managed but never erased or reversed at the levels of circulation and distribution. It is therefore the particular manner in which the capitalist process of production and realization could both develop and surpass the labor theory of value that allowed Marx to perceive an anomaly that can be accounted for only by the theory of surplus value and by the institutionalized class system it presupposes:

Thus, it is an anomaly (i.e. the way "labor" is one-dimensionalized as a factor of production) in relation to a central tenet of the body of knowledge called political economy itself (i.e. the labor theory of value), for instance, which produces a *motive* or *desire* to look beneath political economy's description to see what is really going on. Is the labor theory of value functioning doctrinally and ideologically to legitimize a reality whose operative values and actions are seriously at variance with it? The desire to excavate, to adduce or retroduce "behind" it, as it were, arises out of the anomalous role of what is perceived/observed *in the light of the theory itself.* (Wilson 1991: 121)

VI

Retournons maintenant à nos moutons—or, rather, let us leave now the pastoral confines of Marx's naturalist conceit. Having introduced the theoretical fiction of the ledger (Table 3) while arguing that its conceptual center is the theory of surplus value, we can now return to the logic and sequence of the argument in Marx's 1857–58 studies while specifying some of the empirical variables and institutional frameworks that are implied there. Recalling the historicity of our reading invoked above, we need to consider in more detail some historical data and hypothetical factors drawn from recent accounts of the social structure of late capitalism as a way of testing the limits and possibilities of Marx's model. Like Marx's own critical procedure with respect to the classical political economists, this approach entails developing (and not simply overthrowing) the critical force of his theory in the direction of our own historical circumstances and interests. With reference to key passages from the three main divisions of the *Grundrisse*'s "Chapter on Capital," the following trio of "science fictions" tests the usefulness of the ledger not just as an ideal model for the normal or proper functioning of capitalism, but also as a kind of forgery or fiction—indeed, an ideology of equality and freedom hiding a system of exploitation and domination.

This idea is introduced and then maintained starting from the opening pages of the section on the "production process of capital" (at first titled "Chapter on Money as Capital"), where Marx directs a highly polemical discussion against those French socialists (like Darimon) who assert that "the money system can indeed only be the realization of this system of freedom and equality" (II: 239–50, at 246). In fact, the antiquated and precapitalist merchant ideology of the exchange of equivalents projects an inverted image (*Lichtbild*) of a system that presupposes the nonexchange of surplus values (a figure discussed in the conclusion to this chapter). Marx emphasizes that in the simple exchange of a commodity, such as the worker's labor power for wages, the balancing of equivalents becomes a process of nonexchange and exploitation when the use value of that commodity is consumed in the production process beyond its value:

In the exchange between capital and labor, the first act is an exchange, falls entirely within ordinary circulation; the second is a process qualitatively different from exchange, and only by misuse could it have been called *any sort of exchange at all.* It stands directly opposite exchange; essentially different category. (II. 2/5)

In other words, the ledger's formal calculative rationality positing the exchange of equivalents is shown to be based on the substantive irrationality of nonexchange and even exploitation.[25]

Marx's concern to present this point through a *mathematical formulation* makes it clear that his discovery of the basic necessity of the surplus need not be argued simply on empirical grounds or primarily with reference to ethical principles. His "algebraic" manner of presenting this discovery (the simple production and realization process represented in Scheme I of Table 3) may be read literally as an account of a calculated comparison, counterbalancing, and canceling out (the mathematical meanings of the German word *Aufhebung*) of those variables which factor into the self-valorization processes of labor's exchange of work for wages and then for consumption goods ("small scale circulation" or C-M-C') on the one side, versus capital's investment and production for profit ("large-scale circulation" or M-C . . . P . . . C'-M') on the other. The abstractly logical and mathematical expression for the differential represented by surplus value serves to distinguish a quantitative proportion from such qualitative factors as the needs, desires, interests, and objectives that are contested between and on each side of the class divide. As Marx makes clear (III: 334), only insofar as such factors can be defined within an economy of limits (*Grenze*) and barriers (*Schranke*) does a distinctly mathematical formulation of their disproportion become relevant to the final calculation of the balance.

For the purposes of Marx's argument, it is crucial that such empirical variables and contingencies be both abstracted from and presupposed throughout his analysis (cf. notes 8 and 22 to Part III). For this reason, the relation of "capital in general" to particular capitalists, or of "labor in general" to particular workers, as well as the general relation of each to the other ("this double positing, this self relating to self as alien"), may be understood as "in algebra [where] a, b, c are numbers as such; in general; but then again they are whole numbers as opposed to a/b, b/c, c/b, c/a, b/a etc. which latter, however presuppose the former as their general elements" (IV 41: 450). Marx's aim is to analyze the ratio or proportion of the variable quantities of "capital in general" with respect to "labor in general" apart from any empirical understanding of particular capitalists and laborers, rather than run them together as Ricardo does. In so doing, he does not deny real-world contradictions through the abstract veneer of mathematics, but on the contrary insists on a clear and precise understanding of them through a formal apparatus (ultimately, an algebraically based calculus) that has the capacity to incorporate and even highlight its relation to the real world (Marx [1881b]; Struik 1948; Yonoyovskaya 1983; Zeleny 1980).

Where the algebraic argument presents a mathematical analysis of time (labor-and-circulation time) with its economy of simple production and realization (including the production of a surplus), its counterpart in Marx's "geometric" argument presents a mathematical analysis of space (the distances between the various moments of production, circulation, and distribution) with its economy of expanded reproduction and realization (represented in Scheme II of Table 3). Here the structural disproportion of surplus value is shown to be managed and escalated in actual practice both within and outside of the sphere of production as a kind of "geometrical progression," an expanding and contracting series in which each term varies in a definite ratio from the one preceding it (here, in the ratios designated by profits, wages, organic composition, and so on). Unlike Malthus, Marx does not hypothesize that this progression can go on to infinity, nor does he empiricize these relations into the laws of population and economic growth (I: 197). Rather, he understands such regularities as "natural laws of humanity only at a specific stage of historic development, with the development of the forces of production determined by humanity's own process of history" (VI: 606).

Where the algebraic ratio abstracts from, generalizes, and quantifies empirical particularities by factoring them as variables into a mathematical equation, the geometric argument incorporates the contingencies and results of this process into the conventional premises and hypotheses of a discursive presentation and argumentative demonstration, as in the logical proof that the rate of profit must fall. By contrast, the processes at work in the geometric scheme tend to become reduced to the mechanisms governing the algebraic scheme insofar as capital seeks "to reduce space to time" and time to zero, that is, to pure simultaneity (V: 524, 538–40), an observation that, by the way, later led Marx to study the algebraic foundations of calculus (in Marx [1881b]). The results of each scheme thus reciprocally implicate the other, forming a cycle that is structured through the theory of surplus value, and that thereby presupposes a definite institutional framework of power, wealth, and knowledge, as well as a determinable path of historical development.

We therefore should not assume here that Marx intends the concepts of capital and labor to designate "an undiluted antagonism of a logical contradiction" that he would later transpose into a description of existing industrial society and a prediction concerning its escalating social antagonisms (cf. Nicolaus 1967: 32). On the contrary, it was by following closely the abstract two-step of the Hegelian choreography that Marx was able to analyze in detail the actual historical movements of the capitalist dialectic. Indeed, his economic theory of class outlines the fundamental economic and sociological principles that explain the inevitable emergence and importance of the "unproductive" middle classes within the larger social structure of capitalism (Nicolaus 1967: 46). In this sense, the abstract dialectic of labor and capital already presupposes the three-tiered pyramidal structure displayed in Figure 1, now understood to depict the capitalist class and stratification system that consists of the power elite at the top, white-collar workers in the middle, and the majority blue- (and pink-) collar workers at the bottom (cf. Mills 1956). Of course, as Marx understood, there will be enormous differences between and within each group in the number of hours worked, the amount of money earned, control over working conditions, degree of supervision, and social status, which in turn will vary according to level of education, sex, race, age, and the like.

In Marx's analysis, the development of what he referred to as "fictitious capital" (VI: 657–58), as in the proliferation of banking and credit agencies, joint-stock and insurance companies, advertising businesses, public education institutions, and research and development firms, has in fact become essential to the maintenance and expansion of capitalist enterprise, in the broadest sense of the term (cf. Marx [1861–63]). So, too, have other forms of "unproductive labor," unproductive in the strictly economic sense of the "direct production and realization of surplus value":

The creation of surplus labor on the one side corresponds to the creation of minus-labor, relative idleness (or *not-productive* labor at best), on the other. This goes without saying as regards capital itself; but holds then also for the classes with which it shares; hence of the paupers, flunkeys, lickspittles etc. living from the surplus product, in short, the whole train of retainers; the part of the *servant* class which lives not from capital but from revenue. Essential difference between this *servant* class and the *working* class. In relation to the whole of society, the creation of *disposable time* is then also creation of time for the production of science, art, etc. . . . because *surplus labor* is on one side, therefore not-labor and surplus wealth are posited on the other. In reality the development of wealth exists only in these opposites [*Gegensätze*]: in potentiality, its development is the possibility of the suspension of these opposites. . . . Malthus therefore quite consistent when, along with surplus labor and surplus capital, he raises the demand for surplus idlers, consuming without producing, or the necessity of waste, luxury, lavish spending, etc. (IV: 401–2n)

What has since been called the "law of the rising surplus," namely, the tendency for labor to produce more wealth relative to its own poverty (Baran and

Sweezy 1966: 72), thus entails at the same time a "law of the surplus class," namely, the tendency for capitalism to rely increasingly on its bookkeepers, clerks, secretaries, lawyers, designers, engineers, and salesmen while expanding its "reserve army" of the unemployed, flunkies, paupers, and lickspittles. As fewer people produce more, more people produce less, and as the mass of disposable revenue tends to rise, there is an increase in that part of the surplus which can be expended for the utilization of "unproductive labor" or the expansion of the spheres of "non-labor," although in very different ways and to different degrees during times of exceptionally heavy capital investment or depression (Nicolaus 1967: 38–39).

As latter-day readers of Marx, we are faced with the question of whether or to what extent his conceptual model for analyzing capital/labor relations has been rendered irrelevant by the reorganization of these relations into a more intricate structure of power elites confronting the masses and other class fragments, or by the domination of a "tertiary" or white-collar sector (including the state bureaucracy) that hails the advent of a postindustrial society (Bell 1973). Before any answer is given to this question, however, we need first to test how other variables, such as the balance of trade, national and local budget crises, and the accounting practices of multinational corporations, may also be factored into the equations and calculations of what has become a global process of "double-entry bookkeeping" (*doppelte Buchführung*). In any case, part of the current challenge to modern mathematical economics, econometrics, and equilibrium theories, as well as to complex institutional evolutionary models of economic explanation, should be understood to entail whether they can be made flexible enough to absorb or surpass the achievement of Marx's innovative surplus-value theory (cf. Sekine 1984, 1986). In any case, as both a formal analytical apparatus and a mathematical fiction necessary for capitalism to function, the ledger can be modified to incorporate new historical variables and institutional forces as they are structured through a wide range of class interests and fragments and factored into columns governed by the logics of "capital" and "labor."

VII

We have seen how the very abstractness of the capital/labor balance may enhance its analytic power as a model or prototype for understanding the specifically capitalist character of later stages of capitalism, along with their more complicated class structures. Here we need to specify further the potential uses of this model for understanding the expansion of capitalism into imperialism, its intensification through monopolism and even postindustrialism, and its denationalized and disorganized implosion into postmodern consumerism (cf. Lash and Urry 1987). In other words, where before we regarded the ledger more as a quantitative relation of wealth, here we understand it to express a qualitatively defined balance of power as well, now taking account of its ethical and legal implications.

In the middle of the second section of the "Chapter on Capital," which deals with "the circulation process," and particularly the passages introducing and concluding the discrete "essay on precapitalist social formations" (IV: 456–58; V: 513–14), Marx takes on the role of a litigator. That is, he challenges the legitimacy of the capitalist social system as a whole along with the legality of specific statutes that govern it, what he later refers to as "the bloody handwriting of coercive [legislation] employed to transform the mass of the population, after they had become propertyless and free, into free wage-laborers" (VII: 769). Following many of the *rhetorical conventions of legalistic procedure*, he submits a claim on behalf of the legitimate rights of his main client, "the proletariat," by appealing to the principle of *stare decisis*: that certain historical precedents can be shown to have been illicitly contravened to the detriment of the plaintiff. Marx thus draws upon his extensive knowledge of legal argumentation and historical scholarship in order to put capitalism on trial while defending its victims against counteraccusations and libelous statements.

What he earlier called the "appropriation without exchange" of surplus value, and the formation of "surplus capital II" or capitalist accumulation, he now describes as the "dialectical inversion" of "the law of appropriation" by which each producer was presumed to have a legal right to dispose of the products of her or his labor, "so that on the side of capital it becomes the right to an alien product, or the right of property over alien labor, the right to appropriate alien labor without an equivalent, and, on the side of labor capacity, it becomes the duty to relate to one's own labor or to one's own product as to *alien property*" (IV: 458). What appeared previously as a calculative process of exchanges and (im)balances is here expressed as a general condition recognized by law, posited as an expression of the general will but premised on the separation (*Trennung*) of labor and property or the appropriation of alien labor without exchange or equivalent (V: 514). This inversion constitutes capitalism's continuing *legitimation crisis*, in that the labor theory of value, now given legal expression as the "law of appropriation," can be shown to have been violated and then superseded by what can be called the "law of expropriation," understood as another term for the law of surplus value. By producing and reproducing "the relation of capital and labor itself" (IV: 458) through successive stages of history, capitalism governs itself by quietly revoking or rescinding (legal meanings for the German *aufheben*) the law of equality and freedom that it nevertheless continues to invoke in defense of its own legitimacy.[26]

The implications of Marx's legal rhetoric and historical scholarship here need to be examined in terms of the model he provides for addressing situations beyond those he explicitly addressed. The direction of Marx's procedure has been taken up by political economists influenced by him in their analyses of the institutional preconditions that distinguish later stages of imperialist and monopoly capitalism. Without always articulating their insights under the light of Marx's surplus-value theory, Joseph Schumpeter on the one hand, and Paul Baran and Paul Sweezy on the other, share not only much of Marx's ethical regard for the substantive irrationality of capitalism but also his theoretical vision of how even a "purely" capitalist world, hypothetically operating on purely commodity-economic principles, would not necessarily offer fertile soil for imperialist drives and oligopolist impulses. In different ways, each argues that the so-called higher and more advanced stages of capitalism ultimately draw from, build upon, and shape toward their own ends remnants or survivals from the precapitalist past. Thus, while the principles governing feudalism and mercantilism are revived and refueled in the late capitalist drive toward centralization and monopolism (Baran and Sweezy 1966: 4), "nationalism and militarism, while not creatures of capitalism, become 'capitalized' and in the end draw their best energies from capitalism. Capitalism involves them in its workings and thereby keeps them alive, politically as well as economically. And they in turn affect capitalism, cause it to deviate from the course it might have followed alone, [and] support many of its interests" (Schumpeter 1951 [1919]: 96).

In a similar way, although the capitalist class system indeed serves as a formal presupposition and an essentially structural feature indispensable to the identity of capitalism, it is also itself energized by ethnically and familially based class and caste conflicts that dominate pre- or noncapitalist social formations: "Any study of classes and class situations therefore leads, in unending regression, to other classes and class situations, just as any explanation of the circular flow of the economic process always leads back without any logical stopping point to the preceding circular flow that furnishes the data for the one that is to follow" (Schumpeter 1951 [1927]: 112). An expanded notion of class culture and politics that includes issues involving race and ethnicity, sex and gender, or age and generation must therefore be integrated into an analysis of how definitionally noncapitalist social structures may either challenge or support capitalist legitimation processes.

These larger implications of Marx's historical digression must be kept in mind when considering recent arguments that the "classical" Marxian economic crisis theory must now be abandoned or expanded to accommodate the historical framework of a political or cultural crisis theory. The capitalist exchange principle can no longer be sustained through dogmatic references to the struggle over wages or to the tendency of the profit rate to fall, so it is argued, but must, rather, make way for a more flexible and complicated understanding of normative-legitimation and political-administrative processes. Claus Offe puts the argument in terms of a theory of social systems: "A society based on market exchange cannot function without the family system and the legal system," that is, without what Marxists would call those superstructural value spheres which in their origin or essence appear to be precapitalist or noncapitalist survivals or revivals (Offe 1984: 38).

An understanding of how the latter may be necessary to the capitalist social system allows us to see why imperialist expansion or welfare state policy may in fact seem irrelevant or dysfunctional to capitalist development by paralyzing or even subverting it. Imperialist wars are not always undertaken simply to open new markets for export, investment, and exploitation, for example, but also in order to obstruct processes of emancipation or subversion elsewhere that may be perceived as a threat to capitalist domination. A similar logic may govern welfare policies designed to interfere with the normal functioning of private exchange relationships, but in the name of the system's survival itself. The point here is that in the contemporary context of welfare and warfare, the ideologies of equality, freedom, and justice under "capitalist democracy" may still be upheld within the framework of the capitalist structures of surplus value, that is, of inequality, unfreedom, and injustice, for the very reason that such ideals are deemed to be unattainable in practice.

From a positive perspective, this political model of crisis informs a theoretical view of the dysfunctions inherent in the modern social factory as culturally delegitimizing tactics that may potentially upset capitalist structures of accumulation and disaccumulation, participation and apathy (Habermas 1975; O'Connor 1981; Offe 1984). From a negative perspective, it motivates the theoretical critique of the medical model of crisis by which such dysfunctions are diagnosed as illnesses that may be cured at an economic and social cost. Jacques Donzelot has provided a historical sketch of these issues in terms of the double strategy of sociolegal and medical policymaking that he interprets within the general parameters of the economic model itself. His main example is the current discourse on "pleasure in work," which is now proposed as a way of managing capitalism's ongoing legitimation crisis by remedying such systemic illnesses as disability, unemployment, absenteeism, deskilling, and industrial restructuring at the level of worker psychology.

From early to late capitalism, every individual must negotiate the measure of meaning and value, or pleasure and pain, he or she wishes to give to life against what that society is prepared to concede without significantly compromising its production imperatives. In the new capitalist ledger, or social contract, the social costs of productivity on the one hand—which are defined through a psychopathology of the worker (industrial psychology) and a social pathology of the enterprise (the science of management)—are measured against the economic costs of productivity on the other—expressed as the socioeconomic price of such benefits as social security, work safety, day care, and perpetual retraining (*formation permanente*) that are needed to expand or at least maintain the system:

> In the early part of the twentieth century we thus see the birth of two discourses which divide between them the problem of work, one of them *juridical*, the other *medico-psychological*: two discourses which institute the separation between the *worker* as *subject of rights* and *work* as *object of a science* for which the worker is only a factor; two discourses which organize the partition of production into two relatively distinct entities, the social and the economic. The *social* stands on the side of the *attribution of rights*, of resistance to the logic of production. It sets up the *status* of the worker against the contract which enslaves him to productivity, the solidarity of the employed against the profits of the employer, satisfaction through wages and leisure against the frustration of work. The *economic* stands on the side of the *distribution of forces* for the sake of productivity, the rationalization of jobs in the name of profit, the intensification of work in the interest of increased production. (Donzelot 1981–82: 8)

In other words, from the nineteenth to the twentieth century a new social contract emerges in which the juridical status of persons may be simultaneously upheld and effaced through the redefinition of traditional and liberal rights in medicopsychological terms, thereby substituting the right to political participation and control for the right to "work-satisfaction" or "pleasure in work" (1981–82: 27). The costs of upholding such values as health, education, and welfare are then treated not as matters of civic responsibility or public morality but in the context of the relation of individuals to their productive work, and thus within the basic parameters of the capitalist legitimation process.

The shift from early modern to late modern and even postmodern culture entails not only the generalization, expansion, and intensification of capitalism to previously uncolonized social spheres but also the revaluation of what survives or must be revived from premodernity. Inasmuch as capitalist development marches forward haunted by survivals from its precapitalist past, the critical function of Marxist historiography is thus to recover the sense by which "the dead always rule the living" (Schumpeter 1951 [1919]: 98). When we come to consider such "new" features of the post-1971 global political economy as depoliticized militarism, ethnic nationalization, and economic and cultural disorganization (cf. Lash and Urry 1987), we may therefore need to revise our conception of the emerging postindustrial society through an under-standing of it as the *refeudalization of capitalism*, that is, as a social system refueled by value sources from its past or from cultures viewed as marginal to its "normal" path of development (cf. Negri 1988 [1968, 1980]). The critical and anamnestic purpose of Marx's litigious procedure is thus to recover the ethical and legal problems of succession or inheritance within the historical continuity of an expropriated ancestral legacy. This in turn requires making a case on behalf of certain deeply held beliefs about proprietary relationships, emotional attachments, and loyalties between generations that may serve as the basis for remembering the solidarity of the living with the dead (Lenhardt 1975: 148–52).

VIII

In the early part of the twentieth century, the capitalist ledger was "re-vised"—but not transformed in any essential way—by the Taylorist standard-ization of the workplace, which aimed to pacify the antagonistic relation be-tween employer and employee by shifting attention to find a more efficient relation between worker and machine. When this ideology was superseded by the post-Fordist political economy of corporate capitalism ruled by transna-tional conglomerates rather than monopolies, the focus was only broadened to include the relation between the worker and the "work situation" through the discourse on "pleasure in work." In the "fragment on machines" from the section on "circulation" in Marx's 1857–58 notebooks, Marx provides a model for understanding some of the issues involved here in his argument that the most extreme historical tendency of capitalism is not just to produce surplus value or to accumulate profits, but particularly to replace human beings with machines. Since the basic desire of both capital and labor is to reduce neces-sary labor, the latter by expanding its sphere of autonomy and control over its activities, and the former by extracting more surplus labor through expan-sion and intensification, the basic drive at the basis of the system as a whole is to project a kind of *mechanical construction* in which its very foundations would be canceled out or annulled altogether (both meanings of the German *aufhebt*). As discussed from another perspective in Chapter 1, this futuristic vision is the most progressive feature of Marx's theoretical perspective on the historical development of capitalism, and the dimension that gives it its most poignant critical force and contemporary relevance.

We may identify the basic tendency of capitalism to lie not in its exportation through militaristic imperialism or Third World corporatism; its pathological intensification through chronic unemployment, class antagonism, and wasteful consumerism; or its cyclical breakdowns in commercial, industrial, and legitimation crises. Rather, as Marx understood through his analytical focus on the theory of surplus value and by drawing from his empirical knowledge of nineteenth-century British industrial relations, capitalism strives to re-create all life in the image of a technological automaton:

In speaking of "late capitalism" we have in mind an extreme tendency of early capitalism, rather than any theory of current economic crisis. What is the tendency to which we refer the continuous efforts of capitalism? Despite contrary opinion, we think it is not exploitation, class war, profitability, or human degradation. We do not deny these phenomena. Rather, we think they are embedded in an *extreme tendency of capitalism*, apparent from the early factory system, *to replace human beings with machines*. (O'Neill 1992: 90)

Marx's model for revolution was thus drawn less from directly political class conflicts of the day than from his understanding of "the workers' struggle against machinery" (VII: 708), or rather, from the combination of the idealism of the French Revolution with the materialism of the Industrial Revolution. Besides its repressive effect of chaining human beings to a more highly developed form of slavery, mechanical automation holds out the revolutionary promise of creating a realm of freedom within a realm of necessity, thereby encouraging the free development of the artistic, scientific, and other capacities and sensibilities of "a different subject" (VII: 712). But since capitalism is never really able to realize the scenarios of either its best dreams or worst nightmares, it balances or negotiates the relations between surplus and necessary labor on which it is founded by factoring in new variables or recalculating the equations, or as Marx argues in *Capital*, by redefining class interests through state-administered welfare legislation. Capitalism's more modest aim, then, is to replace the remnants from its prehistory, such as familial or ethnic ties, with a consumer and service industry underwritten by the technologies of law, administration, and medicine, and by the discourses of health, happiness, and security. In this way, the workplace may be further divided along the lines of ethnicity, gender, and generation insofar as the desires and interests of marginalized populations are either included in the official statistics of the system as a whole, brought under its legal protections, or processed through its various machineries in some other way (O'Neill 1992: 91).

Thus, the ledger may now be understood to provide a set of themes and a framework of analysis for understanding the dialectic of promise and defeat, of possibilities and their containment, within the historical cycles of counterrevolution and revolt in late capitalist and postindustrial societies. With explicit reference to Marx's notebooks, Herbert Marcuse has given us an eloquent account of late capitalism's irresolvable paradox of trying to contain political discussion and energies through the administration of social control, while at the same time fostering the "catastrophe of liberation" through the expansion of human needs beyond its own systemic requirements for survival (Marcuse 1964: 34–42; 1972: 1–5). He was thus among the first to read Marx's "fragment on machines" both as a critical commentary on the contradictory historical tendencies of capitalism beyond the factory system of the nineteenth century, and as a visionary projection of the possible fate of late capitalist industrial automation with its governing logic of technical rationality:

Such qualitative change would be [a] transition to a higher stage of civilization if technics were designed and utilized for the pacification of the struggle for existence. In order to indicate the disturbing implications of this statement, I submit that such a new direction for technical progress would be *the catastrophe of the established direction*, not merely the quantitative evolution of the prevailing (scientific and technological) rationality but rather its catastrophic transformation, the emergence of a new idea of Reason, theoretical and practical. (Marcuse 1964: 227–28; emphasis added)

Marcuse interpreted Marx's own reading of political economy from the 1840s and 1850s as itself a kind of "reading" of late capitalist tendencies in the 1960s and 1970s. He was thus able to demonstrate how the very abstractness and unreality of Marx's conceptual framework in many respects anticipate the emergence of a postindustrial era as the practical confirmation of its theoretical insights.

IX

It is precisely in this understanding of the most progressive implications of Marx's thinking, however, that we seem to come up against an insurmountable barrier: Marx himself did not pursue his analysis of the eventual emergence of a relatively automated, postindustrial phase of capitalist development beyond its most general outlines and in the most sparse terms. Rather, he ultimately seems to have been concerned to confine his analysis of the distribution of surplus value to a narrow *textbook account* of the laws of profit, interest, and rent. Indeed, where the passages on large-scale machinery in the *Grundrisse* are concluded in the next section, on profit and interest, the main portion of the first volume of *Capital*, dealing with the history of machinery and working conditions, is superseded in the third volume by a formula showing the tendency of the profit rate to fall (summarized in Scheme II of Table 3 and explained in more detail in the next section).

Even Engels, who edited, rearranged, and published this section from volume 3 and gave it the title "Exposition of the Internal Contradictions of the

Law," seems to have had serious doubts about the general validity and applicability of Marx's law of the profit rate (Seigel 1978: 336–43). And yet Marx explicitly presents his argument not just as the exposition of the contradictions within a particular capitalist "law" (as Engels's title implies) but also as an expression of the most fundamental contradictions and antagonisms inherent in capitalism itself, and clearly stakes the greater part of his scientific theory on it (cf. Sekine 1986: 223–78). Rather than advance his historical investigations further into a critical discussion of capitalism's fiction of an automated society, Marx seems instead to have wished to contain this impulse by regressing to the previous discussions of capitalist legal and mathematical fictions. What, then, does the profit-law theory reveal about the inner workings of capitalism, or about Marx's own interest in developing a theory about them?

To account for these discrepancies, we need first to see whether Marx's insight into the extreme historical tendency of capitalism to replace humans with machines may itself be understood to be simply another expression of Marx's doctrine of the tendential decline of the profit rate. His discovery and first explicit formulation of this law can be found in the third section of the "Chapter on Capital," on distribution, which is punctuated by the following triumphant exclamation: "This is in every respect the most important law of modern political economy, and the most essential for understanding the most difficult relations. It is the most important law from the historical standpoint. It is a law which, despite its simplicity, has never before been grasped and, even less, consciously articulated" (VII: 748).

In the passages that follow, as in all of his later references to the profit law, Marx states explicitly that the law of the tendential decline in the profit rate (defined as surplus value in proportion to the presupposed values of constant and variable capital) entails not just a rise in the mass of profits (that is, the magnitude of surplus value measured against constant and variable capital) but also an increase in both the rate and the mass of surplus value production (see the formula summarized in Scheme II of Table 3 and Nicolaus 1967: 35). Since an increase in the mass of the surplus necessarily includes both constant and variable capital (machinery, raw materials, consumption goods, and so on), the law can be interpreted to include what Baran and Sweezy call the "law of rising economic surplus" (the concentration of constant capital, including the development of science-based technology, monopolies, and consumerism), as well as what Nicolaus calls the "law of the rise of the surplus class" (which would include white-collar workers, the nonwaged and nonsalaried, Third World labor pools, and so on). Most important for our purposes, however, the law also accounts for the proportional increase in the value of constant capital (in the form of machines and raw material, for example) relative to variable capital (expressed in labor costs and wage goods, for example), whether through what

Marx calls the growth of the organic composition of capital or in terms of what Marcuse has discussed as the "technological a priori" (1964: 154).

On both historical and logical grounds, then, we may conclude that Marx's profit law is an expression of capitalism's historical drive toward the technological possession of society. Only on the basis of such an understanding can we grasp not just Marx's feeling of victory over his momentous discovery but especially the extraordinary passage concluding this initial formation of the profit law, which invokes the apocalyptic imagery (already dominating the "excursus on crises," IV: 401–56) of "bitter contradictions, crises, spasms . . . EXPLOSIONS, CATACLYSMS . . . in which momentary suspension of labor and annihilation of a great part of capital violently lead it back to the point where it is enabled [to go on] fully employing its productive powers without committing suicide" (VII: 750).

Nevertheless, the interruption of this explosive vision into Marx's otherwise sober analytical discussion of capitalist historical laws and statistical calculations may ultimately seem to raise more questions than it answers: Why would Marx continue to insist on both the general theoretical validity and the historico-empirical applicability of the profit law, even though this law can almost never hold for long in reality and must almost always be blocked and compromised by countervailing historical, political, and social tendencies? Why did he later choose to concentrate on such capitalist survival mechanisms as the reduction of wages, longer work hours, the introduction of new machinery, the employment or underemployment of the work force, foreign trade, and securities and investments, only to demonstrate the extent to which his scientific abstractions could not hold in reality? Put another way, why was Marx so concerned to synthesize the calculative logic and litigious reasoning he had already worked into his analyses and form them into a scientific law, thereby consolidating his theoretical position into the dogmatic stance of a scientific legislator?

X

Allowing Marx his moment of triumph, I shall argue quite seriously that his profit law, or what I have presented as the crowning touch of the capitalist ledger, is in fact part of a *polemical joke* he is playing on his fellow political economists, and that for this reason whatever scientific and empirical validity it may have is inseparable from its fictional origins and even farcical intentions (cf. Wolff 1988: 61–82). Just as in his historical studies Marx aims to show that capitalism did not create itself out of nothing, summoning the workers out of nowhere with the command "Let there be workers!" (V: 506), and just as the origins of the modern economy cannot be explained away with a wish to "let Robinson appear on his island," so is Marx careful not to let his theoretical discussions on the nature of capitalist exploitation and technological development appear to have been invented out of thin air with a stroke of his pen: "Fiat . . . the surplus value theory!" Marx "discovered" the profit-law theory only at the end of hundreds of pages that soberly summarize, criticize, and then refine the achievements of other political economists, but that ultimately and openly ridicule their unsuccessful attempts to come to terms with either the historical facts or the basic principles of logic.

Almost above all other considerations, Marx wished to test his theory against those of the great English political economists, in particular Smith, Malthus, and especially Ricardo (as the notebooks he filled between 1861 and 1863, the *Theories of Surplus Value*, make abundantly clear), and against the weaker though worthy arguments of such French socialists as Proudhon, Bastiat, and Darimon (who are of particular concern for Marx in his notebooks of 1857–58). In these latter studies in particular, Marx proceeds by using the scientific insights of the English political economists as a foil for the pseudopolitical vanguardism of the French socialists, exposing the political and ideological assumptions behind the latter's static economic categories. Thus, he provides a polemically framed confirmation of his profit theory in terms of his "bilingual" view of the history of political economy, that is, by reconsidering antithetical thinkers who speak English and French, which he had already introduced in the very first lines he wrote of these notebooks (III: 883; see the Foreword).

After elaborating in general terms his "law of the tendential decline of the profit rate," Marx identifies a basic "confusion" in Ricardo's treatment of the key analytical and empirical issues involved. In the *Principles of Political Economy and Taxation* (3rd ed., London, 1821), Ricardo had argued that although the sum of profits and wages may increase as capital grows, "'No accumulation of capitals can *permanently* reduce profits unless an equally permanent cause raises wages'" (cited by Marx at VII 17: 753), a statement Marx at first seems to treat more seriously but no less critically than he did Darimon's proclamation about the precious metals. Against Ricardo, and reiterating earlier arguments regarding the way in which profits and wages do not exist in a "zero-sum" relation to one another, Marx points out that an increase in the value of constant capital (by introducing more sophisticated machinery, for example) necessarily decreases the rate of profit over the long run whether or not wages are increased. In response to Ricardo's qualifying assertion that the decline in the profit rate may be offset by increasing the use value of agricultural labor through technochemical improvements, Marx points out that Ricardo is no longer expounding the principles of political economy at all, but rather "flees from economics to seek refuge in organic chemistry . . . [through] a physiological postulate expressed as a general law" (VII 17: 754). By contrast, Marx is concerned to demonstrate that in spite of historical fluctuations, ground rents and capitalist profits can be treated as analytically identical, as can wages earned through industrial or agricultural labor, at least from the theoretical perspective of the production and distribution of surplus value. So much for Marx's sober refutation of Ricardo.

Somewhat surprisingly, Marx "finishes up" his agile test of the profit law not by going on to consider the arguments of another political economist he admires and respects, such as the French-speaking Jean Charles Sismondi (who with Ricardo marks the "end" of the history of modern political economy; III: 883), but rather by turning to "the witlessness of Bastiat, who expresses commonplaces in a paradoxical way, grinds and polishes them *en facettes*, and hides an utter poverty of ideas under a cover of formal logic" (VII 18: 755). In the *Gratuité du crédit* (1850), Bastiat tries to prove that the "shares" of both capital and labor in the total product can increase absolutely over time, even though "'the proportional part [which goes to capital] diminishes,'" and then demonstrates his proof by way of a "mathematical illustration" that "appears to have amused him greatly." What Marx had earlier called "the unfortunate Bastiat's famous riddle" (*Witz*) (IV 7: 385) is solved here when he shows that Bastiat forgets that capital may in fact produce more than it can sell at a profit (as in the combination of agricultural overproduction and mass poverty that is not uncommon in French history), that capital must always reinvest part of the total product in constant capital (and not just in its own consumption goods), and finally, that the declining profit rate can only result in a proportional decrease in labor's "share" (VII 18: 757; and note 4 to Part III).

Bastiat repeats the same "joke" (*Witz*) when he tries to demonstrate that even if an increase in gross profits is combined with a decreasing rate of profit (so that more products are sold at lower prices), a crisis is automatically avoided because of what he calls "'the law of unlimited decline which never reaches zero, a law well known to mathematicians'" (Bastiat, quoted by Marx in French; VII 18: 755). Where Ricardo retreats into organic chemistry, Bastiat retreats into mathematics: "TO DROP THE PROBLEM IS THEIR GENERAL METHOD OF SOLVING IT" (VII 18: 754). Just as Marx had earlier shown how Darimon's "statistical tableaux" present only a part of the whole picture and have almost nothing at all to do with reality (*du tout*), he now exposes Bastiat's version of the increasing "shares of capital and labor" (*parts du capital . . . du travail*) as itself only a partial illustration (*une part*) of the capitalist class system, and indeed as merely a silly puzzle or laughable joke.

At this point Marx returns yet again to Ricardo's demonstration that the simultaneous growth of capital and decline in the profit rate "is only true for a certain time," thereby showing that the refutation of Bastiat's logical "witlessness" has served to reveal that "Ricardo had anticipated his Bastiat" (VII 18: 755). Quoting one of Ricardo's own lengthy mathematical illustrations on the nature of constant capital "word for word" and in English, Marx ultimately seems to want to use Ricardo's insights into the "unpleasant contradictions and antagonisms" he pursues with "scientific ruthlessness" to make a mockery of what Bastiat can only "water down into WELL-TO-DO HARMONIES" by exposing the Frenchman's mathematical "illustrations" as nothing more than a "joke" (VII 18: 755–56). The real puzzle or joke here, however, may ultimately lie in why Marx would want to consider Bastiat at all, and why he would even suggest that the section "Bastiat and Carey," written earlier, "can be included at this point," when he had already concluded that discussion by dismissing the Frenchman's "nonsense" and by "thereby drop[ping] Mr. Bastiat." Why introduce this especially weak example only to ridicule it mercilessly, and why do it by way of a stronger example that had already been refuted?

Marx is interested in the profit/wage relation proposed by both Ricardo and Bastiat partly because each seems to provide a competing version of Marx's own theory of capital/labor relations, one strong and the other weak, and partly because each exemplifies perspectives that are indispensable to Marx's own analysis of these relations. Thus, where Ricardo's argument represents the "capitalist" analysis of the various component parts of the capitalist process (of machinery, raw material, wages, and so on), Bastiat's "illustration" demonstrates a basic indifference to this perspective that is shared by the perspective of "labor." Marx may therefore be understood here to be playing a prank on both Ricardo and Bastiat, delivering a kind of polyglot punch line to the long and complicated joke he has been telling "with damned seriousness" throughout his notebooks. At various places in this long "droll story" told with a straight face, he seems to betray its absurd and even comical essence, as in the middle or at the end of a long mathematical illustration, a *tableau économique*, or a "highly irksome calculation," where he interjects a kind of punch line (literally a *Witz*), witticism, or joke that expresses his basic "point" (also *Witz*): "der Witz ist daher ebenso" (e.g., IV 1, 7, 27: 373, 385, 425; VI 6, 8, 17: 574, 580, 612). Even later in his studies, when he drew up a first version of the celebrated circulation schemes eventually incorporated into the final chapters of volume 2 of *Capital*, which were based on François Quesnay's great *tableaux économiques*, Marx announced to Engels the "point of the whole exercise" as "the joke of the whole story" (*der Witz des Ganzes geschichte*) (Marx to Engels, 6 July 1863; cf. C2: 179, 268, 435–36). In these ways he announces not only the discovery of what "has never before been grasped and, even less, consciously articulated," but perhaps also the beginnings of a theory of jokes and their relation to political economy.

The point of Marx's profit law may ultimately be that he himself could not rest content with simply exposing the joke he construes Ricardo to be playing on Bastiat without at the same time showing how Ricardo's insight betrays a certain "confusion" or poses a certain "puzzle" that it is left to Marx's own value theory to clarify, solve, or even ridicule. In such moments of hilarity, Marx breaks with the logic of representation embedded in the work of the classical political economists, so that a "certain intertextual stratum—or social activity [gesellschafliche Tätigkeit]" erupts into the scientific seriousness of his writing in a way that anticipates and even calls for our own critical "transformative reading" of it (cf. Mehlman 1977: 8–20). The speculative opposition and rational balancing between capital and labor is broken by the eruption of a third farcical element between them, a heterogeneous, negatively charged instance that exceeds, deviates from, or displaces the closure of the terms of the initial opposition. Marx's pronouncement that "profit is nothing but another form of surplus value, further developed in the sense of capital" (VII 20: 762) is thus the final punch line he delivers to classical (if not contemporary) political economy.

Citing the place where Ricardo demonstrates his "confusion" over the relation between profits and wages, Marx translates a French version of the relevant passage from Ricardo's book (originally written in English) into German. It would appear, then, that Marx will not allow Ricardo's words to stand either in a translated French or in their original English form, even though both editions are certainly available to him and he even cites the English edition of Ricardo's *Principles* on the very same page. Rather, he retranslates Ricardo into German, as if his native tongue in some way could somehow better bring out what for him were the vital points of Ricardo's thought than would have been possible in either the passage's original English or translated French version (cf. Nicolaus 1973: 66, whose translation translates Marx's version back into English). Nevertheless, Marx leaves the word for "wages" in French, referring to *salaire* instead of *Lohn*, as if to continue his polemical prank on Bastiat, or possibly because he could not resist expressing this particular politically charged idea with its distinctively French accent (cf. III 5–7: 889–93). Perhaps, then, we might think to ourselves that Marx's strange contribution to the critique of political economy consists of articulating a theory of *Mehrwert* and a politics of *salaires* in the more familiar language of the laws of *profit*.

• • •

Today even Marxists, if not many bourgeois political economists, tend to look back nostalgically on the clarity of the scientific achievement and empirical application of Marx's theory of surplus value. Insofar as anyone thinks anything about Marx anymore, his work tends to be viewed at best as an impressive speculative venture and at worst as a mere speculation that is now

outdated as much by new scientific revelations of capitalism's inner workings
as by the "illuminated picture" (*Lichtbild*) (II 11: 249) or "inverted image"
(*Gegenbild*) (III: 331) of social reality projected through the smoke screens of its
ideological media. Rather than hear in his work the dissonant strains of utopia
or a violent call for struggle, many readers now tend to cast a melancholy gaze
upon it as a kind of dramatic morality play from some other world or past
life, like spectators who watch a scene unfold without knowing or even caring
whether it is now or ever was real to begin with. His tireless pursuit of a theory
of capitalism now seems to have given way to our more passive enjoyment of
its theater.

Our critical tasks thus seem different from Marx's attempts to conceive the
problem of contemporary ideology through the figure of the camera obscura
(Marx and Engels [1845–47] CW 5: 36), in that we must also try to represent
how social reality appears to be not just inverted but also duplicated through
the *imago machinae* of late capitalism, in which all life is paraded as a continuous commercial spectacle (Debord 1983). Whether the image sells the
commodity, as in advertising, or whether the commodity sells the image, as
in entertainment (Jameson 1991: 278), this latest and possibly last form of
fetishized power forges a new ratio of fact to fiction and of surplus to necessary
labor. Indeed, Marxists must now consider whether the labor theory of value
should be replaced by a leisure theory of value that could be defined in terms
of the relationship or ratio of surplus to necessary leisure, or even whether the
surplus-value theory (SV) may itself have become superfluous and in need of
re-vision through a theory of tele-vision (TV; see Figure 2).

What might be surprising for those critics currently at work on this project
of resisting the postmodern exhaustion of political thought and action is that
Marx's own words may already have shed some light to guide us along this new
historical path:

To the extent that . . . the creation of the objective body of activity happens in antithesis
to the immediate labor capacity—that this process of objectification in fact appears as
a process of dispossession . . . or as appropriation . . . —to that extent, this twisting
and inversion [*Verdrehung und Verkehrung*] is a *real* [phenomenon], not a merely *supposed one* existing merely in the imagination. (VII 44: 831; references to "workers" and
"capitalists" elided)

Marx's own presentiment of a value theory of leisure or concept of *tele-value* to
account for how workers and capitalists alike are rendered increasingly docile
and deluded as control over the conditions of their existence recedes further
from their reach, calls us back to our senses by reminding us that the apparent
inversion and duplication of fact and fantasy is already part of a real historical process. Rather than simply dismiss as mere illusion or idle amusement

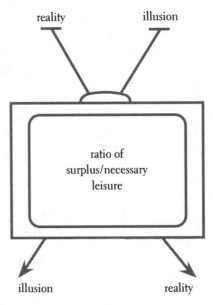

reality   illusion

ratio of
surplus/necessary
leisure

illusion   reality

Figure 2. Tele-value

capitalism's pretension to absorb all opposition and to upset our very sense of reality, Marx tries instead to distinguish the reality effects of the imaginary constructions governing capitalism's political economy, and thus to sketch for us the beginnings of a project for discerning the *specular functions* of capitalism's various media (cf. O'Neill 1991).

I shall not attempt here to pursue all of the empirical and theoretical issues implied in Marx's proto-postmodern invocation of the machinery of alienation and the society of the spectacle as displayed in Figure 2, although any such analysis would have to proceed from his sense of the historical and institutional presuppositions for the production and consumption of surplus value, as analyzed throughout the preceding discussion (and summarized in Table 3). Instead, I shall step back a bit from Marx writing in order to imagine what a minimelodrama of surplus-value-cum-tele-value might look like (perhaps as it would be projected onto Figure 2), notwithstanding the considerable suspension of disbelief this attempt will inevitably entail. Although such a drama might be viewed through any number of today's movies or sitcoms, it might also be seen to unfold in a concealed and uncanny way in one of Marx's favorite "little chefs d'oeuvre" by Balzac, a short story titled "Melmoth Reconciled," which Marx recommended to Engels the year he published *Capital* (Marx to Engels, 25 February 1867; see the epigraph to Part III).

In light of the science fictions Marx incorporated into his critique of political economy, the whole of Balzac's *Comédie humaine*, of which this little masterpiece is a part, may be viewed as a dramatization of, a critical commentary on, and indeed an example of, the principal "specular illusions" that both hide and reveal the inner workings of an emerging capitalist reality.

1. In the drama of *calculations*, the Balzacian search for an absolute value that cannot be quantified or exchanged typically centers on some noble or aesthetic ideal which is nevertheless compromised or extinguished by the baser instincts of the rising working and middle classes.

2. In the drama of *litigations*, the Balzacian ethical and political aporias are frequently played out through the structure of the *mise en abîme*, the staging of a scene within a scene or a story within other stories, that ultimately projects the inevitable submission to a fate.

3. And finally, in the drama of *machinations*, the famous Balzacian character system is constituted not as a syntagma of juxtapositions, diffusions, or contingent associations but as a paradigm of substitutions and exchanges, disappearances and reappearances, that continuously relativize the ratios between historical and fictional characters, and between fact and fiction itself.

In my own retelling of Balzac's story, I hope to display how Marx's conception of what I have called the science fictions that govern modern society may also be viewed as devices of allegorical realism operating within Balzac's *fictional science* of society. Insofar as this argument is convincing, then perhaps the anachronism of showing the postmodern specularization of values by way of a story depicting the spectacles of early capitalist life will at least appear more instructive, if not less ingenuous.

"Melmoth Reconciled" (1835) is constructed as a variation on the classic story of one man's pursuit of passion, power, wealth, and knowledge in exchange for his signature on an infernal contract that stipulates his eternal damnation when his days on earth are over. In this version of the tale, however, a deal has already been struck between the Devil and Melmoth before the story begins, and in this contract there is a special clause that allows someone else to replace the damned one, thereby permitting the latter to seek reconciliation with God. To use Marx's expression when recommending the story to Engels, a "delightful irony" (*köstliche Ironie*) resides in the way in which John Melmoth's replacement, M. Castanier the bank clerk, himself finds a replacement by going one step further than his predecessor, eventually selling the contract on the Paris Stock Exchange, where it is then repeatedly traded until it loses its value entirely.

Indeed, another kind of "costly" irony may also infect Marx's own "delight" in the irony of Balzac's story, in that the substitution for Melmoth by Castanier and the stock-exchange speculators may also be read within the problematic of

Marx's studies in political economy. Thus, by a "certain change in the physiognomy of our *dramatis personae*," Castanier may be seen to appear in the figure of Mr. Moneybags or Mr. Capitalist. Between Marx's text and that of Balzac there may be not just an apparently metaphorical reincarnation or metamorphosis, but also literally an exchange or replacement of the one by the other, so that where Marx becomes a kind of political economist of drama, Balzac becomes the dramaturge of political economy, each providing paradigmatic perspectives on the same science fiction of substitutions. By providing a character sketch, a scenic description, and a set of props for re-presenting the truth of modern reality through the medium of fictional melodrama, "Melmoth Reconciled" both enacts and substitutes for what we may understand to be a kind of *parable of allegorical realism* (cf. Jameson 1971a).

As part of his larger project to elaborate a "natural history of modern man" (Balzac 1956 [1842]), Balzac begins his story by sketching his own peculiar version of the naturalistic fiction of the bourgeois individual—not, however, in terms of Robinson Crusoe alone on his island but as a kind of natural "species" cultivated in the artificial "hothouse" of capitalist *Civilisation*:

There is a variety [*une nature*] of man which Civilization obtains in the social Kingdom as florists create in the vegetable Kingdom through cultivation in a greenhouse, a hybrid species which can be reproduced neither by seeds nor by grafting. This man is the cashier [*caissier*], a truly anthropomorphic product who is watered with religious ideas, maintained by the guillotine, pruned by vice, and who grows to a third stage between an estimable woman and an annoying child. (Balzac 1956 [1835]: 333)

M. Castanier, a less evolved specimen of this species, lives in his modest Paris apartment with his beautiful mistress Aquilina, an "inestimable" woman whom he has saved from a life of prostitution but whose expensive tastes and calculating greed have sunk our hero into the deepest debt (333). In spite of his advanced age and his service to the Legion of Honor, his honorary colonel's degree and his 2,400-franc pension, Castanier has not been granted "the third floor flat, the wife and kids, and all the sweet things of mediocrity" promised him by the modern social charter. Instead, he finds himself on the "debit" side of that "exact balance-sheet [*bilan*] of Talent and Virtue in their relations with the Government and Society," a so-called progressive civilization that "has replaced the principle of Honor with the principle of Money" (335). Trapped in "that city of temptations, that branch-plant of hell," Castanier is desperate to try anything to lift himself out the infernal agony of his current financial crisis.

The opening scene presents us with the image of the solitary Castanier after hours in the office of the bank where he works, studiously bent over his desk, apparently about to complete the balances of the accounts but in fact contemplating the unthinkable: to forge the bills of exchange of the reputable firm of Nucingen. Here Balzac introduces us to the first allegorical device he employs to provide an ironical perspective on the sinister workings of modern civilization. The ledger or *Grand Livre*, he tells us, has replaced the Bible as the primary social contract because it now serves as a bill of faith that guarantees the convertibility or realizability of the belief "that a little scrap of paper with an inscription can be worth an entire domain" (368). By the same token, the stock exchange or *Bourse* has replaced society's Royal Palace, just as the banks and other modern bureaucracies combine to form that "great factory of mediocrities necessary to governments in order to maintain *the feudalism of money* which supports the social contract of the present day" (336; my emphasis). The *Bourse* and the *Grand Livre* thus function as modern society's Universal Church and Book of Eternal Life, the latter providing a *précis de toutes les choses* and the former "a place where one approaches what kings are worth, where one weighs up people, where one judges systems, where governments are brought back to the measure of a hundred-cent shield, where ideas and beliefs are given numbers, where everything is counted, where God himself borrows and guarantees his revenues in souls, because the pope has his running account there" (366). Just at the moment when Castanier finally commits the desperate act he believes will redeem him from his debts, the strange Melmoth mysteriously appears out of nowhere to offer him his pact with the Devil as a substitute for the ultimate sin of counterfeiting the token of trust and bill of faith of the bank.

From here the scenes quickly change to form what comes to be Balzac's second allegorical device for revealing the ironic and demonic conventions of the modern social plot. First, the narrative leads backward in time to the history of Castanier's disastrous love affair with the traitorous and deceitful Aquilina, whom "he had resolved to save from vice to his own profit, by a thought as egotistical as charitable." Her predatory flight to the heights of Parisian society is mirrored by Castanier's swift descent into an "abyss [*abîme*] of debt" that "hurled a column of figures four at a time, when they should have gone innocently three at a time" (346, 342). This historical digression in the narrative brings us up to the day when the desperate Castanier decides in favor of "fraudulent bankruptcy over simple bankruptcy, crime over delinquency," having failed in his efforts to stay his economic woes through those financial maneuvers called *circulations*, those notes "which represent neither goods nor furnished pecuniary values, and which the first endorser pays for the subscriber, a kind of forgery tolerated because it is impossible to verify, and because this fantastic dole only becomes real in the event of a non-payment" (346).

Again the scenes change to yet another *mise en abîme*, this one bringing us beyond the present and into the future, itself played out through the scenes of a theatrical spectacle. When Aquilina and Castanier go to the theater that evening, now accompanied by the sinister Melmoth, our hero does not see *Le Comédien d'étampes* (The Stock-Character Comedian), starring the famous Perlet, as the other spectators do, but rather a five-act drama called *Le Caissier* (The Bank Clerk), starring Castanier himself. To his horror, the play recounts his employer's discovery of his act of forgery that afternoon, Castanier's own discovery that evening of Aquilina's infidelity, and his panicked flight to the border only to be caught by the police and sentenced before a tribunal to twenty years of forced labor. Melmoth's terrible laugh during this piece wrings Castanier's insides and tortures his head enough to make him agree to sign the diabolic pact, a decision whose overtones seem to ring in his ears like the distant strains of celestial music. Returning to the apartment, Castanier indeed discovers Aquilina's lover just as this scene was depicted to him in the play, although this time it is she and her lover who are condemned and banished by Castanier.

The final sequence of scenes in Balzac's story depicts how Melmoth, now relieved of his debt to the Devil, reconciles himself with God and dies in the good graces of the church. Meanwhile, in the course of his search for absolute omniscience and omnipotence, Castanier has found that "possession kills the most immense poems of desire, like those dreams the object of which only rarely responds." Panting breathlessly after "the *Unknown*, because he knows everything . . . seeing the principle and the mechanism of the world, he no longer admired its results, and soon manifested that profound disdain which makes the superior man similar to a sphinx who knows all, sees all, and keeps an immobile silence" (360). Not content with the prospects of possessing the riches, power, and knowledge of the world, and unable to muster enough force to hate and do evil, Castanier then grasps at his last hope for salvation: to find "a man who would submit to the clauses of this contract in order to exercise its advantages." Thus he asks Claperon, the speculator who has had a bad day at the stock market, whether the commerce in souls is "not a business like any other . . . for we are all shareholders in the great enterprise of eternity" (366–67). In this third allegorical device of Balzac's tragicomic epic of the "stock-exchange of the spirit" (Lukács 1950: 59–60), the stock market appears as an infinite substitution machine by means of which one can "traffic in souls as one does commerce in public funds," so that even the soul's salvation is turned into a commodity whose prices are quoted on the market, beginning with a swing toward an excess of supply. By the end of the trading day, the deed has changed hands so many times that "no one believed any more in this peculiar contract, and so purchasers were lacking for lack of faith" (Balzac 1956 [1835]: 369).

In a curious way, Balzac ultimately seems to have wanted his own story of

Melmoth to serve not only as an allegory about the contemporary metamorphosis of ideals and the "specularization" of social values, but also as a kind of
ironical joke on his superstitious German- and English-speaking literary rivals.
As he remarks in a prefatory note, "Melmoth Reconciled" is based on Charles
Maturin's episodic novel *Melmoth the Wanderer*, which in turn takes its inspiration from the same central image or *idée mère* that inspired Goethe's *Faust*
and Byron's *Manfred* (in Balzac 1956 [1835]: 325–26). These sources, along
with Thomas Otway's *Venice Preserved* and others from Balzac's own French
tradition, seem to be ironically commented upon and even subtly ridiculed
throughout the story: in his repeated references to John Melmoth's national
origins ("That man reeks of an Englishman," thinks the simple-minded Castanier when he first senses his presence in the bank [337]), in Castanier's
eventual replacement by a German clerk in Nucingen's bank, and finally, in
the story's cryptic final scene with the appearance of a "German demonologist" who quotes Jacob Böhme (a seventeenth-century visionary writer Balzac
admitted not being able to understand) and refers to Claude de Saint-Martin
(Böhme's French translator, nicknamed the "Unknown Philosopher").

After changing hands hundreds of times on the stock market, Melmoth's
fateful pact has finally come into the possession of a desperate notary clerk,
who spends twelve days of paradise with his beautiful mistress, "thinking of
nothing but love and its orgies which have drowned the memory of hell and
its privileges," only to have them end on the thirteenth day with his mysterious death from a drug overdose, "his dead body turned black like the back of
a mole":

—This estimable young man has been carried away to the planet of Mercury, said the
first clerk to a German demonologist who came to get information on the case.
—I'd willingly believe that, replied the German.
—Ah!
—Yes sir, said the German, that opinion agrees with the very words of Jacob Böhme,
in his forty-eighth proposition on the *Triple Life of Man*, where it is said that "if God
has operated all things by *Fiat*, *Fiat* is the secret matrix which comprehends and seizes
the nature which is formed by the spirit of both Mercury and God."
—That is to say, sir?
The German repeated his sentence.
—We're not familiar with it, said the clerks.
—*Fiat*? . . . said a clerk, *fiat lux*!
—You can convince yourselves of the truth of this reference, the German said, by
reading the sentence on page 75 of the Treatise on the *Triple Life of Man*, printed in
1809 by M. Migneret, and translated by a philosopher, who was a great admirer of the
illustrious shoemaker.
—Ah! he was a shoemaker, said the first clerk. Imagine that!
—In Prussia! replied the German.

—Did he work for the king?, said a boorish second clerk.

—He would have had to add printer's paste-ons to his sentences, said the third clerk.

—That man is pyramidal, cried the fourth clerk, gesturing to the German.

Although he was a first rate demonologist, the stranger did not know what mean devils clerks can be; he went away, understanding nothing of their jokes on him, and convinced that these young men found Böhme to be a pyramidal genius.

—There's education in France, he said to himself. (370–71)

The Black Madonna

Speculations on Aesthetics and
(Post)Marxism

I

The limits of Marxist—and of Marx's—thought are not reached when the materials and topics to which they were traditionally applied no longer hold our critical attention. The recent spectacles of collapsing Eastern bloc economies bidding frantically for a share in the world market, and of Western countries trying to continentalize their economies of welfare and warfare, are not enough to sound the death knell of Marxism or to invalidate the class analysis of these societies that derives from Marx. Instead, such recent historical events serve to displace the theory into new domains of relevance and research, thereby revaluing specific aspects of its analytical framework with respect to a new, transformed context. Marxism is not simply a theory of history, an investigation into the past stages of human development, and a projection of their future direction but also a thesis about the historicization of theory, an open framework that requires its own transformation when confronted with (apparently) new topics of application, political circumstances, and historical tendencies.

Today, when Marxists appear to be faced with both a crisis of relevance for lack of manifestly "objective" conditions for revolution, and a crisis of identity as their own critical science becomes either forgotten or assimilated into the established division of (academic) labor, there is a need to reach into domains quite beyond anything traditional Marxists, if not Marx himself, ever envisioned. In an attempt to gain critical perspective on the dramas played out in the latest stage of postindustrial capitalism, many now take a cultural turn away from the critique of political economy and toward a theory of aesthetics, away from matters that are identifiably economic or political and toward concerns that are manifestly literary or vaguely cultural. Properly understood, the task of this new phase of research is less to redraw the lines between material substructures and ideal superstructures, or to resituate the economic and cultural subsystems of society, than to work against and beyond these traditional analytical distinctions as a way of radically putting one's own habitual disciplinary and political commitments into question (Jameson 1991; O'Neill 1992).

We may treat the simultaneously competing and complementary perspectives of Marxist aesthetics and Marxist political economy as points of access to a single contradictory problematic. In part this is because aesthetics is already bounded by a certain economic logic and in part because political economy is already informed by a certain aesthetic, as I have argued in previous chapters. The orthodox version of the Marxist theory of culture and art has at least implicitly tended to alternate between the following two postulates (cf. Marcuse 1978: 1–21). First, art, including literature, music, and visual media, may be either more or less advanced than existing social relations and productive forces, and may therefore lag behind or anticipate the most progressive possibilities of society, at least in terms of the scope of its vision and the sophistication of its styles and techniques. This *postulate of realism* establishes a determinate relation in principle, if not in practice, between symbolic superstructures and socioeconomic substructures (cf. Chapter 4). And second, the arts mediate an actual relation between the artist-producer and the audience-consumer, as well as a potential relation between the contents of artistic productions and areas of experience outside their immediate spheres of application and influence. This *postulate of political ideology* draws attention to both the class-based situations, consciousness, or world outlooks of artistic productions and the utopian tendencies they prefigure (cf. Chapter 5).

Apart from their somewhat awkward formulation here, these postulates seem to falter to the extent that they not only are limited in specific ways but also presuppose one another in a circular fashion. Thus, the realist intentions of art are often thought to be a function of their political uses, as part of a strategy of realpolitik or in the service of state propaganda, for example, which in turn are believed to be grounded in the "ultimately determining instance" of socioeconomic relations and forces. By contrast, the political ideologies of artists may be challenged either directly or indirectly by movements of cultural subversion and rebellion that are presumed to operate closer to the level of material conditions. A Marxist theory of art thus seems to be condemned either to approach its topics of study as mute realities reducible to a "proven" stock of themes and contents, or to treat them delusionally as fetishes through which reality itself is believed to be captured and communicated through the media that represent it.

What is needed, then, is an understanding of artistic practices that does not deny the unreality of artistic creations or the antirealist intentions of artists, and that acknowledges the limits to the realization of their aesthetic aspirations and their desire to transcend existing social relations in the direction of an as yet unrealized reality. Such a task requires giving up the dream that aesthetics provides some "ultimate" disciplinary specialty (whether within or outside of Marxist research) in favor of a project that seeks to expand the realm of cultural aesthetics in order to restore its dimension of human protest, as Herbert Marcuse argued (also see note 3 to Part I and note 16 to Part III). By preserving a sense of the historical dialectic of repressive and liberating modes of sublimation and desublimation in art (Marcuse 1964: 56–83), and of the complicity of the negative and affirmative characters of culture (Marcuse 1968 [1937]), a Marxist aesthetic strives to discern the political auspices of art on the basis of the aesthetic dimension itself, and thus transcends the legacy of its realist and political orthodoxies (Marcuse 1955: 72–196; 1972: 79–128; 1978).

The elaboration of the aesthetic dimension of Marxism is an essential component of the latter's critical force and political appeal, as Marx implicitly asserts in a classic statement appended to the final section of the "Introduction" to his economic studies of 1857–58: "In the case of the arts, it is well known that certain periods of their flowering are all out of proportion to the general development of society, hence also to the material foundation, the skeletal structure, as it were, of its organization" (M: 110). Rather than give us a rule for interpreting how the arts are bound up with certain forms of social development at various stages of history, Marx goes on to compare the special case of an advanced art that is flourishing in a relatively undeveloped social structure, namely, that of the ancient Greeks (Shakespeare, too, is mentioned in this connection), with the opposite case of an industrially developed society whose art is relatively less advanced. Could a worldview dominated by such omnipotent beings as Vulcan, Jupiter, Hermes, and Fama find a place for the development of such mechanical wonders as self-acting mule spindles, railways, locomotives, and electric telegraphs? Indeed, why did the great inventive minds of the ancient world not apply their profound knowledge and imagination to utilitarian ends, to the development of tools that would alleviate the burdens of work and render it more efficient, or to the invention of machines that might ultimately have replaced the sphere of work altogether?

Marx does not sketch the expected answer to this question: that the ancient world was more interested in defending the sanctity of family life than in developing social relations and expanding productive forces. Nor does he advance the classical Marxist thesis that with their own interests at stake in maintaining the slave industry, the ruling classes ultimately repressed the urge to develop machinery. Instead, he entertains here what might be called the psychohistorical hypothesis that the narcissistic or mythological worldview of the ancient Greeks, by which they sought to overcome and shape the forces of nature through the powers of the imagination, ultimately exerted an inhibiting influence on the expansion of an alienated or technological worldview that was later to search for an instrumentally rational solution to the struggle between human beings and nature. The peculiar character of Greek mythology, as it was unconsciously accepted and modified by the popular imagination and drawn upon in developing the arts, seemed to prescribe an aesthetic and not a utilitarian direction to the advancement of productive techniques (cf. Sachs 1933).

Marx's protopsychoanalytic speculations on the delay of the machine age do not, however, end with this initial assertion of "no direct relation" between the arts and the general development of society. Rather, they take another turn in his consideration of what he calls "another side" of the problem: Are the ancient mythologies with their songs, sagas, and muses at all possible in the age of the printing press, the printer's machine, and the printer's bar? In the age of mechanical reproduction, has the work of art necessarily lost its irreducibly seductive value and its irreplaceable attraction, its enchanting inapproachability and its mythical aura, its cultic uniqueness and distance, "however close it may be" (Benjamin 1968)? Beyond the problem of determining the connection between aesthetic styles or techniques and the progress of science and technology (cf. Raphael 1980), Marx considers here what we might call the *communicative dimension* of ancient art, its capacity to project for us the beautiful image (*schöner Schein*) of another world that seems to transcend its social determination, or even to indict the given reality and strive to emancipate itself from the established universe of discourse and behavior. As Marx puts it, "The difficulty is that [the Greek arts] still afford us artistic pleasure and that in a certain respect they count as a norm and as an unattainable model"— indeed, as a standard (*Muster*) that remains constant in spite of the vicissitudes of history and changes in fashion.

Having glimpsed this "other side," Marx then makes a curious concluding statement, which is all the more surprising in that it entails extending his speculations beyond the critical theoretical framework of political economy and abandoning whatever scientific orthodoxy might have served him up to this point. Beyond his own conceptual model for analyzing the artistic productions and their material conditions, he goes on to speculate on the symbolic value of ancient art by apparently surrendering himself to its seductive charms (cf. Baudrillard 1979), contrasting the magic of the ancient worldview with the disenchantment of the modern outlook by way of that peculiarly German fascination with the modern myth of ancient Greece as the historic childhood of civilization:

A man cannot become a child again, or he becomes childish. But does he not find joy in the child's naiveté, and must he not himself strive to reproduce its truth at a higher stage? Does not the proper character of each epoch come alive in the natural truth of its children? Why should not the historic childhood of humanity, its most beautiful unfolding, as a stage never to return, exercise an eternal charm [*Reiz*]? There are unruly children and precocious children. Many of the old peoples belong to this category. The Greeks were normal children. The charm of their art for us is not in the contradiction to the undeveloped stage of society in which it grew. [It] is its result, rather, and is inextricably bound up, rather, with the fact that the unripe social conditions under which it arose, and could alone arise, can never return. (M 22: 111)

Clearly Marx is not primarily concerned here with synthesizing modern and ancient sciences and worldviews, as he is elsewhere in his work (McCarthy 1990; note 5 to Part II), that is, with incorporating the achievements of Greek thought into a modern theory of ethics and social ontology. Nor does he seem concerned here to acknowledge the specifically modern way of framing the "childishness" of the ancient mythological worldview, or of diagnosing the "narcissistic conflict" in the ancient psyche that limited the development of automated devices to the spheres of play and amusement, rather than in the direction of technical mastery and productive work. Instead, his desire in this concluding statement to his 1857 "Introduction" seems to be to relish this myth for what it might yield of what is permanent and pleasurable in art. To use Marcuse's words, his concern is with the potential in art to express a natural truth that is held fast to one's heart "not as a piece of property, not as a bit of unchangeable nature, but as a remembrance of life past: remembrance of a life between illusion and reality, falsehood and truth, joy and death" (Marcuse 1978: 23). The radical potential of the aesthetic dimension of critical thinking lies in its double aspect as both a seductive and alluring charm (*Reiz*) and a repulsive stimulus or irritation (*Reiz*) that presents the beautiful image of some other form of human existence which is both timelessly past and yet to be realized.

Here we reach the very limits of Marx's thought, if not the outer edges of Marxist theory as a whole, and yet at the same time the residues of something naive, unknown, or unconscious that may yet have moved it all along. If in this juxtaposition of Marxist political economy and aesthetics, each appears to be the other's limit case, this is not due to any privilege one has over the other. It is because the borderline of their meeting is the place where their domains are most radically called into question, and where an eternal charm or repulsive irritation upsets the principles previously assumed to hold each intact.

II

Marx's passage on the childhood of civilization seems to shed an uncanny illumination on the whole of his writing, and even to sound dissonant reverberations throughout the structure and genesis of his thought (cf. note 10 to Part III). As I argued in Chapters 4 and 5 (cf. note 8 to Part III), his theory of the material and ideological mechanisms of modern culture is not intended as a skeleton key or an interpretive grid for understanding primitive societies, and even less is it meant to serve as a map for locating the naiveté or childishness of such cultures. On the contrary, the study of ancient or less developed societies may in fact provide clues for diagnosing the "infantile disorders" of modern societies, including their fascination with primitive arts and rituals as well as their desire to study them scientifically or control them economically. Just as the ancient peoples may appear to us to have naively stood in awe of the uncanny, anthropomorphic movements of those automata they invented for their own entertainment, so have modern-day people exhibited a certain "tomfoolery" (*Narrheit*) in their confusion of capitalist production processes with the mechanical fiction of a perfectly automated society, or of the accumulation of capitalist wealth with the collection of dazzling treasures. This was also Balzac's insight when he so thoroughly studied "every shade of avarice, represent[ing] the old usurer Grobseck as being in his second childhood when he begins to create a hoard by piling up commodities" (C1: 735n; cf. Adorno 1991 [1965]). The derived and secondary character of capitalist childishness and infantile disorders thus exhibits a certain mysticism akin to what Marx elsewhere in *Capital* calls the "fetish-character" of commodities, the structural confusion of treating a social relation between persons as a relation between things, or the symbolic representative of something as the thing itself.

By arguing that modern commodities function as a kind of primitive fetish, Marx critically plays off the nineteenth-century European fascination and obsession with those so-called undeveloped, childish, and savage cultures that were the prime object of imperial expansion, as W. J. T. Mitchell has convincingly argued. Marx's aim is to present modern consciousness as structurally equivalent to what is most inimical to it, "primitive" consciousness. This is a strategic and rhetorical move by which "the figure of commodity fetishism (*der Fetisch-character der Ware*) [becomes] a kind of catachresis, a violent yoking of the most primitive, exotic, irrational and degraded objects of human value with the most modern, ordinary, rational and civilized" (Mitchell 1986: 191).

The radicality of this ambivalence is indicated by Marx through a pun on the two meanings of the word "character" that literally mark the two parameters of industrial society's cultural amnesia: first, the typographic-pictorial and hieroglyphic aspect of the fetishistic imprint as a written character that can be made by human hands and read by human eyes, and second, its figurative or even mystical aspect as an animated character or personification that has been endowed with life and expressive aura (Mitchell 1986: 190).

This understanding of the problem of modern fetishism is thus more subtle than one that tries to grasp an underlying reality hidden by seductive appearances (cf. note 6 to Part III), in that it draws our attention to the communicative relation between symbols and what they represent, and to the rhetorical appeal of things through the words and images they evoke. Beyond Marx's perspective, Mitchell is concerned to reconceptualize the fetish as a kind of hypericon, an image that is not just a particular sign for something but also a figure that symbolizes the process of figuration itself, a picture that allows us to reflect on ourselves as creators of our images and as created in the image of our creator, if not our creations (1986: 158–59).

The notion of ideology thus implies the need for an *iconological analysis*, that is, a theory of icons that can also account for the political uses of ideas. By putting into question the status of the theory as itself a mode of controlling or discerning images and figures, we can then explore the affinities and differences between the techniques of ancient iconoclasm, the Enlightenment battle with the "idols of the mind," and the Marxian critique of ideology. Plundered from Marx's theoretical treasure chest, the critical concept of the fetish may then be expanded, recontextualized, and connected to a new scheme of relevancies that includes the production of commodities as images (as in advertising), the commodification of the imagination (as in entertainment), and more generally, the specularization of all culture, "primitive" and "modern" alike. The problem, then, is to decipher the fetish character of hypericons not merely as stereotypes for decoding the concrete reality behind abstract and reified thought processes, but rather as dialectical images, that is, contested figures, or polyvalent emblems for reflecting on our collective predicament, as if in "a mirror of history and a window beyond it" (Mitchell 1986: 205).

Marx's thesis on the fetish character of commodities points in the direction of new areas of application while calling into question cultural and disciplinary boundaries between the modern sciences of the present and the artistic and religious practices of the past. In arriving at his later formulation of the concept of fetishism, Marx was likely drawing on his early investigations into specialist and often highly technical studies of ancient religious iconography that he had pursued while sketching his critique of the Hegelian philosophy of law in the early 1840s, while translating Aristotle's *De Anima*, and while revising his dissertation on the Epicurean and Democritean philosophies of nature. For example, in Charles de Brosses's study *On the Cult of the Fetish-gods* (1760; 1826 German translation from the French), Marx found a compelling comparison of the fetishistic rituals of the ancient Egyptians with those practiced by modern Africans, and discovered that even the coinage of the word "fetish" betrays a distinctly modern social history and institutional framework. "Invented through the European trade with Senegal, after the Portuguese word, *Fetisso*, that is, a bewitched, divine thing, from *fatum, fari*," the word also suggests such meanings as "to do or make" and shares the same root as such words as "factitious, artificial, or false" (De Brosses, quoted in Marx [1842] MEGA IV/ 1: 320; my translation).

A related study from which Marx copied longer passages was Benjamin Constant's treatise *On Religion* (1826, in French), which provides us with a kind of model for interpreting the modern implications of ancient fetishism in terms of the social "sources, forms, and development" of religion and as an institutional principle of social organization and political control:

> While a human society is formed, a celestial society is formed as well. The objects of worship compose a heaven, just as the worshippers compose a nation [*peuple*]. . . . By a similar necessity, the gods divide the power between themselves. The fetish, being the god of an isolated man, had to satisfy all the needs of its worshipper. All the fetishes thus had the same functions while the gods now have their distinct functions. . . . This revolution is in a way the pendant of the division of labor, which introduces the development of society among men. In the primitive state, each person alone provides for all needs. In civilized society, each is devoted to a circumscribed occupation, and provides in this respect not only for one's own needs, but for those of others as well. Likewise, in fetishism, the fetish is burdened with everything for a single person, while when nascent polytheism succeeds fetishism, each god is burdened with a single thing, but for everyone. . . . For the same reason, the gods then take distinctive denominations, while fetishes do not have particular names. (Constant, quoted in Marx [1842] MEGA IV/1: 350; my translation)

Constant is less concerned here simply to draw analogies between the production of thoughts and the operations of social reality, between the history of images and human history, or between mythology and sociology, than he is to conceptualize fetishism as a kind of social and ideological process and the fetish as a device for organizing social labors and powers. The historical shift from fetishistic individualism (one god and many jobs) to the polytheistic coordination of needs and occupations (one job and many gods) is viewed as both a succession of religious worldviews and a larger historical movement from the "primitivistic" rule by anonymous gods to a "civilized" regime of the production of functionally specific goods, each of which is marked with its own (brand) name.

Whatever the historical or anthropological accuracy of Constant's research, from Marx's perspective its value may derive from its potential use as a model of the fetishistic worldview as it was grounded in a socioeconomic system of class conflicts and power struggles, and governed through a social hierarchy of "enlightened" elites ruling over "superstitious" masses. Where the rulers seize upon "the power of the image [and] the authority of the symbol" as a language in an attempt to control what can and cannot be represented, the superstitious masses are kept in place through faith in their "gods" and "idols," "simulacra which move and cry, speak and predict" (Constant, quoted by Marx [1842] *MEGA* IV/1: 354). Thus, at stake in this struggle is not simply the content of religious art and ritual but also the distribution of power and wealth, and thus the maintenance of social order: "These gods, which would undergo no changes while everything was changing around them, seemed to defy time by their ancient exteriors" (Constant, quoted by Marx [1842] *MEGA* IV/1: 360). In general, then, the metaphysical, mystical, and basically affirmative character of fetish culture functions to ensure the maintenance of and provide the testing ground for the organization of wealth, the distribution of power, and the control over knowledge.

The fetishistic character of religious iconography in particular was explored in more detail by Marx through his readings on the moral philosophy of the church fathers, the figural painting and sculpture of the ancient Greeks, and especially Karl Friedrich von Rumohr's *Italian Investigations* (1827, in German). The latter study presents a discussion of what I shall take to be the exemplary figure of fetishism for Marx (for reasons to be developed here and in the following sections), and what Mitchell might call a hypericon. In a passage Marx copied from Rumohr's book, his image of the childhood of ancient civilization seems to be both represented and completed by a mysterious cultic figure of mythical plenitude:

The old wooden idols that Pausanias attacked, the black Madonnas, especially in the barbaric countries of Christianity where the unmediated presence of the divinities is believed in and honored, are and always were nothing *less than genuine and developed works of art [wirkliche und ausgebildete Kunstwerke]*. By contrast, ancient art appears to be replete with humanity and accessibility, even to the masses insofar as they have achieved life and development, and also to have repelled that attack on polytheistic superstition whose loss was so lamented by so many political moralists of antiquity (Rumohr, quoted by Marx [1842] in *MEGA* IV/1: 294; my translation)

Like Constant and other scholars of the time, Rumohr trades on a two-stage theory of historico-religious change from a barbaric and pagan era characterized by the worship of fetishes to the mythological worldview of the ancients, which attained a high degree of human culture in spite of its polytheistic superstitions. In this account, however, a further complication is introduced in that the Greek geographer Pausanias's scorn for the fetish cults is itself superseded by the attack on ancient polytheistic superstition, and yet both the Black Madonna idols and ancient art are shown to have survived: the former through a belief in the unmediated presence of the deity, and the latter because of its humanity and accessibility. Added to this is Rumohr's remarkable defense of the Black Madonnas as genuine and even sophisticated (*ausgebildete*) works of art in terms usually reserved for the great achievements of ancient Greece. Thus the question becomes how and why the artworks (*Kunstwerke*) from pagan times and antiquity continued to attract such fascination so long after the periods in which they were produced, not just at the dawn of the Christian era but into the nineteenth and twentieth centuries as well. Might the seductive charms of the Black Madonnas even be the result of or enhanced by their inaccessibility and divinity, just as we earlier saw Marx charmed by the undeveloped character and humanity of ancient art?

Much of the literature on the Black Madonnas has been concerned with just such questions, and in particular with how the fascination they continue to draw persists within various stages of history and through various cultural differences. These figures thus bear the traces of an occult history and a kind of heretical Gnostic underground within the official institutions of Christianity, either subverting them or providing them with hidden sources of legitimation (Begg 1985). The double aspect of the Black Madonna figures as both seductive charms and repulsive objects betrays a fundamental ambivalence already latent in the Christian tradition itself, as in the folklore of "wise prostitutes," from the whore of Babylon of the Old Testament to the cult of Mary Magdalene and St. Mary of Egypt in the early Christian era (Quispel 1979). Similarly, such figures may also have served to combine and transform Christian and pagan traditions of the great *Maiestas* or *Sedes Sapientiae*, from the ancient Egyptian myth of Isis, the goddess of wisdom and fertility, to the Christian cult of Mary the mother of God seated on the Throne of Majesty (Eagle 1975). Investigations into the origins and persistence of the Black Madonna cults have thus exposed a cultural history that blends their mysterious and even heretical qualities with an existing class structure of elites and masses and a racially and sexually divided cultural system. Thus, pagan customs like goddess worship are reinterpreted or revalued as they become integrated into rituals of worship practiced in other social and historical contexts. This happens through a process of cultural syncretism by which ethnic identities and sexual differences are not simply obliterated but displaced from their traditional frameworks of meaning into new value spheres and social practices (Moss and Cappanari 1982).

Not only do competing strains of religious history often coexist and overlap, but certain of these layers sometimes provide unintended cultural legitimation for economic expansion, political change, and other secularizing processes, as Max Weber demonstrated in his famous studies of the unevenness of cultural transmission (Weber 1930). Perhaps a similar intuition motivated Goethe to depict a peculiarly anachronistic vision of a Catholic heaven in the final scene of *Faust*, in stark contrast to the immediately preceding narrative of the drama that represents the development of Faust's industrializing projects on a global scale. Legend has it that Goethe modeled this final scene in the "high mountain gorges" of heaven after a description from one of Alexander von Humboldt's travel books of the great cliffs of Montserrat, within which is sheltered one of the most famous and revered of the Black Madonnas (a sight a friend and I could also not fail to be impressed by; see Figure 3).

Presumably, then, some notion of the history of this figure would have been the source of Goethe's inspiration for having the Mater Gloriosa appear to Faust next to Maria Aegyptica (St. Mary of Egypt), along with a heavenly host of other celestial figures. Placing Goethe's aesthetic intuition in the context of the theoretical framework developed by Marx, we might consider whether this example of the Black Madonna phenomenon is also in some way exemplary of how cultural and economic development proceeds unevenly, or at least how ancient artifacts continue to exert a certain charm long after the world that produced them has passed into history. That is, we might speculate on whether this figure may provide a kind of figurative standard or index, an "umbilical chord or gravitational anchor," for marking how the consistency of symbolic systems is institutionalized, or even incited on to new levels of cultural and material transformation (cf. Goux 1990: 114).

What the photograph reproduced here depicts, and what neither Humboldt, nor Goethe, nor Rumohr mentions, is that the Black Madonna holds a child for whom she serves as a kind of *Sedes Sapientiae*, not unlike the one upon which she herself is seated. This ancient figure of the Black Madonna and Child may thus have certain affinities not just with Marx's critical discourse on modern fetishism but also with his reflections on the ancient childhood of civilization that he inserted into his historical introduction to the critique of political economy. Put another way, this figure may be read as providing a kind of *matrix figure* that structures Marx's general conceptualization of the relations between images and things, and between things and social practices. As such, it may be interpretively "revalued" in terms of historical contexts very different from those for which it was originally intended (cf. Figures 1 and 2).

Perhaps the sketch of such a project may already have been drawn for us by Marx in his comment at the end of the "Chapter on Money" of 1857, where he invokes a monstrous vision of capital through the notorious image of the Behemoth, the scarlet beast on which rides the dark-skinned woman of the

Figure 3. The Black Madonna of Montserrat. Photograph by Raimon Camprubì, in d'Osvald Cardona, *Montserrat* (Barcelona: Ediciones Destino, 1977), courtesy Editiones Destino.

wilderness: " 'These have one mind, and shall give their power and strength unto the beast' [Revelation 17:13]; 'And that no man might buy or sell, save he had the mark, or the name of the beast, or the number of his name' (Apocalypse, Vulgate) [Revelation 13:17]" (II: 237; from the Latin). In a curious twist on the history of ancient peoples as interpreted by Constant and Rumohr, Marx may have figured some part of his own critique of modern capitalism through the uncanny image of the civilized child to whom this pregnant wild woman, carried into the desert by a mysteriously marked beast, would one day give birth.

III

As Marx himself might put the matter at this point, looked at from "another side," the real difficulty here may lie not in determining whether a certain ancient fetish may find new expression in later periods of social and material development, but rather in why such figures as the Black Madonna continue to exude a certain charm, why they "still afford artistic pleasure," inspire awe and reverence, or even present us with "a norm and unattainable model." Part of the reason would seem to be that "the unripe social conditions under which it appeared and could alone appear, can never return" (M: 111), and thus that the Black Madonna may gain in mythical importance the more inaccessible she is. But since such a figure by no means appeals to all people living in different historical and cultural contexts, part of the reason may also reside in more properly aesthetic, as well as personal and psychological, domains of reflection. Thus, it may not be surprising to find the Black Madonna reemerging in a few lines Marx penned to his wife, Jenny, just a year before writing the passage on the "eternal charm" and the "most beautiful unfolding" of the "historic childhood of humanity." He declares that only now does he share Rumohr's fascination with these curious images:

My darling Sweetheart,

I am writing to you again because I am alone and because it is irksome to converse with you all the time in my head without you knowing or hearing or being able to answer me. Bad as your portrait is, it serves its end well enough, and I now understand how it is that even the least flattering portraits of the mother of God, the "Black Madonnas," could have their inveterate admirers—more admirers, indeed than the good portraits. At any rate none of these "Black Madonna" images has ever been so much kissed and ogled and adored as your photograph which, while admittedly not black, has a crabbed expression and in no way reflects your dear lovely, kissable, *dolce* countenance. But I put right what the sun's rays have wrongly depicted, discovering that my eyes, spoiled though they are by lamplight and tobacco smoke, can nevertheless paint not only in the dreaming but also in the waking state. There you are before me, large as life, and I lift you up in my arms and I kiss you all over from top to toe, and I fall on my knees before you and cry: "Madame, I love you." (Marx to Jenny, 21 June 1856 MEGA III/8; CW 40)

The significance of such a personal note for us is by no means exhausted by its psychobiographical place in the course of Marx's development as a person in view of what we might recover here of the aesthetic dimensions of his critical theory. Thus, only as a side note will an attempt be made here to document a case for incorporating the "personality system" into Marx's model of the cultural, economic, and political systems of society, especially insofar as we preserve a biographical perspective from within our sense of Marx's sociological imagination (cf. note 2 to Part II and notes 7 and 20 to Part III). What theoretical sense, then, can we make of this expression of an intensely personal and thoroughly pathetic contradiction between Marx's public life and private self, between his aesthetic sensibilities and his scientific rigor (Moss and Cappanari 1982: 72n; Spivak 1984: 35–36)?

I shall suggest that the new dimension glimpsed in these rapturous passages, when placed in the context of Marx's writings as a whole, and of the passage on art and modern society in particular, is a sense of that remembrance of things past and that *promesse de bonheur* which Marx sought in the aesthetic form, and which constitutes an essential source of his ethical and scientific project. Not only may we locate this intensely personal love letter at the very heart of Marx's theoretical and political problematic, but we may also treat its literary and rhetorical features through the techniques of an aesthetic analysis. This approach avoids the seductive traps of psychological reductionism or, as Freud himself might argue, the error of explaining not just the spheres of culture and politics, but also the psychological domain itself, solely in terms of individual and personal experience. At the same time, it provides a means for reformulating the problem of the relations between biography and theory, as well as between art and society, as they are implicitly developed through Marx's analytical project.

To begin with, Marx's letter confronts us with the multiple ironies and fragmentary contradictions that are characteristic of the *lover's discourse*, that rapturous flow of words and emotions whose vicissitudes are largely at the mercy of the presence or absence of the loved one, as Barthes has formulated it (1978 [1977]). By writing while contemplating his wife's picture, Marx implicates this discourse in what Barthes also calls the *photographic paradox*, that is, the perception of a presence through a medium that nevertheless seems to be immediate and continuous with the thing it re-presents "analogically" in its absence (Barthes 1977 [1961]). Specifically, then, the discursive ritual of

Marx's love letter, "all this rhetoric all of a sudden," as he reflects further on with some embarrassment, has been provoked by the circumstance that Jenny has been away for some time, in Trier with her dying mother ("I have been banished from you" [or "by you," as is suggested in a pun on the German *von*], he says), and so he evokes her elusive presence through the rapturous flow of words from his pen and through a melancholic gaze at her photograph.

Both actions are caught in a kind of structural paradox by which their subject somehow communicates a *message without a code* in the intensely personal and immediate significance of Jenny for Karl, but by means of the *coded message* needed to communicate this immediacy, that is, through the techniques of photography and letter writing. The "ineffability" of Jenny's almost pure and unmediated presence, as evoked by the photographic message, thus seems to be repeated and amplified in the love letter itself, which already tends to play out an agonizing game of hide-and-seek complicated by the distortions of proximity and distance: "Temporary absence is good, for in a person's presence things look too much alike for them to be distinguished." Consoling himself with Jenny's imaginary presence in the photograph, Marx rationalizes her absence by imagining the distance between them to yield clarity of perception and a gain of perspective.

Before further specifying some of the implications of this paradox of image and text and this mixture of denotation and connotation, we should note how this particular love letter also suggests its generic affinity with the love poem. Although as a young man Marx had written his own exuberant book of love songs to Jenny (CW 1), here he more tentatively, modestly, and even mournfully asserts that "I could, indeed, even frame verse, German *Books of Sorrow* after the manner of Ovid's *Libri Tristium*" (Marx to Jenny, 21 June 1856). At the very climax of the amorous exhortations cited above, he quotes a line from his friend Heinrich Heine's *Book of Songs*: "Madame, ich liebe Sie!" A look at the poem in which this line appears, "Die Heimkehr" (The Homecoming), and specifically the three sections immediately preceding this line, reveals that nearly all of Marx's letter draws heavily in both form and theme from Heine's verse. Indeed, the poetic expression of details and declarations in the letter might even be captured in Heine's musical rhythms and sentimental words:

26.
I stood and stared at her portrait
    With fixed and dreamy pain,
And the well-loved face most strangely,
    Began to live again.

About her lips was playing
    The wonder of her smile;

And with tears of love and yearning
    Her eyes were bright the while.

My tears began to gather,
    And down my cheeks flowed free.
And oh! I cannot yet believe
    That thou art lost to me.

27.

Ah me, ill-fated Atlas! who must bear
A world, a world of sorrow on my shoulders.
Bear the unbearable the while my heart
Is perishing within me.

O haughty heart, yet thou has chosen so.
Demanding happiness, yes, bliss unending,
Or else unending sorrow. Haughty heart,
And now thy fate is sorrow.

28.

The years are coming and going,
    Generations sleep 'neath the grass,
But the love that burns within me
    Will surely never pass.

Once more would I behold thee,
    And as on my knee I fell,
With my last breath would I tell thee,
    "Madame, I love you well."
        (Heine 1904 [1827]: 148–49; cf. 1960 [1827]: 93–94)

Like Heine's poem, Marx's letter is as much an expression of his love for Jenny as a lament for the loss of things and persons that have touched each of them personally. In mulling over Jenny's portrait he is not only struck with its "uncanny" (*heimliche*) animation and reminded of their happy times together, but also reads in her "sweet countenance . . . my infinite sorrows, my irreplaceable losses" (Marx to Jenny, 21 June 1856), perhaps remembering those "generations who have silently fallen to their graves" in the deaths of three of their children. In a more general sense, Heine's very personal and sentimental poetry seems to represent for Marx, as perhaps for many Germans, a gaping wound in the soul that is the mark of our collective homelessness: "If all expression is the trace left by suffering, then Heine was able to cast his own inadequacy, the muteness of his language, as an expression of rupture" (Adorno 1991 [1956]: 83).

The rest of the letter seems to attest that Marx himself identified with that "ill-fated Atlas" whose destiny was to carry the heavy burdens of the world on his shoulders as his own personal sorrow, and whose lament is presented by Heine in a stanza rendered entirely in prose. Immediately after invoking his own "infinite sorrows," Marx bravely and abruptly concludes his letter with "some facts" bringing Mrs. Marx up to date on the progress of his interminable work, specifically concerning the scandalous events following the Cologne communist conspiracy trial several years earlier, to which Marx had already published his response (Marx 1853a; cf. note 1 to Part III). And yet such prosaic "facts" do not mute the longings of a disciplined but "haughty heart" that continues to demand "happiness, yes, bliss unending / Or else unending sorrow."

Even with Heine's poem to guide us, and several black-and-white photographs of Jenny Marx available in most Marx biographies, both the photographic and the amorous message communicated through the poem and the letter still seem to elude us. A Freudian diagnosis might respond to this apparent inaccessibility by interpreting the projection of the lover's life powers into the object of adoration as a symptom of his symbolic castration and feminization (Freud 1977 [1927]; cf. note 8 to Part III). A "Marxian" reading might add that the sexual frustrations implicit here are also produced from a fatigue wrought by commercial seductions and obsessive overwork (cf. Mitchell 1986: 194–95). Alternatively, the fetishistic perversity expressed in the letter may be read through Marx's own weakened eyes, which he describes as "spoiled . . . by lamplight and tobacco smoke," a description that projects a kind of screen distorting his vision and allowing him to imagine things that are not really "there." From here our attention may then be drawn to the set of connotational systems inscribed in the coded techniques of photography that Marx invokes in his references to the faded image of Jenny's "portrait," "the sun's rays," and her "crabbed expression." These traces of the artifice employed in the mechanical art of photography, its use of light and chemicals, and its techniques of posing and framing, for example, reveal that only an imperfect likeness has been achieved, a flat, black-and-white impression that could never fully make present Jenny's own "lovely, kissable, *dolce* face" except through compensatory fantasies of Marx's wild imagination. Whether through a technical, literary, or poetic scheme of interpretation, Jenny's unmediated presence can be invoked or emoted, contemplated or deciphered only from a distance, or else conjured up in his own mind as an animated character.

For lack of this photographic clarity, the almost auratic or cultic value of Jenny's image is reexpressed by Marx through an analogy with the Black Madonna "portraits" in a way that implicates a modern technology with the fantastic realism of a primitive form of fetishism. That is, the barbaric fascination before an "unmediated presence" now seems to be the property of the rhetorical scheme of photographic idolatry as well. Thus, by means of Marx's apparently arbitrary and purely aesthetic or technical allusions, the ideology of photographic realism here implies a certain iconology that has affinities with the general problematic of fetishism. The peculiar charm of the Black Madonna in particular thus resonates not just with certain personal sentiments and even obsessions, but also within a broader complex of cultural and historical meanings.

IV

Marx's initially passive contemplation of Jenny's portrait is itself framed and then dramatized into a scene he imagines being acted out by both of them: "My eyes may nevertheless paint not only in the dreaming state but also in the waking state." Where in the preceding line photography had been deemed an inadequate medium for representing Jenny, through a kind of imaginary painting her image here seems literally to come to life. Not only does Marx compare the photograph with those Black Madonna portraits, but he also suggests that by "painting" with his tired eyes he might be able to "do better" than the combination of the natural light of the sun with the artificial techniques of modern photography. This older aesthetic medium allows his Pygmalian imagination to create a kind of *tableau vivant* in which the figure of Jenny seems to emerge from the picture's cramped frame, just as Frenhofer in Balzac's story believes that his *Belle Noiseuse* might step out from the surface of his painting (and also compares his beloved to a kind of Black Madonna in the figure of St. Mary of Egypt; Balzac 1956 [1831]: 478).

In the continuation of the passage quoted above, not only are photography and religious iconography, love poetry, and imaginary painting juxtaposed through Marx's ecstatic vision, but they are ultimately blended together through a dramatic frame and a theatrical script:

And love you I do, with a love greater than was ever felt by the Moor of Venice. Falsely and foully doth the false and foul world of all characters construe. Who of my many calumniators and venomous-tongued enemies has ever reproached me with having a calling to play the romantic lead in a second-rate theatre? And yet it is true. Had the scoundrels possessed the wit [Witz], they would have depicted "the productive and commercial relations" on one side and, on the other, myself at your feet. Beneath it they would have written: LOOK TO THIS PICTURE AND TO THAT. But stupid the scoundrels are and stupid they will remain, *in seculum seculorum*. (Marx to Jenny, 21 June 1856 MEGA III/8; CW 40)

Here we become spectators to a kind of dramatic reversal of the relative values of image and text presented in the immediately preceding lines of the letter. To borrow from Barthes's words once again, at this point "it is not the image which comes to elucidate or realize the text, but the latter which comes to sublimate, patheticize, or rationalize the image" (1977 [1961]: 25). Beyond the poetic song of the love letter and the imagined animation of the photograph, the language of the text itself acts to amplify and magnify the image and even to direct it as a dramatic form. The reversal of values is indicated here by the caption that Marx proposes for the tableau he has painted with his mind's eye and that is itself a mixture of image and text. That is, he imagines his own work in political economy—his studies of "the relations of commerce and production"—to be juxtaposed with a romantic love scene between him and Jenny—in the image of "myself at your feet."

These pictures and scenes in turn are framed in a polemical and self-deprecatory way through the caption that here functions as a gibe those scoundrels who are his "many calumniators and venomous-tongued enemies" could use against him had they enough wit or sense of humor to see the joke in it. In general terms, the ironies of the lover's discourse and the photographic paradox here coincide with a certain ethical dilemma at the very heart of Marx's political and scientific commitments. Just when he seemed to want an objective copy or at least an aesthetically neutral and immediate image of Jenny, he employs an analogical procedure in which is implicated his own ideological and scientific investment of values, which thereby put up a resistance or mount an attack against opposing views (cf. Barthes 1977 [1961]: 20). A higher-order realism of loveliness and loneliness emerges here as Marx defends a sphere of happiness and freedom against the harsher realisms of science, religion, and politics: "love, not for Feuerbachian Man, not for Moleschottian metabolism, not for the proletariat, but love for a sweetheart and notably for yourself, turns a man back into a man again . . . let the Brahmins and Pythagoras keep their doctrine of rebirth, and Christianity its doctrine of resurrection" (Marx to Jenny, 21 June 1856).

This romantic love scene is polemically and ideologically contextualized not just by targeting objects of attack but above all by being dramatically framed or staged by way of an analogy with theater, as well as in the very performance of his own writing. By comparing his love for Jenny with the jealous and tragic devotion of Othello (the Moor of Venice) for Desdemona (who also takes a long journey away from her lover), Marx provides a dramatic context and narrative structure for the scene of his rapturous musings over his wife's photograph. This connection is mirrored in the association of the black Othello with the Black Madonna, and is highlighted by the fact that Marx's own dark complexion earned him the nickname "Moor" among his wife, his daughters, and his closest friends. Beyond even this metaphorical dramatization, his love for Jenny is literally "acted out" as a role and performed through his own writing when in the caption to his own self-parody he recites a quotation from the bedroom scene in *Hamlet* (act III, scene 4): accusing his mother of complicity in the rotten turn of events in the royal castle, Prince Hamlet exhorts her to "Look to this picture and to that," the one of his traitorous uncle who is about to marry her, and the other of his father, the dead king whose murder at the hands of his brother provokes the prince's vengeance. In Marx's ironic rewriting of the script, his own "venomous-tongued enemies" seem to have taken on the role of the conscience-ridden Hamlet stirring up a family feud, with Marx playing the role of the uncle jealously guarding his right to love the queen. Like Hamlet, who stages his own little play as "the thing wherein I'll catch the conscience of the King" (his uncle), these scoundrels serve as the playwrights and directors of a "second-rate theatre" in which Marx himself or a character like him would play the "romantic lead," and yet it is Marx himself who here directs not only the actors but also the playwrights.

These polemical and performative dimensions of Marx's writing forge a connection between his private and public life and place them within a distinctly dramatic context or even melodramatic frame of interpretation that implicitly draws not just from literary and other aesthetic sources but from scientific and political ones as well. To consider the broader issues involved there, we may return to Marx's passage on Greek art and modern society, or rather, simply to the mention in it that a similar inquiry might be pursued with respect to Shakespeare and modern society (M: 110). The theme is elaborated not in the 1857 "Introduction," however, but in 1859, in a letter to Marx's sometimes friend and fellow revolutionary, Ferdinand Lassalle.

Here Marx begins by praising Lassalle's recent play, *Franz von Sickingen*, for the emotional effect produced by its composition and action, but then criticizes its political naiveté less for historical reasons than for his inadequacies as a dramatist. The weakness in Lassalle's theatrical representation of the unsuccessful nobles' revolt during the Reformation resides in the way that the title character puts up only a "knightly" fight against the princes and feudal lords, thus making him "in reality only a Don Quixote, even though a historically justified one" (Marx to Lassalle, 19 April 1859; cf. note 22 to Part III). Sickingen failed because "as a *knight* and as a *representative of a declining class* he rebelled against what already existed, or rather, against its new form," in contrast to the peasants, who represent a *rising class* which at that time bore the hopes for the emergence of a new social order (soon to be dashed in the Peasants' War of 1524–25). Nevertheless, it is not upon this orthodox position that Marx ultimately rests his case against the emotional appeal and political relevance of Lassalle's play, but rather on an aesthetic judgment favoring Shakespeare over Friedrich Schiller:

The *noble* representatives [*Repräsentanten*] of the revolution . . . should not have absorbed all interest . . . , but the representatives [*Vertreten*] of the peasants (particularly they) and the revolutionary elements in the cities should have formed a significantly important active background . . . [thus giving] voice to the most modern ideas in their most naive form. . . . You yourself would then have had to *Shakespearize* more, while I chalk up [*anrechne*] against you, as your most important shortcoming, your *Schillering*, that is, your transforming of individuals into mere speaking tubes of the spirit of the times [*Sprachröhren des Zeitgeists*]. (Marx to Lassalle, 19 April 1859)

Marx prefers the "naive viewpoints" presented in the plays of Shakespeare over the "exaggerated reflections of individuals on themselves" that characterize the plays of Schiller. But in doing so, he is not expressing his personal taste or claiming superior literary knowledge as much as he is invoking an *interpretive scheme of representation* for making sense of dramatic situations in which revolutionary potentialities are depicted in refined as well as ordinary ways. The parameters of this scheme are marked by contrasting the meanings of the word *Repräsentanten*, which connotes a pictorial or theatrical "representation" (here used in connection with the role of the nobles), with *Vertreten*, which suggests a political or legal "representation" (here used in connection with the role of the peasants). Thus, in Marx's dramatic theory, the political and theatrical meanings of the act of representation are combined in a way that requires the political significance of dramatic roles to be established not just on political grounds but especially within their own aesthetic dimension.

In a similar way, then, we may interpret Marx's own Shakespearean "performance" in his letter to Jenny in terms of its political as well as its aesthetic significance, and thus within his interpretive framework of "representation" as a whole, rather than just in terms of his personal tastes or ideological opinions. In other words, rather than read his romantic lines in a "Schillering" way, as the "exaggerated reflections of an individual on himself," we should "Shakespearize" them more, that is, approach them as "the most naive expressions which nevertheless give voice to the most modern ideas." Ironically, then, this means that the political implications of his writing are enhanced not when we cast him as the revolutionary Robin Hood–like character of Karl Moor in Schiller's play *The Robbers* (cf. Seigel 1978: 78–83), but rather, according to Marx's own suggestion, as the amorous and even delusional "Moor of Venice" in Shakespeare's *Othello*. This may be how his otherwise private and personal love letter may reverberate profoundly with his other scientific and political studies, which would then reach us not as "mere speaking tubes of the spirit of the times," trapped in their own historical world, but rather as vocalizing the most modern ideas, methods, and themes that we are only now beginning to come to terms with. Marx's role as a lover also enacts a desire for revolutionary activity and critical thought, caught as it is in a movement of history that is articulated through the content and form of his aesthetic theory and scientific insights (cf. Jameson 1971b: 191–95). Thus, it seems all the more incommensurable to us as we "look to this picture and to that."

My strategy here has been to present Marx's own words beyond the personal and historical bounds of the people and times to which they were first addressed—indeed, as a voice that often makes sense only in the context of the most modern or even postmodern practices and intellectual fashions. Thus, when others heap their scorn on or show indifference to Marx's aesthetic theory or critique of political economy, they may only be repeating the joke he himself imagined his "calumniators and venomous-tongued enemies" would play on him if they were to place his scientific works beside a pathetic picture of him at the feet of his wife. Perhaps by placing my own chapter that contains the photograph of the Black Madonna next to and after the chapter discussing Marx's critique of political economy, I, too, have risked a compromising and even embarrassing image of my project here, although in the spirit of Marx's passage on ancient Greek art that he juxtaposes to his discussion on modern economic categories.

Rather than deploy an established stock of aesthetic themes, scientific categories, and political ideologies, I have tried to amplify the communicative dimensions of Marx's writing by making them resonate with my own. Perhaps, then, his writing finds a place in current debates not just because his "theory" has kept up with our history but because we may read in it the trace of some ineffable if irresistible charm that somehow both attracts and repels us. His life and writing may still provide us with a standard, a norm, or even an unattainable model because we find ourselves in much the same relation to Marx as he imagined himself to be with respect to the ancients. This may be why, after reading Marx, we still seem to be left with a melancholic feeling evoked from his humanist vision of the present, and with the quaint ring of his socialist song of the future.

V

Having apparently reached a neat conclusion to these still open speculations on Marx's aesthetics in particular and a (post)Marxist theory of art in general, I still find something more to be said, a supplementary and perhaps excessive comment that seems impossible for me not to bring forward. Perhaps this impulse derives from a sense that the Shakespearean image of Marx evoked above is not entirely convincing, that it might only eclipse the scientific and political vision he fought so hard to achieve, or that our picture of Marx still needs some finishing touch to make it complete.

In the discussion above, I have implicitly drawn from the themes of a certain *family romance*, as if Marx's own enchantment with the charms of the "childhood of humanity" could be complemented by his fascination with the ancient pagan figure of the Black Madonna. What remains to be drawn, then, would be a portrait of the ancestral father in this scene, perhaps even a character sketch of Marx himself in terms that are as exalted and tragic as the "Moor" of Schiller or Shakespeare, or that blend scientific scholarship (*Rumohr*) with mythical fancy (*rumor*) but also project a more ordinary and subdued image of Marx (*ruh' Mohr*) than we might otherwise expect. The risk here is not that we might transgress a sacred taboo against approaching the holy relics of Saint Marx too closely, but on the contrary that we might domesticate, and thus damage, the radical potential of his scientific and political legacy, turning "Marxist theory" into "family research" (Marcuse 1978: 19). Taking this more personal and intimate approach seems to submit to the politically repressive rule of the symbolic father and to an antiquated image of the holy family that thereby sublimates the Marxian concept of alienation (*Entfremdung*) into Weberian disenchantment (*Entzauberung*) and Freudian malaise (*Unbehagen*), perhaps even exhausting the desire for social criticism and revolution in favor of merely individual transformation and psychological renewal.[27]

In spite of these misgivings, I shall consider here another role that may have been Marx's calling to play and that may be even more embarrassing and compromising for him. Along with his "romantic lead in a second-rate theatre," which he acts opposite his wife, he may also be seen to have acted the part of a failed father, indeed, a kind of paternal *faiseur* who unsuccessfully tries to pretend or "make do" for his family, but is ultimately exposed as a charlatan and a quack. In a letter to Engels written just a month after stopping work on his 1857–58 notebooks, Marx paints a graphic picture of his family's desperate financial straits, and even presents the details in the form of a personal account or ledger of his household expenses. He provides these details to Engels, he says, not in order to make "an APPEAL to the already indecent claims on your purse," but so that his friend can "come to a correct decision about THE CASE," although he gives no indication as to what sentence he might expect from his friend's "judgment" (Marx to Engels, 15 July 1858). With the family's modest expenditures already exceeding both the money Engels has sent them and the small fees he receives from the *New York Daily Tribune*, Marx is faced with an impossible dilemma: while tradesmen continue to extend credit to him, creditors press him to pay debts on which interest continues to accumulate, and a landlord, himself hounded by creditors, demands his overdue rent. At the same time, his wife's miserable health and his own utter exhaustion after a winter of hard study project for him "the spectre of an unavoidable final catastrophe" and a scenario that "must end in the ruin of everything":

If I should take the step of reducing expenses to an extreme—for example, take the children out of school, move into purely proletarian quarters, dismiss the maids, live on potatoes—even the auctioning off of my furniture and chattels would not bring enough to satisfy even the neighboring creditors so that I could slip away unhindered into some hiding place. The SHOW of RESPECTABILITY which has been maintained hitherto had been the only means of preventing collapse. For my part I would even ask the devil if only I could find a peaceful hour to pursue my work, even if I had to live in Whitechapel. (Marx to Engels, 15 July 1858)

A decade later, not long before publishing *Capital*, Marx wrote a brief note to Engels that indicates his desperate domestic situation has not changed significantly, now comparing the part he had to play with his landlord that morning to that of Mercadet in Balzac's comedy *Le Faiseur*, which opens with the scene of another delinquent father trying to defer paying the rent so as to forestall imminent financial collapse (Marx to Engels, 25 February 1867; see epigraph to Part III, Balzac 1956 [1848]). Thus, it appears that throughout the period of producing some of his most valuable and lasting work, Marx failed to provide for either his family or himself, insisting instead on the peace and quiet needed to pursue his scientific speculations while trying to "make do" with a "show of respectability" and a confident appearance (cf. notes 7, 19, and 20 to Part III).

Among the last works that Balzac wrote, *Le Faiseur* presents a dizzying portrait of an obsessive but unsuccessful financial speculator who tries every ruse imaginable to avoid his increasingly insistent creditors. In the character of Mercadet, Balzac dramatizes the fate of a man who brings both himself and his family to the brink of financial catastrophe and moral ruin. With the best of intentions, he even speculates on the hand of his own daughter, a devoted but ugly and dark young girl whom he tries to marry off to an unloving, opportunistic, and deceptive suitor with an apparently massive source of income. Balzac's catastrophic and comical family romance of Mercadet, whose very name suggests the purely functional world of the marketplace, and whose simple and virtuous daughter and loyal and honest wife make their own bid for a share of happiness, thus presents a dystopian image of that post-1848 counterrevolutionary society that still held out a hopeful promise to Marx but would have been a sinister nightmare to Balzac, a scenario that was Balzac's insight to have foreseen and Marx's misfortune to have lived.

Balzac thus seems to act for us as a kind of stage director and playwright for a dramatic production that would represent the course and outcome of Marx's fate, with the text of *Le Faiseur* providing the script in much the same way as the demonic Melmoth stages the spectacle of Castanier's destiny (described in Chapter 5). Reading his work before a mesmerized audience at the Comédie Française in 1848, Balzac did not indicate the breaks between acts and scenes, or even the names of the characters, but instead reproduced the energetic dialogue and frequent asides in his own voice and without interruption,

leaving the impression that anyone might play the roles of this almost oper-
atic melodrama which may well serve as the swan song of his own illustrious
career:

He roared and cooed and wept and raged and thundered in every conceivable tone
of voice, while Debt sang a solo supported by a huge choir. Creditors appeared from
everywhere, from behind the stove, under the bed, out of the chest of drawers; they
poured down the chimney, crept through the keyhole and climbed in at the window
like lovers. . . . One had the feeling of a dense army of creditors stretching to the horizon and pressing forward to devour their prey. (Théophile Gautier, quoted in Maurois
1971: 593)

If Marx found a best friend, a scientific colleague, and a revolutionary comrade in Engels (who, by the way, did indeed send him £30 after receiving
the letter of July 1858), he might have found no better (or worse!) a literary
collaborator or dramatic coproducer than Balzac, the conservative monarchist
and Catholic apologist who was also among his favorite nineteenth-century
prose writers (cf. note 17 to Part III). Balzac's drama of Mercadet the speculator and *faiseur* may thus have presented for Marx a kind of *limit-work*, just as
this singular and disconcerting work seems also to constitute for Balzac himself
"at once the secret and the caricature of his creation, suggesting the aberrant
work he has not written and perhaps wanted to write" (Barthes 1972 [1957b]:
77). Perhaps, then, Marx could not "advise" his friend to read this particular
Balzacian piece (as he does the "little chefs d'oeuvre" about Melmoth and
Frenhofer in his note of 25 February 1867) for the very reason that although
he himself could see that he was playing the part of the *faiseur*, he ultimately
could only live it and act it out, but without delight in its ironies.

In a world divided between creditors and debtors, "the latter so ingeniously
called the English" and the former speaking French, as Mercadet puts it,
each awaits the arrival if not of God, then of one's own personal Godeau,
through a fetishistic ritual already remarked upon by Constant. In Balzac's
drama, Godeau is the name of Mercadet's business partner, whom we never
see or hear but whom we are made to believe has swindled Mercadet out of
the shares (*actions* in French) in the company they owned together in order
to avoid catastrophe and make his fortune abroad. By the end of the play,
Godeau's apparently imminent return is so anxiously anticipated that he even
seems expected to fulfill the role of a savior or redeemer (*racheteur*), although
he may yet be revealed to be nothing more than another cynical invention of
the financial *faiseur*. Mercadet himself seems at times to believe in the return
of his former friend and business partner, hoping against hope that he may go
on speculating recklessly, or else retire quietly to the country. He cannot see
that at the limits of the search for wealth, the will to power, and the desire

for knowledge, the modern social pact may also require us to recognize ourselves as both debtors and creditors to our families, and will not allow us to wait for yet another Godeau. "*Will* burns us, *power* destroys us, but *knowledge* leaves our frail organism in a perpetual state of calm" (quoted in Barthes 1972 [1957b]: 77, unattributed).

. . . .
. . . .
. . . .

Appendixes

Bibliographical Note on Reading Marx

Reliable and nearly complete collections of Marx's works now exist in German and English editions. Nevertheless, they all present problems for a reader who wants to try to follow both the sense of Marx's lifework as it was conceived and written by him, and the manner in which that sense is preserved, distorted, or transformed by publishers, editors, and translators, not to mention political, academic, and journalistic commentators. To complicate matters even further, Marx himself often revised, modified, or even disowned his works in the course of developing his ideas, frequently leaving important manuscripts unfinished and almost indecipherable. Legend has it that when the young Karl Kautsky asked Marx whether he would consider assisting in putting together an edition of his complete works, he replied that "they would first have to be *written*." Indeed, none of Marx's major works can be considered complete, except perhaps certain shorter occasional pieces. Even those works already written would first have to be made legible, as David Ryazanov, director during the 1920s of the newly created Marx-Engels Institute in Moscow, found after taking on the project of editing and translating all of the writings of Marx and Engels. Marx often had to be translated twice, he said: first from the manuscript, deciphering his handwriting into legible German, and then from German into Russian (Tucker 1978: 74). What is more, once such works were made legible, they would still have to be made readable, that is, made accessible to a readership and presented in a way that allows them to be understood with reference to the context in which they were written.

The fate of Marx's works in the twentieth century has shown that the problems of collecting, editing, translating, and publishing his works in accessible editions were indeed not only of a technical nature but political as well, since many works were held back or allowed only limited circulation by the Institute, which had procured nearly all of the manuscripts and first editions. In later years, English and German editions were often based on their Russian predecessors, creating a situation where Marx's works had to be "translated" yet again, this time out of Russian. Nowhere are many of these issues more marked than in those rougher texts that highlight Marx's career: the 1844 *Manuscripts*, the 1857–58 *Grundrisse*, and the 1861–63 *Theories of Surplus Value*. Each set of unfinished manuscripts was written in an almost indecipherable handwriting and grammatical style, each uses a difficult mixture of foreign languages, each was first edited and published only long after Marx's death (in the 1930s, 1940s, and 1950s, respectively), and each was not made available in accessible German, French, and English editions until even later (in the 1960s and 1970s). However, that we are now finally able to read these works with some sense of how they were conceived and written does not necessarily bring us closer to the "original" Marx, nor does it authorize us to read him "to the letter . . . complete" (Althusser 1970: 13), as if he were the holy scribe of a sacred text. His hurried and often careless reading and writing are an integral part of his methods of research and presentation, so any attempt to "polish" them would tamper with an essential part of their significance (cf. Nicolaus 1973: 65).

Since 1975, the Berlin Institute, in cooperation with its counterpart in Moscow, has taken on the project of meticulously editing Marx's works from his manuscripts, source materials, first and revised editions, and translations, taking into account the most subtle differences in published versions, and even making note of the color of his papers, how they are bound, his use of different writing utensils, and his marginal doodles. If it is ever finished, the *Marx-Engels Gesamtausgabe* (MEGA) will be the most complete and scholarly edition of the works of Marx and Engels in any language, building on and revising the multivolume *Marx-Engels Werke* (MEW) begun in 1956, itself based on the 39-volume Russian edition of 1955. When the English version of the *Collected Works* (CW) began to appear in 1975 (see the "General Introduction" in CW 1: xviii), a steady flow of selections in readers and paperback editions in English had been published since the 1960s. Many of these editions are still in print, more available and affordable, and better edited and translated, than the versions appearing in the *Collected Works*, in particular those selections of Marx's works collected in the Pelican series (and published by Vintage and Penguin Books). Since the 1970s, Robert C. Tucker's *Marx-Engels Reader* has introduced many readers to Marx in English, even though Tucker's editorial comments are often incorrect or questionable, almost no selection appears complete, and translations are sometimes inferior to those available elsewhere (Tucker 1978). Better selections and translations can be found in David McLellan's *Karl Marx: Selected Writings* (1977, Oxford: Oxford University Press). Where Tucker's *Reader* presents a magisterial view of Marx from "philosophical roots" to "revolutionary strategy," McLellan's *Selected Writings* sticks to a chronological order of presentation and encourages a style of research that is closer to Marx's own. The selection and collection of extended excerpts with appended commentaries and bibliographies confronts us with a difficult task similar to the one Marx faced: trying to get a sense of the whole through imperfectly connected and constructed pieces.

List of the *Grundrisse*'s "Foundational Passages"

The selections from Marx's 1857–58 notebooks labeled A–G below are the focus of much of my discussion, either directly, when I consider Marx's own arguments, or indirectly, when I apply the interpretive model Marx seems to have used to a wide range of different issues. In the latter case, I have treated them as "foundational passages" largely in an ironical and metaphorical sense: not only are they places where Marx establishes his own "grounds" or "reasons" (*Gründe*), but they also provide "ways" or "passages" for moving beyond perspectives originally opened by him.

The selection and naming of these passages is discussed in notes 2 and 12 to Part III. The location of passages C–G within the major divisions of the *Grundrisse* is presented in Table 2B; Chapters 4 and 5 discuss each of these passages in terms of the literary structure of the whole work. As indicated by the cross-references, each passage has also been used as a model for a part of my text.

A: "Avant-propos" on economic harmonies (review of Bastiat and Carey; III 1–7: 883–93); see Foreword
B: Notes on Greek art and modern society (M 21–22: 110–11); see Chapter 6
C: Digression on precious metals (I 28–34: 173–86); see Chapter 2
D: Excursus on crises (IV 15–44: 401–56); see Chapter 4
E: Essay on precapitalist social formations (IV 44–V 15: 456–515); see Chapter 5
F: Fragment on machines (VI 43–VII 6: 690–714); see Chapter 1
G: Remark on alienation (VII 44: 831–33); see Chapter 3

Excerpts on "Gold-Weighing Machines"

Not long after stopping work on his notebooks of 1857–58, Marx copied the following excerpts from George Dodd's book *The Curiosities of Industry and the Applied Sciences* (London, 1854; VII 64, CW 29: 254–55). The title above is Marx's own, and the passages are in English, with the exception of a few German words and phrases that he added. For a discussion, see Chapter 4 (section IV), Chapter 5 (section III), and note 12 to Part III.

Mr. Cotton's machine . . . the most delicate ever yet constructed for weighing gold coin. Adopted *von der* [by the] Bank of England. *Scheidet die Schaafe von den Böcken* [divides the sheep from the goats (Matt. 25:32)]. . . . In the transactions between the Bank of England and the public, the weighing of gold coin has been a most anxious and tedious process. As between the Bank and the Mint, the labour is not so minute, for 200 sovereigns being first accurately weighed, all the rest are weighed in groups of 200. The Mint officers are allowed a deviation of 12 grains in about 50 sovereigns; but they generally work to within half of this amount of error; and if the groups of sovereigns are correct within the prescribed limits no closer weighing is adopted. In the transactions between the Bank and the public, however, matters must be treated in more detail. It is no satisfaction to Smith to know that if his sovereign is light, Brown has a correct one and Jones a heavy one, so that therefore the Bank is just in the aggregate; each one demands that *his* sovereign should be of proper weight. . . . If a difference of even $\frac{1}{100}$ of a grain existed between 2 sovereigns, it is said that this machine would detect it. On a rough average, 30,000 sovereigns pass over the Bank Counter every day; each machine can weigh 10,000 sovereigns in 6 hours; and there are 6 machines; so that the Bank can weigh all its issues of gold by these means, and have reserve power to spare. Between 1844 and 1848 there were 48 million gold coins weighed by these machines at the Bank. . . . These machines save £1000 a year to the Bank in weighers' wages. (A child can turn the handle, but the machine judges for itself, *wirft die vollwichtigen sovereigns auf 1 Seite, die leichten auf die andre* [casts the full-weight sovereigns to one side and the light ones to the other].) (*Früher* [formerly] liability of error on the part of the weighers (the "personal equation," as the astronomers would term it) *nicht* [not] equal.) An expert weigher could weigh about 700 sovereigns in an hour by the old balance; but the agitation of the air by the sudden opening of a door, the breathing of persons near the apparatus, the fatigued state of the hand and eye of the weigher—all led to minute errors. (pp. 19–21)

Curiosities des Geldes [of Money]. When society rises above the level of mere barter[ing] transactions, any substance which is equally valued by buyer and seller may become money; . . . One of the earliest *cattle*, but this is obviously a coin inapplicable to small purchasers, for it would puzzle the seller to give change out of an ox. *Shells* are used to a great extent as money, in India, the Indian islands, and Africa; the *cowry shells* of India have a value of about 32 to an English farthing. *Cocoa-nuts, almonds, maize,* have all had to do duty as money. In hunting countries *skins* . . . *salt.* . . . *Dried fish* [is] often the money in Iceland and Newfoundland; *sugar* has at times been a West-India money.

Gold very solid and dense; divisible or separable in an extraordinary degree; very little affected by air or moisture, or ordinary usage, etc. (its supply very limited).

Wearing away of gold coin, by the constant friction to which it is exposed. No one can say whither the worn particles go. . . . When gone, somebody must bear the loss. A baker who takes a sovereign one day, and pays it away to his miller the next does not pay the veritable sovereign itself; it is a lighter one than when he received it. . . . *Nach* [according to] Jacob each gold coin in England bears an annual loss of about $\frac{1}{900}$ by friction (little more than a farthing in the pound). In silver coins the loss is supposed to be 5 or 6 times greater, owing to the more unceasing circulation of silver than gold, and to the less fitness of the metal to bear friction. (pp. 14–17)

Post-Marks

Notes on Notes

I have made a considerable effort in these pages to capture the spirit of Marx's writing by integrating and even imitating in my own way his often unruly methods of working out his thoughts: his habit of breaking off his writing in order to pursue a digression, sometimes in midsentence and for long passages that may take him several sentences or even pages to complete, of quoting articles and books while interjecting his own parenthetical comments, of mistranslating his sources according to his own interests, of developing a thought or working out a calculation at the bottom of a page, in the margins, between lines, on the back of a page, or on the cover of a notebook. Needless to say, just as it has been impossible to reproduce these idiosyncrasies in published versions of his work, so it would be pointless to try to imitate or even understand all the intricacies of what have been called his sibylline and labyrinthine passages. My own remarks on Marx, which these notes formulate in a different way, are my attempts nevertheless to explore the specific functions of Marx's note-taking habits and some of their broader implications. My writing is thus curiously caught between what Marx wrote and what others have written since, or what is still left to be written.

I have tried, then, to go further than Marx did by allowing my own notes to take on a life of their own, thus tipping the balance in my favor as I weigh and measure Marx's text like a "machine [that] judges for itself" (VII 64). Through a kind of dialectic gone wild, the number of endnotes corresponding to each of the three parts of my work itself progressively increases from three to a power of three—as Melmoth might say, hurling out columns of text four or five at a time when they should have come two or three at a time—thus, three notes in Part I, nine (or three times three) in Part II, and twenty-seven (or three cubed) in Part III. Like inflationary banknotes that continue circulating because they cannot be converted or redeemed, they exceed my main fund of writers, examples, and themes even as I attempt to reinvest topics already addressed with more meaning or to speculate on them in new ways.

Sometimes following Marx, and sometimes not, I have come to conceive of the proliferating notes that appear below as devices for self-clarification, as spaces for working out problems and showing my work as one would for a mathematics assignment, and as vehicles for exposing my thoughts to directions I have not pursued or am not (yet) capable of pursuing. These aims have forced me to construct these notes in a way that allows them to be read independently of one another and of the main text, as competing versions of the same topic or issue, or as otherwise quite unrelated perspectives operating within very different frameworks. It is in part because Marx's writings of 1857–58 are too often dismissed as a mere collection of indecipherable notes, having less value the further they appear to be from anything polished or "worked out," that I have put some effort into shaping my own essay into a kind of note-book that would explore and exemplify the implications of this way of writing out ideas while enhancing their pedagogical effect. By breaking up the apparently seamless systematism of thought into independent topics ordered numerically (a practice only slightly less arbitrary than the alphabetical list of a bibliography, since here the notes loosely follow the order of the text), my hope is that these notes will provide occasions for someone else's note-taking.

For better or for worse, this hope has led me to try to accent the musical dimension of note composition as an essential part of what I have called in these pages the *melodramatics* of Marx's work. I have argued that this literary and generic characterization may be understood to determine the communicative effectiveness of Marx's writing in particular, and the rhetorical or political affectivity of Marxism in general, much as Friedrich Nietzsche sought to turn sober philosophy into a kind of "gay science" by presenting his work with a prelude in rhymes and an appendix of songs (Nietzsche 1974 [1882]). No aspect of text construction seems better suited than notes are for amplifying the musical dimensions and the almost symphonic orchestration of multiple voices in written texts. While parenthetical references may function as style markings and as notations for phrasing and dynamics, footnotes may provide baseline accompaniment to the main melody or tonal colors to the dominating (dis)harmonies, and endnotes may serve as background instrumentation or percussion, as a coda to the whole piece, or as overtones that are heard only afterward and when we concentrate on them. In this sense, my notes are composed to preserve and to privilege the musical element in the art of melo-drama (a kind of musical theater) as it was practiced in the eighteenth century, in which songs were interspersed with the theatrical performances and the actors were accompanied by orchestral music appropriate to the situations represented (cf. Prendergast 1978). Perhaps, then, Marx's notebooks of 1857–58 may one day be heard in a musical piece that has yet to reach human ears.

However, I have not thereby become tone-deaf to the more common and popular nineteenth- and twentieth-century uses of melodrama. On the contrary, I have sought to recover this earlier form of the art in order to emphasize further the dilemmas and the possibilities its later versions pose to us. Indeed, I have even wanted to identify and enhance through this work those aspects of Marx's writing which function according to the now classic melodramatic themes of "the triumph of moral virtue over villainy, and the consequent idealising of the moral views assumed to be held by the audience" (Frye 1957: 47). This is our usual sense of those characteristic features of melodrama which exploit fantasy and excess, exaggeration and implausibility, or uncontrolled luridness and shameless sensationalism, in a vicious circle that aims to root out the residual elements of social evil in the name of goodness (Brooks 1976).

This use of the genre thus seems to serve a purely conservative function in providing an escape route from the repressions, boredom, and deprivations of the established order, thereby amplifying the hysteria of protest while containing the politics of rebellion. By pandering to the basest, most regressive, and least emancipatory popular sentiments; by capitalizing on the pervasive fears and hopes of the masses; and by profiting from the eclectic market of ideas, melodramatic literature and science are often reduced to the predictable reassurances of an unreal dream life and the impotent absurdities of mob violence, or even pressed into propagandistic service for the police state (Mehlman 1977; Prendergast 1978). When these are the effects of Marx's own melodramatic prose, the great monument of Marx's "open and supplemented dialectic" (LaCapra 1983: 272n) seems to be defaced, ruined, or irretrievably sealed by the very aesthetic form that gives it life, critical force, and communicative power: "Archetypal melodrama, erupting into the materialist dialectic, throws into question the status of the act—the revolution—within the Marxist system. The ascetic mechanism, the transposition to myth, the theatrical climax have abbreviated the dialectic and may have damaged it irreparably" (Sypher 1948: 439; also see notes 12 and 27 to Part III). Instead of advancing our sense of the potential for human freedom in history, and instead of communicating a human truth across the borders of class and competence, the critical force and analytic power of Marx's revolutionary prose would then ultimately seem to have been dulled by the "outmoded" character of his revolutionary music.

Thus, my notes have sometimes been composed to carry a melody or develop a story line in a different direction than the ones Marx pursued through his writing, to provide digressions that nevertheless illuminate his sense of the direction (*Sinn*) or forward march of history, as Lukács might say (see note 16 to Part III). Notes that are directly bibliographical and that are put in parentheses in the main text (or expressed discursively, as in Appendix A) might therefore be read as road signs that indicate the direction of alternate routes one may acknowledge without pursuing. Other notes that might otherwise have been put at the foot of the page but for their length serve a more humble, penitential duty of bearing the text forward as carriers (*Träger*) of key ideas in the main text, in relation to which they are subordinate or even parasitical. They may provide a kind of resting place for gaining one's footing, a step from which to move the argument or the story along, a pivot for turning it in new directions, or a spur by which the reader and the writer who straddle the text may combine their efforts to incite it toward some new terrain. Or perhaps, like the perfect foot peeking out from the chaotic brush strokes of the unknown masterpiece described in Balzac's short story, such notes may present a kind of unfulfilled promise of something that still seems unknown or imaginary but may one day be realized. They are "hors-textes" indicating the way to an adventure out of a study that has become confining or has reached a dead end.

In fact, however, my notes appear not at the foot of the text but rather at the end or behind it as its "posterior," often projecting an almost opposite image from the one Marx intends to depict. Just as he imagines a parodic diptych in which his work on "the relations of production and commerce" would appear on one side, with a scene of him kneeling at his wife's feet on the other, we might also say about these notes: "Look to this picture and to that" (Marx to Jenny, 21 June 1856, quoting *Hamlet*). Like so many of his own works and so many passages in them, such notes often project an image from within the text, *Stück in Stücken*, a play within a play, a piece within another piece, thereby upsetting our sense of the plot we have been following and forcing us to implicate ourselves in a new one.

As much for the reader's as for my own enjoyment in writing them, my notes below and above (or on this side and the other, depending on how they are looked at) may provide places of embellishment, little bits and pieces born of obsession, fetishes originating from what seemed to be an untenable idea that I have nevertheless clung to and now offer in their rough form for the reader's disposal (cf. Barthes 1975, 1978 [1977]). But the freedom I have exercised in these fragments has not kept me from facing an ethical obligation, both scholarly and political, to acknowledge the relatively autonomous existence of these points as marks of the inherent limits of my own writing (to which I draw attention by giving each note its own title). Often I found that the only way to enhance the moral responsibility of the conversation I was trying to provoke or inscribe myself in was in some side note that would ultimately undermine, subvert (in the sense of "turn under"), or reroute the direction and flow of my own argument. The price of such an ethic has been that I am able to provide only a rough and damaged piece of what I am trying to communicate, something that may therefore appear more like a prayer or a promise than a theoretical point (cf. Adorno 1974, 1991 [1956, 1959]). At their best, however, my notes, both in the fragments below and in the chapters above, may serve to open up that holistic space of communicative praxis in which the sometimes refined and esoteric exercises of reading, writing, and thinking can find their place in a community of argument and in the hub of human interests (cf. O'Neill 1989a; Schrag 1986). This is the sense, then, in which they are not notes at all, but only "postmarks" on notes that have already been sealed and sent but have yet to reach their destination.

Notes

FOREWORD

1. In the spirit of the intellectual autobiography presented in the "Preface" (Marx 1859) that Marx wrote not long after completing the *Grundrisse*, I should remark that my own book is part of a larger investigation into the human sciences of reading and writing titled "Faust's Study," of which this forms the first installment of a trilogy—or the bottom layer of a threefold composition. The other two works will deal with Weber's essays "Science as a Vocation" and "Politics as a Vocation," and Freud's case history of "Dora." In spite of their apparent eclecticism, these studies are connected thematically through specific scenes of writing inspired by passages from Goethe's tragedy that each writer cites in order to dramatize the dilemmas of "scientific man," and methodologically by the deployment of hermeneutic procedures and literary genres characteristic of each writer that I display in figures and tables as well as through my own discourse. I hope that my efforts here and in the larger project may contribute to our sense of the trust as well as the courage involved in academic work, and to indicate not just the steep slopes of science but also its open doors (cf. Marx 1859 CW 29: 265, quoting Dante's *Inferno*).

PART I

1. *Productive misreadings (the Habermasian reading of Marx)*

Strategic, reductive, and seductive misreadings of Marx are often produced from textual cuts that chop up the totality of a particular work, or even his lifework as a whole, in order to reconstruct it according to the reader's own interests. Notwithstanding his better sense of the challenges to Marxism within the context of late capitalism, Jürgen Habermas's interpretation of the "fragment on machines" from Marx's 1857–58 notebooks has its sources in two crucial interpretive cuts that allow him to redirect its sense toward his own ends (cf. note 2 to Part III).

1. By separating Marx's discussion of machinery and living labor from the polemical and even theoretical context of much of the rest of the *Grundrisse* (cf. Appendix B), Habermas is able to treat it as "an interpretive scheme" that contains the "program for the instrumentalist translation of Hegel's philosophy of Absolute Knowledge" already contained in what he takes to be Marx's "synthesis" of philosophy and economics in the 1844 manuscripts (Habermas 1971: 43). Thus, he cannot see that Marx is here working out a theory of surplus value while also trying to show the limits of the classical formulation of this theory by developing the problematics of fetishism and use value, as he states explicitly in the preceding section on "small-scale circulation" (VI: 673–90; cf. Negri 1984; Rovatti 1973).

2. In a long footnote, Habermas discusses the opening sections of Marx's 1857 "Introduction" as if they constituted "one of the few detailed references to the method of political economy in Marx," although in fact he does not discuss the penultimate section, "The Method of Political Economy" (1971: 326–29, on M: 83–100). Thus he is able to treat Marx's critique of the abstract "textbook" discussions of the economic categories as if Marx himself were elaborating his own "categorical framework" or "model of instrumental action" for comprehending "the entire life process . . . from the perspective of production" (i.e., instrumental or purposively rational action). Here, Habermas cannot see that this discussion is only a pretext for Marx's subsequent articulation of the nonidentity of the concrete totality with all theoretical efforts to conceptualize it (M: 108–9).

Each of these moves provides Habermas with the grounds for his later reevaluation of Marx in the essay "Technology and Science as 'Ideology'" (1970), which explicitly places his own categorical framework of work and interaction (later reformulated in terms of the broader concepts of system and lifeworld) over the often more subtle and supple distinctions operating throughout Marx's work. Nevertheless, in the conclusion to his monumental study *The Theory of Communicative Action*, he returns to a reading of Marx's work that is more sensitive to its "double perspective" and even its "bilingual character" in combining and bringing to the "critical point" accounts of resistance and struggle and those of autonomous systematization and steering (1987: 338). Indeed, on the very last page of that study he is finally able to find "a special case of the transference of communicatively structured domains of action over to media steered interaction" in Marx's methodological argument from the 1857 "Introduction," where Marx argues that even the most abstract and universal categories, such as "labor pure and simple," may be most valid and "true in practice" only within the most modern conditions, such as in the United States (1987: 401–3, on M: 105). Habermas thus leaves unexplored much of the long journey undertaken in Marx's (and his own) theoretical practice.

2. *The Pied Piper (an allegory of reading, Marx contra Goethe)*

To read Marx through Goethe cannot simply be a matter of poeticizing Marx's prose or of setting his words to the music of Goethe's verse, any more than reading Goethe through Marx would only entail working out the scientific and sociological dimensions of Goethe's poetry, his music, and his epic drama (cf. Lukács 1968). The main task is

to find the common ground on which each writer stands, and even more is it to illuminate their differences and to amplify their dissonances, as Goethe himself might put
it: "People say: between two opposed opinions the truth lies in the middle. Not at all!
Between them lies the problem, what is unseeable, eternally active life, contemplated
in repose" (quoted in Sepper 1988: ix). In the spirit of Dennis L. Sepper's study of
Goethe's polemic against Newton concerning the new science of color, we might say,
then, that our task is both to search through the "shadowy underworld" which sustains
their sense of science, and to find well-defined concepts in the poetic consciousness
each writer exhibits. As Sepper points out, the very problem may well lie in insisting
on the opposition between science and poetry, rather than in considering the legitimate
claims and different concerns raised within each field of inquiry (Sepper 1988: 4–9; cf.
Ronell 1986: 139–57).

Let us then briefly "contemplate in repose" the problem that lies between Marx and
Goethe through the "unseeable, eternally active life" depicted in a story with which
both writers would certainly have been familiar from their childhood. The legend of
the Pied Piper of Hamelin, with its themes of childish delusions and vengeful recognition, its dramatic figure of the seductive music leading listeners into life or death,
and its moral lesson about broken promises, may stand for us as an allegory of reading
about the contested land that stands between Marx and Goethe:

> *There came into the town of Hamel in countrey of Brunswyc an od kynd of com-*
> *pagnion, who for the fantastical cote which hee wore beeing wrought with sundry*
> *colours, was called the pyed pyper; for a pyper hee was, besides other qualities. . . .*
> The leaders of the town offered him a large reward if he could rid them of the
> rats that had lately infested their houses. When he played a strange tune upon
> his pipe, the vermin were lured out of their holes, down the street, and to their
> deaths in the waters of the River Weser: *And it seemed as if a voice / (Sweeter*
> *by far than by harp or by psyltery / Is breathed) called out, "Oh rats, rejoice! The*
> *world is grown to one vast dysaltery! / So munch on, crunch on take your nun-*
> *cheon / Breakfast, supper, dinner luncheon!"* . . . When the piper returned to the
> town leaders, he found that the bargain they had made with him was not in
> earnest: *"But as for the guilders, what we spoke" /* they said, *"Of them, as you*
> *well know, was in joke"* . . . So with a last blow on his pipe, he produced yet
> another strange melody that now drew all the children of the town out of their
> houses, whence he led them to the foot of the Koppelberg Hill: *When, lo, as*
> *they reached the mountainside, / a wondrous portal opened wide . . . to a joyous*
> *land . . . where waters gushed and fruit trees grew.* The children followed him
> within the open rift of the hill, which closed behind them, and neither child nor
> piper was ever heard from again. . . . *In memory whereof it was then ordayned,*
> *that from thence-foorth no drum, pype or other instruments should bee founded*
> *on the street leading to the grate through which they passed.* (italicized excerpts
> from Verstegen 1979: 85–87; and Browning 1981: 384–91)

Of course, there is no denying the important influence of Goethe on Marx, or Marx's
polemical intentions in quoting Goethe in several places in his work (e.g., VII: 702).
Nor should we close our ears to the fact that the works of both men have been subject to

what Marx once referred to as "the gnawing criticism of the mice," or to the possibility that both may ultimately have been led by that chorus of Europeans leaping to their feet to sing the strange song of the proletarian revolution: "Well worked, old mole!" (Marx 1859 CW 29: 264; 1852a SE: 237, paraphrasing *Hamlet*).

3. *Two souls in one heart (Lukács reading Faust)*

We need to understand the lifework of the now much-maligned Georg Lukács through its inconsistencies and contradictions, as well as through the tragic sensibility and the spiritual generosity with which he tried to understand his own cultural heroes, both fictional and historical. The prefaces he later wrote to his early works provide us with an initial standard by which to evaluate the contradictions between his political activism and his ethical idealism with which he struggled for most of his life: "If Faust could have two souls within his breast, why should not a normal person unite conflicting intellectual trends within himself when he finds himself changing from one class to another in the middle of a world crisis?" (1971 [1922]: x, new preface 1967). As in his portrayal of Lenin, it is less a question here of simply mapping out Lukács's shifting political affiliations and intellectual interests than of approaching his life and work through a holistic study of "the unity of his thought."

Like the painter in Balzac's story who burned the great "unknown masterpiece" he labored over for so long after showing it to an unappreciative and baffled audience, Lukács publicly disowned even his greatest works in Marxist philosophy and aesthetics when they drew criticism from official Marxists, in what some have interpreted as a kind of career-long *sacrifizio dell'intelletto*. But while Lukács's "studies" sometimes seemed to take the form of a kind of search for the "absolute," especially in his later work, he never lost his sense of the tragic impossibility or "incommensurability" of the ideals of humanism as the very mark of realism. Rather than attempt to mediate forms of literary, philosophical, and sociological discourse with each other and with the "level" of social reality, Lukács combines the descriptive and narrative aspects of his work so that his literary studies may provide a vehicle of communication for his philosophical and sociological ideas, while the latter illuminate ideals otherwise expressed through art and literature (cf. Jameson 1971b, 1988 [1977]; notes 16 and 18 to Part III).

Perhaps the Faust legend in particular suggested to him the quintessential expression of the problematic relation of thought and action posed in terms of the claims of a religious (Lutheran) orthodoxy that viewed as sinful the (Faustian) demands for power, knowledge, and pleasure. Lukács praises Christopher Marlowe's dramatic depiction of "the original greatness of the Renaissance legend" but criticizes him for lacking "sufficient poetic and intellectual force," and thus for weakening its effect by dwelling too often on "external aspects (the witchery, the grandiloquence, the magical and the mystical)" (Lukács 1968: 165). Nevertheless, Lukács's own profound sense of Goethe's "incommensurable work" may have already been exemplified in Marlowe's wonderful portrait of a Faustus who has the power to do anything but only thinks up banalities, so that precisely these slapstick and phantasmagoric aspects of the legend best preserve its radical realism as a scholar's tragedy that both begins and ends in the scene of the study. Only in the freedom and the limitations of the study can a principle of absolute play

(Marlowe) come to inform a principle of hope (Goethe, Marx, Lukács) for the future of an emancipated humanity (Greenblatt 1978; Guy-Bray 1991).

PART II

1. *The reflective scholar (on the young Marx)*

A hermeneutic perspective on the unity of Marx's lifework as a process of reading and writing puts us in a position to understand an early and relatively neglected phase of Marx's career in which the three main periods (1840s, 1850s, and 1860s) may be seen to have their origins. In an eloquent letter to his father after his first year of university, Marx reports on his initial excitement with his studies in literature, aesthetics, ancient mythology, philosophy, and legal studies above all others, pausing for a moment to "take the liberty to examine my situation and, in general, my view of life, which I consider an expression of reflection in all directions—in science, in art, in private endeavors" (Marx to his father, 10 November 1837). Nevertheless, he reports, all this book learning now seems to have amounted to little more than the construction of "a writing desk with drawers which I later filled with sand."

So begins Marx's own Faustian study scene, in which he vented his youthful frustrations through a wide range of early poetic and dramatic experiments (translated in CW 1) that express his longing to experience and perceive things directly, as they are, not just as they are read in a book or dreamed up in a library:

I have pursued, alas, philosophy,	Habe nun, ach! Philosophie,
Jurisprudence, and medicine,	Juristerei und Medizin,
And, help me God, theology,	Und leider auch Theologie!
With fervent zeal through thick and thin.	Durchaus studiert, mit heissem Bemühn.
And here poor fool, I stand once more,	Da steh ich nun, ich armer Tor! Und bin so klug als wie zufor.
No wiser than I was before.	(Goethe's *Faust*, ll. 354–59)

Like Faust's adventure, Marx's eventful career appears to have begun in the 1830s and 1840s, not with an exclamation of triumph but with a sigh: "Habe nun, ach!" (cf. Kittler 1990). Like Faust, he pursued the four traditional faculties of the university to the point of exhaustion, including the theological ideas revived by the Young Hegelians under the slogan of "Criticism," Marx's first object of attack. Like Faust at his desk studying with Lutheran resolve: "Da steh ich!," so Marx and Engels seemed to have imagined themselves to be translating Adam Smith, the "Luther of political economy" (Marx [1844b]), into the discourse of humanistic science. And like Faust, who refers to himself as both a "fool" and a "gateway" (by a pun on the word *Tor*), Marx wished to pass outside of his study and through the city gates, as if woken from his dream of the "childhood of humanity" by the tolling of a bell on a bright Easter morning: "Two souls, alas, do dwell within his breast, the one ever parting from the other" (ll. 1112–13, quoted in Marx C1: 741; cf. M: 111; cf. Berman 1988: 41–50).

2. *Prometheus unbound (on Marx's sociological imagination)*

Marx's reading practices do not need to be demythologized or given a strictly scientific or philosophical formulation (Tucker 1961); rather, they need to be revised and made explicit with reference to Marx's own view of the relations between personality, society, and scientific thought (cf. O'Neill 1982: 43–58). Beginning from Marx's procedure in his famous 1859 "Preface" of presenting his own intellectual autobiography within a sketch of the "materialist conception of history," we should try to present a portrait of Marx that resists the reductionism of both ego psychology and economic determinism. Where Jerrold Seigel offers a useful interpretation of Marx's fate partly as a function of his personal development and biopsychic "complexes," David McLellan presents an account of Marx's struggle with "Marxism" in terms of the breaks, turning points, interruptions, and deferrals in his life that have personal as well as political and economic dimensions (Seigel 1978; McLellan 1973; cf. notes 5, 7, 20, and 26 to Part III). At issue here is our sense of the author in the text and of the text in its historical and political context, as C. Wright Mills had already outlined in his conception of the promise and task of the sociological imagination: "The sociological imagination enables us to grasp history and biography and the relations between the two within society. . . . It is the quality of all that is intellectually interesting in Marx" (1959: 6). Rather than appropriate Marx's work as a myth and then pass this reconstituted version off as "the essential Marx" (Tucker 1978), we need instead to approach it more carefully, in terms of the Promethean character of toil and rebellion that informs it.

3. *Spinning metaphors (on Marxist literary structuralism)*

Perhaps a Marxian procedure of reading might proceed not by making categorical declarations on science versus ideology, but by determining how the identities of these domains are both constituted and called into question, as Gayatri Spivak argues in defense of Althusser: "I would submit that, in the spirit of a critique of positivism, Althusser *bricole-s* or tinkers with the name of science itself, reconstellates it by spinning it out (*filer*) as a convenient metaphor even as he establishes Marx's claim to be a scientist rather than merely a philosopher of history" (Spivak 1987 [1985]: 292–93, citing Althusser 1971: 38–40, 61, 66).

Nevertheless, it seems more likely that in his own reading of Marx, Althusser's project is predicated on not seeing that such a "spinning out" is already at work throughout Marx's text (cf. O'Neill 1982: 1–17). With reference to a particularly revealing example from the opening chapters of *Capital*, Samuel Weber has pointed out that "the most frequently used example of the labor process in the general discussion of Volume I is that of the fabrication of fabrics (weaving, spinning, carding, etc.). As the text wears on, however, the "fabrication" begins to assume the double meaning it also has in English: the production of a product on the one hand, but also *an imaginary, a deluding, and deluded activity* on the other" (Weber 1979: 174). Thus the denotative level is undermined by the connotative, so that the sentence "Der Spinner hat gesponnen und das Produkt ist ein Gespinst" is first read literally as "The spinner has spun and his product is something that has been spun," and then metaphorically as "The madman has spun [a story] and his product is a figment [of the imagination]."

I would submit that by ignoring the literary features of Marx's own textual weave, readers like Althusser must spin their own unseen threads (*unsichtbaren Fäden*) and weave them into Marx's discourse in order to render more productive and compelling their theoretical constructs or *Hirngespinst* (figments of the mind; III 13–14: 304–6). This in part is how they are able to establish the communicative appeal or interpellation (what Max Weber in a more useful way calls the *Beruf*) of their theoretical practice to a reading public. What we get then is another spun-out Marx (Tucker's in the United States, Althusser's in England) who is cut off from the guiding thread that runs through the totality of his lifework (Marx 1859 CW 29: 262).

4. *Humanist hermeneutics (on responsible readings of history)*

The hermeneutic conception of Marxism as a tradition of rival readings, itself grounded in the perception of the direction of history, was developed in Merleau-Ponty's reflections on the "Communist problem" during the post–World War II era: "Marxist politics is not primarily a system of ideas but a reading of ongoing history" (1969 [1947]: 52). In his study *Humanism and Terror*, Merleau-Ponty distinguishes several kinds of ideological readings in order to contrast them with a more careful and courageous one mindful of its responsibility to history: (1) uncareful readings of Arthur Koestler's influential novel *Darkness at Noon*, which deals with the Moscow Trials of 1939 (1969 [1947]: 2); (2) hasty readings of the published proceedings from the court trials themselves (58–59), including the interpretation of them presented in Koestler's novel; and (3) nonreadings of Merleau-Ponty's own arguments against the above readings by critics from both the Right and the Left (xxxiv). Merleau-Ponty intends his critique of Marxist literary scientism to serve as a basis for proposing rules for an intellectually responsible reading of pre- and postwar political events and the intellectual debates surrounding them (178–89).

Without claiming any self-evident or a priori scientific status for his own reading of Koestler's novel, transcripts of the trial, and rival interpretations of both, Merleau-Ponty's "reading" of world events thus provides both an example of and a model for a critical interpretation of competing political ideologies, and of their scientization within modern institutional structures and categories of thought. His early study thus anticipates recent attempts to elaborate Marx's theory and practice of reading as part of a critique of the ideological practices of the sciences, and invites us to approach the hermeneutic conception of Marxist debate as a thoroughly practical problem: "We may think of the Marxist tradition as a set of rival reading practices that have to be understood as the very issues of Marxist politics, and not simply as glosses upon events intelligible apart from such practices" (O'Neill 1982: 124).

5. *The stink of history (on Marx's Aristotelianism)*

The humanist concept of essence that implicitly informs Marx's discussion of the method of political economy in his 1857 "Introduction" had been articulated in more explicitly philosophical (that is, Hegelian and Aristotelian) terms in his manuscripts of 1844. Marcuse's classic essay "The Concept of Essence" (1968 [1936]) is an early but by no means exhaustive investigation into the ontological dimension of Marx's thought. Recent studies have more thoroughly developed Marx's own thinking on the critical significance of the ancient Greek conception of social ethics and ontology for his critique of modern political economy, what Marx in the "Introduction" suggests in terms of the "charm" of the "historic childhood of humanity" for modern thinkers (M: 111; Gould 1978; McCarthy 1990). Others have explored the implications of Marx's approach to the ancient metaphysics of atomism for the critique of modern empiricism, especially as the latter may be understood through Marx's theoretical framework of organic "holism" or the dialectics of the "concrete totality" (M: 100–103; Kosik 1976; Meikle 1985). The aim of such studies is to elaborate on Marx's understanding of thought as a form of praxis, and of conceptual formalism as embedded in a reality that includes it and gives it cultural, collective, and historical relevance (Wilson 1991; Zeleny 1980).

They might be contrasted to others that are at pains to avoid what are assumed to be the "pitfalls" of essentialism, the latter believed to compromise the "relative autonomy" of literary, discursive, and ideological analysis with respect to the "level" of historical reality understood as an "absent cause" (cf. Jameson 1981; note 3 to Part I; note 18 to Part III). Rather than articulate the concept of essence (*Wesen*) as the memory of what was (*gewesen*) and continues to be within the aesthetic dimension of history and critical thinking (Marcuse 1978), for example, Marxist literary critics like Fredric Jameson seem to keep their noses to the open book of "textuality," invoking a largely unexamined conception of how unconscious historical necessities and political realities are uncovered by cracking the appearances of language. With reference to the negative legacy of post-Althusserian Marxism in particular, Scott Meikle has countered that the difficulty in accounting for the problem of necessity in history "is made even less attractive by the fact that, having faced up to it, you are immediately plunged into an even more malodorous unmentionable: essence" (1985: 7). Perhaps this is the sense behind the joke circulating among graduate students who refer to Jameson's *Political Unconscious* simply as "p-u."

6. Political theater (reading "Capital" dramatically)

Recent attempts to invoke the dramatic spirit of Marx's theoretical practice often keep a fair distance from the letter of Marx's text. Lyotard's approach to Marx as a writer through the characters of the little girl, the lawyer, the defendant, and the prostitute, for example, is inspired less by Marx's works than by Lyotard's own imagination, although such speculations may indeed be supported with textual and biographical evidence he does not provide (Lyotard 1974: 117–88; cf. notes 5, 7, 20, and 26 to Part III).

A similar inattention is exhibited in more directly political readings of Marx, as in Harry Cleaver's no less dramatic interpretation of the first chapter of *Capital* through what he calls a "strategic reading" that proceeds from the perspective of "working class power" and actual "working class struggles": "We must bring to bear on a reading of this first chapter all our knowledge and interpretations of the rest of *Capital* and of the class struggle it analyzes" (Cleaver 1979: 69). By taking an apparently less "literary" and more straightforwardly "political" approach, he sees no need to give a "separate analysis of Section 4 of Chapter One on fetishism simply because . . . this whole essay involves the work of going behind the appearances of the commodity-form to get at the social relations" (1979: 69). Indeed, from the very first page of his reading, Cleaver is impatient with Marx's concern with "deceptive appearances," and thus with the barriers to communication to which they give rise. After quoting Marx's famous opening statement in *Capital* that it makes sense to begin with the analysis of the commodity because " 'the individual commodity *appears* as [capitalism's] elementary form,' " Cleaver "clarifies" Marx's meaning by "reiterating" the point that Marx "begins with the commodity because it *is* the elementary form of wealth in capitalist society" (1979: 71; my emphasis). But Marx's concern with the deceptions of language and appearance is crucial here, as he himself emphasizes by putting supplementary quotation marks around the key phrase. Thus, Cleaver cannot account for the rhetorical aspect of Marx's critical procedure that addresses the illusions and prejudices of both the working class and the political economists as his target readership, and thus the paradoxes of the communicative situation in which readers and writers alike are implicated.

To be sure, it is not my intention here to argue that the political and dramatic appeal of Marx's discourse must always be found by attending to the letter of Marx's text. For example, the main character in Robert Paul Wolff's study of the literary structure of *Capital*, "our friend Mr. Moneybags," does not in fact appear in Marx's text until 1887, four years after Marx's death and twenty years after *Capital*'s first publication, when Samuel Moore and Edward Aveling translated Marx's German phrase "müsste unser Geldbesitzer so glücklich sein" as "our friend Mr. Moneybags must be so lucky" (not retained in Ben Fowkes's 1976 translation of *Capital*; C1: 270). Although this characterization does not literally belong to Marx, it is theoretically and theatrically quite appropriate to his argument here, in that the chapter in *Capital* titled "The Buying and Selling of Labor-Power," which begins with the passage on Mr. Money-bags/*Geldbesitzer*, concludes by announcing a change in the "physiognomy of our *dramatis personae*"—indeed, a dramatic shift in "scenes" from the sphere of circulation to that of the production process of capital. In short, Marx's understanding of economic and political theory is often expressed by him through the metaphor of the theater of political economy.

7. *Historical ghosts (hallucinatory readings of revolution)*

Besides criticizing the texts of political economy and philosophy, Marx developed at the same time a procedure for reading the events of ongoing history, such as those surrounding the revolutions of 1848. Here I shall cite just two episodes in which Marx deployed this early hermeneutic theory in his attempts to show how the ghostly "character" of revolution seems to haunt the current political scene.

First, *interpretive castration*: in the famous opening line of the *Communist Manifesto*, the communist "specter" or "spook" (*Gespenst*) that is now haunting Europe is invoked as the sign or character of the emerging communist revolution. Later in this text, Marx ridicules the manner in which this ghost is conjured up by the "German, or True Socialists," who take their "solemn schoolboy tasks" so seriously by translating the slogans of the French Socialists into their own stereotyped language. For these Germans, it is not only a question of misreading the French through a translation that characterizes original ideas but also of rewriting those ideas through a translation that ritually emasculates:

> The work of the German *literati* consisted solely in bringing the new French ideas into harmony with their ancient philosophical conscience, or rather, in annexing [*anzueignen*] the French ideas without deserting their own philosophic point of view. This annexation [*Aneignung*] took place in the same way in which a foreign language is appropriated, namely by translation. It is well known how the monks wrote silly lives of Catholic Saints *over* the manuscripts on which the classical works of ancient heathendom had been written. The German *literati* reversed this process with the profane French literature. They wrote their philosophical nonsense beneath [or behind, *hinter*] the French original. For instance, beneath the French criticism of the economic functions of money, they wrote "Alienation [*Entäusserung*] of Humanity," and beneath the French criticism of the bourgeois state they wrote "Dethronement [*Aufhebung*] of the Category of the General," and so forth. . . . The French Socialist and Communist literature was thus ceremoniously emasculated [*entmannt*]. (Marx and Engels 1848 *MEW* 4: 486; R48: 91)

Second, *interpretive amnesia:* four years later, in *The Eighteenth Brumaire of Louis Bonaparte*, the historical "character" of the spirit of revolution is again invoked with a French accent. In spite of the failure of the 1848 revolutions, it is not communism that is dying but rather those "Napoleonic ideas" which merely express the attitudes of the peasant smallholding, and which are therefore only "the hallucinations of its death agony, words made into phrases, spirits made into ghosts" (Marx 1852a *SE*: 244). Early in the text, Marx parodies those revolutionary "actors" of 1852 who merely caricature their counterparts in earlier periods of revolutionary crisis, unable as they are to forget the mother tongue of oppression in order to articulate the foreign language of revolution:

> [They] anxiously conjure up the spirits of the past to their service and borrow from them names, slogans, and costumes in order to stage the new scene of world history in this time-honored disguise and this borrowed language. . . . In the same way, a beginner who has learnt a new language always translates it back into his mother tongue, but he has appropriated the spirit of the new language and can freely express himself in it only when he can manipulate it without re-calling the old and forgets his native tongue in the use of the new. (Marx 1852a *MEW* 8: 115; *SE*: 146–47)

Marx's early model of the fetishistic practice of reading and writing about politics and history in many ways anticipates his later critical theory of the fetish character of capitalism generally, where relations between things are imbued with a mystical "character" as if they were relations between persons (C1: 163; cf. Freud 1977 [1927]; note 8 to Part III).

8. *Literary democracy (Marx and the reading public)*

The communicative appeal of Marx's writings to a reading public may be studied in connection with the more general problem of the democratization of reading and the commercialization of literature in the nineteenth century. For example, Christopher Prendergast has shown that a key event in transforming the reading public in the early days of capitalism was Émile de Girardin's attempt in 1836 dramatically to increase daily newspaper sales by expanding advertising and reducing their price from 80 to 40 francs. Eventually, serialized literature in journals, marketed in a similar way, became the most popular and profitable avenue to reach a more massive readership beyond (but by no means excluding) the men and women of the privileged classes: "The *roman-feuilleton* becomes a symbol, representing and crystallizing in extreme form many of the dominant forces and tendencies at work in the emergence of Sainte-Beuve's *démocratie littéraire*; and the whole question of popularity and relations with the reading public, of standards and values of 'popular' culture, will be debated time and time again against the background of this particularly symptomatic phenomenon" (Prendergast 1978: 19).

Balzac stands out as an especially contradictory and even ambivalent figure in this development. Not only did he try to exploit and profit from this new trade that mediated and expanded the relationship between reader and writer, but in his own books (notably *Lost Illusions*) he also critically represented the devastating effects of this trend on the principles of literary integrity and public morality (cf. note 15 to Part III). At the same time, he often imagined his own Promethean struggle to create the perfect chef d'oeuvre in direct opposition to the crass and often more popular productions of his rivals, especially Victor Hugo and Eugène Sue. In the scientific book trade, in political journalism, as well as in the other arts, the profound influence of this increasingly competitive market was felt by producers and consumers alike, as Marx himself points out: "In Paris the great demand for vaudevilles and novels brought about the organization of work for their production, [which] at any rate yields something better than its 'unique' competitors in Germany" (Marx and Engels [1845–47] CW 5: 415). And yet for him it could not simply be a question of avoiding the compromises required by the capitalist book trade, but rather of encouraging and defending through his own literary practice a critical ideal of democratic communication.

9. *Textual orthodoxy (reading Marx beyond Marxism)*

A fresh reading of Marx's writings in terms of their literary appeal or their scientific validity does not need to be separated from our sense of the political relevance of Marxism for contemporary social and theoretical concerns. Martin Nicolaus's approach to the problems involved here with respect to Marx's *Grundrisse* has been challenged by several critics for what they take to be his ideological "orthodoxy" (Nicolaus 1973). Some argue that his rigid use of Marxist categories does not allow for the "reconstitution" of Marxian theory as required by its own historical character. In his argument against Nicolaus, Paul Piccone nevertheless employs a revealing metaphor that may not be altogether "a matter of indifference," to use Marx's phrase in his account of the use of gold as money: "In the concrete thematization of these new problems, the *Grundrisse* appears as *a gold mine* for the precious theoretical material needed to finance the slum clearance of Marxist ideology such as Nicolaus' and the reconstitution of a viable and meaningful Marxist theory" (Piccone 1975: 252, my emphasis; cf. Postone and Reinicke 1974–75; and I: 145). In a similar vein, John Keane and Brian Singer have waged a more general attack against what they take to be Nicolaus's project for a "conceptual archaeology by which Marxism is to be reinvigorated by unearthing the treasured 'What Marx Really Said'" (Keane and Singer 1974–75: 149). The ambivalence of these arguments (perhaps intended) may be grasped if we consider how Marx's text might indeed be useful both as a gold mine for financing a better Marxist theory of politics and as a slum clearance of ideology of all kinds, both as a site for recovering lost treasures of Marx's thought and as itself an archaeological dig into the buried layers of wealth, poverty, and historical memory (cf. notes 2, 3, and 6 to Part III).

By contrast, a more "animated reading" of Marx's *Grundrisse* against the grain of Marxist orthodoxy has been undertaken by Roslyn Bologh in her attempt to "formulate the rationality of the text" in terms of its "omissions and silences," and to imagine "the form of life that provides the text's sense for the reader" as the condition of its possibility. In situating her own reading of Marx, however, Bologh nevertheless restricts herself methodologically to the categorical formulation of antipositivist rules and their application to Marx's "text." Although freed from the ideological burdens hampering other readings of Marx (1979: 233–74), she risks another kind of textual orthodoxy that loses sight of Marx's own expanded vision of what it is to "read" both the rationality of the capitalist social system and the texts that are its rational creatures: "In reformulating political economy, Marx invites us to reconsider the rationality of political economy. Similarly, in reformulating Marx's theorizing, I invite the reader to reconsider the rationality of Marx's work" (Bologh 1979: 19). As H. T. Wilson remarks with respect to Bologh, "There is more to [Marx's] procedure than 'anti-positivism' because these rules are to be applied to the key substantive concepts, whether theoretical, disciplined, or common-sense, that are employed by given disciplines, professional practices and common-sense parlance in the present social formation (capitalism, Society), *not just to the work of Marx*" (1991: 215n). In reading Marx, we must also consider how the open character of his methods of research and presentation necessarily expands any narrow orthodox understanding of what constitutes "the work of Marx."

PART III

1. Secret societies (notes on the "unknown Marx")

As with any so-called prolific and notorious writer, a secret history could be written on the "unknown Marx" based on his private letters, relatively ignored or unpublished works and documents, or even reminiscences and rumors. This history would be parallel to but also structurally inseparable from what is usually taken to be the "official" one, as Georg Simmel notes in his brilliant study of "the secret society": "The secret offers, so to speak, the possibility of a second world alongside the manifest world, and the latter is decisively influenced by the former." Marx's correspondence reveals for us the curious paradox by which "the objective elimination of all warranty of secrecy" may be combined with "the subjective intensification of this warranty," and may even mark him as noteworthy to us precisely through what is concealed there (Simmel 1950: 330–37, 352–55; cf. Payne 1971). A single line from just one such letter that Marx wrote to Engels may allow us a glimpse into some of the issues involved here, which are complicated further by the fact that the line itself refers to another letter: "Letter from Kugelmann enclosed" (Marx to Engels, 25 February 1867).

In 1867 there occurred a curious though not unusual episode in Marx's life in which the confidential exchange of private letters between him and two of his closest friends, and a public exchange of letters to the editors of a German newspaper, happened to coincide with his plans to publish his magnum opus on political economy. In February of that year, not long before the first volume of *Capital* issued from the presses, Dr. Ludwig Kugelmann, a German physician, a member of the First International, and a good friend of Marx and Engels, had written to Marx informing him of allegations, recently made by the liberal Hannover newspaper *Zeitung für Norddeutschland*, that Marx was on his way to the Continent to plan a Polish insurrection. Marx then wrote a letter to the newspaper refuting the allegations and demanding a retraction, worried that the authorities would block his passage to Hamburg, where he was soon to conclude the contract with Meissner for the publication of volume 1 of *Capital*. Kugelmann later sent the *Zeitung's* retraction with a letter to Marx, who then sent both the letter and the retraction, along with a brief note, to Engels (cf. CW 42: 645). Thus, by the end of this flurried but not atypical exchange of letters, everyone could rest assured that the paper's "lie" had been exposed, and that Marx could safely travel to Hamburg to bring his great work on political economy to print.

This single line from Marx's brief note seems to connect a number of points between the "official," "public," and "known" Marx and the "other," "unknown," and "secret" history of Marx, even as it also reads like a line from a mysterious episode in the early history of Marxism as a "secret society." As a revolutionary, Marx indeed had to involve himself with many covert groups whose intrigues often rendered him complicit with those secret dealings he was elsewhere determined to expose, as in his relatively unknown polemical tracts titled *Revelations Concerning the Communist Trial in Cologne* (1853) and the *Revelations of the Diplomatic History of the Eighteenth Century* (1856), and later in his libel suit against Herr Vogt (*Herr Vogt* 1860). Not only may these pieces be read as parallel texts to his economic and journalistic studies of the same period, but they are also curiously reminiscent of such great Balzacian fictional histories as *Les Chouans*, *Une Ténébreuse Affaire*, *Histoire des treize*, and *L'Envers de l'histoire contemporaine*, as several critics have pointed out (Lukacher 1986; Mehlman 1977; cf. Prendergast 1978). Indeed, many of Marx's works seem to contribute to that melodramatic genre of detective novels and secret-society fictions cultivated by Sue, Hugo, and Balzac, just as the latter often strike readers as uncanny portrayals and realistic revelations of secret societies precisely insofar as we "know" they are fictional, guesswork, and even compensatory fantasies, "as though every sentence of [their] industrious pen[s] were constructing a bridge into the unknown" (Adorno 1991 [1965]: 122). Thus, instead of just feeding the intellectual rumor mill with new facts of personal documentation on a "great" writer, we may explore the elaborate hermeneutics involved in such a theme as the "unknown Marx."

2. Panning for gold (an excursus on the foundational passages)

Any text that is more often cited than read tends to be understood through a series of "foundational passages" which eventually get sifted out from the main flow of the argument, characterized, and even canonized as representing that work's major themes. The selected translations of Marx's *Grundrisse* by Eric Hobsbawm (1964) and David McLellan (1971), for example, have served precisely this function, as have the brilliant readings of this text that have been presented by Antonio Negri (1984), Herbert Marcuse (1964), and Jürgen Habermas (1971), each of whom emphasizes the centrality of what Italian Marxists refer to as "the fragment on machines" (cf. Appendix B; and note 1 to Part I). To take another example, rather than situate Marx's "essay on precapitalist economic formations" within Marx's developing theories of circulation, crisis, and surplus value, Hobsbawm's introduction to the translation of this text places it in the context of Marx's historical scholarship and in terms of recent debates over the so-called Asiatic mode of production. Thus, such selections are not neutral but reflect the implicit or explicit interests by which such writers comb through this unruly text and single out certain passages for special emphasis.

My own list of foundational passages from these notebooks is guided by an interest in examining Marx's scientific and analytical procedure through highlighting its aesthetic dimensions and rhetorical structures (see Appendix B; cf. note 12 to Part III). If any one passage best characterizes my own interest in this text as a whole, it would probably be the one I call "the digression on precious metals" (Appendix B, passage C, I: 173–86). Where McLellan excludes this passage, apparently because it seems to represent only a technical digression, Negri considers it only as a historical "parenthesis," without commenting on its ironic and polemical function as a critique of the gold fetishism of the French socialists. By contrast, this particular discussion may be understood to provide an allegory for how the historical and hermeneutical process of selecting these passages itself takes place, in a way analogous to the "revaluation" of gold and silver as money through a long history of sifting and refinement. Perhaps a similar idea has inspired others who have approached the *Grundrisse* as a kind of "goldmine for the precious theoretical material" needed to reinvigorate a viable and meaningful Marxist science (Piccone 1975: 252; cf. note 9 to Part II).

3. Cutting the perfect diamond (the layout of Marx's work site)

Implausible as it may seem at first, in Marx's chaotic notebooks of 1857–58 we may catch a glimpse of that perfect conceptual structure which is at the very core of the whole of his scientific project, from the 1844 *Manuscripts* (including his "Excerpts from James Mill") to the three volumes of *Capital* (1867–83). As Thomas Sekine has demonstrated, the three volumes of *Capital* that were already planned out in the notebooks logically present the major categories of bourgeois economics in the triangular shape of Hegel's *Science of Logic* (1812), with the doctrine of Being substituted for that of Circulation, Essence for Production, and the Concept for Distribution (1984: 102–8, 250–58; 1986: 2–9; see Table 2C). With reference to the *Grundrisse*, Gayatri Spivak has shown that Marx's capital logic does not just employ and stand in for the science of logic, but its morphology of value also questions the latter's "philosophical justice" (1987 [1985]: 158; see Table 2B). In any case, from the *Grundrisse* on, Marx tried to contain theoretically the empirical "contingencies" of capitalist history through the "fictitious" assumption that use values are always and everywhere produced and realized as (exchange) value, that is, for exchange on the capitalist market (note 8 to Part III). This approach was already anticipated in Marx's *Manuscripts* of 1844, where Hegel's logic is employed to study the limits of classical political economy, which he indicates by dividing his text into three equal columns on wages, profits, and rents before abandoning them in favor of a more general discussion of human alienation (MEGA I/ 1; see Table 2A). The social phenomenology of values, sketched here in terms of such issues as private property, the division of labor, and money, is grounded in the same humanist notion of the historicity of "essence" that informs the later notebooks (cf. note 5 to Part II).

Unlike *Capital* and the 1844 *Manuscripts*, Marx's *Grundrisse* does not appear in the form of a triangle or as the columns of a building, but ultimately projects the image of a diamond, each aspect in perfect symmetry with the other, refracting the incoming light into a rainbow of different colors. Marx's project in this text was thus to mine this diamond and then to grind, cut, and polish it *en facettes* in the solitude of his study. Faced with the impossibility of this task, however, and noting the dismal failure of such writers as Bastiat in attempting the same thing (VII: 755), he turned his workshop into a theoretical mine for exploding such gems as were buried in the works of others, defacing their smooth surfaces but thereby allowing them to project a very different spectrum.

4. *Tantalizing trees (the "organic" composition of capital)*

Along with the image of the human body, the figure of the tree provides for Marx a set of organic metaphors in terms of which he conceives the multidimensional composition and growth of capital as a "living totality." While much effort has since been spent on addressing the reductionist implications of Marx's "naturalism," such criticisms have rarely been able to see the forest for the trees. We need to concern ourselves with how such metaphors enhance both the imaginative dimensions of Marx's writing and its scientific import, which incidentally owe much to the influence of Darwinian biology generally and to the *Origin of Species* (1859) in particular (cf. Hyman 1962: 11–78; Lukács 1970; O'Neill 1982: 97–108; Wilson 1991: 120–46).

It is interesting, therefore, to note the interpretive implications that follow when Martin Nicolaus omits one of these metaphors in his translation of the *Grundrisse*, specifically, in Marx's image of "trees which will not be allowed to grow [too far] over the workers' heads [*um dem Arbeiter die Baümer nicht über dem Kopf wachsen zu lassen*]" (VII 19: 757). Here Marx seems to be painting a picture of workers who lay out (*anlegen*) a garden or plant an orchard, and later stretch to pull at or draw down (*ziehn*) the fruits of the harvest, at least insofar as such fruits continue to grow within reach. However, Nicolaus's translation abandons the image of the tree for the idea that the capitalist system "leave[s] little danger of the workers being *overwhelmed by abundance*" (my emphasis). He thus preserves Marx's understanding of the structural relation between poverty and wealth, but not the suggestion conveyed in the metaphor that the real "danger" (a word not used here by Marx, although its meaning may be implied) for capitalism would not consist of giving the poorer classes too much (the "overwhelming abundance" in Nicolaus's translation) but of giving them too little or nothing at all.

Although the difference between the two versions is not crucial to Marx's understanding of the structure of the capitalist distribution and production of wealth (cf. Nicolaus 1972), its empirical application is what is at stake here, and incidentally in Marx's so-called immiseration thesis generally. In particular, Marx's argument here is that Bastiat should know better than to think that even in periods of agricultural overproduction the workers ever really get much to eat, and implies that by starving the workers, the capitalists may in fact increase the level of agitation and put their interests in danger. It appears, then, that the altered translation projects a kind of "American" ideology of abundance onto the historical reality of French poverty (in contrast to Ernst Wangermann's more "English" version, "undue affluence," in the *Collected Works*).

In an early article titled "Debates on the Law on Thefts of Wood," Marx undertook a brilliant analysis of the economic, legal, and metaphorical significance of trees as a way of illuminating the material and theoretical relations between peasants and property owners:

> Nature itself presents as it were a model of the antithesis between poverty and wealth in the shape of the dry snapped twigs and branches separated from organic life in contrast to the trees and stems which are firmly rooted and full of sap, organically assimilating air, light, water, and soil to develop their own proper form and individual life. . . . Human poverty senses this kinship and deduces its right to property from this feeling of kinship. (Marx 1842 CW 1: 234)

I am suggesting that in his later works, Marx literally "cultivates" or "develops" the metaphor of tree-growing into a figure for capital's "organic composition," that is, its capacity continuously to "bear fruit" while perpetuating a class structure which ensures that the harvest is distributed unequally. In other words, the legal claims of the peasants of the right to gather (in German: *lesen*) wood presented to Marx a model he later used in his critical reading (*lesen*) of the political economy of capitalism (cf. Marx 1859 CW 29: 262; Illich 1977). In the context of today's global political economy, the figure of the capitalist hothouse with its tantalizing trees might help us to shift our focus on the distribution of power and wealth from the east/west axis of capitalist versus socialist countries to the north/south axis of First World versus Third Worlds.

5. The house of prostitution (Marx and the universal market)

What Marx refers to as the colonial "hothouse" (*Treibhaus*) when describing the expansion of capitalism into a global system frantically searching for the "representatives" of wealth and power (II 2: 225), could also be understood to be a house of prostitution (also *Treibhaus*), that is, a global warehouse and whorehouse where everyone and everything can be bought and sold in the capitalist market:

> (The exchangeability of all products, activities and relations with a third, *objective* entity which can be re-exchanged for everything *without distinction*— that is, the development of exchange values (and of money relations) is identical with universal venality, corruption. Universal prostitution appears as a necessary phase in the development of the social character of personal talents, capacities, abilities, activities. More politely expressed: the universal relation of utility and use. The equation of the incompatible as Shakespeare nicely defined money. Greed as such impossible without money; all other kinds of accumulation and of mania for accumulation appear as primitive, restricted by needs on the one hand and by the restricted nature of products on the other (*sacra auri fames*)). (I: 163)

Picking up on Marx's less "polite" expression, Lyotard has speculated in a deliberately scandalous way on the significance of the figure of the prostitute in Marx's writing, drawing above all from the discussions of prostitution that appear in connection with his arguments against "crude communism" (in the 1844 *Manuscripts*) and the bourgeois family (in the *Manifesto*). He thus describes Marx's theory of money as an effect of his simultaneous fascination and disgust with what it can buy: "this horror of money, of the world of money that sells to buy and buys to sell, of the world of capital as a Milieu of universal prostitution, is the *horror* (thus concupiscence) *before the 'perversion' of the partial drives*" (Lyotard 1974: 167; my translation). But Lyotard often seems to confuse what he takes to be Marx's own ethical and emotional prurience with what should also be understood to be one of his basic analytical insights: that capitalism seeks to colonize and replace a kinship system based on the structural exchange of women and men through marriages between families, with an economic logic that puts everyone on the exchange market and in the factory, but not without revaluing certain activities and people as polluted and abject. That is, the "world's oldest profession" is necessarily valued differently depending on the historical context, whether inside or outside kinship relations, or as an (imperfect) manifestation of capitalism's tendency to subsume all human activities under its own machineries of production and exchange (cf. O'Neill 1991: 79–98).

6. *Excavating the pyramids (toward a Marxist archaeology)*

There must be more than merely symbolic significance in the fact that Marx's own studies, from 1850 until his death in 1883, were often undertaken in the library of the British Museum, which houses one of the world's largest collections of ancient artifacts from Egypt, South America, India, Greece, and elsewhere. Perhaps this alone is enough to open a speculation on how Marx's scientific studies might offer a perspective on the history of archaeology and museumology in the nineteenth and twentieth centuries.

In a way that combines historico-archaeological metaphor with sociopolitical analysis, Peter Berger anticipates but does not himself pursue such an inquiry in his account of the history of the pyramid at Cholula, a small town in the Mexican state of Puebla. This colossal structure was built over several centuries as a holy place of temples by successive empires, from the Teotihuacas in the third century, to the Aztecs up to the sixteenth century, until Cortés (at first revered by the Aztecs as a resurrected Quetzalcoatl) buried it and built a Christian church on top with hundreds of others around it. Only in the twentieth century was this great pyramid excavated and put under the custody of the National Institute of Archaeology and History, an agency of the Mexican government, which had discovered the political usefulness of making a cult of its pre-Columbian past (Berger 1974: 1–6). By contrast, the artifacts dug out of the Egyptian pyramids, including mummies, sarcophagi, treasures, and manuscripts, have circulated outside their place of origin, but again in the interests of science and profit, as in the King Tut road show, the permanent Egypt/Nubia exhibition at Toronto's Royal Ontario Museum, and the British Museum's famous collection of Egyptian artifacts.

The archaeological history and museum culture of the pyramids as exemplified in these two cases may therefore be understood in the context of the globalization of markets and the proletarianization of developing countries. In other words, what Marx described as the restless expansion of the colonial "hothouse" may also be figured as a First World museum and a Third World archaeological site. Beginning from what others have criticized as "a conceptual archaeology [for] unearthing the treasured 'What Marx Really Said'" (Keane and Singer 1974–75: 149; cf. note 9 to Part II), we might here anticipate a way of developing a distinctly Marxian archaeology of knowledge, power, and wealth.

7. The daughter's hand (the domestic economy of Marx's mind)

Let us imagine something like the "desire named Marx" to be embodied in the life and mind of a little girl: *la petite Marx* is horrified or even brutalized by the monstrosities of "capital," and yet her burgeoning prepubescent drives leave her confused, fascinated, and seduced by it (Lyotard 1974: 165–74). Perhaps the textual evidence for this fanciful conceit (which Lyotard lacks) may literally be found on the very surface of Marx's 1857–58 notebooks. That is, the signature of Marx's youngest daughter, Laura, graces the back of the cover of Notebook M, which contains the 1857 "Introduction," since apparently she had originally intended to use it for school (see frontispiece). On the cover of the last notebook (VII) her handwriting appears again, this time "With a hoop dedoodeuu Doo" after her father's name written in her hand in its English or French form as "Charles Marx" (facsimiles in *MEGA* II/1: 19; *Apparat*: 777; CW 28: 20, 53). These cryptic markings might be imaginatively construed to raise questions about whether Marx's notebooks may not in fact have belonged to his daughter Laura, whether this little girl and not the older man might have laid a claim to them by placing her marks on the first and last of them. Under whose name—"Karl," "Charles," or "Laura"—should we read "Marx"?

As tempting as it may be to pursue these speculations, we need first to consider the implicit notion of a domestic economy that informs Marx's critical writings on political economy. Marx's own theory of the alienation (*Entfremdung*) and uncanniness (*Unheimlichkeit*) of bourgeois social structures may thus be interpreted partly in terms of the Marx family's perpetual state of "foreignness" and of "being away from home." Following a lead given by Marx in the intellectual self-portrait sketched in his 1859 "Preface," we might read Marx's own poverty-ridden domestic economy within the context of the capitalist economy of the nineteenth century through a pattern of interruption and exile. First, through his own intellectual work Marx aimed to intervene in the alienating social conditions about which he was writing. At the same time, the desperation of such conditions was interrupting his studies and interfering with his own well-being and that of his family, forcing them to live in poverty and ill health and to move further and further from Germany. Finally, family time and home life constrained Marx's reading and writing, inducing him to work late into the night and to write for journals in order to support himself, his wife, his maid, and his three daughters.

The role of Engels's friendship and financial resources in alleviating this situation cannot be overestimated, for he often played the role of the angel (*Engel*) of good news with every £20 note he sent to his best friend. Nor should the significance of Helene Demuth be overlooked, since she was the servant for whom the family held the deepest respect and reverence and who provided an anchor of humility (*Demut*) as well as a source of scandal when Marx fathered her child (his only surviving son) in the early 1850s (McLellan 1973; Seigel 1978; cf. note 2 to Part II). Finally, Marx's beloved daughters, each with her own set of endearing nicknames, were the very image and pride of their parents, so much so that Marx could not help trying to prevent his youngest daughter, Laura, from losing her family name to the "Creole," Paul Lafargue, who in 1866 asked for her hand in marriage. Interpreting Marx with Freud (1977 [1905]; cf. Kemple 1989) and in the direction of Lyotard, we might here begin a proper study of the "psychic household" or "domestic economy of the mind" (*psychische Haushalt*) that informs Marx's writings (cf. note 27 to Part III). Such an investigation would need to incorporate such issues as the ambivalent status of "domestics" inside and outside of the bourgeois household, and the sociological significance of the transformation of the patronymic into a family name.

8. Finding the fetishes (the catachresis of use value)

The most radical disharmonious note or catachresis sounded in Marx's theoretical scheme or composition is transported by way of the concept of use value (cf. Baudrillard 1975; Sekine 1984; Spivak 1987). Marx's economic analysis of exchange value does not simply leave out, but rather presupposes, both a theoretical analysis of commodity fetishism and an anthropological inquiry into use values. Indeed, his critical perspective calls for such a cross-cultural and historical approach, not as an interesting literary digression but as a propaedeutic to political economy, even when he himself does not pursue it (Rubin 1973: 5–6; cf. note 22 to Part III, on Marx's planned "Book on Wage-Labor").

Rather than jump into a "post-Marxist" position, we need first to discern the function and intention of Marx's strategic exclusions or to trace the form and location such issues took in his work. An important area of future research will therefore be to look into the waxing and waning of Marx's interest in the history and anthropology of noncapitalist societies. Indeed, his pursuit of these latter studies seems literally to "frame" the edges or margins of his entire career: from the excerpts he made in Bonn in 1842 on the history of art and religion (in *MEGA* IV/1) to the ethnological notebooks he kept in London from 1879 to 1883. Only a few Marx scholars have appreciated the significance of such an approach, notwithstanding the debates on the "Asiatic mode of production" (cf. the introduction to Marx [1879–83] in Krader 1972; and Mitchell 1986). In the final analysis, however, the problematic of use value in Marx's writings will need to be tied to his concept of fetishism, as well as to some understanding of his own personal and theoretical "fetishes," including his obsessive avoidance of an examination of use value within his study of political economy proper (partly an effect of his scientific aspirations), combined with his irresistible attraction to perspectives that provide critical insights from outside the system (partly an effect of his political commitments). Only in this way will we be able to "see what is not there" without disavowing (*Verleugnung*) its existence (cf. Freud 1977 [1927]).

9. A hieroglyphic script (deciphering a notebook by its cover)

Marx's 1857–58 notebooks are literally covered in signs that, with some practice and specialist knowledge, may be deciphered as a kind of hieroglyph, that is, an arrangement of images and signs that form a text which tells a story (cf. note 7 to Part III). For example, the editors of the *Gesamtausgabe* note that the outer cover of Marx's Notebook I, which contains the "Chapter on Money," is literally covered with cryptic markings. Each of them may be arranged and then "deciphered" to reveal its logical and narrative connection with respect to the contents of the notebook itself, and thus show themselves to be anything but arbitrary, indifferent, or meaningless signs (*MEGA* II/1; *Apparat*: 781–82, 783 facsimile; cf. I: 145).

Hieroglyph 1: "Heft I." This designation expresses a connection with the other six notebooks from 1857–58, implying that the entire text forms an organic whole in its own right. But this sense of the work's completeness and independence is upset by *Hieroglyph 2: "A" (corrected from) "C," "Heft a."* Each of these headings seems to relate to notebooks B' and B, which contain drafts for the *Critique of Political Economy* published in 1859, suggesting that these notebooks form only part of a series. That the "C" may refer either to later studies in the theory of capital or to some earlier set of notebooks is implied by *Hieroglyph 3: "Wirth, Tooke."* The works of these two authors whom Marx studied in 1852, the former's *History of the Germans* and the latter's *History of Prices*, indicate his use of specialist histories to "fill in the blanks" (as he puts it) of his developing theory of political economy. That such studies might also pose new perspectives on or challenges to his conceptual framework is hinted at by *Hieroglyph 4: schema of the shifting of consonants.* Grimm's *History of the German Language*, of which Marx made a conspectus in 1856, may have suggested to him that, like the use of precious metals for money, the history of alphabetic signs is neither "arbitary" nor a matter of "indifference" (I: 145), since even subtle shifts and substitutions may indicate that a new language is being articulated (as in the emergence of English from German). The formal principle of displacement embodied in this schema seems to be even more perfectly presented in *Hieroglyph 5: arithmetical calculations, and a right tri-*

angle whose smallest angle is bisected several times. Marx's critical theory largely draws from both an algebraic-arithmetical conception of time and a geometrical conception of space, which inform but are analytically distinct from his empirical studies of circulation, production, and distribution (cf. Marx [1881b]; Struik 1948). Since numbers in mathematics need not refer to anything in reality, and letters may designate any and all numbers, we may thus repeatedly return to the cryptic signs of the other hieroglyphs in order to imagine more creatively what else they might mean . . .

The very surface of Marx's text thus seems to provide a key for deciphering its contents insofar as the signs that cover it either designate specific subjects discussed inside or indicate a formal scheme of interpretation for treating these subjects. It is less a question here of delighting in superficial trivialities than it is of employing a specialist knowledge to offer fresh perspectives on what at first appears to be strange, or perhaps to disrupt our complacent sense of familiarity.

10. *Illuminating the text (introduction to Marx's semiology)*

Let us excavate a particular image from the depths of a text and use it to reconfigure that work as a whole, both what it is and what it is about. The figure of the pyramid may project for us a kind of neon sign illuminating Marx's text from within, while lighting a way outside it as well (VII: 769). This concept-metaphor may therefore exude a "general illumination which bathes all the other colors and modifies their particularity . . . a particular ether which determines the specific gravity of every being which has materialized within it [here: Marx's text]" (M: 107). The method in this madness consists of extending and reapplying the insane rationality of Marx's object of study, the capitalist money system, to the crazy logic of his own study of it.

Marx himself may have dug the figure of the pyramid not just from his knowledge of history but also from the history of philosophy as told by Hegel. That is, the semiology by which Marx tried to understand the fungible signs of the capitalist money system may derive from the treasure chest of Hegel's philosophical "Concept" of the sign, which Jacques Derrida shows is imagined by Hegel through the figure of the pyramid. The word "pyramid," Derrida argues, comes to function for Hegel as "the semaphore of the sign, the signifier of signification": "The sign—the monument-of-life-in-death, the monument-of-death-in-life, the sepulchre of a soul or of an embalmed proper body, the height conserving in its depths the hegemony of the soul, resisting time, the hard text of stones covered with inscription—is the *pyramid*" (Derrida 1982: 83). In short, Hegel seems to have arrived at a concept of the sign—that is, at a "sign" for the philosophical "Concept"—by way of the figure of the pyramid. Derrida's "archaeological" concern here is to "excavate" Hegel's text to find out the extent to which the symbolism of Egyptian pyramids and hieroglyphics poses the problem of an image-text that "resists the movement of dialectics, history, and logos," and that may thereby disrupt the dominant phonotext of Western metaphysics.

Marx may have been writing from a similar deconstructive impulse in his frequent use of analogies that show how "the money form is structured like writing" (Spivak 1987: 34). Where the pyramid literally presents the graphic sign of an ideal or divine presence, so, too, does money serve as a kind of "visible god that solder'st close impossibilities and mak'st them kiss," as Marx puts it, quoting Shakespeare's *Timon of Athens* (I: 163; cf. Burke 1966 [1963]). By a similar confusion of verbal and visible signs, the iron bar used in the Barbary Coast as a value standard seems to present us with an " 'ideal' imaginary standard [that] is nothing but an imagined real value":

> an imagined notion, however, which, because the monetary system has not de-
> veloped its further determinants—a development depending on quite different
> relations—achieves no objective reality. It is the same as if, in mythology, one
> were to consider as the higher religions those whose god-figures are not worked
> out in visible form but remain stuck in the imagination, i.e. where they obtain
> at most an oral but not a graphic presence. (VII: 795)

The polemical context of this passage shows that Marx is concerned here to criticize the idealist and empiricist prejudices of the political economists (David Urquhart in particular), and so he is careful to specify that it is only "as if" the graphic presence of visible god figures constitutes a higher mode of thought. He thus implies that his own theory of generalized "writing" would entail a critique of the "phonocentric" metaphysics of philosophy or political economy, which would thereby deconstruct the traditional binarism of written proofs over and against oral mythologies. Indeed, his own practice of writing, especially insofar as it is read as an exemplary piece of imaginative literature or even melodrama, combines the graphic presence of science with the oral resources of a mode of folk theater that may be "musically" interpreted as a kind of vocal score.

11. *The theater of catastrophe (episodes in French melodrama)*

Marx envisions the death of capitalism through a theory of crisis that is staged as a theater of catastrophe. His "advice" to "this last form of human servitude . . . to be gone and to give room to a higher form" is also a call for the destruction of modern reality through a dramatic vision of "explosions, cataclysms, crises, . . . [and] catastrophes" (VII: 749–51). These disruptions in the flow of his argument show very little of the contemplative sobriety of the English political economists or German philosophers who usually guide him, but seem inspired, rather, by the explosive rhetoric of the nineteenth-century English radicals (cf. Marx 1856b) and especially the hysterics of such French writers as the soothsaying Proudhon and the doomsaying Balzac. As Lukács notes, the latter's catastrophic sense of the revolutionary events of 1848 projected the "vision of an imminent cataclysm, of the imminent destruction of culture and of the world, [which] is the idealistically inflated form which a presentiment of class extinction always takes" (1950: 39).

Recent dramatizations of this "theater of catastrophe" seem to find their most elaborate expression in the writings of the French post-Marxists, especially among those intellectuals writing in the wake of 1968. The critical trope in Baudrillard's theatrical script, for example, is to have posed the problem of (post)modern realism by addressing the scenes and symbolisms of modern death as a problem that reaches beyond the mere "reality" or "fantasy" of death, beyond the personal hysteria over biological death or the global panic over nuclear holocaust. Instead of assuming that the fact of death is the opposite of the dream of death, he shows how "*symbolic* death is at the origin of the *reality* of death" (Baudrillard 1976: 226). The modern reality principle has less to do with any verisimilitude of representations to reality than with the reality effects that are produced from our fascination with the destruction or imagined loss of our sense of reality, that is, with our memory or dream of the episodic scenes in a symbolic theater of death:

> Behind power, or at the very heart of power and of production, there is a void which gives them *a last glimmer of reality*. Without that which reverses them, cancels them, and seduces them, they would never have attained reality. . . . It is *the imaginary catastrophe* standing behind them that sometimes makes reality and the truth fascinating. Do you think that power, economy, sex—all the real's big numbers—would have stood up one single instant without a fascination to support them which originates precisely in the inverted mirror where they are reflected and continually reversed and where their imaginary catastrophe generates a tangible and imminent gratification? (Baudrillard 1987: 46; emphasis added)

Baudrillard wants to highlight the horror and fascination animating the dramatic spectacle of imploding reality in order to criticize what he takes to be the scientific mythology that governs the residual realism in Foucault's historical studies of the scenarios of madness, sexuality, crime, and death. These studies affect us, he argues, precisely because and insofar as we are fascinated by the passing away of the horrible "truths" and institutional principles on which modern social institutions are founded. In spite of Lyotard's charge that Baudrillard himself seems really to believe in the "real" existence and distinctive value of "primitive societies" as an alternative to modern death culture (Lyotard 1974: 126–33), both writers seem to share the same delirious sense of political economy as a seductive spectacle of libidinal flows and desires, as well as a scenic epiphany of primitive exchange and sacrifice. Thus, whatever their ultimate position on the problem of modern realism, each of these writers (Foucault included) might be seen to trade roles as actors and scriptwriters for virtually the same *theatricum philosophicum* played out with a distinctively French accent.

To follow the episodes in this theoretical drama, we need to give up trying to understand these writers as if they are or should be doing more conventional sociological analysis, political economy, or critical theory, and instead abandon ourselves to their "postmodern primitivism" and delusional mythologies (Kroker 1992; Kroker and Cook 1987), and attend to the theatrical form of their writing along with its dramatic content (Genosko 1992). The same is true when we read Marx's own writing for the way it is given over less to the familiar Victorian (or Dickensian) scenes of cruelty and violence between individuals (cf. Hyman 1962: 132) than to the almost nihilistic, French (or Balzacian) projections of the extinction of a class and the death of an entire culture: not bourgeois shock therapy but a melancholic gaze into the superficial abyss of lost illusions.

12. *Gold-weighing machines (a second excursus on the foundational passages)*

Marx's science is both informed by and itself a contribution to the literary genre of melodrama. Just as he once considered expounding the *Rationale* in Hegel's *Logic* "to make it understandable to the common man" (Marx to Engels, 16 January 1858), so, too, did he want his economic science both to be realistic and to affect real people through its emotional appeal to an often poorly educated reading public (see note 8 to Part II). Hyman has gone so far as to argue that "We get closer to the essential nature of *Capital* if we deal with it, not just as social science or polemical exhortation, but as imaginative literature," and in particular, as an exemplary piece of Victorian melodrama (1962: 132). His interest is in developing the earlier observations of Wylie Sypher's "Aesthetic of Revolution" (1948) and of Bernard Shaw in his "The Illusions of Socialism," each of whom uses literary insight to criticize the delusional character of Marxist politics: "the dramatic illusion of struggle . . . which presents the working-class as a virtuous hero and heroine in the toils of a villain called the capitalist; suffering terribly and struggling nobly, but with a happy ending for them, and a fearful retribution for the villain, in full view before the curtain on a future of undisturbed bliss" (Shaw, quoted in Hyman 1962: 146). More sympathetic than Shaw to the political dimensions of Marx's work, Hyman argues that Marx could not in fact write the last "act" of the melodrama staged in *Capital*, since "only the proletarian revolution could produce that final curtain." He is thus less given to hallucinating a future of undisturbed bliss into Marx's text and instead appreciates the political implications of its essential incompleteness.

Nevertheless, by avoiding the specifically economic content of Marx's project, each of these writers overlooks how Marx's literary imagination also informs his sense of both the political communicability of his ideas and their scientific accountability. With a focus on key texts or foundational passages (cf. Table 2B; Appendix B), for example, Marx's economic studies of 1857–58 may be understood to sketch the plot outlines of an epic melodrama, complete with an overture and opening chorus on economic harmonies, five acts that reach a crescendo in the death of a monstrous mechanical creation in its struggle with a multitude of slaves, and a final coda and chorus that ironically reveal not the secret behind this story but rather its essential mystery. What I take to be the final image of this melodramatic mystery, presented in the excerpts on "gold-weighing machines" that appear on the last page of the notebooks (VII 64; see Appendix C), brings together under one metaphorical figure several important political and economic themes presented throughout these studies: the politics of justice, the economics of science and technology, and the dominant aesthetic of nineteenth-century bourgeois mythology.

The figure of gold-weighing machines also seems to provide an allegory for characterizing my own approach to this work through the selection and use, or balancing and scaling, of key foundational passages that for me set the standards for constructing the episodes of Marx's drama (cf. note 2 to Part III). The short section in which Marx presents this image consists of two slighty doctored excerpts in English from George

Dodd's book *Curiosities of Industry and the Applied Sciences* (1854; a title that Marx corrupts at one point as CURIOSITIES *des Geldes*). Perhaps it is significant that Nicolaus's English translation of the *Grundrisse* is incomplete insofar as he does not include the last page of the last notebook on which these excerpts appear, with the page on "I Value" (VII 63: 879–80) apparently completing the earlier chapters "II Money" and "III Capital." The section "GOLD-WEIGHING MACHINES," which appears only in the CW and MEGA editions of the late 1970s and was thus not available to Nicolaus, upsets this false sense of completeness by apparently regressing to the fragment on machines earlier in the seventh notebook and the studies of the precious metals in the first. Indeed, it seems to belong both inside and outside the structure of Marx's plan, to serve as an epigraph or epilogue to his melodrama, and perhaps even to provide the true English title for the *Grundrisse* that Nicolaus lacked, since Marx himself provided the heading to this section in English. Perhaps, then, it also functions as a kind of counterweight or balance to the unevenly layered foundations of the revolutionary plot that he could only sketch without completing, or provides enough friction by rubbing against the foundations of Marx's thinking to make us wonder why this text still wears on us.

13. The ABCs of biographical portraiture (studies in the "agreeable customs of life")

Marx's "Balzacian" flair is not limited to his appreciation for that writer's realistic prose style; it is also integral to his critique of the socialist and bourgeois aspects of French culture generally. Indeed, his first critical target in his studies of 1857–58 is Alfred Darimon, whose book on the reform of the banks during the financial crisis of 1856 presents to Marx a curiously hybrid self-portrait of a bourgeois socialist worthy of Balzac (a role played out to its absurd conclusion when Darimon later switched allegiance from Proudhon to Napoleon III). Specifically, Darimon is indignant over the banks' practice of withdrawing their services "precisely at the moment when the public most needs them," and thus of failing in their "duty" to provide gold and silver currency at affordable rates of exchange. Marx thus gives the socialist Darimon a simple lesson in the laws of supply and demand, reminding him that the cost of supplying precious metals will rise as demand increases, so that those "philanthropic" grain merchants who pay high prices for withdrawing gold do so only in order to exchange it more profitably in foreign markets: "And do not the gentlemen who represent the 'public' *vis-à-vis* the bank follow the same 'agreeable customs of life'?" he asks (I 3: 119). Thus, what economists understand in terms of "general economic laws of supply and demand," and what Darimon expresses as "the rule of gold and silver," Marx calls "the agreeable customs of life." Perhaps, then, Marx is here proposing a direction for his own economic "studies in modern manners" ("die angenehme Gewohnheit des Daseins," as he puts it, paraphrasing Goethe's *Egmont*), much as Balzac devoted the greater part of the *Comédie humaine* to what he called his "études de moeurs," consisting of scenes from private, provincial, Parisian, political, and military life.

Much of Marx's work is indeed taken up with just such Balzacian studies depicting the decay of Napoleonic and post-Napoleonic France, but often in the more grand style of Goethe's exemplary portrayal of the dramatic conflict between popular customs and heroic aspirations depicted in *Egmont* (1787). Throughout the 1850s, for example, besides pursuing his economic studies and writing articles on current events for the *New York Daily Tribune*, Marx wrote short pieces for the *New York Cyclopaedia* (1857–62) dealing mostly with post-Napoleonic military figures. These biographical portraits can be read in light of Marx's developing sense of the place of historical biography within the critique of political economy, along with his other relatively marginal polemical tracts of the 1850s on shady diplomacy and absurd political figures (Marx 1852b, 1853a, 1853b, 1856a, 1860; cf. note 1 to Part III). His articles on post-1848 France, for example, reveal a montage of post-Napoleonic historical figures whose *differentia specifica*—as in the contrasting roles played by Napoleon and Louis Bonaparte— are nevertheless subject to the broader social system of post- and counterrevolutionary French capitalism, as Jeffrey Mehlman (1977) has shown.

Less interested in these historical figures for themselves, Marx came to approach them as the bearers (*Träger*) of economic categories. Usually putting his scientific studies first, he left the larger part of the *Cyclopaedia* work to Engels (who wrote all of the "A" section), and eventually contributed only to the "B" entries. More concerned with the ABCs of money as a system for exchanging equivalents as well as for changing names under the rule of capital, Marx wanted to develop a general theory for explaining how all social values become subsumed under the same name, regardless of their unique or intrinsic characteristics. As he puts it, if through exchange value A can be exchanged for B, B for C, and so on, we can say that "in money all [exchange values] are equinominal or same-named [*gleich-namig*]" (I 35: 189; VII 30: 791–92). Thus, the farce of counterfeit leaders parading under the name Bonaparte betrays a more "sinister anonymity" (*unheimliche Anonymität*) in the machinations of capitalist social processes (Mehlman 1977: 5–41), and suggests to Marx a "story [that] further recounts a violent misnaming, a situation where the circuit of the names becomes more important than the presentation of the things signified" (Spivak 1987: 31).

If Marx and Engels's tireless studies of the agreeable customs of life ultimately seem to be connected through a kind of elementary reasoning, a mother tongue, or an ABCs, this is not because they are reducible to any single factor, to a *précis de toutes les choses*, a *kurzgefasstes Compendium* (I: 218; cf. Kittler 1990), or a *dictionnaire biographique des personnages fictifs*. Rather, it is because they share with Balzac's *études de moeurs* that cynical and sinister sense of the unity of the modern historical drama as a relentless *comédie humaine*.

14. *Raphael redivivus (Balzac's search for the absolute)*

In the opening and closing arguments of his 1857–58 economic studies, Marx expresses his contempt for the laughable abstractionism and dull dryness exhibited in the statistical "tableaux" and "illustrations" of two French socialist economists, Darimon and Bastiat (I: 115; VI: 755). Depicting the social landscape in only its barest outlines or in pathetically "lurid colors," these unimaginative writers delude themselves into believing that their numerical schemes and arguments can capture the multidimensional contradictions and shades of modern social life. No better are the tenuous poetic analogies employed by those bourgeois economists who "defile all the sciences with their liquorice-sweet filth," those "belletristic sophomores" (still green before the ugly realities of bourgeois life: *belletristische Grünfärber*), "empty chatterboxes" (babbling into the blue: *Schwätze ins Blau*), and "whitewashing sycophants" (painting over the harsh realities of life in fine colors: *schönfärbenden Sykophanten*) (III 9: 293). Rather than view the world through rose-colored spectacles, Marx casts a penetrating eye across the many facets and deep recesses of the social landscape, hoping thereby to paint a vivid tableau that could portray its vast array of character types from multiple perspectives and in all their dimensions.

Such an achievement Marx found in another Frenchman, Honoré de Balzac. In the "Avant-propos" to the *Comédie humaine* that Balzac drafted in 1842, he envisioned the entire social tableau to be mounted in his monumental work in triple form, that is, through a three-layered pyramidal structure he had already conceived in 1834 but was never able to complete:

> As the work spirally achieves the heights of thought, it becomes pressed together and condensed. If twenty-four volumes are needed for the *Studies in Manners*, only fifteen will be needed for the *Philosophical Studies* and only nine for the *Analytical Studies*. Thus, man, society, and humanity will be described, judged, and analyzed without repetitions, and in a work which will be like the *Thousand and One Nights of the West*. (Balzac to Mme. Hanska, in 1956 [1842]: 38)

This pyramidal image might be seen in another way in one of Balzac's greatest masterpieces, *La Peau de chagrin*, which he wrote just a few years before the letter to his lover, Mme. Hanska, and which he describes in his "Avant-propos" as a crucial link between his philosophical studies and his studies in manners, and indeed as "the ring of an almost oriental fantasy where Life itself is painted at grips with Desire, the principle of all passion" (1956 [1842]: 72). Like the shape of the *Comédie humaine* itself, the oriental inscription on the "wild ass's skin" that gives the story its title is also triangular but in reverse image, its point turned downward. The skin bestows on its young owner the Faustian power to have all of his desires realized, but at the fatal price that it, along with the possessor's own life energies, must progressively weaken and shrink with the fulfillment of each wish.

Just as in "Le Chef d'oeuvre inconnu," another philosophical study begun the same year, in which the young painter Poussin is depicted at the threshold of glory when he, too, is tempted by the demonic *recherche de l'absolu*, so also in this tale of the demise of a young student named Raphael we might be expected to ponder the unfathomable implications if the artistic man of genius who was his namesake had also died young, that is, the Raphael who was Balzac's favorite painter. Balzac's fascination with painting and his own wish to be praised as a kind of "more or less faithful, more or less happy, patient or courageous painter of human types" (1956 [1842]: 67) indicates the manner in which he considered his own grand design (*dessein*) to consist of a montage of characters and figures that would form a monumental social tableau (cf. Maurois 1971: 285–97).

But herein lies the profound difference between the painter and the writer: "In order to create many virgins, one must be Raphael. Literature is perhaps, in this connection, beneath painting" (Balzac 1956 [1842]: 72). Thus, not unlike Marx's sense of the ambivalence of modern social mores, the *Comédie humaine* is informed by Balzac's vision of both the holy family, which offers a hope of forgiveness that may render human life sublime and civil, and the social pact, through which human passions are given over to the pursuit of vulgarity and viciousness (cf. note 27 to Part III). At the center of this literary and political vision are not just unsteady symbolic fathers but also the great maternal imago who is likewise a figure for the most delightful seductions as well as the most repulsive horrors (cf. Moore 1991).

15. The lost illusions of reality (on Balzacian Marxism)

A fictional work should not be used simply to produce a psychological study of real-life personal dilemmas or to provide literary illustrations for a scientific theory (note 17 to Part III), any more than the latter should be employed simply to reveal the real foundations of such situations that literary writers face in their own lives and depict through their fiction. For example, not only does Marx appreciate Balzac's "profound grasp of real conditions," including their political and economic foundations, but he also shares with Balzac a deep understanding that real life itself literally "works" by way of the illusions and fantasy demands people have about it:

> In a social order dominated by capitalist production, even the non-capitalist producer is dominated by capitalist ways of thinking. Balzac, a novelist who is in general distinguished by his profound grasp of real conditions, accurately portrays in his last novel, *Les Paysans* [The Peasants], how the small peasant eager to retain the good-will of the money-lender performs all kinds of services for him unpaid, yet does not see himself as giving something for nothing, as his own labor does not cost him any cash expenditure. The money-lender for his part kills two birds with one stone. He spares cash expenditure on wages and, as the peasant is gradually ruined by depriving his own fields of labor, he enmeshes him even deeper in the web of usury. (C3: 138)

The "web of usury" here is a figure for the systematic production of illusions on which capitalism depends and that Marx elsewhere calls ideology, that "rule of abstractions" and "reign of ideas" which express only an "objective dependency, which, incidentally, turns into certain definite relations of personal dependency but stripped of all illusions" (I: 164–65). For Marx it is not a question of positing the rule of the philosophers or litterateurs, but rather of showing how they, too, draw from the abstractions and ideas, illusion and disillusionment already operative in the social relations they describe. What interests Marx in Balzac is as much the realism with which his literary counterpart is so often credited, as that fantastic element by which Balzac is able to show that our illusions about reality may themselves be illusory, and that the loss of illusions may itself be an illusion sustaining the reality of the status quo.

As Lukács once remarked, this "fantastic element" derives from the fact that Balzac "radically thinks through to the end the necessities of social reality, beyond their normal limits, beyond even their feasibility" (1950: 60). For Balzac it is not a question simply of seeing or depicting reality clearly, but above all of assessing the mystifications and disillusionments that form a part of and constitute social reality. In his best-conceived novel, *Illusions perdues* (Lost illusions), for example, the naive and simplistic ideals of the printer David Séchard are not simply contrasted with the poetic ambitions of Lucien de Rubembré through the dramatic portrayal of a strained friendship. First and foremost, the ideals and illusions that both characters share are shown to be episodic final chords in the generalized capitalization of literature, whereby the capitalist exploitation of technical progress in the printing press is completed by the market manipulation of literary standards by desperate writers and capitalist publishers (Lukács 1950: 51). Balzac's fiction thus refers to, depicts, and takes as its subject matter a historical process (capitalization) that is actually taking place, thereby showing how his own work is itself both an example of the prevailing reality principle and a model of the situations portrayed in the novel (cf. note 8 to Part II). A Balzacian-Marxist sense of the role of social fictions within social reality transcends merely literary interests, envisioning rather a political project that the critique of such illusions might incite: "To call upon [people] to give up their illusions about their conditions is to call upon them to give up a condition that requires illusions" (Marx 1843–44 SE: 244).

16. *The highway of history (the case for Lukács)*

An intellectual journey is almost never without its side routes and detours, its twists and its turns, and its bumpy rides. Jeffrey Mehlman has criticized Georg Lukács's Marxian reading of Balzac as an almost obsessive attempt to avoid getting lost in the labyrinths of texts by conservatively opting for "an interpretive tendency which functions as a pressure to inhibit . . . the text's strongest moves." He argues that such a restrained approach may be understandable partly because it is already operative in Balzac's fictional historical interpretations (as in the conflicts between royalists, republicans, and police in *Les Chouans*). By contrast, Marx's own historical accounts are often much less inhibited, as in a text like the *Eighteenth Brumaire of Louis Bonaparte*, whose strongest moves can be seen to lie in the unwieldy "Bonapartism" and other tangential eruptions that emerge unexpectedly into his writing, in spite of his efforts to control them through the "philosopheme of representation" (Mehlman 1977: 117–18).

Mehlman rejects what he takes to be the reserved Lukácsian style of Marxian interpretation because it prefers the more direct highway of scientific history with its speed limits, laws, and signposts, resisting the temptation to take off on literary side routes when the ride gets rough:

> Respect for the classical heritage means that Marxists look for the true high-road of history, the true direction of its development, the true course of its historical curves, the formula of which they know, and because they know the formula they do not fly off at a tangent and at every hump in the graph, as modern thinkers often do because of their theoretical rejection of the idea that there is any such thing as an unchanged general line of development. (Lukács 1950: 5)

But when quoting this statement in his argument against Lukács, Mehlman elides the opening and closing phrases, that is, "Respect for the classical heritage" and "modern thinkers" (cf. Mehlman 1977: 116), which indicate the polemical context of Lukács's own argument. With the view through his windshield restricted in this way, Mehlman does not see that the Lukácsian-Marxian respect for classical literature may itself serve as a kind of road sign requiring detours, digressions, or tangents that diverge less from history's high road than from those modern thinkers like Mehlman who would seem to reject any such idea of the true direction of history. Thus, in spite of the fact that both of these drivers (modern thinkers) occupy the same road (history) and obey most of the same rules (respect for the classical heritage), where Lukács appears to Mehlman to be one of those extremely defensive, inhibited, and pressured highway speed demons who drive according to a set formula, Mehlman would appear to Lukács to be among those careless drivers who get bored with the monotony of the ride and thus fly off on a tangent and at every hump in the road: for Lukács, such drivers need either to have their (Marxist) licenses revoked or to be sent back to (Marxist) driving school.

Taking a longer view of the Marxist road of history, and a closer look at Lukács's own long career, we might ask whether it is possible to pursue an interpretive course that is attentive to the forward direction of history but does not prohibit digressions from historical-political analysis into literature (Mehlman). "The case for Lukács" must therefore be packed like Lukács's own traveling case for finding the meaning of Marxism, not as a "Baedeker of history" but as "a signpost pointing the direction in which history moves forward" (Lukács 1950: 4). Lukács's long "road to Marx" (as he called it) did not proceed along some kind of shortcut or one-way street that made him leave behind the distracting stories of his youth (Lukács 1971 [1964 "Preface"]). It is rather the case that his twisting and winding path through literary criticism eventually came to intersect with Marx's own digression into a "story" about the politics and economics of how such roads are built (V: 525–33).

17. Splendors and miseries of the bourgeoisie (the unconscious Marx)

In 1865 Marx made his "Confession," that is, a list of his likes and dislikes as part of a parlor game that was all the rage among Londoners. In it he listed Balzac among his favorite prose writers, along with Diderot, Goethe, and Lessing (1 April 1865, in CW 42). Marx was enamored of the panoramic view of the murky depths and dazzling heights of French social life that provides unity and dramatic structure to Balzac's Comédie humaine. His personal experiences and scientific studies would surely have reminded him of characters and scenarios he was reading in Balzac, as he himself occasionally remarked in his writings and private letters. From the other side, his readings of the many character types that figure prominently in the Balzacian literary universe would have jogged memories of his own years as a young political journalist, an ambitious revolutionary, or a would-be poet and dramatist. Likewise, Marx was probably deeply moved when he reflected on the tragedy of Balzac's personal failure to complete his writings, in spite of the Promethean sacrifices he made on their behalf, or his having died before seeing his worst fears proved true (in the rise of Napoleon III) or his best hopes realized (cf. Maurois 1971; Seigel 1978).

In his reminiscences about his father-in-law, Paul Lafargue notes that Marx had planned to write a critical review of Balzac's entire Comédie humaine after completing his economic studies. He thus confirms our sense of Balzac's intractable place at either the unknowable core or the ill-defined outer edges of Marx's scientific consciousness. But in exploring this relatively unconscious and unknown dimension of Marx's thought we should not limit ourselves to considering why Marx would want to turn (or return) to Balzac's work simply because it could provide illustrations for personal and historical dilemmas he otherwise sought to represent through science. In spite of their differences in political ideology and intellectual craft, Marx may have been able to find in Balzac a theory or model of representation that accounts for the limits, ironies, and rhetorical effects of representation (cf. note 15 to Part III). Ned Lukacher comes close to such a consideration when he reads Marx's polemical writings of the 1850s as "a retreating forwards . . . toward a notion of philosophy for which he did not have a name" (1986: 253). Indeed, it seems that insofar as Marx could not yet give his own name to the thought he was developing in the 1850s, we may need to read Marx beyond Marxism, perhaps by reading "Marx as Balzac," or even as the painter Frenhofer in Balzac's "Chef d'oeuvre inconnu" (Seigel 1978: 363–92). The Balzacian frame of Marx's life and work can be glimpsed not just through wild literary speculation but also through our sense of Marx's own appreciation of particular works by Balzac, through which he himself may have sought to develop a theory of reading and interpretation that would delve into the unknown or unconscious dimensions of human life.

18. *The stone of reality (the Marxist unconscious)*

It is one thing to read literature for the way it distorts reality or leaves out certain real considerations: Balzac, for example, exploited his literary license in the pursuit of historical truth, while Marx was often disturbed by the unrealistic depictions of "socialist" writers like Eugène Sue (Marx and Engels 1845; cf. notes 1 and 15 to Part III). But it is quite another thing to posit historical reality as the unarticulated, unconscious, or ultimate ground of literature. In the final analysis, Jameson's concept of literature's "political unconscious" seems to rest on just such an unexamined (though eloquently stated) notion of "reality" and "the ultimate ground of history" as the intractable and compelling "subtexts" of "literature":

> The literary work or cultural object, as though for the first time, brings into being that very situation to which it is also, at one and the same time, a reaction. It articulates its own situation and textualizes it, thereby encouraging and perpetuating the illusion that the situation itself did not exist before it, that there is nothing but a text, that there never was any extra- or contextual reality before the text itself which generated it in the form of a mirage. One does not have to argue the reality of history: necessity, like Doctor Johnson's stone, does that for us. (Jameson 1981: 82)

In spite of this particular formulation, with its somewhat crass appeal to the hard realities of historical necessity, Jameson's more detailed literary analyses of Balzac's work (e.g., 1971a, 1990) discern in a much more subtle way the manner by which that writer's authorial libidinal and ideological investments—as in the careful construction of his descriptions and prologues—themselves produce "reality effects" through which he attempts to control reader responses. Jameson is thus able to show how an essential aspect of Balzac's realism may be understood to be "allegorical," in the way that he employs and exaggerates the very illusions and mirages that are operative both in his own compositional practice (as in the construction of an apparently neutral description) and in the workings of social reality itself (as in the illusions and ideologies that govern social relations). Jameson's concept of the political unconscious thus seems to entail an "archaeological" project of recovering subjugated discourses buried within other apparently formal—but in fact highly ideological—layers of discourse (cf. Foucault 1973; note 6 to Part III).

Ultimately, however, Jameson really does seem to be concerned with the intractable necessity of stumbling over "Doctor Johnson's stone," and thus really to believe in its unspeakable powers and its transcendent unknowability. By contrast, Marx is usually more concerned with the social fiction of this "stone" and thus with its social functions, whereby, for example, "the possession of money places me in exactly the same relationship towards wealth (social) as the philosopher's stone would towards the sciences" (II: 222). It would appear, then, that we may also need to dig out the Marxist unconscious as a subjugated discourse within Jameson's own discourse on the political unconscious (cf. note 5 to Part II).

19. *Democritus redivivus (Marx's search for the absolute)*

The whole of Marx's lifework—from his doctoral dissertation to his work on volume 3 of *Capital* in his final years—might be read as a tireless attempt to grasp all of reality through knowledge, and then to present that knowledge in his own perfect "masterpiece." At least that is the judgment of Jerrold Seigel in his psychobiographical study, *Marx's Fate: The Shape of a Life*. Marx thus became like the old antique dealer in Balzac's *Peau de chagrin* who lives in fascination and fear of the "wild ass's skin," traveling the world in order to learn of its mysterious powers but in the end selling it to a desperate and suicidal young student. Even more did Marx become like the insane painter in Balzac's "Chef d'oeuvre inconnu," who considers searching the globe to find the world's most gorgeous woman so he can finish his sublime masterpiece but in the end settles for a young painter's beautiful lover to pose for him. In his interminable search for absolute knowledge and for the perfect outer expression of his inner vision, "Marx's fate" was ultimately to have become like the worldly Democritus whom he himself had so severely criticized in his doctoral dissertation:

> Driven by the light in his mind and the pale reflection of his vision which reality offered, Democritus had also travelled the world in search of evidence. "Cicero calls him a *vir eruditus*. He is competent in physics, ethics, mathematics, in the encyclopedic disciplines, in every art." So did Marx become a *vir eruditus*, extending his learning to some of the same disciplines Democritus cultivated. His notebooks and manuscripts bulged with accumulated knowledge. He did not, like Democritus, travel "through half the world in order to exchange experiences, pieces of knowledge, and observations," but he learned new languages and constantly expanded the scope of his reading. He wrote to friends at vari-

ous times that *Capital* could not be completed until he had at hand one more piece of information—from Belgium, or Russia, or the United States. Marx's self-induced illnesses were less radical and violent than Democritus' blinding himself, but their self-destructiveness served a similar purpose, preserving the theoretical vision underlying *Capital* from the threatened revelation that the empirical reality of market relations might not correspond to it. (Seigel 1978: 388–89; quotations from Marx [1840–41])

While Marx never relented in his search for the correct empirical expression for the ideals and insights that continuously guided his work, and was indeed torn by the compromise these conflicting research principles demanded of him, he nevertheless did not hope to achieve—nor did he despair over the impossibility of realizing—an absolute identity between his theoretical representation of reality on the one hand, and the actual processes of historical reality on the other (cf. Wilson 1991). Rather than believe that his work had to culminate with the Democritean construction of a comprehensive table of social knowledge, Marx wanted above all to express his vision through an Epicurean principle of beauty, happiness, and pleasure. More likely to identify with the young student and the aspiring painter in Balzac's stories (Raphael and Poussin respectively), Marx would probably have delighted in the ironic failure of the aging masters (the antique dealer and Frenhofer) in their ruthless search to find the secret principle of life, just as he had earlier ridiculed Democritus's aspirations to be the great *vir eruditus*. And yet a certain ambivalence may lie at the heart of his Epicurean search for the absolute that is mirrored both in Poussin's triumphant rise to glory and immortal fame, and in its tragic counterpart in the exhaustion and death of the young Raphael (cf. Miles 1992).

20. *The writer as a masturbating masochist* *(sacrifice and pleasure in Marx's work)*

It is well known that Marx often sacrificed his health, happiness, and well-being, along with those of his family, to a kind of Promethean singleness of purpose he expressed through his work and acted on through his political commitments. As if to live by Adam Smith's version of Jehovah's curse on Adam—"In the sweat of thy brow shalt thou labor!"—he conducted his colossal labors through long days and sleepless nights that he seemed to offer up to some as yet only partly articulated ideal: "In his normal state of health, strength and activity, and with the common degree of skill and facility which he may possess, he must always give up the *identical portion of his tranquillity, his freedom,* and his *happiness*" (Smith, quoted by Marx VI: 610–11). Nevertheless, in a project like his economic studies of 1857–58, Marx seemed determined to make his tireless efforts at constructing his great theoretical monument count for more than just an imaginary, pure expenditure of time or investment of energy that could not be realized in this world, as with "the Egyptian kings or Etruscan priest-nobles [and their] pyramids, etc." (IV: 432). In only a limited sense, then, is the sacrificial aspect of his theoretical work like the historic form of "*repulsive . . . external, forced labor*" among slaves, serfs, and wage workers, and even less is it like the "worthless castigation and flagellation" that characterizes the monk's sacrifice to the gods: "The negation of tranquillity, as mere negation, ascetic sacrifice, creates nothing . . . [it] can also be called the sacrifice of laziness, unfreedom, unhappiness, i.e. negation of a negative state" (VI: 613). Rather than simply suffer under capitalism's production imperatives, Marx's desire was both to take his place in the work of history and to project a future realm of freedom beyond degrading work.

To be sure, this aspiration could not end for him in a world of "freedom and happiness . . . mere fun, mere amusement" (VI: 610–11), although he himself exercised many liberties and took great pleasure in what he produced. And while he would certainly not have wished his writings to be read as the unproductive "delusions of a madman" (*Narre*) (III 14: 305), his writing certainly exemplifies many insane qualities. Lyotard has speculated on both the madness and the pleasure in Marx's work by irreverently asking what a proper Marxist would never ask: What was Marx's left hand doing while his right hand took notes and wrote books? Invoking the figure of "the writing masturbator, capitalist apparatus par excellence" (1974: 174), Lyotard may be understood to be putting Marx himself among "those sycophantic economists . . . [who] . . . want to demonstrate to [the bourgeois] that it is productive labor when somebody picks the lice out of his hair, or strokes his tail [*den Schwantz reibe*], because for example the latter activity will make his fat head—BLOCKHEAD—clearer the next day in the comptoir [office]" (II 21–22: 273). In spite of the counteraccusations we might expect each writer to make against the other at this point, their scandalous polemics draw our attention to the larger question of whether the eroticism of one's literary labors may be realized not as accidents and deviations within the writing process, but rather among its sources and effects. Instead of conceiving his work through the bourgeois notion of "pleasure in work" (cf. Donzelot 1981–82) by which the political economy of capitalism is only intensified through the libidinal economy of desire, Marx wanted to exercise all of his faculties through writing as a form of "really free working, e.g. composing [*Komponieren*], [which] is at the same time precisely the most damned seriousness, the most intense exertion" (VI 17: 611). Thus, with both hands he strove to make his work an example of that unity of sense and intellect whose social form would be communism, and the real possibility of which he could only glimpse in the present as a hopeful sign of the future.

21. Untitled (Marx's advice, Balzac's dedication)

In a short note Marx sent to Engels in 1867, he advised his friend to read Balzac's short story "Le Chef d'oeuvre inconnu," telling him that "it is full of the most delightful ironies" (Marx to Engels, 25 February 1867). Through its depiction of the unsuccessful efforts of a painter named Frenhofer to capture reality itself through art, the story indeed provides an ironical commentary on the general problem of realism with which Marx and Engels were also concerned in the presentation of their scientific studies. Although we can only guess whether Engels indeed took Marx's advice, or whether the irony was lost on him if he did, we do know that Engels was profoundly impressed by the ironic combination of Balzac's success as a literary writer with his failure as a political thinker, as he notes in his celebrated letter to Margaret Harkness:

Well, Balzac was politically a Legitimist; his great work is a constant elegy on the irretrievable decay of good society; his sympathies are all with the class doomed to extinction. Yet his satyre is never sharper, his irony never bitterer than when he sets in motion the very men and women with whom he sympathizes most deeply—the nobility. . . . That Balzac thus was compelled to go against his own class sympathies and political prejudices, that he *saw* the necessity of the downfall of his favorite nobles, and described them as people deserving no better fate; and that he *saw* the men of the future where, for the time being, they alone were to be found—that I consider one of the greatest triumphs of Realism, and one of the grandest features in old Balzac. (Engels to Margaret Harkness, April 1888; from Engels's draft in English)

Lukács later deepened this analysis by showing how far this ambiguity of political blindness and literary insight resonates through the problem of realism itself. Balzac's literary realism thus succeeds not in spite of its failure to represent reality "as it is," but because and insofar as it fails (Lukács 1950: 21). Indeed, it is this expressive inadequacy and literary incommensurability that is the very mark of realism. This understanding of realism may already be intimated in Marx's reference in his note to Balzac's story as itself a little "chef d'oeuvre": like Frenhofer's impossible "masterpiece," the story itself necessarily fails to present anything new about the historical Poussin but succeeds in its perfect depiction of a thoroughly impossible and fictional failure. Perhaps, then, the irony of Balzac's story carries over not just to Marx's advice to Engels but also to the projects with which both men were concerned. That is, the elaborate phantasmagorias of fiction may actually come closer to the truth than the hard-core realisms of history, sociology, and politics that Marx believed to be Engels's forte (cf. Levine 1975).

In a different way, Balzac himself seems to acknowledge these paradoxes in his cryptic dedication of his story simply "To a LORD," followed by five unexplained lines of dots. As the editor points out, Balzac's dedication and mysterious "epigraph" seem to provide a strange commentary on the title and contents of the story, raising questions about whether this unnamed "Lord" may know some secret about the unknown masterpiece that is not divulged in the story, perhaps even suggesting that these dots may themselves be the ironical "point" of the narrative itself: "Indecipherable, secret, these lines have a mysterious value; unveiled, divulged, as are Poussin's mistress and Frenhofer's canvas in the story, they are nothing more . . . than an object whose value is degraded in passing from the solitary and unknown life of the heart and the spirit to public life, from the interior sky to the social inferno" (Balzac 1956 [1831]: 474, editor's note). It seems, then, that the "Lord" to whom Balzac dedicated his story has no more right to a proper name than Balzac's story itself may lay claim to a proper title, just as Marx's best works, and his "Grundrisse" in particular, may in the end not be entitled to any other designation than simply "rough drafts" or "notebooks" (cf. note 12 to Part III): in both instances we seem to be confronted with a nontitle not unlike Diderot's "Ceci n'est pas un conte" (This is not a story). (Diderot was a favorite writer of both Balzac and Marx.) Rather than carry titles, then, these literary pieces by Marx and Balzac are headed by a friendly word of advice and a cryptic dedication that also serve as epigraphic reminders of the nonidentity of the reader with what is already written and of what is written with what each hopes to express in writing. In these references to the best friend and the unnamed (and perhaps unknown) Lord we might therefore locate the most distinguishing mark of realism: the search by the writer for a reader, since only between them lies any hope of finding the truth.

22. Sancho Panza's suffering (on the ledger's mythopoetics)

Throughout his career Marx continuously produced outlines and plans that may be read as metacommentaries projecting different versions of his project as a whole. They not only present arguments that seem to be complete in themselves—and so can be analyzed and judged according to what they actually contain—but they also sketch points that are to be elaborated later and can therefore only be supposed to be true or imagined to be necessary. This dynamic tension and potential structure in his work give it an almost delusional character even as they also illuminate the path of Marx's long scientific quest.

Concentrating on Marx's 1857–58 notebooks, Roman Rosdolsky has presented an indispensable analysis of Marx's proposed and revised "plans," beginning from the original six-part systematic analysis and critical presentation of bourgeois economics and ending with the three-volume plan of *Capital* (1977: 55–56). He demonstrates, for example, that when drawing up an early plan for his critique of political economy, Marx had wanted to write a separate "Book on Wage-Labor" after *Capital*. He thus shows how the notebooks appear to constitute simply a stage in the development of a more perfect, refined, and harmonious work in which the theory of wage labor would eventually be "subsumed" into the theory of capital, thus explaining how the "Book on Wage-Labor" eventually came to "fit" into *Capital* as a chapter of volume 1 (and was partly left aside in an unpublished manuscript, Marx [1862]; Rosdolsky 1977: 57–62, 282–313).

Arguing against Rosdolsky's conclusions, but also using these notebooks as his point of departure, Antonio Negri convincingly stresses the unique importance of Marx's proposed "Book on Wage-Labor" as the irreplaceable presupposition and key antithetical form of Marx's entire theory of capital. He provides a list of the major points by which (he insists) from the *Grundrisse* to *Capital* "the theory of capital can only base itself and develop by way of the theory of the wage" (1984: 129–30). Showing how the latter cannot simply be incorporated into the former, Negri presents a reading of these plans that is attentive to both their topical proportions and their thematic layers. He shows, for example, how the effect of this proposed book on wage labor would have been to highlight the political intentions of Marx's entire critical presentation of capital, how a phenomenology of worker subjectivity always already informed Marx's theory of objectifying economic structures, and how Marx himself understood the concept of wages to play a dissonant role within the economic harmonies of such economists as Bastiat (III 5–6: 889–93).

Marx's outlines and plans are so many ways of framing a reality that must always exceed and be at variance with any representation of it. However, their sometimes "delusional" or even "quixotic" implications derive less from any resemblance Marx's scientific quest might have to Don Quixote's search for Dulcinea than they do from his critical understanding of the errant knight's haughty disavowal of Sancho Panza's suffering (cf. III: 891).

23. *Robinson Crusoe and the birth of "economic man"* *(on the ledger as a moral inventory)*

In Marx's view, if the fiction of Robinson Crusoe alone on his island presents a kind of primal myth of the origins of the "Natural Individual" as conceived by eighteenth-century economists, this is not because this story itself represents any "reaction against over-sophistication and a return to a misunderstood natural life, as cultural historians imagine." The "Natural Individual" is only an ideal taken from the present and pro-jected into the past, and so merely expresses a precapitalist myth that represents "the anticipation of 'civil society'" with its division into economic classes (M 1: 83). It is this "anticipatory" aspect of the Crusoe myth that puts it at the center of Marx's own account of what may be called his critical fiction of "the birth of 'economic man.'" Crusoe, then, is not the noble savage frolicking in the Garden of Eden, but neither is he simply a greedy speculator ready to exploit the raw wealth of the wilderness: "the most covetous griping miser in the world would have been cured of the vice of covetousness if he had been in my case; for I possessed infinitely more than I knew what to do with" (Defoe 1965 [1719]: 140). Thus, in spite of the boundlessness of nature, Crusoe bud-gets his time, rations his resources, and keeps a strict account of the tools he has been able to save from the shipwreck in a way that does not exemplify but only prefigures the logic of investment and savings which will later drive the expansion of capitalism: "This boundless greed after riches, this passionate chase after exchange-value, is common to the capitalist and the miser; but while the miser is merely a capitalist gone mad, the capitalist is a rational miser" (C1: 254).

As Max Weber argued in his famous study of the origins of economic rationalism, Defoe's story from the early eighteenth century carries the traces of that same monastic and Protestant asceticism which provided a religious source and moral force for the economic ethics shared by both modern capitalists and wage laborers. Thus, by shut-ting the door on the cells of the Catholic monks of the Middle Ages, who rationalized divine salvation into a temporal economy of credits and debits, the Puritan outlook could stand "at the cradle of modern 'economic man'" and watch his growth from Bunyan's Pilgrim, who must "hurry through the market place of vanity in his lonely spiritual search for the Kingdom of Heaven," to Defoe's Robinson Crusoe, "the isolated economic man, who carries on missionary activities on the side" (Weber 1930: 176, 174). Perhaps, then, we should not be surprised to find that the ledger Crusoe began to keep shortly after being shipwrecked does not simply function for him as an eco-nomic catalog; it also provides him with a moral inventory through which he conducts a quasi-religious examination of conscience:

> and as my reason now began to master my despondency, I began to comfort my self as well as I could, and to set the good against the evil, that I might have

something to distinguish my case from worse, and I started it very impartially, like debtor and creditor, the comforts I enjoyed against the miseries I suffered, thus:

Evil	Good
I am cast upon a horrible desolate island, void of all recovery.	But I am alive, and not drowned as all my ship's company was.

[etc. . . .]

I have no soul to speak to, or relieve me.	But God wonderfully sent the ship in near enough to the shore, that I have gotten out so many necessary things as will either supply my wants, or enable me to supply myself as long as I live.

. . . and let this stand as a direction for the experience of the most miserable of all conditions in this world, that we may always find in it something to comfort our selves from, and to set in the description of good and evil, on the credit side of the account. (Defoe 1965 [1719]: 83–84)

Crusoe's "prayers and the like" do not simply constitute a kind of "recreation" for him, as Marx seems to assume (C1: 169); they also secure the moral and religious foundations of the economic balances of the ledger he must now use to guide his life, his new "Good Book" in which is contained any hope he has of finding his way back to civilization.

24. The dialectician's credo (on the ledger's logical structure)

One of Marx's most lasting achievements was the manner in which he distinguished a logical ideal on the one hand, and those value-laden interests which may be held for ethical or aesthetic reasons on the other. His logical ideal of capitalism is intended to clarify, but not to prove in any ethical or empirical way, the intractable injustice of that system, and even to highlight those features in it that are ugly or beautiful. Concepts that are constructed according to a formally rigid logic may be of interest to the sociologist, the political activist, and even the artist precisely because and insofar as they are at variance with empirical reality, prevailing ethical values, or aesthetic standards.

This point is at least implicitly made in the introduction to Thomas Sekine's study *The Dialectic of Capital*, when he states that use value constitutes "the true limitation of capitalism, even in its ideal state" (Sekine 1984: 98–99). However, the word "even" here might obscure the basic analytical gain that is otherwise to be had from such theoretical abstractions as the "ideal state of capitalism." In his efforts to situate the theoretical abstraction of his presentation with respect to Marxism as an ideological and critical enterprise, Sekine is not always explicit about the extent to which his operative scientific ideals, that is, the "assumptions" or "fictions" he must sustain throughout his systematic presentation, may function in other contexts as evaluative or even aesthetic ideals. To be sure, the unclarity resides not in the nature of his "Marxism" as a critique of capitalism or as a political commitment, but in the potential evaluative conclusions or actual empirical (or interpretive) uses to which such theoretical abstractions may in fact be put, as when we study the "fetish character" of use values rather than their conceptual containment in capitalism, or when we approach the problem of wages as the expression of human needs and desires rather than as "the value of labor power" (cf. notes 8 and 22 to Part III). In this respect, Max Weber was much more explicit about the uses and abuses of the constructs of "pure economics," "a theory that is 'apolitical,' which asserts 'no moral evaluations' . . . which is 'individualistic' in its orientation . . . and which is and will always be indispensable for analytical purposes," for the very reason that its "fictions" are indeed illuminating in their unrealism (Weber 1949: 44). But Weber was never able to elaborate anything as logically systematic as Sekine's (or Marx's) theoretical presentation of capital, and he himself always seemed ambivalent about the ultimate place of scientific and logical ideals with respect to value judgments.

My argument here is that "the logical possibility of capitalism . . . a far from obvious credo to start with," itself needs to be counted explicitly among the "sustained fictions" of the "pure theory of capitalism," especially insofar as the scientificness of the exposition is at some ultimate point grounded in a kind of credo or confession of faith: "I believe that, in principle, there can be only one real totality capable of complete self-synthesis, and that totality is capitalism whose inner logic the dialectic of capital copies" (Sekine 1984: 57). To be sure, it is not a question here of either hiding or extorting confessions of faith, whether political, religious, or otherwise (cf. note 17 to Part III). Rather, it is a question of acknowledging the extent to which logic itself must operate from a principle of faith or a sustained fiction that may be invested with very different values and meanings within various contexts of human praxis and perception, including contiguous fields of empirical, normative, and even aesthetic inquiry (cf. Zeleny 1980).

25. *The accountant's balance sheet (on the ledger and calculative reason)*

Toward the end of his 1857–58 economic studies, in which he first elaborated the theory of surplus value and illustrated it with a few mathematical examples, Marx wrote to Engels requesting a sample of the balance sheets he used to manage his textile firm in Manchester, apparently hoping to see how his theory would work in reality. In fact, Marx spent much of the rest of his life pursuing more empirically grounded and systematic inquiries, understanding a large portion of his work to consist of little more than such menial calculations as would characterize any capitalist accounting scheme. The revival of Marx's studies in mathematics at this time was thus motivated not only by his theoretical interests but by his practical and empirical ones as well (cf. Marx [1881b]; Struik 1948; Zeleny 1980).

Marx did not aim simply to ground capitalist accounting practices in the theoretical abstractions of the labor theory of value, but rather to specify the set of empirical factors and organizational principles that are both implied and presupposed in the uses of such calculations. This interest also guided Max Weber's studies on the origins and specificity of Western capitalism, which he defines sociologically in terms of the systematic pursuit and peaceful acquisition of profit through exchange, as well as the "rational capitalist organization of (formally) *free labor*" (Weber 1930: 17). Such practices as budgeting and accounting, bookkeeping and balance sheets, he argues, thus provide the basic structure of the capitalist social system in their ideal function as a "précis de toutes les choses" or a "concise compendium" of things that can be calculated in terms of money, produced in industry, and exchanged on a market (cf. I 48: 218):

> Where capitalistic acquisition is rationally pursued, the corresponding action is adjusted to calculations. This means that the action is adapted to a systematic utilization of goods or personal services as a means of acquisition in such a way that, at the close of a business period, the balance of the enterprise in money assets (or, in the case of a continuous enterprise, the periodically estimated money-value of assets) exceeds the capital, i.e. the estimated value of the material means of production used for acquisition in exchange. . . . Everything is done in terms of balances: at the beginning of the enterprise an initial balance, before every individual decision a calculation to ascertain its probable profitableness, and at the end a final balance to ascertain how much profit has been made. (Weber 1930: 18)

Contrary to what many Marxists might believe, Marx did not simply read into this formal and calculative rationality the empirically verifiable and ethically objectionable principle of an organization based on "substantively *unfree* labor." His main theoretical concern, rather, was to demonstrate in rigorously logical terms the structural disproportion and essential anomaly specific to Western capitalism, which he elaborated in terms of the theory of the capital/labor relation and expressed mathematically in terms of the concept of surplus value.

Marx's empirical studies of the nineteenth-century factory system may thus be coordinated with Weber's sociological and historical investigations into the rise of the Western bourgeois class and the reciprocal and uneven development of capitalism, science-based technology, bureaucratically organized law and administration, and rationalized arts. To be sure, as Herbert Marcuse notes (1968 [1964]), Weber was more concerned to understand (*verstehen*) the calculative and technical institutions of capitalism "in their own terms" than he was to take a critical stance on their rationality, and so may ultimately have viewed Western reason as a fatality, if not indeed as a form of unreason. Thus it was left to the Marxian theoretical vision to show how the "ruptures" in this reason may open up a new field of possibility.

26. Grand Inquisitors (on the ledger as a legal convention)

Let us imagine Marx as a great prosecuting attorney, "delegated to the accusation of the perverts and to the 'invention' of a convenient lover (the proletariat)": Marx the lawyer thus "begins to study the dossier of the accused capitalist" only to become as horrified as he is fascinated by the evidence he finds there (Lyotard 1974: 118). Whatever the seductive appeal of such a fanciful conceit, it may itself be studied for the way that a certain legal rhetoric informs Marx's work. Indeed, this rhetoric may often lend to our sense of him as a writer the character not only of a prosecuting attorney but also of a defense lawyer, judge, legislator, and especially the accused, called upon to bear witness either in his own defense or in solidarity with others who have also been put on trial (as in the second section of the *Communist Manifesto*). By far the most elaborate deployment of Marx's litigious procedure appears in the main section of the first volume of *Capital*, "The Production Process of Capital," which consists largely of a detailed legal argument for the legislative recognition of the working class, toward which the passage of the ten-hours' bill in 1847 in England was an important milestone. Indeed, this entire section may be read as the report of a landmark court case dealing with "the mortgage on labor-power foreclosed" (Hyman 1962: 146; cf. note 12 to Part III), and as a testimony to how the nineteenth-century poor laws themselves served to define the "working poor" as an object of scientific knowledge (Green 1983).

Marx was training in jurisprudence when he first began to study philosophy and political economy during his student days. His competence in legal argumentation is abundantly evident from his article "Debates on the Law on Thefts of Wood" (1842; cf. note 4 to Part III), and later in his defense of the communist movement after the revolutions of 1848. During the Cologne communist trial, for example, Marx was called upon to defend his own revolutionary activities as well as those of his fellow German émigrés. Ten years later one such émigré turned around to accuse Marx himself of extortion, forgery, spying, and slander. The yearlong court battle, during which Marx tried to sue the *National-Zeitung* and the *Daily Telegraph*, which published the accusations, forced him to interrupt his economic studies so that he could defend himself in an elaborate polemic entitled *Herr Vogt* (1860). Through a series of self–cross-examinations and personal confessions, Marx tried to preserve his honor, and nowhere more vigorously than in a letter to the Berlin lawyer he hired to represent him in the case: "Since I am myself the son of a lawyer (the deceased legal counsellor Heinrich Marx of Trier, who was a long time chief officer of the court there, and who was distinguished both by the purity of his character and by his legal talent), I know how important it is for a conscientious jurist to be completely in the clear about the character of his client" (Marx to Weber, 3 March 1860). The relevance of this episode for understanding Marx's isolation and anxiety after the chilly and silent reception given to his *Critique of Political Economy* in 1859 has been suggested in Jerrold Seigel's psychoanalytic reading of Marx's letters from this period (although he does not go far in exploring the sociolegal aspects of the episode that are evident from Marx's reference to his father as a lawyer while consulting with his own defense attorney). After being deprived of recognition for his intellectual achievements, in the Vogt affair Marx then embarked on "a compulsive demonstration that he embodied the moral purity his father's ethic demanded" (Seigel 1978: 382), the latter being the young Karl's highest personal standard as well as the most critical judge of his character.

Beyond this psychobiographical line of inquiry, we might further speculate on the historical and interpretive implications of the chance occurrence that the lawyer who defended Marx when he was called upon publicly to defend himself happened to have the same family name as another Berlin lawyer whose work, along with Marx's, was a major influence on the subsequent development of Western social science: Weber. The sense in which Marx may be understood to have been one of *Max* Weber's own sociological "cases" (or "ideal types," of which Weber was always concerned to argue both sides) is often forgotten in the Weberian tradition of American sociology that has rested its case against Marx on the spurious grounds that he did not have a properly empirical understanding of sociolegal institutions other than as merely epiphenomenal "superstructures" (Parsons 1967; cf. Mills 1959; O'Neill 1972; Wilson 1977). By contrast, while the German Marxist tradition also tends to approach issues in the social sciences and philosophy through the interpretive frameworks provided by Weber, it often does so more as a way of putting Marxism on trial rather than either to accuse or defend Marx (cf. Habermas 1984, 1987; Lukács 1971 [1922]; Marcuse 1964; cf. Merleau-Ponty 1969, 1973; cf. note 4 to Part II). Thus, it has usually been left to others to plead the case for Marx against his grand inquisitors, before the final judgment has already been made, or at least to begin asking the right questions: What crime has been committed? Who is the criminal? What evidence do we have? By what authority do we judge?

27. The holy family (the final scene of Marxism)

Lately it seems that Marxists and non-Marxists alike sense that the final scene or last act of Marxism may be unfolding before us not in the spectacle of authoritarian or collapsing socialist economies but rather through a more singular and disconcerting vision: the exhaustion of heroic passions that have their world-historical expression in work and war, reason and revolution, and humanism and freedom (Dunayevskaya 1958; Marcuse 1941); the domestication of these grand struggles into the private sphere of family life; and their fragmentation into psychic disorder and social narcosis (cf. Deleuze and Guattari 1977; Lyotard 1984). Perhaps Lukács had this shift in mind when he criticized the epilogue to War and Peace for the way the heroic narration of the great events and deeds of the Napoleonic Wars had been superseded by a restrained, prosaic depiction of family life with its placid mood and its "nursery atmosphere": "The love which occupies the really central place in Tolstoy's world is love as marriage, love as union (the fact of being united, of becoming one, being more important than who it is that is being thus united), love as the prelude to birth, marriage and the family as a vehicle of the natural continuity of life" (Lukács 1971 [1915]: 148). For Lukács, such expressions of love ultimately seem to rest on a profound disillusionment, insofar as the community of feelings among human beings is reduced to the conventional rhythms of birth and death that pacify "everything that is great and noble in man." Truly human compassion is thus framed polemically, nostalgically, and so remains abstract or becomes absurd (cf. Ley 1972): "Nothing is left of what was there before, as the sand of the desert covers the pyramids, so every spiritual thing has been swamped, annihilated, by animal nature" (Lukács 1971 [1915]: 149). Perhaps Marx himself had already envisioned this exhaustion (and thus redoubled his fight against it) when he studied the demise of the great critical tradition of Hegelian negative thinking into the comedy of Critical Criticism and the banalities of second-rate melodrama (Marx and Engels 1845).

By contrast, Balzac's work seems to stage a grand representation of this last act and final scene as a historical movement that extends well beyond his nineteenth-century–bound literary imagination. Perhaps the core structure of his vision may be characterized as a sociosymbolic generalization of the holy family in terms of its myth of paternity and its genealogy of family life as the essential principle of the modern social contract. The radical subversion of this mythical and symbolic structure is dramatized throughout the *Comédie humaine* in the proliferation of renegade or rejected fathers (Goriot and Hulot), and particularly in the pervasiveness of absent, impotent, or even falsely omnipotent fathers (Godeau and Mercadet). These figures are the sign of a rupture in this contract that is usually elaborated negatively by Balzac as the recomposition or destruction of family alliances, their replacement by the formation of sinister leagues, or their postmortem resurrection by authoritarian decree (cf. Prendergast 1978; note 1 to Part III). Only in rare moments of bliss and optimism does he elaborate on the possible formation of a new social pact through the great maternal figures of his stories (Mme. Claes and Mme. de la Chanterie), and even then only in an impossibly abstract and utopian way.

Balzac seems to belong neither to the world about which he wrote nor to that Marxian world whose promise he might have sensed but could never articulate, much less embrace, which is why a closer analysis of his works lies beyond the scope of this study (cf. Lukács on Dostoyevsky 1971 [1915]: 152–53). Perhaps his greatest works are not identical to his understanding of them, but rather provide some future world with the outlines of its theater, sketches for its paintings, or scores for its musical pieces. It may therefore be the task of later generations to decide whether these materials can be collected into some new great aesthetic composition, thereby completing a project begun by him, or whether they might find their true meaning only in some other world whose sciences and arts have been redeemed by that hope for forgiveness which renders us sublime (Balzac 1956 [1842]: 71).

Works Cited

Square brackets denote dates of first publication or composition. Editions of Marx's works are listed in the Note on Abbreviations, Citations, and Translations, pp. xiii–xv.

Adorno, Theodor. 1974 [1951]. *Minima Moralia: Reflections from Damaged Life.* Trans. E. F. N. Jephcott. London: New Left Books.
———. 1991 [1956]. "Heine the Wound." In his *Notes to Literature,* vol. 1. Trans. Shierry Weber Nicholsen. Ed. Rolf Tiedemann. New York: Columbia University Press.
———. 1991 [1959]. "On the Final Scene of Faust." In his *Notes to Literature,* vol. 1.
———. 1991 [1965]. "Reading Balzac." In his *Notes to Literature,* vol. 1.
Althusser, Louis. 1969 [1965]. *For Marx.* Trans. Ben Brewster. New York: Vintage Books.
———. 1970 [1968]. *Reading Capital.* Trans. Ben Brewster. London: New Left Books.
———. 1971. *Lenin and Philosophy, and Other Essays.* Trans. Ben Brewster. New York: Monthly Review Press.
Balzac, Honoré de. 1956 [1831]. "Le Chef d'oeuvre inconnu." In *La Comédie humaine: Études philosophiques.* Vol. 14 of his *Oeuvres complètes.* Paris: Club de l'Honnête Homme.
———. 1956 [1835]. "Melmoth réconcilié." In *La Comédie humaine: Études philosophiques.* Vol. 14 of his *Oeuvres complètes.*
———. 1956 [1842]. "Avant-propos de Balzac pour *La Comédie humaine.*" In vol. 1 of his *Oeuvres complètes.*
———. 1956 [ca. 1848]. *Le Faiseur.* Vol. 20 of *Oeuvres complètes.*
Baran, Paul, and Paul Sweezy. 1966. *Monopoly Capital: An Essay on the American Economic and Social Order.* New York: Modern Reader Paperbacks.

Barthes, Roland. 1972 [1957a]. "Myth Today." In his *Mythologies*. Trans. Annette Lavers. London: Jonathan Cape.

———. 1972 [1957b]. "*Will* Burns Us. . . ." In his *Critical Essays*. Trans. Richard Howard. Evanston, Ill.: Northwestern University Press.

———. 1974 [1970]. *S/Z*. Trans. Richard Miller. New York: Hill and Wang.

———. 1975 [1973]. *The Pleasure of the Text*. Trans. Richard Miller. New York: Hill and Wang.

———. 1977 [1961]. "The Photographic Message." In his *Image, Music, Text*. Trans. Stephen Heath. London: Fontana Press.

———. 1977 [1968]. "The Death of the Author." In his *Image, Music, Text*.

———. 1977 [1970]. "Musica Practica." In his *Image, Music, Text*.

———. 1978 [1954]. *Michelet*. Trans. Richard Howard. New York: Hill and Wang.

———. 1978 [1977]. *Fragments of a Lover's Discourse*. Trans. Richard Howard. New York: Hill and Wang.

———. 1986 [1968]. "The Reality Effect." In his *The Rustle of Language*. Trans. Richard Howard. New York: Hill and Wang.

———. 1989 [1971]. *Sade, Fourier, Loyola*. Trans. Richard Miller. Berkeley: University of California Press.

Baudrillard, Jean. 1975 [1973]. *The Mirror of Production*. Trans. Mark Poster. St. Louis: Telos.

———. 1976. *L'Échange symbolique et la mort*. Paris: Éditions Gallimard.

———. 1979. *De la Séduction*. Paris: Éditions Galilée.

———. 1987 [1977]. *Forget Foucault*. New York: Semiotext(e).

Begg, Ean. 1985. *The Cult of the Black Virgin*. Boston: Arkana.

Bell, Daniel. 1973. *The Coming of Post-Industrial Society*. New York: Basic Books.

Benjamin, Walter. 1968 [1936]. "The Work of Art in the Age of Mechanical Reproduction." In his *Illuminations*. Trans. Harry Zohn. Ed. Hannah Arendt. New York: Schocken Books.

Berger, Peter L. 1974. *Pyramids of Sacrifice: Political Ethics and Social Change*. New York: Anchor Books.

Berman, Marshall. 1988. *All That Is Solid Melts into Air: The Experience of Modernity*. New York: Penguin Books.

Bloch, Ernst. 1970 [1963]. *On the Philosophy of the Future*. Trans. John Cumming. New York: Herder and Herder.

Bloom, Harold. 1973. *The Anxiety of Influence: A Theory of Poetry*. London: Oxford University Press.

———. 1975. *A Map of Misreading*. London: Oxford University Press.

Blumenberg, Hans. 1985 [1979]. *Work on Myth*. Trans. Robert M. Wallace. Cambridge: Massachusetts Institute of Technology Press.

Bologh, Roslyn W. 1979. *Dialectical Phenomenology: Marx's Method*. Boston: Routledge and Kegan Paul.

Brooks, Peter. 1976. *The Melodramatic Imagination: Balzac, Henry James, Melodrama, and the Mode of Excess*. New Haven: Yale University Press.

Brown, Norman O. 1966. *Love's Body*. New York: Vintage Books.

Browning, Robert. 1981 [1842]. "The Pied Piper of Hamelin: A Child's Story." In *Robert Browning: The Poems*. Ed. John Pettigrew. New Haven: Yale University Press.

Burke, Kenneth. 1966 [1954]. "Goethe's *Faust*, Part I." In his *Language as Symbolic Action: Essays on Life, Literature, and Method*. Berkeley: University of California Press.

――――. 1966 [1963]. "*Timon of Athens* and Misanthropic Gold." In his *Language as Symbolic Action*.

――――. 1966 [1965]. "*Faust* II: The Ideas Behind the Imagery." In his *Language as Symbolic Action*.

Cleaver, Harry. 1979. *Reading 'Capital' Politically*. Brighton, Eng.: Harvester.

Darwin, Charles. 1871. *The Descent of Man*. New York: A. L. Burt.

Debord, Guy. 1983 [1967]. *Society of the Spectacle*. Detroit: Black & Red.

Defoe, Daniel. 1965 [1719]. *The Life and Adventures of Robinson Crusoe*. Ed. Angus Ross. New York: Penguin Books.

Deleuze, Gilles, and Félix Guattari. 1977 [1972]. *Anti-Oedipus: Capitalism and Schizophrenia*. Trans. Robert Hurley, Mark Seem, and Helen R. Lane. New York: Viking.

De Man, Paul. 1979. *Allegories of Reading: Figural Language in Rousseau, Nietzsche, Rilke, and Proust*. New Haven: Yale University Press.

Derrida, Jacques. 1978 [1967]. "Freud and the Scene of Writing." In his *Writing and Difference*. Trans. Alan Bass. Chicago: University of Chicago Press.

――――. 1981 [1972]. "Outwork Prefacing." In his *Dissemination*. Trans. Barbara Johnson. Chicago: University of Chicago Press.

――――. 1982 [1971]. "The Pit and the Pyramid: Introduction to Hegel's Semiology." In his *Margins of Philosophy*. Trans. Alan Bass. Chicago: University of Chicago Press.

Donzelot, Jacques. 1981–82. "Pleasure in Work." *Ideology and Consciousness* (Winter): 3–28.

Dunayevskaya, Raya. 1958. *Marxism and Freedom*. Preface by Herbert Marcuse. London: Pluto.

Eagle, Judith. 1975. "The Mystery of the Black Madonnas." *Country Life* (Dec. 18): 1744–45.

Elson, Diane. 1979. "The Value Theory of Labor." In Diane Elson, ed., *Value: The Representation of Labor in Capitalism*. Atlantic Highlands, N.J.: Humanities Press.

Foucault, Michel. 1973 [1966]. *The Order of Things: An Archaeology of the Human Sciences*. New York: Vintage Books.

――――. 1977 [1969]. "What Is an Author?" In his *Language, Counter-Memory, Practice*. Trans. Donald Bouchard and Sherry Simon. Ithaca, N.Y.: Cornell University Press.

――――. 1977 [1971]. "Nietzsche, Genealogy, History." In *Language, Counter-Memory, Practice*.

Freud, Sigmund. 1977 [1905]. "Fragment of an Analysis of a Case of Hysteria." In *The*

Pelican Freud Library. Vol. 8. Trans. James and Alix Strachey. Harmondsworth, Eng.: Penguin Books.

————. 1977 [1927]. "Fetishism." *The Pelican Freud Library*. Vol. 7. Trans. James Strachey. Harmondsworth, Eng.: Penguin Books.

Frye, Northrop. 1957. *Anatomy of Criticism*. Princeton: Princeton University Press.

Genosko, Gary. 1992. "Bar Games: Baudrillard's Encounters with the Sign." Ph.D. diss., York University, Toronto.

Gill, Stephen, and David Law. 1988. *The Global Political Economy: Perspectives, Problems, and Policies*. New York: Harvester.

Goethe, Johann Wolfgang von. 1976 [1770–1831]. *Faust*. Trans. Walter Arndt. Ed. Cyrus Hamlin. New York: W. W. Norton.

————. 1986 [1770–1831]. *Faust*. Stuttgart: Phillip Reclam.

Gould, Carol C. 1978. *Marx's Social Ontology: Individuality and Community in Marx's Theory of Social Reality*. Cambridge: Massachusetts Institute of Technology Press.

Goux, Jean-Joseph. 1990 [1973, 1978]. *Symbolic Economies: After Marx and Freud*. Trans. Jennifer Curtiss Gage. Ithaca, N.Y.: Cornell University Press.

Green, Bryan. 1983. *Knowing the Poor: A Case Study in Textual Reality Construction*. London: Routledge and Kegan Paul.

————. 1988. *Literary Methods in Sociological Theory: Case Studies of Simmel and Weber*. Chicago: University of Chicago Press.

Greenblatt, Stephen J. 1978. "Marlowe, Marx, and Anti-Semitism." *Critical Inquiry* (Winter): 291–307.

Guy-Bray, Stephen. 1991. "The Civilization of Eros: A Study of Christopher Marlowe." Ph.D. diss., University of Toronto.

Habermas, Jürgen. 1970 [1968]. "Technology and Science as 'Ideology.'" In his *Toward a Rational Society: Student Protest, Science, and Politics*. Trans. Jeremy J. Shapiro. Boston: Beacon Press.

————. 1971 [1967]. *Knowledge and Human Interests*. Trans. Jeremy J. Shapiro. Boston: Beacon Press.

————. 1975 [1973]. *Legitimation Crisis*. Trans. Thomas McCarthy. Boston: Beacon Press.

————. 1984. *The Theory of Communicative Action*. Vol. 1. Trans. Thomas McCarthy. Boston: Beacon Press.

————. 1987. *The Theory of Communicative Action*. Vol. 2. Trans. Thomas McCarthy. Boston: Beacon Press.

————. 1989 [1962]. *The Structural Transformation of the Public Sphere*. Trans. Thomas Burger. Cambridge: Massachusetts Institute of Technology Press.

Hegel, G. W. F. 1969 [1812]. *Science of Logic*. Trans. A. V. Miller. Atlantic Highlands, N.J.: Humanities Press.

————. 1977 [1807]. *The Phenomenology of Spirit*. Trans. A. V. Miller. Oxford: Oxford University Press.

Heine, Heinrich. 1904 [1827]. "The Homecoming." In his *Book of Songs*. Trans. T. Brooksbank. London: William Heinemann.

————. 1960 [1827]. "Die Heimkehr." In his *Buch der Lieder*. Ed. Ralph Tymms. Manchester, Eng.: Manchester University Press.

Hobsbawm, Eric. 1964. "Introduction." In Eric Hobsbawm, ed., *Pre-Capitalist Economic Formations* (excerpt from Marx's *Grundrisse*). New York: International.

Hyman, Stanley Edgar. 1962. *The Tangled Bank: Darwin, Marx, Fraser, and Freud as Imaginative Writers*. New York: Atheneum.

Illich, Ivan. 1977. "Tantalizing Needs." In his *Toward a History of Needs*. London: Bantam Books.

Jameson, Fredric. 1971a. "*La Cousine Bette* and Allegorical Realism." *PMLA* 86: 241–54.

————. 1971b. *Marxism and Form: Twentieth Century Dialectical Theories of Literature*. Princeton: Princeton University Press.

————. 1981. *The Political Unconscious: Narrative as a Socially Symbolic Act*. Ithaca, N.Y.: Cornell University Press.

————. 1988 [1977]. "Reflections on the Brecht-Lukács Debate." In his *Ideologies of Theory, Essays 1971–1986*. Vol. 2. Minneapolis: University of Minnesota Press.

————. 1990 [1976]. "The Ideology of Form: Partial Systems in *La Vieille Fille*." In Martin Kanes, ed., *Critical Essays on Honoré de Balzac*. Boston: G. K. Hall.

————. 1991. *Postmodernism, or, the Cultural Logic of Late Capitalism*. Durham, N.C.: Duke University Press.

Keane, John, and Brian Singer. 1974–75. "A Reply to Postone and Reinicke." *Telos* no. 22 (Winter): 148–53.

Kemple, Thomas M. 1989. "Dora from A to Z: A Fragmentary Misreading." *Social Discourse/Discours social* 2, nos. 1 and 2 (Summer–Fall): 35–44.

Kittler, Friedrich A. 1990 [1985]. "The Scholar's Tragedy." In his *Discourse Networks 1800/1900*. Trans. Michael Meteer and Chris Cullens. Stanford, Calif.: Stanford University Press.

Kosik, Karel. 1976 [1961]. *Dialectics of the Concrete Totality: A Study in Problems of Man and World*. Trans. Karel Kovanda and James Schmidt. Dordrecht, Netherlands: D. Reidel.

Krader, Lawrence. 1972. "Introduction." In *The Mathematical Notebooks of Karl Marx, 1879–1883*. Assen, Netherlands: Van Gorcum.

Kroker, Arthur. 1992. *The Possessed Individual: Technology and the French Postmodern*. Montreal: New World Perspectives.

Kroker, Arthur, and David Cook. 1987. *The Post-Modern Scene: Essays in Excremental Culture*. Montreal: New World Perspectives.

LaCapra, Dominick. 1983. *Rethinking Intellectual History: Texts, Contexts, Language*. Ithaca, N.Y.: Cornell University Press.

Lafargue, Paul. 1890. *Karl Marx: His Life and Work*. Toronto: Progress Books.

————. 1907 [1883]. *The Right to Be Lazy, and Other Studies*. Trans. Charles H. Kerr. Chicago: Charles H. Kerr Cooperative.

————. 1970 [1883]. *Le Droit à la paresse*. Rev. from 1880 version. In Jacques Girault, ed., *Textes choisis*. Paris: Éditions Sociales.

Lange, Oscar. 1934–35. "Marxian Economics and Modern Economic Theory." *Review of Economic Studies* 2: 189–201.

Lash, Scott, and John Urry. 1987. *The End of Organized Capitalism*. Cambridge: Polity Press.

Lefebvre, Henri. 1968 [1966]. *The Sociology of Marx*. Trans. Norbert Guterman. New York: Vintage Books.

———. 1984 [1967]. *Everyday Life in the Modern World*. Trans. Sacha Rabinovitch. New Brunswick, N.J.: Transaction Books.

Lenhardt, Christian. 1975. "Anamnestic Solidarity: The Proletariat and Its *Manes*." *Telos* no. 25 (Fall): 133–54.

Levine, Norman. 1975. *The Tragic Deception: Marx Contra Engels*. Oxford: Clio Books.

Ley, Ralph J. 1972. "Compassion and Absurdity: Brecht and Marx on the Truly Human Community." In *Studies in German Literature in the Nineteenth and Twentieth Centuries*. 2nd ed. Ed. Siegfried Meios. Chapel Hill: University of North Carolina Press.

Lukacher, Ned. 1986. *Primal Scenes: Literature, Philosophy, Psychoanalysis*. Ithaca, N.Y.: Cornell University Press.

Lukács, Georg. 1950 [1948]. *Studies in European Realism*. Trans. Edith Bone. London: Merlin.

———. 1968 [1947]. *Goethe and His Age*. Trans. Robert Anchor. London: Merlin. New preface 1967.

———. 1970 [1936]. "Narrate or Describe?" In his *Writer and Critic, and Other Essays*. Ed. and trans. Arthur Kahn. London: Merlin.

———. 1971 [1915]. *Theory of the Novel*. Trans. Anna Bostock. Cambridge: Massachusetts Institute of Technology Press. New preface 1964.

———. 1971 [1922]. *History and Class Consciousness: Studies in Marxist Dialectics*. Trans. Rodney Livingstone. London: Merlin. New preface 1967.

Lyotard, Jean-François. 1974. *Économie libidinale*. Paris: Éditions de Minuit.

———. 1984 [1979]. *The Postmodern Condition: A Report on Knowledge*. Trans. Geoff Bennington and Brian Massumi. Foreword by Fredric Jameson. Minneapolis: University of Minnesota Press.

Macpherson, C. B. 1962. *The Political Theory of Possessive Individualism: Hobbes to Locke*. Oxford: Oxford University Press.

Marcuse, Herbert. 1941. *Reason and Revolution: Hegel and the Rise of Social Theory*. Boston: Beacon Press.

———. 1955. *Eros and Civilization: A Philosophical Inquiry into Freud*. Boston: Beacon Press.

———. 1964. *One Dimensional Man: Studies in the Ideology of Advanced Industrial Society*. Boston: Beacon Press.

———. 1968 [1936]. "The Concept of Essence." In his *Negations: Essays in Critical Theory*. Trans. Jeremy J. Shapiro. Boston: Beacon Press.

———. 1968 [1937]. "The Affirmative Character of Culture." In his *Negations*.

———. 1968 [1964]. "Industrialism and Capitalism in the Work of Max Weber." In his *Negations*.

———. 1972. *Counterrevolution and Revolt*. Boston: Beacon Press.

———. 1978. *The Aesthetic Dimension: Toward a Critique of Marxist Aesthetics*. Boston: Beacon Press.

Maurois, André. 1971 [1965]. *Prometheus: The Life of Balzac*. Trans. Norman Denny. Harmondsworth, Eng.: Penguin Books.

McCarthy, George E. 1990. *Marx and the Ancients: Classical Ethics, Social Justice, and Nineteenth Century Political Economy*. Savage, Md.: Rowan and Littlefield.

McLellan, David. 1971. "Introduction." In *Karl Marx's Grundrisse: Selections*. Ed. and trans. David McLellan. London: Macmillan.

———. 1973. *Karl Marx: His Life and Work*. London: Papermac.

Mehlman, Jeffrey. 1977. *Revolution and Repetition: Marx, Hugo, Balzac*. Berkeley: University of California Press.

Meikle, Scott. 1985. *Essentialism in the Thought of Karl Marx*. London: Gerald Duckworth.

Merleau-Ponty, Maurice. 1969 [1947]. *Humanism and Terror: An Essay on the Communist Problem*. Trans. John O'Neill. Boston: Beacon Press.

———. 1973 [1955]. *The Adventures of the Dialectic*. Trans. Joseph Bien. Evanston, Ill.: Northwestern University Press.

Miles, Geoff. 1992. "Gravida-Gradiva: Pregnancy and Death-work in Freud's Pompeian Fantasy." Ph.D. diss., York University, Toronto.

Mills, C. Wright. 1956. *The Power Elite*. Oxford: Oxford University Press.

———. 1959. *The Sociological Imagination*. Oxford: Oxford University Press.

———. 1962. *The Marxists*. Harmondsworth, Eng.: Penguin Books.

———. 1963 [1955]. "On Knowledge and Power." In Irving Horowitz, ed., *People, Power, Politics*. New York: Ballantine Books.

Mitchell, W. J. T. 1986. *Iconology: Image, Text, Ideology*. Chicago: University of Chicago Press.

Moore, Carol. 1991. "The Maternal Imago: A Psychoanalytic-Feminist Study of Unconscious Representations of the Mother and Their Role in Women's Complicity in Their Own Oppression." Ph.D. diss., York University, Toronto.

Moss, Leonard W., and Stephen C. Cappanari. 1982. "In Quest of the Black Virgin: She Is Black Because She Is Black." In James J. Preston, ed., *Mother Worship*. Chapel Hill: University of North Carolina Press.

Negri, Antonio. 1984 [1979]. *Marx Beyond Marx: Lessons on the Grundrisse*. Ed. Jim Fleming. Trans. Harry Cleaver, Michael Ryan, and Maurizio Viano. South Hadley, Mass.: Bergin and Garvey.

———. 1988 [1968]. "Marx on Cycle and Crisis." In his *Revolution Retrieved: Selected Writings on Marx, Keynes, Capitalist Crisis and New Social Subjects, 1967–1983*. London: Red Notes.

———. 1988 [1980]. "Crisis of the Crisis State." In his *Revolution Retrieved*.

Nicolaus, Martin. 1967. "Proletariat and Middle Class in Marx: Hegelian Choreography and the Capitalist Dialectic." *Studies in the Left* 7, no. 1: 22–49.

———. 1972 [1968]. "The Unknown Marx." In Robin Blackburn, ed., *Ideology in Social Science: Readings in Critical Social Theory*. Suffolk, Eng.: Fontana/Collins.

———. 1973. "Foreword" and "Note on the Translation." In *Grundrisse*, by Karl Marx. Trans. Martin Nicolaus. London: Penguin Books.

Nietzsche, Friedrich. 1967 [1887]. *The Genealogy of Morals*. Trans. Walter Kaufmann and R. J. Hollingdale. New York: Vintage Books.

———. 1974 [1882]. *The Gay Science ("Gaya Sciencia")*. With a prelude in rhymes and an appendix of songs. Trans. Walter Kaufmann. New York: Vintage Books.

O'Connor, James. 1981. "The Meaning of Crisis." *International Journal of Urban and Regional Research* 5, no. 3: 317–29.

Offe, Claus. 1984 [1973]. "'Crises of Crisis Management': Elements of a Political Crisis Theory." In John Keane, ed., *Contradictions of the Welfare State*. Cambridge: Massachusetts Institute of Technology Press.

O'Neill, John. 1972. "The Hobbesian Problem in Marx and Parsons." In his *Sociology as a Skin Trade: Toward a Reflexive Sociology*. New York: Harper and Row.

———. 1976. "Critique and Remembrance." In John O'Neill, ed., *On Critical Theory*. New York: Seabury Press.

———. 1982. *For Marx Against Althusser, and Other Essays*. Washington, D.C.: Center for Advanced Research in Phenomenology and University Press of America.

———. 1985. *Five Bodies: The Human Shape of Modern Society*. Ithaca, N.Y.: Cornell University Press.

———. 1987. "Marx's Humanist Theory of Alienation." In Ernest Joos, ed., *Georg Lukács and His World: A Reassessment*. New York: Porter Lang.

———. 1989a. "Postmodernism and (Post)Marxism." In Hugh J. Silverman, ed., *Postmodernism—Philosophy and the Arts*. Continental Philosophy III. New York: Routledge.

———. 1989b. "The Textual Cogito." In his *The Communicative Body: Essays in Communicative Philosophy, Politics, and Sociology*. Evanston, Ill.: Northwestern University Press.

———. 1991. *Plato's Cave: Desire, Power, and the Specular Functions of the Media*. Norwood, N.J.: Ablex.

———. 1992. "Religion and Post-modernism: The Sense of an Ending, with an Allegory of the Body Politic." In his *Critical Conventions: Interpretation in the Literary Arts and Sciences*. Norman: University of Oklahoma Press.

Parsons, Talcott. 1967. "Some Comments on the Sociology of Karl Marx." In his *Sociological Theory and Modern Society*. New York: Free Press.

Pasco, Allan H. 1991. *Balzacian Montage: Configuring "La Comédie Humaine."* Toronto: University of Toronto Press.

Payne, Robert. 1971. "Introduction." In Robert Payne, ed., *The Unknown Karl Marx*. New York: New York University Press.

Perron, Paul, and Roland Le Huenen. 1990 [1984]. "Reflections on Balzacian Models of Representation." In Martin Kanes, ed., *Critical Essays on Honoré de Balzac*. Boston: G. K. Hall.

Piccone, Paul. 1975. "Reading the *Grundrisse*: Beyond 'Orthodox' Marxism." *Theory and Society* 2: 235–55.

Postone, Moishe, and Helmut Reinicke. 1974–75. "On Nicolaus' 'Introduction' to the *Grundrisse*." *Telos* 22: 130–48.

Prendergast, Christopher. 1978. *Balzac: Fiction and Melodrama*. London: Edward Arnold.

Quispel, Gilles. 1979. *The Secret Book of Revelation: The Last Book of the Bible*. Toronto: Gage.

Raphael, Max. 1980 [1933]. *Proudhon, Marx, Picasso*. Trans. Inge Marcuse. Ed. John Tagg. Atlantic Highlands, N.J.: Humanities Press.

Ronell, Avital. 1986. *Dictations: On Haunted Writing*. Bloomington: Indiana University Press.

Rosdolsky, Roman. 1977 [1968]. *The Making of Marx's "Capital."* Trans. Pete Burgess. London: Pluto.

Rovatti, Pier Aldo. 1973. "The Critique of Fetishism in Marx's *Grundrisse*." *Telos* 17 (Fall): 56–69.

Rubin, I. I. 1973 [1928]. *Essays on Marx's Theory of Value*. Trans. Milos Samardzija and Fredy Perlman. Montreal: Black Rose Books.

Ryazanov, David. 1925 [1923]. "Neueste Mitteilungen über den literarischen Nachlass von Karl Marx und Friedrich Engels." *Archiv für Geschichte des Sozialismus und der Arbeitbewegung*, Karl Grünberg, ed., 385–400.

Sachs, Hans. 1933. "The Delay of the Machine Age." Trans. Margaret J. Powers. *Psychoanalytic Quarterly* 2: 404–24.

Schrag, Calvin O. 1986. *Communicative Praxis and the Space of Subjectivity*. Bloomington: Indiana University Press.

Schumpeter, Joseph. 1951 [1919]. "The Sociology of Imperialism." In his *Imperialism and Social Classes*. Ed. Bert Hoselitz. Trans. Heinz Norden. New York: New American Library.

———. 1951 [1927]. "Social Classes in an Ethnically Homogeneous Environment." In *Imperialism and Social Classes*.

Seigel, Jerrold. 1978. *Marx's Fate: The Shape of a Life*. Princeton: Princeton University Press.

Sekine, Thomas T. 1984. *The Dialectic of Capital: A Study of the Inner Logic of Capitalism*. Vol. 1, *The Doctrines of Circulation and Production*. Tokyo: Yushindo.

———. 1986. *The Dialectic of Capital*. Vol. 2, *The Doctrine of Distribution*. Tokyo: Toshindo.

Sepper, Dennis L. 1988. *Goethe Contra Newton: Polemics and the Prospect for a New Science of Color*. Cambridge: Cambridge University Press.

Simmel, Georg. 1950 [1908]. "The Secret and the Secret Society." In *The Sociology of Georg Simmel*. Trans. Kurt H. Wolff. London: Free Press of Glencoe.

———. 1978 [1900]. *The Philosophy of Money*. Trans. Tom Bottomore and David Frisby. London: Routledge and Kegan Paul.

Smith, Dorothy E. 1987. "The Everyday World as Problematic: A Feminist Methodology." In her *The Everyday World as Problematic: A Feminist Sociology*. Toronto: University of Toronto Press.

———. 1990. "The Ideological Practice of Sociology." In her *Conceptual Practices of Power: A Feminist Sociology of Knowledge*. Toronto: University of Toronto Press.

Spivak, Gayatri Chakravorty. 1984. "Love me, love my ombre, elle." *Diacritics* (Winter): 19–36.

———. 1987 [1985]. "Scattered Speculations on the Question of Value." In her *In Other Worlds: Essays in Cultural Politics*. New York: Methuen.

———. 1987. "Speculations on Reading Marx: After Reading Derrida." In Derek Atteridge et al., eds., *Post-Structuralism and the Question of History*. Cambridge: Cambridge University Press.

Struik, Dirk. 1948. "Marx and Mathematics." *Science and Society* 12: 181–96.

Sypher, Wylie. 1948. "Aesthetic of Revolution: The Marxist Melodrama." *Kenyon Review* 10, no. 3 (Summer): 431–44.

Tucker, Robert C. 1961. *Philosophy and Myth in Karl Marx*. Cambridge: Cambridge University Press.

———. 1978. "Preface" and "Introduction." In Robert C. Tucker, ed., *The Marx-Engels Reader*. New York: W. W. Norton.

Van Russum-Guyon, Françoise. 1990 [1981]. "Metadiscourse and Aesthetic Commentary in Balzac: A Few Problems." In Martin Kanes, ed., *Critical Essays on Honoré de Balzac*. Boston: G. K. Hall.

Verstegen, Richard. 1979 [1605]. *A Restitution of Decayed Intelligence in Antiquities*. Norwood, N.J.: Walter J. Johnson.

Weber, Max. 1930 [1920]. *The Protestant Ethic and the Spirit of Capitalism*. Trans. Talcott Parsons. New York: Charles Scribner's Sons.

———. 1949 [1917]. "The Meaning of 'Value-Freedom' in Economics and Social Science." In his *Methodology of the Social Sciences*. Trans. H. Finch. Ed. Edward Shils. Oxford: Oxford University Press.

———. 1976 [1909]. *The Agrarian Sociology of Ancient Civilizations*. Trans. R. I. Frank. London: Verso.

Weber, Samuel. 1979. *Unwrapping Balzac: A Reading of "La Peau de Chagrin."* Toronto: University of Toronto Press.

Wilson, H. T. 1977. *The American Ideology: Science, Technology, and Capitalism as Modes of Rationality in Advanced Industrial Societies*. Boston: Routledge and Kegan Paul.

———. 1983. "Technocracy and Late Capitalist Society: Reflections on the Problem of Rationality and Social Organization." In S. Clegg, G. Dow, and P. Boreham, eds., *The State, Class and the Recession: Issues for the 1980s*. London: Croom Helm.

———. 1986. "Critical Theory's Critique of Social Science: Episodes in a Changing Problematic from Adorno to Habermas." Parts I and II. *History of European Ideas* 7, no. 2: 127–47; no. 3: 287–302.

———. 1991. *Marx's Critical/Dialectical Procedure*. London: Routledge.

Wolff, Robert Paul. 1988. *Moneybags Must Be So Lucky: On the Literary Structure of "Capital."* Amherst: University of Massachusetts Press.

Yonoyovskaya, S. A. 1983. "Introduction." In *The Mathematical Notebooks of Karl Marx, 1881.* London: New Park.

Zeleny, Jindrich. 1980 [1968]. *The Logic of Marx.* Trans. and ed. Terell Carver. Oxford: Basil Blackwell.

Index

In this index "f" after a number indicates a separate reference on the next page, and "ff" indicates separate references on the next two pages. A continuous discussion over two or more pages is indicated by a span of numbers. *Passim* is used for a cluster of references in close but not consecutive sequence.

Library of Congress Cataloging-in-Publication Data

Kemple, Thomas M.

   Reading Marx writing : melodrama, the market, and the
"Grundrisse" / Thomas M. Kemple.

      p.   cm.

   Includes bibliographical references and index.

   ISBN 0-8047-2408-3 (acid-free paper) :

   1. Marx, Karl, 1818–1883.   2. Marx, Karl, 1818–1883.
Grundrisse der Kritik der politischen Ökonomie.   I. Title.

HX39.5.K388   1995

335.4′12—dc20   94-42468

                                                      CIP

⊗ This book is printed on acid-free recycled paper.